DON ADAMS & ARLENE GOLDBARD

COMMUNITY, CULTURE
AND GLOBALIZATION

A PUBLICATION OF
THE ROCKEFELLER FOUNDATION
CREATIVITY & CULTURE DIVISION

Published in 2002 by The Rockefeller Foundation,
420 Fifth Avenue, New York, New York 10018-2702

Book Design: Landesberg Design Associates, Pittsburgh

Don Adams and Arlene Goldbard / Editors

   Community, Culture and Globalization

   p.   cm.

   Includes bibliographic references.

   ISBN 089184-063-X

Cover: Indonesian migrant workers take part in a creative dance and movement workshop
in Hong Kong. © Asian Migrants' Theatre Company, 2000

Table of Contents

Introduction

The Rockefeller Foundation is a knowledge-based, global foundation with a commitment to enrich and sustain the lives and livelihoods of poor and excluded people around the world. Since its founding in 1913, the Foundation has based its support for creativity and culture on the belief that the free expression of creative individuals is indispensable to strong societies. As the Foundation refocuses its strategy to address today's challenges of globalization, the Creativity & Culture program aims to enhance the imaginative talents of individuals and communities through the preservation and renewal of the cultural heritage of poor and excluded people, and the involvement of artists and humanists in the creation of democratic and inclusive societies.

Globalization refers to the rapid and massive movement of capital, goods, people, ideas, institutions and images across the globe. Although this process has been occurring for centuries, its speed and scale have accelerated over the last 50 years. In both a moral and a practical sense the Rockefeller Foundation seeks to ensure that poor and excluded people are included in the benefits of globalization and protected from the worst of its negative consequences.

It is a fundamental tenet of the Creativity & Culture program that the arts and culture have a vital and powerful role to play in using the globalization process to push forward an agenda of equity and inclusiveness. We recognize and support the positive aspects of globalization, including increased access to and innovative use of new technologies in the arts and media, the re-emergence of folk traditions and the creation of "imagined communities" that unite people across geographic boundaries through shared experiences. At the same time, we support and celebrate the multilingual, multifaceted and, above all, independent artistic and cultural expressions and movements that warn of the homogenizing influences of globalization.

In May 2001, officers from the Creativity & Culture program invited artists and activists from the field of community cultural development around the world to come together for several days at the Foundation's conference center at Bellagio, Italy. They were brought on, in contributing author Martha Ramirez's words, "a trip around the world meeting very incredible people with parallel experiences, who devote [their] sweat, tears, laughter, and passion to create an art that helps heal and strengthen our suffering communities." The result was a wealth of insight into the many varied, inventive, creative, educational, charged and sometimes ingenious ways in which these artists challenge the threat of homogeneity in a globalizing world.

Brought together in this anthology, their stories illustrate an amazing diversity of creativity, a resilience and strength of identity and culture, and an affirmation of self-expression as a form of community activism. These essays bring to life the crucial role that the arts can play in lifting the human spirit, bringing about understanding and nurturing social development. This collection sounds the call for a greater recognition of this field of work in the United States and throughout the world.

We thank all of the authors who participated in this rich exchange of views in Bellagio, and who give so much to their communities throughout the world. We are especially grateful to the editors, Don Adams and Arlene Goldbard, for all they have done to shape this volume and the field of community cultural development.

Tomás Ybarra-Frausto
Associate Director, Creativity & Culture
The Rockefeller Foundation
April 2002

1

Community, Culture and Globalization

by Don Adams and Arlene Goldbard

In May of 2001, the authors represented in this anthology met at the Rockefeller Foundation's Bellagio Study and Conference Center on Lake Como in northern Italy. The villa and its grounds are beautiful, especially when adorned by spring's profusion of leaf and blossom. Succumbing to spring fever, from time to time we abandoned the conference room for a wide lawn overlooking the lake.

One afternoon, Maribel Legarda, artistic director of the Philippine Educational Theater Association (PETA), volunteered to lead theater exercises as a demonstration of PETA's work, kicking off a discussion that was to touch on privatization and commercialization of cultural development. Following Maribel's instructions, everyone assembled by world region into five groups: we joined one that included several people from the United States, one Canadian, one Peruvian and one Mexican. Other groups were just as polyglot: the Asian cluster included someone from Hong Kong, two members from India and three Australians (one born in Vietnam). Our eventual assignment turned out to be silly, ironic and hilarious: devising and performing a mock television commercial for community cultural development. But for a warm-up, Maribel had each group choose a Beatles song to perform with enthusiasm. If memory serves, our group chose "All You Need Is Love." Another group belted out "Yellow Submarine." Without conferring or even knowing the choices the other groups had made, each picked an entirely different Beatles tune.

Here, in microcosm, we have the dialectic of globalization: two dozen community arts practitioners and theorists come from 15 countries on six continents to a meeting in Italy. The meeting's purpose is to share experiences and ideas gleaned from their own work in communities, exploring commonalities as well as differences. Before the meeting, they conduct an introductory dialogue in English via e-mail to introduce themselves and their work, together beginning to formulate an agenda of issues for their face-to-face meeting. At the meeting, their presentations are earnest, diverse, often amazing and about as multifarious as can be imagined: a community dance project in which construction workers performed a pas de deux for tractors; a half-mile-long mural commemorating the suppressed history of southern California; a Vietnamese youth theater; a youth-created video game on unemployment; and many, many more. Their common aims are to help people wrest a meaningful and grounded sense of cultural identity from the jaws of a rapacious market culture and, by engaging with ideas, feelings and expression, to catalyze social action. But when they search for a lingua franca, they turn to the products of that market, from the Beatles—one of the most successful franchises of the commercial cultural industries—to the formulas of television advertising, familiar to each and all.

——

This anthology was created to raise the profile of community cultural development practice around the world by offering a rich mixture of experiences, ideas and stories that demonstrate the validity of this work as a stimulus to pluralism, participation and equity in cultural life, and as a response to globalization's pull toward the standardization of commercial culture. Our hope has been to create a tool that can be used by anyone to understand the community cultural development field, a book that can serve as a resource for both training and practice.

"Community cultural development" describes the work of artist–organizers ("community artists") who collaborate with others to express identity, concerns and aspirations through the arts and communications media, while building cultural capacity and contributing to social change. In community cultural development work, community artists, singly or in teams, use their artistic and organizing skills to serve the emancipation and development of a community, whether defined by geography (e.g., a neighborhood), common interests (e.g., members of a union) or identity (e.g., members of an indigenous group). The work is intrinsically community-focused: while there is great potential for individual learning and development within its scope, it is aimed at groups rather than individuals. Individual issues are considered in the context of collective awareness and common interests.

Culture—the sum total of signs, beliefs, artifacts, social arrangements and customs created by human beings—is both the container and the content of this work. To be human is to make meaning. Powerful meanings attach to even the smallest matters: the fate of a species of bird or a plot of land; the way a regulation is interpreted or the outcome of a particular court case. Social life offers infinite opportunity for organizing, as is seen wherever people protest against laws and policies they oppose or rally support for their chosen causes. But culture subsumes them all. When we speak of culture, we describe a people's "operating system," to borrow an analogy from one of humanity's most suggestive creations, the computer. Culture underpins all choices, all outcomes. It contains the means of expressing all thoughts and emotions. It enables all associations. And within this encompassing realm, the purest and densest meanings are conveyed through art, through individual and collective creations driven by the desire to express and communicate, unencumbered by extraneous objectives.

Thus, culture rather than a particular art form is the true medium of this work. Within the community cultural development field, projects are remarkably diverse. All artistic media and styles are adaptable. Projects have employed visual arts, architectural and landscape design, performing arts, storytelling, writing, video, film, audio and computer-based multimedia. Activities include structured learning, community dialogues, community mapping and documentation, oral-history collection, the physical development of community spaces and issue-driven activism, as well as the creation of performances, public art, exhibitions, moving-image media, computer multimedia and publications. In all this work, the powerful experience of bringing to consciousness and expressing one's own cultural values is deemed worthwhile in and of itself, apart from the outcome.

Despite superficial differences, the field's internal diversity reflects strong common principles and values. The following unifying principles originally appeared in "Creative Community: The Art of Cultural Development," a companion volume to this international anthology, focusing on community cultural development's definition, history, theoretical underpinnings and current conditions in the United States. (Copies are available free of charge from the Rockefeller Foundation.) Community cultural development projects aim to realize these common principles:

- Active participation in cultural life is an essential goal of community cultural development.

- All cultures are essentially equal, and society should not promote any one as superior to the others.

- Diversity is a social asset, part of the cultural commonwealth, requiring protection and nourishment.

- Culture is an effective crucible for social transformation, one that can be less polarizing and create deeper connections than other social-change arenas.

- Cultural expression is a means of emancipation, not the primary end in itself; the process is as important as the product.

- Culture is a dynamic, protean whole, and there is no value in creating artificial boundaries within it.

- Artists have roles as agents of transformation that are more socially valuable than mainstream art-world roles—and certainly equal in legitimacy.[1]

[1] Don Adams and Arlene Goldbard, *Creative Community: The Art of Cultural Development* (New York: Rockefeller Foundation, 2001), p. 14.

Many of the authors whose work is included here are based in the developing world or in marginalized communities within the industrial world. Considered as a group, they represent a departure from the stereotype of the deracinated intellectual described by commentators from Fanon to Naipul, alienated by education and training from heritage culture, yet unable to enter fully into or find deep satisfaction within the transnational imposed culture. Rather than surrender to permanent alienation, these artists and activists have grasped the power inherent in their simultaneous roles of participant and observer. Understanding the new reality of multiple identities and multiple belonging, they serve as catalysts and conduits, dedicating their skills to the development of their communities, to the articulation of suppressed voices.

Although their particular locations differ greatly, these authors respond in their work to realities that now transcend all national boundaries. Every current society is multicultural due to the penetration of virtually all cultural barriers by colonization, immigration and the nearly universal proliferation of electronic media. Every chapter of this volume touches on some of the many and varied challenges this presents. Although most projects described here take place within the bounds of a particular location, every one reflects the reality that community cultural development work is intrinsically trans-national and multicultural in scope and outlook—from the work with migrants described here by Judy Baca and Mok Chiu Yu to the second-generation immigrant cultures depicted by Tony Le Nguyen and Gary Stewart to the many depictions of populations straining to shoulder the cultural impact of industrialization.

More fully than any other artistic endeavor or development approach, community cultural development embodies the deep appreciation of cultural diversity described in the first three articles of the "UNESCO Universal Declaration on Cultural Diversity" adopted in November 2001:

Article 1

Cultural diversity: the common heritage of humanity

Culture takes diverse forms across time and space. This diversity is embodied in the uniqueness and plurality of the identities of the groups and societies making up humankind. As a source of exchange, innovation and creativity, cultural diversity is as necessary for humankind as biodiversity is for nature. In this sense, it is the common heritage of humanity and should be recognized and affirmed for the benefit of present and future generations.

Article 2

From cultural diversity to cultural pluralism

In our increasingly diverse societies, it is essential to ensure harmonious interaction among people and groups with plural, varied and dynamic cultural identities as well as their willingness to live together. Policies for the inclusion and participation of all citizens are guarantees of social cohesion, the vitality of civil society and peace. Thus defined, cultural pluralism gives policy expression to the reality of cultural diversity. Indissociable from a democratic framework, cultural pluralism is conducive to cultural exchange and to the flourishing of creative capacities that sustain public life.

Article 3

Cultural diversity as a factor in development

Cultural diversity widens the range of options open to everyone; it is one of the roots of development, understood not simply in terms of economic growth, but also as a means to achieve a more satisfactory intellectual, emotional, moral and spiritual existence.[2]

2 www.unesco.org/confgen /press_rel/21101_clt _diversity.shtml

Collectively, the essays in this volume assert community cultural development's value as a response to the homogenizing effects of the complex phenomenon known as "globalization." The increasing economic irrelevance of national boundaries and growing interdependence of worldwide trade, capital and population have been a boon to markets, hugely escalating the global penetration of new technologies and cultural products. That practitioners from 15 different countries were able to conduct a pre-conference dialogue via e-mail and to enter so easily and enthusiastically into a global Beatles medley at Bellagio attests to this new reality. These same phenomena have also raised serious concern that commercial considerations will override efforts to protect our cultural commonwealth—from local seed stocks to indigenous architecture to homegrown music—resulting in a world society more reminiscent of a hypermart than a garden of human possibility.

Globalization is a newish term (the Oxford English Dictionary lists the first use in 1962); but to see the phenomenon as entirely novel would be to mistake the label for the contents. In fact, the community cultural development field came into being in response to earlier social forces we now group under the label globalization.

Consider the international phenomenon known as Theater for Development, discussed in David Kerr's essay, Masitha Hoeane's interview and elsewhere. By the early 1970s, community workers and artists in the developing world had conducted extensive experiments in the use of theater to educate and involve community members in campaigns to improve their quality of life in the face of economic and social concerns. As Ross Kidd and Martin Byram wrote in their 1978 how-to manual for such work:

> Popular theatre can be used for extension work and adult education. As entertainment it can catch and hold the interest of large numbers of people. As a dramatic way of presenting local problems, it makes people in the audience see these problems in a fresh way. Through discussion (which follows every performance) people can talk about these problems with others and see what can be done about them. Often this leads to action.[3]

Their work was shaped by new geopolitical conditions—the restructuring of local economies, the decline of traditional cultures, the rise of insurgent indigenous movements and governments' repressive responses, all in the setting of post-colonial Africa. Among the typical local problems the Kidd and Byram manual lists are those now associated with globalization:

> Young people drift to towns. Women and old people left in villages…
> People forgetting traditional practices…
> Unemployment…
> Inflation…[4]

This early community cultural development work—called by many names, including popular theater, Theater for Development, people's theater—was shaped both by the unique conditions facing each locality and by inspiring examples circulated throughout the growing international network of practitioners.

In preparing this essay, we retrieved from our archives a thick folder of documents from the Third World Popular Theatre Network, a now defunct international alliance that published its first newsletter—composed on an electric typewriter—in January 1982. Some readers may not recall the difficulty of international networking in the years before the advent of the Internet. Some of these archival materials are tissue carbon copies or hand-written letters; still others are mimeographed. All were received by post operating at the snail-like pace of the international mails of two decades ago. The obstacles were formidable: it took a year to compose and circulate the newsletter's first two issues. But around the globe—most actively in Asia and Africa—practitioners of Theater for Development struggled to document and share what they had experienced.

[3] Ross Kidd and Martin Byram, *Laedza Batanani: Organizing Popular Theatre: The Laedza Batanani Experience 1974–1977* (Gaborone: Institute of Adult Education, University College of Botswana, 1978), p. 5.

[4] Ibid., p. 15.

Where conditions permitted work to develop, itinerant theater programs grew out of universities, community organizations and development agencies: Laedza Batanani in Botswana, programs directed at farmers emerging from Ahmadu Bello University in northern Nigeria, the impressively ambitious programs of PETA (still going strong and represented in the present volume by Maribel Legarda), Sistren in Jamaica. Even in its earliest days, Theater for Development's powerful ambitions emerged side-by-side with its populist critique:

> Chikwakwa Theatre and Theatre-for-Development attempted to take theatre to the marginalized groups of Zambian society but they have not been able to convert theatre into a tool which popular groups and organizations can use in challenging oppression and victimization in Zambian society. Theatre for Development remains a means for imposing technocratic solutions on the rural and urban poor rather than a tool for analyzing the class contradictions in Zambian society and the real sources of urban and rural poverty.[5]

Holding their own work to this challenging standard, every accomplishment of the international network was matched by a painful setback. Partners from India, Bangladesh, Nigeria, Zambia and the Philippines, aided by first-world partners, pulled off an "Asia–Africa Popular Theatre Dialogue" in Bangladesh in February 1983. The statement adopted by participants called for many of the same elements of support that community cultural development practitioners still feel are needed to advance their work, including "Popular theatre networks…at national, regional, and inter-regional levels."[6]

Next to this statement in our file is a bright green flyer urging recipients to send cables to Philippine President Ferdinand Marcos to express concern at the disappearance of Karl Gaspar, a pioneering popular-theater worker. During the two years when Gaspar was held in military detention in the early '80s, international attention was focused on his situation through the efforts of the network; in 1984, for example, he received the J. Roby Kidd Award of the Toronto-based International Council for Adult Education. Next in the file is a rumpled, fawn colored paper dated 1983 addressed to President Daniel Arap Moi of Kenya and other government officials; it exhorts them to release political prisoners and end repression against groups such as the theater of the Kamiriithu Community Educational and Cultural Centre, home base of the imprisoned and exiled playwright N'gugi Wa Thiongo, now Erich Maria Remarque Professor of Languages at New York University.

Or consider an even older example from the United States: President Franklin Delano Roosevelt's New Deal created employment and subsidy programs to put people back to work during the Great Depression of the 1930s, including massive Works Progress Administration (WPA) programs with major divisions covering visual art, music, theater, writing and history. Artists and scholars employed by the WPA painted murals for public buildings, tramped through cotton fields to collect slave narratives and record folk music, wrote and

[5] Dickson Mwansa, "Theatre for Community Animation in Zambia," *Third World Popular Theatre Newsletter*, Vol. 1, No. 1, Jan. 1982, p. 35.

[6] Statement of the Popular Theatre Dialogue, International Workshop, Koitta, Khaka, Bangladesh, Feb. 4–16, 1983 (collection of the authors).

performed plays on social issues and much, much more. New Deal cultural programs were created in response to massive unemployment in those sectors hardest hit by the Depression. Artists suffered in those years in part because of the Depression's general effects: people had less discretionary income to spend on things like theater tickets and art exhibits, so artists earned less income. But the main cause of unemployment in the performing arts was structural and coincidental to the general economic collapse: the new technology of motion pictures was displacing live performance, putting countless authors, actors, designers and technicians out of work. The richness of visual art, theatrical production, music and narrative that emerged from communities during the New Deal—and that inspired so much community cultural development work in succeeding generations—was at bottom a publicly funded response to the encroachment of capital-intensive industrial development in the arts sector.

In other words, before the term globalization came into common usage, community cultural development work was called into being around the world by the same complex of social forces and social dangers known outside the United States by another name: Americanization. While the United States remains the "golden land" that animates the dreams of countless immigrants, to scholars and social critics abroad, Americanization has for decades represented the decline of traditional, participatory cultural practices in favor of consuming their commercial counterparts.

Commentators on both left and right are still making this correlation. For example, here's how Francis Fukuyama (professor of public policy at George Mason University, consultant to the RAND Corporation and author of "The End of History and the Last Man") responded to the question of whether globalization is really a euphemism for Americanization:

> I think that it is, and that's why some people do not like it. I think it has to be Americanization because, in some respects, America is the most advanced capitalist society in the world today, and so its institutions represent the logical development of market forces. Therefore, if market forces are what drives globalization, it is inevitable that Americanization will accompany globalization.

> However, I think that the American model that people in other cultures are adopting is from the America of two or three generations ago. When they think of globalization and modernization, many people think of America in the 1950s and '60s: "They put a man on the moon," John Wayne, and "Father Knows Best." They're not thinking of the America of the Los Angeles riots and O. J. Simpson. The culture that we exported in the '50s and '60s was idealized. It really presented quite an attractive package. The culture we export now is cynical, and a much less attractive model for other nations to follow.[7]

[7] From "Economic Globalization and Culture: A Discussion With Dr. Francis Fukuyama," www.ml.com/woml /forum/global.htm, ©2001 Merrill Lynch & Co., Inc.

As the essays and interviews in this volume affirm, certain aspects of the phenomenon called globalization have positive, liberating potential. Advocates of cultural freedom in Asia can use the Internet to contact counterparts and supporters in Africa, Europe and the Americas, making it much harder for the perpetrators of human rights abuses to keep their misdeeds secret and much more likely that they will be called to account—if not in an official forum, then in the court of global public opinion. Mok Chiu Yu's essay about Asian popular theater lists a dazzling array of transnational collaborations, suggesting that the problems of migrant workers—enormously exacerbated by globalization—can be addressed by a joint international effort to use theater as an organizing tool, an effort that would undoubtedly be supported by the Internet and other transnational communications and support systems. Martha Ramirez Oropeza is interested in using new communications media to protect and restore indigenous Nahuatl culture in a way that transcends the Mexico–United States border. Gary Stewart's interview describes working with young people to use music sampling and recording technologies to portray their Asian–British–international youth culture in London, thereby addressing the racism of British society. Dee Davis's essay describes efforts to document, preserve and valorize rural culture using the tools of mass communications.

Yet both the preservationists among community cultural development practitioners and those who celebrate the syncretic fluidity of contemporary cultural mixing are up against the same formidable opponent, a key assumption underlying the course that globalization is taking: that the cultural products, customs and values of the U.S. marketplace are precisely what the rest of the world should and will have. Here's how Maude Barlow, national chair of the Council of Canadians watchdog organization, characterizes it:

> The entertainment-industrial complex…sees culture as a business, a very big business, and one that should be fiercely advanced through international trade agreements, like the World Trade Organization. This industry combines giant telecommunications companies, movie studios, television networks, cable companies and the Internet working together in a complex web that includes publishing, films, broadcasting, video, television, cable and satellite systems, megatheatre productions, music recording and distribution, and theme parks.

> Mass produced products of American popular culture are the U.S.'s biggest export according to the United Nations' 1999 Human Development Report. A huge, well organized coalition has formed that links the U.S. entertainment, media and information-technology sectors together in a "common front" to oppose cultural protectionism. Companies like Time-Warner and Disney have powerful friends on Capitol Hill and in the White House and they work closely with the U.S. Government which in turn has taken a very aggressive stand in protecting their interests.

She goes on to sum up the ambitions of globalization:

> The corporate assault on cultural diversity is part of a larger political, social and economic global watershed transformation. Economic globalization is the creation of a single global economy with universal rules set by big business for big business in which a seamless global consumer market operates on free-market principles, unfettered by domestic or international laws or standards.[8]

According to the *Computer Industry Almanac,* there were more than 550 million Internet users around the world at the end of 2000, with users in the United States making up just under one-third of the total.[9] Various sources have estimated that from 80 to 87 percent of the approximately five million Web sites active at this writing are in English.[10] Indeed, the online dialogue that laid the foundation for our Bellagio meeting was conducted in English, as was the conference itself. Clearly, a common language can be an advantageous instrument, facilitating international exchange and economies of scale that would be prohibitive if the costs of translation had to be borne.

But even the ubiquity of English can be seen as expressing a single nation's program of internationalizing its perceived self-interest. The fact is that for an increasingly large proportion of this planet's residents, the cultural products of the United States are an omnipresent, distorting mirror. Filmmaker and scholar Manthia Diawara describes the power of this "unified imaginary" to shape perceptions in Africa:

> There is a globalized information network that characterizes Africa as a continent sitting on top of infectious diseases, strangled by corruption and tribal vengeance, and populated by people with mouths and hands open to receive international aid. The globalization of the media, which now constitutes a simultaneous and unified imaginary across continents, also creates a vehicle for rock stars, church groups, and other entrepreneurs in Europe and America to tie their names to images of Afro-pessimism for the purpose of wider and uninterrupted commodification of their name, music, or church. Clearly, the media have sufficiently wired Africa to the West, from the public sphere to the bedrooms, to the extent that Africans are isolated from nation to nation but united in looking toward Europe and America for the latest news, politics, and culture.[11]

The vast majority of community cultural development practitioners would welcome the globalization—the universal extension—of human rights, self-determination, the means to livelihood, health and safety. But it is the globalization of consumerism, as Fredric Jameson has written, that inspires dread:

> ...the destructive forces...are North American in origin and result from the unchallenged primacy of the United States today and thus the "American way of life" and American mass media culture. This is consumerism as such,

[8] From "Can National Cultures Survive Globalization?," a talk delivered at the Globalization and the Live Performing Arts conference in Melbourne, Australia, June 23, 2000, available from the Council of Canadians, at www.canadians.org /publications/publications -speeches.html.

[9] www.c-i-a.com /pr0701.htm

[10] www.nic.at/english /geschichte.html

[11] Manthia Diawara, "Toward a Regional Imaginary in Africa," in Fredric Jameson and Masao Miyoshi, *The Cultures of Globalization* (Durham: Duke University Press, 1998), p. 103.

the very linchpin of our economic system, and also the mode of daily life in which all our mass culture and entertainment industries train us ceaselessly day after day, in an image and media barrage quite unparalleled in history. Since the discrediting of socialism by the collapse of Russian communism, only religious fundamentalism has seemed to offer an alternative way of life…to American consumerism. But is it certain that all of human history has been, as Fukuyama and others believe, a tortuous progression toward the American consumer as a climax? And is it meanwhile so sure that the benefits of the market can be extended so far as to make this new way of life available for everyone on the globe? If not, we will have destroyed their cultures without offering any alternatives…[12]

[12] Fredric Jameson, "Notes on Globalization as a Philosophical Issue," *The Cultures of Globalization*, pp. 64–65.

———

Community cultural development practice is based on the understanding that culture is the crucible in which human resilience, creativity and autonomy are forged. As everyone knows, an unexamined life is indeed possible: any of us might move through our lives in a trance of passivity, acted upon but never acting as free beings. The root idea of community cultural development is the imperative to fully inhabit our human lives, bringing to consciousness the values and choices that animate our communities and thus equipping ourselves to act—to paraphrase Paulo Freire—as subjects in history, rather than merely its objects.

The practitioners and thinkers represented in this volume do not suggest that making theater or murals can substitute for the other social and political acts that create a humane and equitable society. But these community cultural development activities are demonstrably the best available tools to teach the skills and values of true citizenship: critical thinking, interrogating one's own assumptions, exercising social imagination and creative problem solving, simultaneously holding in mind one's immediate interests and the larger interests of the community as a whole.

The computer metaphor invoked earlier may help to make the point clear: many forms of social activism in essence tinker with the surface of society, as one edits a document—substituting this piece of legislation for that one, this social program for that one—meaningful activity, but also often self-contained. When a particular accomplishment of this type is in place—when the edited document is complete—the task begins anew. In contrast, community cultural development work aims to change individuals' (and thereby society's) "operating system," providing new and fundamental tools of comprehension, analysis and creative action that inform all constructive social endeavor. The prospects for improving any social system, no matter how flawed it may be at first, are vastly increased when citizens enter into the tasks of social imagination and cultural development with consciousness of the work to be done and their own roles within it.

Community cultural development theory and practice have been influenced by activist movements for civil and human rights and by theoreticians of liberation including Frantz Fanon, a psychiatrist born in Martinique who formulated his revolutionary ideas on the psychology of the colonized and colonizer while practicing in Algeria during its struggle for independence from France; Paulo Freire, the Brazilian educator whose "pedagogy of the oppressed" was shaped by literacy campaigns with landless peasants in northeast Brazil in the years preceding his expulsion following the military coup of 1964; and Brazilian theater director Augusto Boal (who at one time served in Rio de Janeiro's municipal legislature), creator of the social-dramatic forms known as Theater of the Oppressed, Forum Theater and Legislative Theater, among others.

Many liberatory ideas converge in community cultural development practice, which asserts each human being's value to both the local and the world community. The heart of the work is to give expression to the concerns and aspirations of the marginalized, stimulating social creativity and social action and advancing social inclusion. Inherent in this approach is asserting the value of diversity, fostering an appreciation both of difference and of commonality within difference. In valuing community cultural assets both material and nonmaterial, community cultural development deepens participants' comprehension of their own strengths and agency, enriching their lives and their sense of possibility. By linking the personal and communal, community cultural development brings people into the civic arena with powerful tools for expression and communication, promoting democratic involvement in public life. Essential in an era of globalization, it creates public, noncommercial space for full, embodied deliberation of policies affecting citizens. And as the essays in this volume amply demonstrate, the work is inherently transnational, with strong roots in immigrant communities and deep commitments to international cooperation and multidirectional sharing and learning.

At community cultural development's core is Freire's concept of "conscientization" (from the Portuguese *conscientização*). This describes the process by which one moves from "magic thinking" toward "critical consciousness," breaking down imposed mythologies in order to reach new levels of awareness through dialogue, thus becoming part of the process of changing the world.

Within the community cultural development field, a parallel has been drawn between community artists' efforts to protect local cultures from unwanted market interventions and developing countries' efforts to resist the economic and social interventions of agencies of globalization such as the World Bank, the International Monetary Fund (IMF) and, more recently, the World Trade Organization (WTO). The most passionate critique of these interventions has emanated from impoverished countries where citizens have discovered that the price of securing World Bank largesse is too high to be borne. Typically, in exchange for certifying governments for much-needed international credit, the IMF has demanded such measures as reductions in public expenditure (often achieved through job cuts, wage freezes or cuts in health, education and social-welfare services); privatization of public services and industries; currency devaluation and export promotion, leading to a conversion from local food production to cash crops, which in turn leads to greater impoverishment as citizens are forced to buy imported food; and so on. For example, here is one account of the impact of such policies on Africa:

> Globalization in Africa involves one fundamental project: that of opening up the economies of all countries freely and widely to the global market and its forces.
>
> To this end, it is demanded that, whatever the nature of their economies, their level of development, and whatever their location in the global economy, all countries must pursue a common set of economic policies. In particular, they must permit the free and indiscriminate operation of transnational corporations in their economies: open their economies freely and indiscriminately to imports and concentrate on exporting what they are supposed to be good at; reduce the role of governments in the economy to that of supporting the market and private enterprise; and leave the determination of prices of goods, currencies, labour, as well as the allocation of resources to the operation of the market. Seen in this way, globalization is primarily not an impersonal process driven by laws and factors of development—such as technology—operating outside human control and agency. Rather it is a conscious programme of reconstructing international economic and political relations in line with a particular set of interests (the profit motivations of the businesses, especially the transnational corporations of the advanced industrial countries) and vision (the dogma of the primacy of the free market and of private enterprise in all processes of human development).
>
> For Africa, all the central planks of the process of globalization have been implemented over the past decade-and-a-half as structural adjustment programmes. Countries have deregulated foreign investment, liberalised their imports, removed currency controls, emasculated the direct economic role of the state, and so on. The results have been to further undermine the internal, national productive capacity, social security and democratic integrity of these countries. So that is basically how globalization has impacted on Africa.[13]

Following much the same pattern, globalization of culture inculcates consumerism, substituting mass-produced imported products for indigenous cultural production, and encourages privatization of public cultural-funding apparatus. The result is that market forces determine what aspects of culture will be preserved and supported, and, as in the advanced industrial economies,

[13] Fridah Muyale-Manenji, "The effects of globalization on culture in Africa in the eyes of an African woman," in *Echoes*, No. 12 (Geneva: World Council of Churches, 1997), pp. 13–14.

much of the cultural particularity that continues to exist is expressed through purchases of clothing, recordings, concert and film tickets—through a process of market segmentation—rather than active participation in community cultural life.

It is not that such choices are meaningless: to the contrary, a powerfully evocative recording or insightful film can have great meaning in the life of an individual, and affinities for such products can be part of the basis for even intimate connections. The point is that as an act, consummating purchases can never express the breadth or depth of meaning that inheres in heritage culture or that we invest in our own creations. But the particulars of what is purchased are incidental to the main impacts of the act—enriching the consumer cultural industries and placing our roles as consumers at the center of our lives and communities. By reducing culture to commerce, globalization robs us of so much: our connection to our own histories with their reservoirs of resilience and creativity; our ability to reconceive the past for the benefit of the future; the ease of exploring our boundless creativity.

We opened our meeting at Bellagio by asking each participant to envisage cultural democracy: What are we working for? What are the conditions we hope to bring about through community cultural development? People's responses give a flavor of the group—its members' pragmatic idealism, their uncanny ability to engender hope and possibility where others might see cause for despair.

Tony Le Nguyen: To give an alternative voice to the community. To allow and accept a different way of thinking and doing things and making decisions.

Munira Sen: Not just to respect and tolerate other cultures, but to celebrate other cultures.

David Diamond: It has to do with creating the space for authentic voices in the midst of a growing corporate voice. To be in true dialogue is a human right.

Judy Baca: What we're struggling with is the creation of a kind of homogeneity that is going across the world, and what we're trying to do is preserve the specificity of various cultures and to amplify those voices in such a way that they become valued.

Nina Obuljen: Giving space, on different levels, from individuals to small groups, nations, and eventually coming into something that is globally appreciated.

Dee Davis: Finding strategic ways to take cultural voices and frame public discourse.

David Kerr: I am interested in cultural exchange, and a big problem is unequal exchange, like when Paul Simon comes and gets Ladysmith Black Mombazo to work on his record, it's not really an equal cooperation. My point is trying to create conditions in which cultures can exchange on an equal basis.

Liz Lerman: One aspect of our work is to insist that art making is a central, critical and crucial aspect of decision making within the culture, and it's not marginal.

Prosper Kampoare: To facilitate the empowerment of the population to be actors in their own development.

Nitin Paranjape: To create spaces where multiple flows of information are possible, to empower people to believe in themselves, their own values, their own personal strength.

Mary Marshall Clark: To create ways of communicating across cultures and all other kinds of barriers; people communicating to create community.

Maribel Legarda: We've seen that the political and economic spheres have not really contributed to finding resolutions to our problems. The cultural sphere is the last bastion of trying to struggle against globalization. Coming from culture being an appendage—a thing we did to support political and social issues—the cultural sphere takes the lead role in the changes, insurrections and struggles that we need to be able to let mankind survive.

Tony Stanley: For me it's all about connectedness—us as individuals helping other people connect with their own imaginative lives. But more important perhaps is the connectivity between people and through that, the building of cultures and the sustainability of cultures.

Gary Stewart: Young people around the world tend to be the most consistent targets of negative global practices. The way I envision cultural democracy is for those young people to have ways of articulating their concerns and ideas with each other that aren't mediated necessarily through adults or other agencies.

Norm Horton: Given that there's a lot of economic and cultural and social development that's happening around us all the time, protocols should be established that are particular to place, so that development work is actually informed by the specific place where it's acting and that drives it.

Sarah Moynihan: Being able to create a space for dialogue between or amongst the mainstream and all the marginal groups, so that can start to impact on more appropriate development.

Mok Chiu Yu: We should work toward everyone becoming active creators of art, not just passive consumers. Cultural democracy means people have control of their lives.

Brian Holmes: Discovery—people discover themselves in relation to a community or a group. Expression, confrontation.

Iman Aoun: To break the silence and develop the art of listening. By breaking through the walls of each self, we might create a bond.

Paul Heritage: I believe in inclusion, but cultural democracy is about exploring the margins. We should watch the margins change as our cultures develop, and find a safe place for the excluded.

Bárbara Santos: The challenge is to find the means to stimulate people to find themselves and find their own futures.

Azril Bacal: Globalization has bred a lot of hopelessness: how to breed hope? And how to reappropriate and democratize cultural definition and development?

Masitha Hoeane: Looking around the room I see the diversity of humanity. In that divergence, those differences, there is a convergence. It is important to redefine culture and how it is perceived.

Martha Ramirez Oropeza: To find ways of motivating through participation. The way to motivate the original part within us as well as indigenous people and communities is through self-esteem. Globalization is destroying self-esteem.

Arlene Goldbard: To awaken compassion, a passion for justice and freedom.

Don Adams: There is a fundamental way we understand our participation in culture. Most people do not think, "What I see around me is a direct result of what I do."

———

Most community cultural development work is conducted in microcosm, at the level of the individual in community. Paul Heritage's and Bárbara Santos' essays share experiences of prisoners and guards in Brazil's penal system; Liz Lerman talks about employees of a shipyard in Portsmouth, New Hampshire; Judy Baca recounts the experiences of gang members in East Los Angeles, California. The localism and particularity of this work is both its strength and its vulnerability.

On the one hand, there is no way to mass-produce transformation of consciousness: the individuals who make theater out of their own lives or unearth their own cultural heritage as preparation for creating a history mural or a computer game come to consciousness of the roles they may play in changing the world precisely because their own minds and bodies are directly engaged in the process of self- and community-discovery. The labor-intensive, time-consuming effort that Maribel Legarda describes in creating a youth theater in Smokey Mountain—a mountain of garbage near Manila where children endanger their health working as scavengers—or that Sarah Moynihan and Norm Horton recount in discussing their work in creating a database of local cultural information with the people of Dajarra—a small, remote, predominantly Aboriginal township northwest of Brisbane, Australia—has dynamic transformative impact that can't be reached by any shortcut. The work's power and its enduring effects stem from its intensely personal nature.

But one of the impacts of globalization has been a cheapening of the local and the particular in favor of the general, and especially whatever gives "more bang for the buck." What is distended through mass replication or swollen with its own putative significance shows up on the "globalized information network" to which Manthia Diawara refers. Everything else—such as community cultural development projects on the ground in Australia, Mexico, India or Britain—is too small to signify. As one consequence, this democratic community cultural development movement, with its tremendous potential to respond successfully to the negative effects of globalization, has been marginalized by its invisibility in the mass media, and thus lacks the resources to realize that potential. This is a pity, because right now many of those who wish to oppose globalization's most dangerous effects can be seen as acting them out, if only inadvertently.

Consider what has come to be known as the anti-globalization movement, the decentralized network of many thousands of activists who have demonstrated in Seattle, Montreal, Genoa and beyond against the World Trade Organization and other multinational attempts to regulate trade at the expense of local livelihood and culture. Part of the critique of globalization is the globalized media's cynical manipulation of symbols to disguise its real impact: the very concept of "free trade" reduces the meaning of liberty to little more than corporations' unfettered access to world markets. Yet the centerpiece of the anti-globalization movement's campaigns has been symbolic action transmitted through sound bites and film clips on CNN: smashing the windows of a McDonald's, spray painting slogans on the facade of a Gap outlet, temporarily shutting down a world capital's business district in time for the evening news. Certainly these efforts have publicized the fact that there is a serious opposition to the globalization of corporate interests. Certainly they have forced international trade meetings to seek out more remote and secure meeting places. But it is hard to argue they have done much beyond that to slow the advance of globalization's harmful effects or hasten the realization of its liberatory potential.

Many of the essays in this volume were completed during September 2001, as can be discerned from some authors' mention of the appalling terrorist acts that cost so many lives in New York and Washington. In the aftermath of those tragedies, commentators at all points along the political spectrum have remarked that the World Trade Center was chosen as a target because it was a symbol of American capitalism—just as the Pentagon is a symbol of American military might. As we write, a few months later, pre–September 11 photos of the New York skyline evoke tears, and the twin towers of the World Trade Center have come to symbolize thousands of lost lives. In this context, spray painting anti-capitalist slogans on a McDonald's may read one way to a committed North American or European anti-globalization activist, but how does it read halfway around the world? Consider this account of Asian young people's consumer preferences:

> A new GenerAsians survey asked 5,700 children, between the ages of 7 and 18, in 18 cities in 12 Asia-Pacific countries, about their activities, aspirations, food, drink and entertainment. The survey was sponsored by Turner Broadcasting's Cartoon Network, and conducted by ACNielsen in March and April of 1998.

Food & Drink

"What's your favorite fast food restaurant?"
"What's your favorite soft drink?"

Australia	McDonald's, Coca-Cola
China	McDonald's, Coca-Cola
Hong Kong	McDonald's, Coca-Cola
India	Suvarna Bhuvan, Coca-Cola
Indonesia	McDonald's, Coca-Cola
Japan	McDonald's, Coca-Cola
Malaysia	KFC [Kentucky Fried Chicken], Coca-Cola
Philippines	Jollibee, Coca-Cola
Singapore	McDonald's, Coca-Cola
South Korea	Lotteria, Coca-Cola
Taiwan	McDonald's, Coca-Cola
Thailand	KFC, Pepsi [14]

[14] Reported in "End Games," *Adbusters*, Vol. 6, Iss. 4, Winter 1999, p. 42.

The perpetrators of the September 11 attacks, the corporations targeted on that day and the anti-globalization movement all have this in common: their activities have been staged for the global media network, which they have used to disseminate one-way messages that—whether or not one agrees with any of them—have no organic relationship to communities' own aspirations for their development. Neither embracing nor rejecting consumerism constitutes a cultural identity nor a platform for social change. Nor can it be demonstrated that the global media themselves have the power to bring about real social change. To the contrary, it has been convincingly argued that their main impact is to solidify the existing social order by broadcasting a continuous stream of official pronouncements and reactions to them, so that there is absolutely no confusing the "center" from which authoritative messages originate with the "margins" where the less powerful reside.

As has so often been pointed out, mass media are fascinated with images of destruction because spectacle—fire, explosion, blood and agitated crowds— makes "good television." In the days following September 11, news footage of the World Trade Center towers was repeated on CNN with such disturbing frequency that the Red Cross ran public-service announcements during commercial breaks exhorting viewers to limit their TV news watching, thus avoiding the trauma that might result from a permanent mental imprint of the horror. During the demonstrations accompanying international trade meetings in Seattle, Montreal and Genoa, images of demonstrators smashing shop windows and blocking streets and of police smashing demonstrators' heads were broadcast with proportionate repetitiveness. So far as we have seen, no one has even suggested that the result of these image-wars will be positive social change. Indeed, the main result traceable to both seems the same: an escalation of the barrage of symbols asserting the desired status quo; and new and expanded security measures that promise to constrain the lives of ordinary citizens, if not to deter terrorists.

In times of stress and upheaval, pundits are forever tempted to divide the world into easy dualities: two popular versions are Benjamin Barber's "Jihad vs. McWorld," and Samuel P. Huntington's "clash of civilizations." In the current fashion, Islamic fundamentalism is placed on one side of the dividing line, with a version of the West characterized by post-Enlightenment ideals of rationality on the other. Implicit in these divisions is the assumption that modernity can only be opposed by the oppressive nostalgia of fundamentalism. But funda- mentalism, protectionism and nationalism are based on the fortress paradigm of the walled city discussed in Dee Davis' essay, something impossible to achieve given the interpenetration of realities already accomplished through globalization. Nationalism and essentialism create disconnection, asserting that a separate destiny somehow awaits each people. But the fate that unchecked globalization threatens would be truly encompassing, rendering all cultures dispensable in the face of market imperatives. Rather than attempting to wall cultures off from each other, the urgent question now is how it will be possible to construct dynamic relationships between communities and the larger world, relationships that allow for agency on all sides.

In community cultural development practice—and this is also supported by what we now know about human consciousness and learning processes—it is understood that no ideological platform can accomplish the shift needed to expand freedom and equality in the world. Declarations inevitably evoke counter-declarations. The only meaningful dividing line is between received ideologies that demand to be swallowed whole and regurgitated intact and the process of questioning that defines human intellectual and spiritual freedom. The passion for global justice does not attach to the human spirit as a good idea: it is acquired through first-person experiences that concretize concepts such as freedom and equality, allowing them to be integrated and to lead to constructive social action. When Nitin Paranjape writes about tribal children in the Indian government's Ashram Schools discovering their own agency by publishing a "wall paper" in their own words, he shows us this process.

There is infinite scope for books, films and broadcasts about globalization and its discontents. There is infinite room for interesting ideas and analyses, for quotable scholarship and theoretical exploration. It is altogether a good thing that the process of globalization be examined and interrogated, that room be made to assert its constructive powers and condemn its destructive forces. But the only real promise for ordinary people in their own communities to have a say in how their cultures will be affected by the process of globalization lies in efforts like those described in this volume, in which the process of conscientization—discovering one's own voice and learning to speak one's own words—emancipates those who experience it, equipping them to enter the public sphere and take action to realize their ideals.

The community cultural development field is still taking shape. As we wrote of the U.S. field in "Creative Community," there is as yet no consensus on definition or nomenclature. Many different names are in simultaneous use:

> **Community arts.** This is the common term in Britain and most other Anglophone countries; but in U.S. English, it is also sometimes used to describe conventional arts activity based in a municipality, such as "the Anytown Arts Council, a community arts agency." While in this document we use "community artists" to describe individuals engaged in this work, to avoid such confusion, we have chosen not to employ the collective term "community arts" to describe the whole enterprise.

> **Community animation.** From the French *animation socio-culturelle*, the common term in Francophone countries. There, community artists are known as *animateurs*. This term was used in much international discussion of such work in the 1970s.

Cultural work. This term, with its roots in the panprogressive Popular Front cultural organizing of the '30s, emphasizes the socially conscious nature of the work, stressing the role of the artist as cultural worker, countering the tendency to see art making as a frivolous occupation, a pastime as opposed to important labor.

"Participatory arts projects," "community residencies," "artist/community collaborations"—the list of labels is very long. Even though it is a mouthful, we prefer "**community cultural development**" because it encapsulates the salient characteristics of the work:

- **Community**, to distinguish it from one-to-many arts activity and to acknowledge its participatory nature, which emphasizes collaborations between artists and other community members;

- **Cultural**, to indicate the generous concept of culture (rather than, more narrowly, art) and the broad range of tools and forms in use in the field, from aspects of traditional visual- and performing-arts practice, to oral-history approaches usually associated with historical research and social studies, to use of high-tech communications media, to elements of activism and community organizing more commonly seen as part of non-arts social-change campaigns; and

- **Development**, to suggest the dynamic nature of cultural action, with its ambitions of conscientization…and empowerment and to link it to other enlightened community-development practices, especially those incorporating principles of self-development rather than development imposed from above.

Within the community cultural development field, there is a tremendous range of approach, style, outcome—in every aspect of the work.[15]

[15] *Creative Community,* pp. 4–5.

Researching the current state of the global field in order to identify participants for the May 2001 Community, Culture and Globalization conference, we began with archival resources. At first, we searched through Web sites and publications for organizations that had been fairly prominent in years past. Some of these—for example, the Third World Popular Theatre Network mentioned above—had effectively disappeared from view. Later, during the online dialogue that preceded our conference, David Kerr e-mailed this story:

> In 1983 popular theatre workers from all over the "Third World" meeting in Koitta, Bangladesh, tried to set up IPTA (International Popular Theatre Alliance), to help mobilise work at a global level, with an annually rotating leadership. The first chair was to be Karl Gaspar.…Unfortunately, shortly after Karl's return to the Philippines, he was detained by the Marcos regime, and his files confiscated.…IPTA was in disarray. Several others in the original organisation had problems. The police in Malawi simply confiscated virtually

all my mail for two years (my postal arrest I called it!). Dickson Mwansa in Zambia did try to pick up the mantle, and did draw attention to abuses against popular theatre workers (Karl's case, arrested student actors in Malawi, etc.), but it was very difficult. The inertia of involvement in local struggles made it hard for us to unite at a global level.

Such are the conditions faced by many community cultural development workers, making continuity and coordination a perpetual challenge. But we were heartened that even though earlier networks had disintegrated, it proved possible to trace the progress of some of their constituent parts, and thus we were able to learn a little about who is active now and what they are doing.

Within the field as a whole, development has been uneven. Without question, the most vigorous and well-established branch of the community cultural development field today centers on Theater of the Oppressed and other dramatic practices originated by Augusto Boal: fully a third of the essays in this volume touch on such work, and that is representative of the community cultural development work evident around the globe. Related but independent popular-theater practices—such as PETA's "Basic Integrated Arts Workshop," used by many Asian people's theater workers—have had tremendous staying power, enabling community artists to work effectively with an enormous range of social and age groups. As Paul Heritage's essay points out, the effectiveness of such work has been recognized even in sectors that don't normally interact with community cultural development practitioners, such as prisons, and this recognition has aided its expansion.

Co-created public works of visual art—mainly but not exclusively murals— have also had staying power as "sites of public memory," a rubric coined by Judy Baca. Video production has been a viable platform for community cultural development projects since the first portable and relatively low-cost cameras and editing technologies began to emerge in the 1970s. As new media penetrate visual-arts practice, community artists have begun to create Web sites, CD-ROMs, video games, databases and new software as the virtual equivalent of public art, monuments in cyberspace to community cultural development. After popular theater, practices centering on the creation of static or moving-image media expressing community identity and concerns appear to be second in scale within the global field. Approximately a quarter of the essays and interviews in this volume touch on work in these sectors.

As already noted, community cultural development work is adaptable to any arts medium and virtually any style or technical approach. But for complex reasons, there is not as much activity in dance as in theater, not as much work that results in writing as in murals. One factor may be that these artistic practices tend to have higher thresholds for competence. For instance, as Bárbara Santos' essay points out, participants (including those with underdeveloped literacy skills) who engage enthusiastically in theatrical improvisation and character development may easily be daunted at the stage where an improvised script becomes a written document. This anthology contains only one essay dealing with dance, and one that treats oral-history practice, a specific form of literary production often used in other forms of arts work.

No collection of 21 chapters could possibly do justice to this movement in all its diversity and variation. There are significant gaps here in terms of world regions, types of practice and approaches—gaps we sincerely hope will soon be filled by other publications that will contribute to a composite picture of a field full of promise and badly in need of support to realize that promise. In the meantime, consulting the Web sites and publications mentioned in this volume and in the Further Resources section of "Creative Community" will lead any curious reader to more accounts of community cultural development practice.

2

The Tonalmachiotl,
the Sun's Stone or Aztec
Calendar, as portrayed
in a drawing by
Martha Ramirez Oropeza.

Universidad Nahuatl-Mascarones, A.C.
Tlacopan 10, Barrio Tlacopan
Ocotepec, Morelos, Mexico
Telephone: (73) 82-13-80
Fax: (73) 13-42-10
E-mail: uninahuatl@hotmail.com
Web site: www.universidad-nahuatl.com

Martha Ramirez Oropeza's
professional work is as a mural
painter, performer and creator
of indigenous/popular theater
and as a researcher into ancient
Nahuatl manuscripts called
codices. She serves as vice-
director of the Mascarones
Theatre Group, with which she
has worked for 30 years, and
as cofounder, administrator and
designer of the pyramid campus
of the Nahuatl University that
Mascarones and its supporters
created in Ocotepec, a small
community close to Cuernavaca,
in the Mexican state of Morelos.
She also teaches at Nahuatl
University and promotes cultural
exchange with faculty and
students from universities based
in the United States.

Her own biography embodies
many of the contradictions of
globalization, from her childhood
as a migrant farmworker, picking
prunes from the age of four in the
California agricultural fields—
and having to relearn Spanish
after it had been driven out of
her head by a second-grade
teacher who washed her mouth
out with soap. Growing up in the
violent Pacoima barrio of Los
Angeles, she took part in the
militant awakening of La Raza,
of the Chicano[1] movement,
participating in a victorious
hunger strike for the United
Farmworkers Union, designing
posters for anti-war demonstrations, painting her first murals,
studying with maestro David A.
Siqueiros and, in 1971, joining
Mascarones.

This essay is remarkable for its
seamless fusion of ancient
cultural symbols and contemporary
realities, reflected throughout
Mascarones' work. The expan-
sive nature of the group's vision
and its aim of cultural recon-
struction seem to embody an
understanding of culture's
encompassing nature, the way it
is possible to draw from the well
of cultural tradition and use what
is learned to move forward. The
sheer ambition, enterprise and
zeal required to create a university
—all in the service of community
cultural development—inspires
awe. Here's a bit of the information she contributed in the spring
of 2001 to the online dialogue
among the authors represented
in this volume:

*Speaking in terms of my own
country, if we want to seriously
counter the negative effect of
globalization, this neo-colonization,
we must start by working with
our youth, especially indigenous
youth, to promote self-esteem,
pride of our identity…But how
to feel pride of being the sector
of Mexicans that live in the
worst possible conditions, all
they want is to someday be able
to escape this extreme poverty.
This is one of the most important
tasks our Nahuatl University
has taken on in our town….
When we arrived here in 1989,
the local authorities asked me*

[1] Chicano: Term used to
identify people of Mexican
heritage who suffer
discrimination in the
United States and struggle
against it.

to paint a mural which reflected the historical past of the town on the walls of the government office. This wonderful personal experience led me to the idea of teaching Nahuatl culture directly in the elementary school.

So, 12 years ago, after consulting with the local authorities, ... teachers and parents, we instituted an annual spring festival, "Xopanixtli," to celebrate the new year in the ancient Nahuatl calendar. ... Each year, we work with 500 students, teaching them myths, poems, Aztec dances, and especially the national anthem in the Nahuatl language. Because of the latter, the school has received recognition and prizes in state competitions. When the TV or radio comes to interview them, these children, who are daughters and sons of farmers, are now proud to say they are Nahuatl.

And the children go home to sing and speak Nahuatl to their grandparents, who still speak the language. The middle generation, the children's parents, forced to forget Nahuatl, to learn Spanish, also begins to "remember."

Addressing the specific situation of indigenous people in Mexico, this essay provides useful insight into the homogenizing tendencies of globalization and how they might be resisted.

Huehuepohualli[2]

COUNTING THE ANCESTORS' HEARTBEAT

by Martha Ramirez Oropeza

The indigenous culture of Mexico has survived repeated waves of colonization because our ancestors preserved their worldview in a highly disciplined oral tradition. This is a tradition that recognized the ordering principle of number as the invisible structure of visible time, the expression of the seasons of life that bind individuals into a living community. Many centuries before the European invasion, the indigenous cultures of Mexico devised a writing system based on the ritual calendar that governed the community's relationship with the agricultural and spiritual forces that sustained human life and spirit. By unifying the ritual life of the community in the traditional day-count of the calendar, our ancestors bequeathed us a vision of the organic unity of the world and our original place within that world.

With this in mind, I wish to make use of the ancestors' vision here to describe our own community development work. As their descendants, Mascarones'[3] work in the fields of theater, visual arts and education cannot help but reflect the perceptions and beliefs of those whose great communal works call to us from the past which lies on the other, unwritten side of history.

Although the Tonalmachiotl,[4] or Aztec Calendar Stone, is a monumental work that incorporates all the elements of the ritual calendar, its particular emphasis is on the cyclic ages by which the world is created and transformed. Each of its five Ages[5] or Suns depicts a distinct period in the development of the world itself, providing us with a model by which to encounter, evaluate, resist, adapt to and ultimately influence the forces of dehumanization that penetrate our communities.

[2] Huehuepohualli (*huehue*: ancient; *pohua*: to count; *li*: essence): The essence of the counting of the ancient. This concept (used in the title, "Counting the Ancestors' Heartbeat") is a way of applying the structure of the calendar to tell the history of Mascarones.

[3] Mascarones: The name of the Mascarones Theatre Group originated in a high school that operated in Mexico City within a neo-colonial building with masks on its walls. Because of these masks, the popular name for *Preparatoria No. 6* was *Prepa Mascarones*, "preparatory school of the masks."

[4] Tonalmachiotl (*tonal*: energy; *machio*: map, model; *tl*: essence): What is popularly known as the Aztec Calendar. A monumental sculpture of great importance can be seen in the National Museum of Anthropology. It contains the cycles of Earth, Venus and the Moon, as well as the cycle of the five Suns, or Ages.

For this reason, the Tonalmachiotl appears to us as a map for strategic action in the face of mounting pressures as Mexico struggles to defend itself against the newest wave of colonization: globalization. Because the implicit intent of those who wage the cultural war known as globalization is the cultural conquest of poorer nations lacking the economic and media resources to compete on the same field, we resort to our greatest natural resource: the wisdom of our ancestors and the vision of unity and harmony inspiring their descendants.

In the five sections that follow, I will attempt to show how our endeavor has been guided—sometimes consciously, sometimes intuitively—by the enduring vision of transformation our ancestors inscribed on the Stone of the Five Suns.

Because the shifting figure of "the Other" has evolved from its earlier form of colonizer into its current form of globalizer, our work has had to take on different manifestations in order to survive as a community-development group. In 1962, we formed the Mascarones Theatre Group under the direction of Mariano Leyva. Developing from a high-school drama class into a professional, award-winning theater group, Mascarones began recording albums of choral poetry and classical plays. The turbulence of the late 1960s politicized Mascarones, sculpting us into an institution committed to advocating for the rights of workers and indigenous people in Mexico.

What set Mascarones apart from other theater groups—and assured our survival—was our economic independence: rather than relying on universities, the government or elite funding agencies, we appealed directly to the popular needs and concerns of the time. Factory workers would set aside money from their unions to pay for a play; the farmworkers and indigenous community organizations would give us sacks of corn or beans and transport us in their tractors or trucks; political parties would set aside money for community culture activities; and in some cases, we would simply pass the hat. Furthermore, Mascarones was the first independent popular theater group to produce records, posters, books and audio tapes for supplementary income and as a means of cultural diffusion. During the past 40 years of uninterrupted community cultural development work, Mascarones has evolved a unique style of theater that responds to actual circumstances—because many of the poor and disenfranchised do not go to formal theater settings, we take our work to towns and villages.

By the late 1980s, our work had become more narrowly focused on the rights of indigenous peoples, inspiring us to create an institution that would preserve and disseminate our ancestors' culture in such a way as to increase awareness of and respect for our historical identity. Toward this end, we founded the Nahuatl[6] University.

THE JAGUAR SUN: ENCOUNTERING THE OTHER

This First Age is guided by the creative force named Tezkatlipoka,[7] or Smoking Mirror, who is identified with the obsidian mirror he carries in his chest — a mirror in which all who face him must look into their own hearts and see themselves as they truly are.

From this we learn that in order to encounter the Other it is necessary to know our own heart: before we can meet the Other face-to-face, it is necessary that we grasp the continuity of our collective identity. By confronting the ancestral memory within the Smoking Mirror, we do not allow our identity to be defined by the Other. Remembering who we are in our totality, however, requires that we educate ourselves about the essential experience that makes us one.

In 1990, we founded the Nahuatl University as a means of crystallizing theatrical experience into a deeper expression of community identity. Based on the oral tradition of the ancient *kalmekak*,[8] or centers of higher learning, we designed a curriculum with a dual objective: (1) for the urban community, 80 percent of whom have lost our native language yet deeply desire to find answers to modern problems with the ancient wisdom of the past; and (2) for the rural and indigenous community, to be supported in their struggle to retain their identity and resources. Both objectives result in increased awareness and pride in our original cultural roots.

Toward these ends, we constructed four pyramids in the traditional architectural model: standing in the four cardinal directions, the pyramids face a central plaza and ceremonial space. Within the Western pyramid of Zihuatlampa,[9] or Region of the Feminine Force of Transformation, we incorporated a traditional *temazcal*, or steam-bath, for the purpose of conducting rites of purification and self-knowledge. By inviting healers from various indigenous communities to guide our *temazcal* ceremonies, we have found our own sense of purpose arising from spiritual roots running much deeper than intellectual curiosity.

Over the past 10 years, more than a thousand individuals have been introduced to these same ceremonies and shared our sense of self-discovery. Countering the emptiness and isolation people often find in their daily routines, the *temazcal* experience reawakens their sense of belonging to a higher community. For those who re-enter the womb of the earth represented by the *temazcal*, the elements of night, fire, water, steam, medicinal plants, nurturing companions and ancient chants combine to provide participants a clearer vision of what a meaningful life entails and the steps they wish to take in order to achieve it. Because the *temazcal* itself exists within the context of a ceremonial center, surrounded by four pyramids painted with murals and other artwork,

[7] Tezkatlipoka (*tezkatl*: mirror; *i*: his; *poka*: smoke): The smoking mirror. Ancient memory, inner knowledge.

[8] Kalmekak (*kalli*: house, community; *mekatl*: rope; *k*: the place): The place of the continuity of the traditions. A school for higher learning, where young people were trained to become leaders and spiritual guides.

[9] Zihuatlampa (*zihua*: woman; *tampa*: region): The region of women, the West. It refers to the place where the Sun metaphorically sleeps with the Earth.

Nahuatl University buildings are pyramids decorated with traditional symbols.

the vision that emerges is one of wholeness: as an act of healing the fragmented identity, individual and collective, the *temazcal* reunites its participants with their natural, cultural and spiritual heritage.

Complementing this form of traditional medicine are various courses of study that Nahuatl University has instituted as part of its curriculum. The following courses in pre-Hispanic culture provide us with the basis by which to define an authentic boundary between ourselves and the Other.

By presenting classes in the Nahuatl language, for instance, we work to preserve our native tongue and to demonstrate its central role in the formation of our ancestors' thought and cultural expressions. Not only is Nahuatl a language in which words come to convey complex and multiple meanings by compounding simpler morphemes, it also produces a thought and culture of harmony and beauty: those who learn to read and speak it not only discover their cultural origins, they take its logic and poetry as inspiration for their own creative expression.

Because much of our oral tradition is handed down in the form of historical stories, myth, song and dance, these make up a substantial body of performative art we have incorporated into our theater work. Toward this end, we present workshops to teachers and community theater groups, since they have ready-made audiences with local concerns and needs. For more than 10 years now, each one of our members has directed his or her studies from the experience of theater toward a more specific area within the Nahuatl culture. As an example, I devoted my studies to the interpretation of the glyphs in ancient manuscripts, pre-Hispanic murals and sculptures. This quest brought me into connection with the research of other teachers and with indigenous artists and spiritual guides themselves. In our intensive workshops, I introduce the symbols in a classroom situation, showing slides as well as manuscripts. For instance, a special focus is interpreting the astrological calendar symbols. The day after I have introduced the symbols, students have the opportunity to paint their own particular symbols on *amatl*, the original paper used by the ancients. Or, if time permits, they make masks with their own spiritual images. Finally, the cycle culminates with a visit to Xochicalco, the National Museum of Anthropology, where they can find a meaningful relationship in the present with the greatness of the past.

By way of example, the community of Amatlan[10] had no voice by which to recount its historical drama as the birthplace of the great culture hero, Ketzalkoatl.[11] At the town's request, our theater group accepted responsibility for creating a play to commemorate the birth of Amatlan's most honored child, some 1,200 years ago. After 17 years of annual performances, our group was able to pass on the responsibility to a newly established theater group from Amatlan. This transition was accomplished in several stages: (1) members of our group designed a special two-month workshop to prepare the local group for their first theater performance; (2) we then taught them the play, rehearsed it with them, and helped them design and make their costumes and masks; (3) our final performance of the play was presented jointly with members of the local group; and (4) we publicly transferred our responsibility to the local group in a moving and solemn ceremony.

This example demonstrates how theater can *be* community identity—and how the act of reclaiming one's sense of historical self elevates the institution of theater beyond mere commodity or art form. Similar examples can be drawn from other classes that the Nahuatl University offers in the arenas of written history and its Nahuatl writing system, Mayan[12] mathematics, traditional medicine and nutrition, mural production, indigenous philosophy and poetry (or Flower and Song) and comprehensive studies of the ritual calendar as recorded in the painted manuscripts of our ancestors.

Through our efforts in the Nahuatl University, we strive to provoke in those we touch a sense of identity that reaches back to our mother culture and forward to our shared destiny—and a foundation from which to encounter any other culture as an equal.

[10] Amatlan (*amatl*: tree from which sacred paper was made; *tlan*: abundance): The land where there is an abundance of trees for making paper. The name of the town in the state of Morelos, close to Tepoztlan, where Ze Akatl Topiltzin Ketzalkoatl was born.

[11] Ketzalkoatl (*ketzal*: the quetzal bird; *koatl*: the snake): The balancing principle needed for creativity. This refers to three aspects. In cosmic terms, it indicates the planet Venus, the morning and the evening star; in terms of intelligence, it indicates great wisdom; and in myths that refer to the creation of the human being of the Fifth Sun, it indicates a degree of wisdom, as well as all of the guides prepared in this philosophy and discipline toward great wisdom, such as Ze Akatl Topitzin Ketzalkoatl.

[12] The great ancient Mayan culture developed in the southeastern region of Mexico and Central America. The flourishing culture is recognized as having created one of the most exact calendar systems, as well as discovering the concept of zero.

THE WIND SUN: EVALUATING THE OTHER

 This Second Age is guided by the creative force named Ketzalkoatl, or Plumed Serpent, who is identified with both the penetrating wind of intelligence and the wisdom of the serpent who perpetually renews itself—a wise intelligence that neither becomes narrow nor stagnant, but rather encompasses ever-widening vistas from constantly refreshed points of view.

From this we learn that in order to evaluate the Other, it is necessary to establish a viewpoint that places our efforts within the contemporary cultural context of the balance between justice and injustice: before we can assess the strengths and weaknesses of the Other, it is necessary that we develop the historical perspective to understand how its institutions of power have evolved. By exercising the conscious discernment of Ketzalkoatl, we do not allow our objectives and ideals to be defined by the Other. Creating new allies, however, requires that we point out injustices for all to see.

Holding a mirror up to the culture of dehumanization in all its many guises, our plays are intended to be participatory experiences in the sense of providing historical or mythological dramas that parallel the audience's contemporary concerns. An example of such a work is our dramatization of the life and death of Emiliano Zapata,[13] based on a series of related ballads or *corridos*[14] that arose around Zapata during the 1910 Mexican Revolution.[15] Its performance carries the audience from a time of injustices and hopelessness, through a time of rising social consciousness and hope, then into a time of popular victory tempered by betrayal and the institutionalization of a new form of exploitation.

The drama opens with the birth of Zapata in the indigenous community of Anenecuilco in the state of Morelos. Central to the mythic structure of the play is the fact that Zapata was born with a birthmark in the shape of a hand on his heart. The *corrido* begins:

> The tradition recounts that when Emiliano was born
> A hand engraved on his heart marked his greatness.

When the midwife notes aloud that the child has a sign on his heart that looks like the symbol for the community of Anenecuilco, his mother becomes alarmed. Reassuring her, the midwife reminds her of the date and forecasts the child's destiny in the manner of the ancient ritual calendar:

> He will be a guide and a companion for his people, reawakening the vision of
> a better life. His spirit will become a guiding force for our people's happiness.

[13] Emiliano Zapata: Best-loved Mexican revolutionary of 1910. Born in the state of Morelos. His example of great love for the field workers has inspired many social and political movements.

[14] *Corridos*: Ballads composed and made popular in the Mexican Revolution of 1910, encompassing ancient rhythms, oral history and the arrival of the guitar in Mexico. These songs became the popular way of sharing significant happenings of the revolutionary years when there were few other means of communication.

[15] 1910 Revolution: After more than 30 years of the dictatorship of Porfirio Diaz, the people of Mexico revolted in what was known as the Agrarian Revolution of 1910. It changed the structure of the government, although later on was betrayed. Nevertheless, it brought about important social and political reforms that benefited the people.

The author appears in a scene from the play "The Life and Death of Emiliano Zapata" by the Mascarones Theatre Group. Photo by Raul Aguilar.

The social conditions facing those who work the land is the subject of the next scene, dramatized by depicting Zapata at age 13, witnessing his father being unjustly beaten by the foreman. Confronting the social status of the land workers, which amounted to little more than slavery (symbolized by his father's shame), Zapata announces:

> When I grow up I will return the land to those who work it!

The next scene shows Zapata at 30, in a meeting with the community's council of elders. In a solemn ceremony, Zapata is handed several ritual objects that confer upon him the rank of *kalpulelke*, or leader of his people: the ancient land documents marking the boundaries of Anenecuilco; the ancient staff signifying the ancestor's wisdom; and the antique rifle carried by his predecessor. In response, Zapata hands back the staff of wisdom, saying:

> This staff will serve our cause better in your hands—but I will take this rifle in order to return the land to its rightful owners.

Then comes a montage of scenes depicting the exploitation of the land workers, their voicing of grievances, the violent reaction of the landowners and the acceleration of the revolution. The montage culminates with a meeting between Zapata and Francisco Madero, the new president of Mexico. As the liberal replacement for the deposed tyrant, Porfirio Diaz, Madero promises to fulfill the land reforms but covertly insists that Zapata accept a large land grant as a bribe. Zapata forcefully rejects the bribe, intuitively understanding that Madero will eventually betray the cause: they part ways as inevitable enemies.

There follows a scene in which Zapata's land-reform manifesto is read aloud. Because Zapata and his immediate circle spoke Nahuatl rather than Spanish, the manifesto was translated and signed by Spanish-speaking supporters— an act that permitted city dwellers far removed from the lives of the land workers to understand and support Zapata's struggle for land rights. In an uncompromising defense of land reform, Zapata's manifesto declares war against the new government of Madero. As the *corrido* relates—

> I am a rebel from Morelos,
> I will fight for the manifesto of San Luis.
> I am a rebel from Morelos
> Because Madero has not fulfilled his word.
> With my horse, my rifle, and my bullets,
> With my Virgin of Guadalupe as my shield,
> I will make the manifesto of Ayala come true,
> Or I will die in the effort.
> Wealth corrupts a man
> And estranges him from his people.

While the new government consolidates its power, Zapata implements a model of the agrarian land-reform movement: claiming most of the state of Morelos in the name of the land-reform movement and keeping his promise to return the land to the land workers, Zapata redistributes rights to the land so as to re-establish communal ownership.

In order to pacify the nation by forcing the institutionalization of the revolution, Venustiano Carranza, the new president, sets out to assassinate Zapata. The *corrido* recounts the treachery of Guajardo:

> They left from Tepalcingo in the direction of Chinameca.
> Zapata was with Guajardo because he believed him to be trustworthy.
> I will sleep in Water-of-the-Ducks,
> You and your men go on ahead to Chinameca.

The next scene shows Zapata sleeping with his wife, then awakening from a nightmare in which the birthmark over his heart has disappeared. In a flash of insight, his wife recognizes this as a portent of his death. Although she tries to stop him from rejoining Guajardo, Zapata departs and falls into Guajardo's ambush:

> Little bubbling stream, what did that carnation have to say?
> It says that our leader has not died, that Zapata shall return.
> And that this is the end of the *corrido* of the inconceivable treason
> By which Emiliano Zapata lost his life.

For the contemporary citizen of Mexico, this story is no less relevant today than 90 years ago. Repeated promises of reform have consistently been broken. Those who sacrifice for reform have consistently been betrayed. The need for widespread and deep-seated reform has consistently been ignored.

By attuning ourselves to the enduring myths of our people, the Mascarones Theatre Group has endured to tell and retell those stories that allow contemporary audiences to judge the acts of their exploiters and take sides against them.

THE LIGHTNING SUN: RESISTING THE OTHER

 This Third Age is guided by the creative force named Tlalok,[16] or Drink of the Earth, who is identified with the rainstorm and its attendant lightning—a nurturing and animating force that ensures survival under even the harshest conditions.

[16] Tlalok (*tlalli*: land; *oktli*; drink): The sacred drink of the land, rain. The masculine waters. The powerful force of a storm. Lightning, thunder, rain.

From this we learn that in order to resist the Other, it is necessary to both find strength in the ritual life of our ancestors and foster that same strength in the community as a whole: before we can mount a credible resistance to the culture of the Other, it is necessary that we experience how our indigenous culture instills in us a wise face and wise heart. By embodying the vitality and fortitude of Tlalok, we do not allow our inner experiences to be defined by the Other. But holding on to our way of life requires that we re-enact our traditions as if our people's survival depended on it.

The last days of October and the first two days of November have since ancient times been celebrated in Mexico by the ritual called Mikiztli, or Day of the Dead: over a period of two weeks, all of Mexico coexists with the spirits of the deceased. Preparations begin nine days before the Day of the Dead with making of skeletons, traditional foods and public and private altars; through the use of rosaries and fireworks, the living guide the spirits of the deceased home. Five days before the Day of the Dead, the spirits of those who have died violent deaths are remembered and consoled. One day before the Day of the Dead, offerings are set out for the spirits of those who have died as children. On the Day of Dead itself, special attention must be paid to the spirits of family members who have died in the past year. An all-night vigil ensues where family and friends visit with the spirits of their loved ones, and the following day each family takes their offering to the cemetery to share it with the deceased. The nine days after the Day of the Dead are again accompanied by rosaries and fireworks in order to help guide the spirits back to Miktlan, or the Land of the Dead.

One of the most recent manifestations of the cultural war is the encroaching tide of mass-produced masks, costumes and candies typical of the "trick-or-treat" aspect of Halloween as celebrated in the United States. Because Halloween falls near the most important dates of the Day of the Dead ceremonies, its appeal to urban children threatens the continuation there of this ancient tradition into the next generation. Innocuous as the trick-or-treat holiday may appear, its masks and costumes are almost universally of a frightening or ugly nature, presenting a demonic or evil aspect to the deceased and death itself. Likewise, mass-produced candies and related paraphernalia threaten to replace the traditional hand-made and home-made papier-mâché skeletons and ceramic toys and figurines. Because the burgeoning population of Mexico represents such a large market for the products of global consumer culture, the economic forces driving the entry of Halloween merchandise into urban Mexico are considerable. Visits to urban supermarkets and malls during the past few Day of the Dead seasons have revealed that a minimum of 60 percent of the floor space dedicated to seasonal merchandise is for Halloween and trick-or-treat products.

For the past 35 years, our theater group has performed "Las Calaveras de Posada" ("The Skeletons of Posada"), a play we adapted based on the characters created by the great engraver Jose Guadalupe Posada. Using skeletons to comment on contemporary social and political conditions at the time of the Mexican Revolution of 1910, Posada combined art and satire to criticize the powerful—a combination that inspired the Mexican muralist tradition a generation later. Mascarones' production of this play has proven to be our most popular and enduring—a fact we attribute to its reflection of a purer time in which the Day of the Dead celebration had not been trivialized by the culture of globalization.

The scope of the play carries the audience from pre-Hispanic times, in which the skeletons quote the great Nahuatl poet–philosopher Netzahualcoyotl; through the European invasion, in which the skeletons relive the attempt to exterminate their civilization; through the colonial period, in which the skeletons recount three centuries of oppression at the hands of foreign kings; through the War of Independence from Spain, the French Intervention, the U.S.–Mexican War and the Agrarian Revolution of 1910, in which the skeletons pay homage to Posada and describe the social conditions that brought about the revolution; into modern times in the form of a debate between two popular characters, the Pulquera, a witty, truth-telling drunkard, and the Catrina, a snobbish, prissy member of the nouveau riche; and finally the play ends with all the skeletons throwing a big party and inviting the audience onto the stage to dance.

Characteristic of the play's theme is the following verse, spoken by a female skeleton who is explicitly identified with the Mexican conception of Death:

> Here am I, represented in another form,
> Without scythe or hourglass,
> As the final place of dwelling.

Through the use of pathos, humor and biting satire, the play builds one catharsis upon another to produce the laughter and tears that fortify the heart against the perennial cycles of invasion.

THE WATER SUN: ADAPTING TO THE OTHER

 This Fourth Age is guided by the creative force named Chalchiuhtlikue,[17] or Jade Skirt, who is identified with lakes, rivers and streams—a nurturing force that adapts to circumstances without losing its essential nature.

From this we learn that in order to adapt to the Other, it is necessary to subvert its institutions of power to our own ends: before we can chart our own course across the landscape of the Other, it is necessary that we ensure our own objectives and goals will never be subverted by success or recognition. By making ourselves as resilient and versatile as Jade Skirt, we do not allow the way we interact with our surroundings to be defined by the Other. Crossing the most desolate terrain without losing our way, however, requires that we keep our gaze fixed on the guiding star of our core values and principles.

As the Mascarones Theatre Group grew and evolved, we sought ways to achieve economic stability that would not pressure us to sacrifice our vision of social transformation. In 1984, we were invited by the governor of the state of Morelos to create a Commission for Cultural Development that would benefit primarily the rural population of the state. Despite a limited budget, Mascarones organized 11 troupes of artists who traveled between the 400 towns of rural Morelos, creating a new audience and, thereby, a renaissance of popular theater. Our relationship with the government lasted for 13 years, proving beneficial to the rural areas, the government and ourselves.

An important aspect of our cultural-development work was the production of murals under my direction as Mascarones' vice-director and longest-standing member. After apprenticing with the master muralist David A. Siqueiros, I joined Mascarones in 1971 and have since produced approximately 20 murals. An example is the large-scale mural "Kuauhtemok"[18] that occupies the local government office in the indigenous township of Tetelcingo, whose citizens contributed to the mural's theme by sharing the stories making up their local oral history.

[17] Chalchiuhtlikue (*chalchihuitl*: jade, precious stone; *kue*: skirt): Jade Skirt. The feminine waters. The penetrating rivers, lakes, seas.

[18] Kuauhtemok (*kuauhtli*: eagle; *temok*: descends): The Eagle That Descends. Last Tlahtoani (governor) of Mexico. A young man of only 21 years who confronted the Spaniards in 1521, guiding his people in a heroic defense of the nation. Undoubtedly the most powerful symbol against foreign intervention.

In the mural "Emiliano Zapata," the agrarian revolutionary hero rides on horseback with machete in hand to defend Koatlikue, Mother Earth, and the right to "Tierra y Libertad" (Land and Freedom). The mural was done with community artists directed by Martha Ramirez in the Agricultural Collective Government Building in Yautepec, Morelos. Photo from the Mascarones Archive.

I produced a previous version of that mural's theme in 1988 for the State Auditorium of Morelos. That mural spanned two large panels, each 25 feet high and 40 feet wide, depicting an indigenous couple engaged in acts of their traditional way of life. Located in the most important public auditorium in the state, the mural came to play an important role in the public rallies and celebrations of its citizens.

Seven years after the mural was painted, a new governor created a unified State Institute of Culture that assimilated all existing state-funded cultural development commissions, including our own. One of the first acts of the new Institute was to remodel the old state auditorium and convert it into a modern movie theater. Without notifying us, the director of the new Institute of Culture ordered the murals irrevocably destroyed by painting over them. Ironically, the reason given was that the new director believed they would distract audiences from the movies being shown in the darkened theater.

A public outcry ensued, fueled in part by the fact that the new director had come from Mexico City after an assignment as cultural attaché in France. The community of Cuernavaca found the director's arbitrary destruction of indigenous symbols so insulting that the State House of Representatives inquired into the matter in one of their hearings, during which the director of the Institute of Culture accepted full responsibility for the destruction of the mural.

At this juncture, Mascarones had a critical decision to make: either we safeguard our longstanding theater contract with the government by not joining the public outcry, or we forfeit the economic stability of the past 13 years by filing a lawsuit against the government for the destruction of the mural. We decided to file the lawsuit, and one week later our contract with the state government was terminated.

Not abandoning our ethics, not abdicating our responsibility to protest, proved to be the right decision: six months after we filed our lawsuit, the governor was impeached after having been linked to kidnappings and narcotics trafficking. When a new governor took office and appointed a new director of the Institute of Culture, we were once again approached to participate in the Institute's program. The new government settled the lawsuit filed by Mascarones, offering both financial restitution and another public space within which to produce a new mural with themes similar to the original. Work is currently underway on that mural in the State Public Education Building, the theme of which is the role of the *tlamatini*, or makers of wise faces and strong hearts, who were the teachers in the ancient Nahuatl culture.

The outcome of this battle was not so much a victory as a vindication: while defeating a corrupt and powerful officialdom is rewarding, we found that holding to our convictions and maintaining our dignity was infinitely more fulfilling. While the pitfalls of participating in the institutions of power of the Other are many, we negotiate our way through them by staying to the path of our original vision.

Another example of our adapting to the culture of the Other and turning its artifacts to our own use involves computer technology and its communications adjunct, the Internet. Like many other community cultural-development groups, the Nahuatl University has found the Internet to be a useful tool. Specifically, it enables us to: (1) communicate with groups and individuals who share our ideals; (2) offer courses and information to those seeking to learn about Mexico's indigenous culture; and (3) provide an innovative means by which indigenous professors receive computers in exchange for teaching Nahuatl.

Three professors from indigenous communities approached us, seeking advice on how they might acquire computers by which they could produce text-books for their courses in Nahuatl. In response, we organized a month-long course in Nahuatl and announced over the Internet that people could receive instruction in exchange for donating used computer equipment in good condition. In reply, we received enough interest to provide each of the communities with the needed computers and printers.

Small-scale projects like this are rewarding for all concerned, touching individual lives in ways ultimately more meaningful than the straightforward exchange of money for services. It is equally rewarding, however, to see indigenous communities taking up the cultural products of the Other in order to preserve their own.

THE MOVEMENT SUN: INFLUENCING THE OTHER

This Fifth Age is guided by the creative force named Tonatiuh, or Shining Sun, who is identified with the light and heat of the Sun as it soars above the Earth—a transformative force that dispels the shadow of ignorance and self-interest by unwaveringly expressing the ideal of universal equality and justice.

From this we learn that in order to influence the Other, it is necessary to win the hearts and minds of those whose loyalties have not yet been settled: before we can change the course of the Other, it is necessary that we recruit allies from its own base of support. By shedding light on the equality of all cultures just as Shining Sun does, we do not allow our sphere of influence to be defined by the Other. Moving others to act with a greater sense of ethical responsibility, however, requires that we expand their vision of what is possible.

[19] 1968 saw a political student movement in Mexico, as in other parts of the world, that awoke the nation into change. The government led by Diaz Ordaz massacred thousands of students in Tlatelolco, frustrating the movement. Yet it set the basis for a deep transformation within the political structure and for the creation of a powerful wave of new political parties.

As a result of the social and political unrest of 1968,[19] Mexico began evolving a more democratic form of government in which independent political parties were tolerated and allowed to seek popular support. By the 1980s, parties representing the interests of urban and rural workers began actively seeking the support of artists and intellectuals in an effort to make their message more accessible to a wider range of voters. As a result, Mascarones was invited to contribute to a party primarily representing the interests of rural land workers.

Feeling that the time had come for us to erase all boundaries between our political and artistic efforts, we channeled our group's experience in the visual and theater arts into a political campaign. Our artistic approach to campaigning proved to be successful, eventually leading to the election of our group's founder, Mariano Leyva, to the Federal House of Representatives. His three-year term was highlighted by his proposal to reform education for indigenous people by mandating that elementary schools provide education in the indigenous language of its students. Forcing debate of such a disregarded problem was a historic victory in and of itself—and it proved to be a precursor to current efforts of the legislature to address national and international demands for indigenous rights.

As a result of the social and political unrest of the 1960s, migrant farmworkers in the United States began organizing a union in order to obtain adequate living conditions. Under the leadership of Cesar Chavez, the farmworker movement attracted supporters from nonpolitical arenas—among whom was Luis Valdez, founder of a new theater company, Teatro Campesino. Teatro Campesino became the artistic voice of the Farmworkers' Union, evolving from its initial drive for farmworkers' rights into a wider understanding of its indigenous roots.

Center image of the Aztec Calendar, showing the five Suns surrounding the face of Tlaltekuhtli, the Creative Force of the Earth, which receives the influence of the cosmos. The four squares represent four Suns: counterclockwise from the upper right, they are Jaguar, Wind, Rain of Fire and Water. The fifth Sun is Naui Ollin, Four Movements, represented in the sign of movement, the two symmetrical bars that connect two Suns each, coming together in the center, and in the four circles next to each Sun. Drawing by Martha Ramirez Oropeza.

In 1970, Teatro Campesino invited the Mascarones Theatre Group to participate in a cultural exchange with Chicano theater groups from California. One outgrowth of this festival was TENAZ (Teatro Nacional de Aztlan, or Aztlan National Theater), a transnational association cofounded by Mascarones that organized an annual festival and promoted the creation of new theater groups, more than 50 within the United States and Mexico within the 1970–74 period alone. That momentum culminated in the Fifth Annual TENAZ Festival hosted by Mascarones in Mexico City and attended by 700 people, representing 50 theater groups from North, Central and South America.

The opening ceremony of this festival took place in Teotihuacan, or Where the Creators Gather, the greatest ceremonial site of Central Mexico. Amid the great pyramids and temples of Teotihuacan, the hundreds of participants heard the unity speeches spoken in four different languages—English, Spanish, Nahuatl and Portuguese. The spirit of the opening ceremony pervaded the rest of the festival: because the shared origins of our identity were represented by the power and majesty of Teotihuacan, a profound sense of belonging began to emerge. The following days provided an exchange of experiences that helped bridge the gap between Chicanos and Mexicanos. By performing their plays before a Mexico City audience, Chicanos were able to feel themselves part of a family separated only by a political boundary, and their Mexican counterparts were able to hear in their stories of alienation the Chicanos' struggle to recover their history and culture.

During the final days of the festival, theater troupes were transported to rural villages in the state of Veracruz, where they performed before indigenous audiences. The experience culminated in a closing ceremony at the ceremonial

An audience of 2,000 attends Mascarones Theatre's performance of "Don Cacamafer" at the Casa del Lago theater in Mexico City's Chapultepec Park during the 5th Annual TENAZ Festival in 1974. Photo by Alejandro Stuart.

[20] *Tajin* (thunder): An important ceremonial center in the state of Veracruz.

center of Tajin[20]: following an indigenous wedding ceremony uniting a couple from Teatro Campesino, farewells brought us together in a vision of belonging to a single continent.

By reintroducing Chicano theater groups to their cultural heritage, Mascarones was able to play an instrumental role in the development of a shared identity and purpose. By helping newer groups in the United States organize, Mascarones was able to extend its voice and vision beyond the borders of Mexico. By demonstrating that a theater group can survive even as it holds up a mirror to commonplace injustices, Mascarones advocated for the role of the artist in the development of an international community.

During the past 20 years, there has been a growing interest in indigenous studies worldwide. This is particularly keen in the United States, where many people are now more interested in exploring the native cultures of our continent than the cultures foreign to it. To meet this growing need, the Nahuatl University has been presenting courses and workshops outside of Mexico. In this way, we are able to reach those who are unable—or unprepared—to travel to our campus.

By exposing people to a worldview that they might never otherwise encounter, the Nahuatl University attempts to provide them with an alternative way of thinking and feeling about their lives. By bringing our ancestors' way of life to those in other cultures, the Nahuatl University attempts to expand the influence of our original culture. By increasing awareness of our heritage, the Nahuatl University attempts to inspire those in other cultures to act in a way that reflects their belief in the equality of all cultures.

CONCLUSION: RECOUNTING THE ANCESTORS' HEARTBEAT

The song of the wind calls from the ancient conch, the beat of the *huehuetl*[21] drum unifies our steps: the Jaguar Sun guides us to encounter, the Wind Sun guides us to evaluate, the Lightning Sun guides us to resist, the Water Sun guides us to adapt—and as we follow the ancients' wisdom, we are moved to move others. Without this *topializtli*,[22] or teachings that we must pass on, to guide us, our actions would merely be reactions to injustice, and our outrage would have no creative purpose.

We look back at these 40 years with a sense of satisfaction. Mascarones' modern version of choral poetry was embraced by the public school system, introducing poetry into the lives of millions of children. Within Mexican professional popular theater, our survival is an example for other groups linked to the struggles and lives of the community. We have pioneered making effective statements in the National House of Representatives to preserve the indigenous language and culture; and we have founded the Nahuatl University, the first of its kind, to research and reconnect ancient wisdom with the indigenous people of today. Our institution has branched out into other forms of art and education, inspiring others by presenting murals and Nahuatl courses beyond our borders. Yet, there is much to do toward protecting each of our respective *topializtli* through international collaboration.

For those of us whose communities and cultures are at risk of being overwhelmed by the rising tide of products and images pouring out of the global commercial culture, it is of the utmost necessity that we pool our efforts to preserve our autonomous identities. Of course, this is not a battle we will win in our own lifetimes, but one that our children and theirs will have to continue. Because the military, economic and media resources of the Other are so many times greater than our own, we survive through solidarity with those of like mind—and sustain the hope of an ultimate victory by changing minds wherever we can.

[21] *Huehuetl* (*huehue*: ancient; *tl*: essence): The *huehuetl* is a sacred drum that gathers the dancers, circling the heartbeat of a united spiritual healing ritual. It is made with a hollowed tree trunk.

[22] *Topializtli* (*to*: our; *pia*: to guard, to protect, to hold; *liztli*: the essence of an action): The essence of what we must guard and pass on to the new generations. The wisdom we inherit for our children.

3

Liz Lerman (third from left) with a cross-generational group of dancers. Image originally created as an illustration for her book *Teaching Dance to Senior Adults* (1984). Photo by Dennis Deloria.

Liz Lerman Dance Exchange
7117 Maple Avenue
Takoma Park, Maryland 20912 U.S.A.
Telephone: (301) 270-6700
Fax: (301) 270-2626
E-mail: mail@danceexchange.org
Web site: www.danceexchange.org

Liz Lerman is the founder and artistic director of the Liz Lerman Dance Exchange, a cross-generational performance company and learning institution based just outside Washington, D.C. As she explained in the online dialogue carried out by the authors of this volume in the spring of 2001:

We began 24 years ago with these questions: who gets to dance? what are we dancing about? where is the dancing happening? and who cares? Answering these and other inquiries is at the basis of the work my company does both on stage and in community.

The Dance Exchange's work consists of formal concerts, interactive performances, specialized community workshops and participatory events, and training that encompasses the technical, aesthetic, community and process-dimensions of its practice. Company residencies—conducted at home in the Washington, D.C., area, at sites around the United States and abroad—seek to include all of these activities.

This essay describes a path into the community cultural development field that begins in the conventional training institutions of "mainstream" arts practice and—finding that practice inadequate or even threatening to the true purposes of the

artist's work—takes a turn into trailblazing collaborative endeavors in which the artist is first and foremost a partner with other community members. In the U.S. community cultural development field, some have perceived a tension between community and art, often expressed in the requirement that practitioners defend their work against a "dilution" that funders and policymakers fear will attach to collaborating with nonprofessionals. In this essay, Liz Lerman offers a truly substantive response, one that may surprise readers who may never have considered that such collaborations could strengthen artistry rather than diminish it.

As part of the editorial process, we asked Liz if working with a defense industry—the Portsmouth, New Hampshire, shipyard project described below—had presented a political or ethical dilemma. Here's how she replied:

One day in 1993, I got a phone call from an arts presenter in Portsmouth, New Hampshire: would we be interested in considering a residency that

would help the community face up to the very likely possibility that the shipyard would be closed as part of government cost-cutting measures? The presenter explained that among other things, the shipyard was on the federal government's "Superfund" toxic waste clean-up list. Some families in town had worked at the yard for 12 generations. I found it very complicated and very interesting, despite the fact that I considered myself anti-military and an environmentalist.

This raised questions: Who has the right to tell their stories? Who has the opportunity to discover new things about themselves and their world? Who gets to tell the history of their families? Who gets to participate in a project affording an opportunity to reconsider their ideas about neighbors or co-workers who may be of different racial or class backgrounds, sexual orientations, or political ideologies? As my father liked to remind me as I was growing up: look carefully. Things are rarely as one-dimensional as they seem.

Art and Community

FEEDING THE ARTIST, FEEDING THE ART

by Liz Lerman

When I first began teaching dance in a senior-adult residence in 1975, I was struck by the number of well-meaning friends, colleagues and guests whose response upon visiting me at work was to pat me on the head and say, "Isn't that good for them?"

Now actually, it *was* good for many of the older people who found their way into the class I taught for 10 years at Washington, D.C.'s Roosevelt Hotel for Senior Citizens. The physical range of their bodies increased as they found the joy in moving; their imaginations became animated as they learned new mind/body connections; their trust in each other grew as they partnered in dance; and their self-esteem blossomed as they made works of art. They were strengthened as a community as well: when the residents of the building staged a rent strike against the management, it was the dance-class regulars who organized it.

But it puzzled me that while observers immediately recognized the social good of this practice, they never conceived of the possibility that my work at the Roosevelt was also good for me as a person, as a teacher and as an artist—and ultimately not only good for me, but good for the art form of dance as well.

In the following pages I will describe through stories, anecdotes and observations how working in a variety of community settings has informed and vitalized my artistry and that of the countless dancers who have traveled with me over the past 25 years. This is not to suggest that the social and political good that emerges from such projects is unimportant. It is vital, and I have lots to say on the subject. But I consider this an opportunity to unveil a point of view which is not talked about very much: making art in community settings forges better artists; and it can also help to forge interesting and important art.

This essay is drawn from my own experiences and path. Trained in classical ballet and modern dance from childhood through my student days at Bennington College, I always expected to take my place in a conventional modern-dance company. After much turmoil and experimentation and many attempts to quit, I claimed a place for myself in the world of dance by merging my interests in making art and making community.

The Dance Exchange, the dance company I founded in 1976, has been committed to exploring the relationship between professional artists and community life, and to the principle that each is made better when informed by the other. Over its long history we have examined myriad ways of playing along this dynamic continuum. We are still trying to understand it. Of course, the basic context of our work is grounded in the culture and society in which it was born: late–20th-century contemporary art making in the United States. All of our language, questions and assertions are of that time and place, and are not meant to relay a completely global picture.

As a way of examining this premise, I want to divide the subject of an artist's evolution into three overlapping categories. Perhaps by pulling them apart, we can find a framework and an evolving curriculum to make the relationship of artistic practice and community interaction a way of life, not a burden; a means of building strengths, not interrupting aesthetic will.

- **Artist as technician.** What constitutes the craft of dancing, and how is it taught and learned? What aspects of this training can be taught outside the technique class and why?

- **Artist as performer.** When and how do dancers learn the skills they need to excel on the stage? In addition to academic curricula, what other avenues can prepare and sustain an artist's growth in this area?

- **Artist as choreographer.** As the dance field in the United States continues to explore methods to develop imaginative, challenging and strong choreographers, what value do community projects have as a learning playground?

TECHNIQUE: ARTIST AS TECHNICIAN

I first noticed that a community setting might actually be a wonderful place for training in dance technique when I was in graduate school at George Washington University in Washington, D.C., in the mid-'70s. As a graduate teaching assistant in dance, I was responsible for training relative beginners along with more advanced dance majors. At the time I taught a technique class similar to hundreds I had taken myself. It was designed to give students a warm-up, impart information on how their bodies could achieve more physical range and teach certain stylistic dance patterns that would allow them to actually dance for the latter part of the class.

I had grown up with structures like this. I understood what was expected between student and teacher. But I also found myself questioning some of the conventions we practiced in these technique classes. I considered them an odd form of American folk dance; you stood in lines, facing the mirror, separated and never touching, always trying to best the next dancer by getting the leg higher, turning one more revolution or looking thinner. I thought these classes were a far cry from why most of us had begun to dance in the first place. But they were and are the accepted form of learning Western-style concert dance.

My contribution to the form of technique classes was to try to make them a safe environment for people to discover what was important to them about becoming better dancers, then how to push themselves to achieve their goals. Also, unless dancers are in a company or involved in a project, class is the only time they can really dance. So I tried to make sure that at some point in the hour-and-a-half of the lesson, people could enjoy their dancing selves.

I spent a lot of time making sure everyone knew each other's names, since I had noticed that I danced better when my teacher could name me. I worked on focus because I was tired of going to dance concerts where the dancers' inner-directed focus made them seem like automatons. I wanted the students to look like people dancing instead of little machinelike technicians. I encouraged my students to find pleasure in what they were doing and to support the struggles of those around them. I taught them what I had learned by then about how the body can function in time and space in recognizable classical Western forms.

It was at this time that I also began teaching at the Roosevelt Hotel for Senior Citizens, a residential facility commonly known as the Roosevelt Hotel. My mother's recent and rather sudden death from cancer had propelled me into an emotional period of loss and reflection. Although still fairly new to

Liz Lerman Dance Exchange leads a workshop at a senior center in the early 1990s. Photo by Stuart Bratesman.

choreography (I had at that time made one formal piece for the concert stage and many informal works for my high school students in a previous teaching job), I realized that I needed to make a dance about what my family and I had gone through. I was interested in finding older people to be in that dance. My search led me to the Roosevelt Hotel, and after much discussion and good humor on the part of the staff, I was allowed one night each week to teach a class in modern dance to anywhere from 20 to 50 older adults.

Suddenly, everything I believed in was called into question—especially everything that I believed about how to train a person to become a dancer. What exercises did these folks need? How and what could I ask them to achieve? What made them look beautiful? In fact, I began to question accepted notions of who and what was beautiful. I found each class a struggle and an inspiration. I discovered new ideas and new processes at every moment. Slowly I realized that my own teaching was changing, and I brought these changes with me back to the academy.

For example, the older people danced harder, with more investment, if they understood the source of the movement. From this discovery, these older dancers and I began to develop what was to become for me a whole methodology of talking and dancing, storytelling and dancing, text and dancing. I tried similar approaches with my more sophisticated college students and found they evoked a new investment and curiosity in their dancing as well.

But the real changes occurred when I brought the college dancers to the senior center. I encouraged each of them to move around the room before the class actually began, meeting the older people and learning their names. They were greeted with great smiles and often with direct, outspoken comments about their looks, such as, "You are so pretty," or "What a great body you have!" I had become used to this type of conversation, but I was unprepared for the positive impact it had on the women students.

I also warned them that, because of the hearing and vision impairments that affected some of the older people, they might have to exaggerate their presence to make connections. I noticed that some of the shyer students were laughing, talking loudly (in order to be heard) and in general participating at a very high level. The older people made it so easy to extend oneself, converse with strangers and be big about it all. I wondered if I hadn't stumbled into a way of teaching dancers how to project character on stage. If dancing is primarily a mute form, perhaps we had found a way to evolve performance personality that was both authentic and larger than life.

At the Roosevelt, I taught a modified technique class. We began seated in chairs, working our way to standing while holding onto the chairs as a kind of barre. Eventually we would gather in a circle in the middle of the room and do some kind of extended improvisation with the goal of keeping the older dancers on their feet for as long as possible.

I made sure that everyone could and did participate at the beginning of the class. But I also made sure, as the class became progressively more physically demanding, that those who had reached their limits could become encouraging observers, able to re-enter the movement whenever they saw fit. I also encouraged all to keep adapting the movement so that even as many of us stood up, others could continue seated.

I realized that the participants were learning theme and variation in this way; when I posed all of this as artistic practice, the participation level soared. What became evident to me is that conventional technique classes assume that every student's body will proceed at the same pace as the teacher's. (I've known many dancers who would come to a certain class early to warm up so that they could be ready for the teacher's warm-up, for example, making clear the inaccuracy of this assumption.)

A favorite improvisational structure late in the class was a kind of free-form dance done in the center of the circle with each person taking a turn to solo. I always shadowed these solos, making sure dancers had plenty of room to move while remaining available to them in case of a balance problem.

Sometimes, in the excitement of the music or the audience's appreciation, the older dancers would find themselves close to falling. I wanted them to stay aware, but I also found shadowing them an interesting form of partnering.

This exercise is where I noticed the biggest change in my students. Everybody had to take a turn in the center of the circle, including the visiting dance students. Taking their turns, they danced more freely and more beautifully than I had ever seen in class. On the way back to campus they were full of excitement: "I was never able to do triple turns before. What happened?" or "My leg has never gone that high and with so much ease." This happened over and over.

I traced this new ability and agility on the part of my college students to the loving environment of the class and their audience at the senior center. I realized that in our professional training we were never in a context which was not hypercritical. The moment these young women entered the room they were considered beautiful; this was probably the only time in their dance career they had such an experience of affirmation. Instead of personal feelings of loathing about imperfect bodies, they found an opportunity to dance with people who were free with their appreciation. That in turn affected the dancers' technique, so they danced better.

I began to experiment. What happened when my students started from a place of positive feedback, a way to appreciate what they had accomplished? I observed that if they could name something particularly meaningful for themselves in what they had done, they could more easily take the next step, isolating a particular technical problem they wished to work on. It wasn't just a global, "I need to be better," but rather, "I want to work on the way I swing my leg in my hip socket."

But my larger concern as a teacher of dance was how to get my students to be human as they worked on their technical deficiencies. I have heard the same thing from other teachers, not just in modern dance but in ballet and in classical music too. Just recently I had a conversation with a ballet master who said, "We train them to be phenomenal technicians, and then we damn them because they have no passion or personality when they perform." I had tried numerous approaches in college classes, mostly various partnering schemes, where facing each other students had to accomplish difficult physical tasks. It seemed they could handle either seeing their partners or working on their technical assignments, but not both at the same time.

Professional company members (left to right) Pene McCourty, Margot Greenlee, Martha Wittman and Marvin Webb perform in "Hallelujah," a 1999–2002 project of Liz Lerman Dance Exchange. Photo by Lise Metzger.

So back to the Roosevelt we went. (An interesting aside is that when I brought my students from George Washington University with me to the Roosevelt, the number of older participants might double. It was as if they could smell young people in the building. Perhaps many of the residents came just to socialize, but eventually they were all dancing, which led to wild events with as many as 100 people cutting loose.) I began to push the older people more in their physical prowess by experimenting with the idea of shadowing. I paired everyone up early in the class, reminding my college students that they had to keep dancing while keeping an eye out for their partners' health, balance and technique. As the exercises became more demanding, problems for the young dancers increased. If they stopped dancing in order to be sure their partners were okay, they found their partners quit too. So they had to find ways to be externally involved with someone else while maintaining their own physical work.

We had spent time both at the college and at the senior center talking about what was meant by a safe environment. I had become convinced that a safe environment meant not just a nurturing place, but also a place where people were challenged to do better. The older people didn't want to be commended just because they could raise their arms at the age of 80. They wanted to learn how to do it better, bigger, in unison, with dynamism. They wanted to improve. The older people took pride in the fact that some of them were able to do push-ups, dance for a full hour, turn or jump. I didn't realize how important this was until I brought the younger dancers to class.

The question for me and my young students was whether we should dance to our full capacity, or in effect to "dumb down" in the hope of making older partners feel better about their own limitations. What we discovered was, for me, revolutionary.

My young students began to develop real skills as they partnered the older dancers. They learned how to dance fully while remaining aware of someone else. They learned how to be in support roles and how to step forward into leadership roles, whether partnering or taking a solo turn. They learned how to focus outward even as they listened to their own inner stories. They figured out how to read a room for space, for personality, to spark new movement ideas. But above all, they learned how to be themselves, to be human as they danced.

I began to talk about the work in senior centers as a training ground for professional dancers. I talked about how it was like money in the bank: the experiences we had at the senior center could serve us later in so many capacities in the dance world.

PERFORMANCE: ARTIST AS PERFORMER

I first met Keith Antar Mason at a national gathering of artists interested in community-based work. Originally set up as a way for artists from the American Southeast to congregate, Alternate ROOTS (Regional Organization of Theatres–South) had expanded to include people from all over the country, making it possible for this Los Angeles–based artist to come and perform. His performance was explosive. He is a very tall, very broad African-American theater artist and was, at that time, also very angry. In the performance he stalked the stage, moved with enormous speed and power, screamed, confronted the audience and compelled us to think about our own experience of race and racism in the United States.

I saw Keith again just 18 months later. In this later performance, he lay on the floor and moved very slowly, then rose just as slowly into a kind of ethereal dance. I was just as shocked as I had been the first time I saw him. I asked him directly, "What happened? How could you change your movement range so drastically?" His answer went something like this: he had spent the previous six months working with young offenders in the juvenile justice system. If he moved fast, percussively or with quick changes of direction (all formerly standard practice for Keith), he terrified the young people, causing them to respond with hostility. So he had to learn to move more quietly. He said it was practically a matter of life and death.

To me, this illustrates the reality of working in community. There is no pretense. Craft joins necessity to force artists to become our fully capable selves. Keith could not afford *not* to learn to move differently. He had to expand his craft, and that in turn changed and charged his performance.

Keith's story is a dramatic and very tangible example of how working in community can affect performing artists' range. Here are a few more.

For most of the '90s, my choreographic work focused on issues of identity. With my company, I did a series of works that allowed us to look at questions of belonging. In "The Good Jew?" I was put on trial to judge whether I was "Jewish enough." In "Shehechianu," we explored our own individual family and tribal histories, examining their impact on our stories in the present. In "Safe House: Still Looking," we worked with various communities in Wilmington, Delaware (on the east coast of the United States), to examine the local history of the Underground Railway,[1] as well as contemporary issues of safety and comfort. In each of these works, we carried on community projects in association with the formally staged performances. In some cases we were joined by our community partners, which in this case included local professional dancers and students, young people from a primarily Latino urban arts program, and a gathering of local storytellers. Sometimes the community and performance events happened within the same time frame, but not in the same space. Because we worked so intently on both concert and community projects, we discovered many ways in which each informed the other.

Describing the particulars of the work "Safe House: Still Looking" will help to explain these relationships. "Safe House" was originally commissioned by the University of Delaware. We were asked to spend time in Wilmington, the largest city in the state of Delaware and about a 20-minute drive from the university. The commissioner hoped we would make a work that celebrated something about the city. One common thread in all of our conversations was how proud people were of the city's role in the history of the Underground Railway. That got us to thinking about contemporary connections to running away, aiding refugees, the comfort of the known and the fear of the unknown. I would describe the structure of the dance we made as "big story, little story," where we look for our own personal stories inside the larger fabric of history. This dance was constructed as a series of solos in which each dancer told a contemporary, personal story that revealed something about these questions. These in turn were interspersed with larger-group sections that contained either fierce dancing, stories taken from narratives of escaped slaves or sections involving the whole group in a kind of prayer.

[1] The Underground Railway was a network of safe houses and individuals who helped runaway slaves reach free states in the northern United States and Canada. It operated from about 1840 to 1860, most intensely after the passage of the Fugitive Slave Act in 1850 enabled slave hunters to pursue runaways onto free soil.

One characteristic that marked the period of making and performing "Safe House" was the work's site-specificity, meaning we found ourselves performing in many places other than stages. Although we had been doing this for some time, our work in "Safe House" grew because we connected the content of the dance with the conditions and situations of the sites in which we performed. Whether dancing in someone's home, swimming pool or church, the events proved engaging, fruitful, surprising, useful and delightful for our audiences. Subtle changes happened to the dancers and their performing, and again it is these changes I would like to discuss.

One form of site-specific engagement we evolved in this period is what we call "house parties." These are intimate performances held in someone's home for audiences of 50 to 100. We will often try new ideas at house parties or use segments of longer stage works for these small and intimate portraits. Both of these processes are of great importance to our choreographic explorations, teaching us so much about the dances and about ourselves as performers.

So we found ourselves making a dance about historical safe houses while also performing in houses. One of these performances took place in a rather small home, which meant that most of the dancing occurred in very tight spaces. At one point in the evening, the dancers scattered throughout the house to perform their solos from "Safe House." Each reported how strangely real it became to try to move expansively in small spaces and to tell stories of running in the night, terror, escape and comfort while dancing in a linen closet, a tiny space under the stairs, behind a door or in a dark bathroom. All reported that it changed the way they next performed the work on stage. Partly it was a matter of scale, of having to force large physical movements into tiny spaces, making the experience of the concept much more real.

The final performance of "Safe House" in Delaware took place in the Quaker Meeting House where Thomas Garrett and Harriet Tubman did so much of their work on the Underground Railway together. He was a member of the Quaker Meeting and is buried in the courtyard. She led many escaped slaves through Wilmington, often relying on his protection. At the conclusion of the performance, we taught the audience a simple dance made up of some of the gestures they had just seen. We again mentioned the incredible strength of these two individuals. We asked the audience to think of their own ancestors who they would wish to "walk with them" in this life. Then we invited everyone outside to perform the dance in the courtyard in close proximity to Garrett's grave. Suddenly the first movement of the dance, reaching down and touching the earth, had concrete meaning; it was no longer just a symbol. Likewise, the gesture of reaching back to make a beckoning circle of the lower arm took on new meaning, as if we were calling Mr. Garrett and Ms. Tubman to join us in the present.

What happens to the performance ability of a dancer asked to research stories about a time and place, live with these stories over the course of a year, work with people in many settings to aid them in discovering their own stories, perform these stories in a house and on a stage and in a place where the actual events happened? I believe that the accumulation of physical, emotional and historical meaning leads the dancer to a new level of investment and a different understanding of what the movement itself might mean and convey to another person. In a world as abstract as the world of movement, such experiences carry enormous weight.

For me, an excellent dance performance includes the following: the dancers are 100 percent committed to the movement they are doing; they understand why they are doing what they are doing. And something is being revealed in that moment: something about the dancer or about the subject, about the relationship of the dancers or about the world in which we live. Something is revealed. Too many dance concerts lack these elements. When I think about our dance training, I realize how little time and encouragement we receive to develop our skills in finding such meaning in dance.

This is precisely the information so many professional dancers lack as they take the stage in dance after dance without knowing the meaning of their movement. Given no compelling reason to make one movement instead of another, a kind of ennui sets in, and both audience and performer are relegated to perceiving the movement in purely physical terms, and therefore often only able to measure its success against a standard of virtuosity.

As one company member explained to me recently, the impact of working in community and then bringing the resulting images to the stage is in part that she has a much better and truer picture in her mind as she performs. When she has a true picture, she feels her own performance is more nuanced, and she believes audience members can find their own pictures sooner. As the piece gets performed over and over in different settings, there is an opportunity for the performer to reflect and synthesize anew the information she receives from her interactions with sites and audiences. This keeps the dance fresh and the performing experience unique, and that is always a blessing.

Lastly, interaction with community folks on stage requires a delicate balance that sustains multiple levels of excellence and authenticity. Each company member must constantly solve the dilemma of being a person who dances and has high technical capacity, who must both play a role and remain aware while onstage. This is the synthesis that artists at the Dance Exchange attempt to make at all times. This is what makes them such interesting and beautiful performers.

CHOREOGRAPHY: ARTIST AS CHOREOGRAPHER

There is a symbiotic relationship between choreographing in community settings and for the stage. In my artistic practice, the way they inform each other is complete. But this wasn't always true for me, and so I will try to document some of the more salient moments of change.

My experience in making art within community settings has evolved over time. In the beginning, I taught people a dance I had made for them. The most successful of these dances (which we still perform) is called "Still Crossing." The company performs the first part of that dance alone. At the end they are joined onstage by many others who have all learned the same dance. Originally choreographed for older adults, we now do the piece as a large community effort that makes it possible for diverse groups to work together quickly and with satisfaction. While we always teach the dance so as to ensure that the movement has real meaning for the performers, in "Still Crossing" they are not the originators of the movement.

Over the years, however, I began to feel that I could intensify the art-making experience for all of us if I worked differently. During the "Safe House" period, we began to integrate new stories into an existing work. As we toured, we included community members onstage with us telling stories of their own that we had curated for the performance. But after awhile, this too felt formulaic.

When we got a commission to work with the Portsmouth Naval Shipyard (a 200-year-old federal facility in New Hampshire, on the east coast of the United States), we decided to enter the community with no preordained idea of structure or content or even the form of the culminating event of our collaboration. Through months and months of conversation, participatory workshops and small gatherings, including little performances, the final event took shape. This opened up a whole new world of choreographic exploration which, as I write, is continuing to unfold.

With this approach, the community is a full artistic partner from the beginning: what we do, how we do it, who does it, what it is about—all questions are resolved in the context of time spent in the community devising the dance together. We still make many artistic decisions, but these decisions are taken in dialogue with the participants.

Many interesting aesthetic challenges emerge from this process, and I would like to focus on two that involve the kind of artistic process native to the rehearsal studio. The differences in our approach concern who is involved and how public the processes become. The first I would categorize as naming and defining. The second is about choreographic structure.

It is inspirational to work with people who are untrained in artistic practice, yet totally committed to making art together. One of my jobs in this equation is to communicate where we are in the creative process—sometimes to apathetic listeners or curious but skeptical onlookers—and to help people understand why we are doing what we are doing. Once people commit to joining us, they are in for quite an emotional and intellectual journey. As a schoolteacher in Portsmouth said to me several years after we had finished our work there, "You taught me that I didn't need to know the ending before getting started at the beginning. This is a great life lesson. In fact it has changed my life completely." I am convinced that her confidence in us came about in part through our willingness to explain the artistic process as it unfolds, to name the experience as it happens. We don't do this alone. There is ample time for reflection by the participants as they begin to discover their own ability to acknowledge to each other their personal and collective experience.

But this naming process has a peculiar and I think useful effect on me too. The act of naming helps me understand my own choreographic methods better, to repeat them as needed in other settings and to pass them on to my students and colleagues. It doesn't mean that I act in a rote way, but rather that I have become accustomed to communicating with my collaborators as either intuitive leaps or familiar methods lead us to our goal.

Sometimes I think this naming feels counterintuitive and frightening, especially for artists who are trained to equate inarticulateness with the mystery of art. Quite the contrary, I have found that the more I can describe and name, the more mysterious and miraculous it all becomes. Indeed, it appears that this very understanding makes it easier for me to take on risk. Comprehension leads to freedom in quick problem solving that gives me the courage to enter even more complex and challenging circumstances. It helps me to work quickly, which is good because so often there is very little time and people are busy.

As I enter communities and begin conversations and experiential workshops, the people with whom I am working often introduce me to interesting and subtle choreographic ideas. These are ideas I would not have had alone, nor if I had stayed in the studio working only with my wonderful company. For me, this is where it gets so exciting, because the more I think I understand, the more mysterious the road in front of me becomes.

The brevity of our initial encounters and the short time span in which we often make and craft work with community partners has taught me much. Often those first encounters allow me to develop "muscles" that come in handy as the projects unfold. For example, when we were asked by the major performing arts center in Portsmouth to come and work on the shipyard project, I was surprised, delighted, scared. Over a period of three years we made many visits, eventually carrying out a weeklong festival with events occurring both in the shipyard and in the community beyond the yard. It took constant attention to introduce the idea of a modern dance company working with the history and stories of a shipyard and the people who lived there. We continuously enlarged the circle of participants. I want to describe four different encounters where the naming of our process brought me insight and where—simply by explaining something about how dance might be used—I learned new choreographic tools from the audience.

First, our initial public meeting brought out a very diverse crowd, including retired engineers, older community members who had worked with us before, several arts professionals, a relative of someone lost in a submarine accident of enormous consequence to the yard and some folks from the staff of the Music Hall, the presenter who had commissioned this work. I talked about how we might develop the project and gave people a sense of what I imagined might take place. During a question-and-answer period, one of the engineers asked if I knew how submarines worked. I didn't. As he began to explain, his hands flew through the air with a delicacy that belied his size. Other engineers jumped in with their own explanations, and again hands danced through the air as they made me see the physicality of the boats and the design elements that allow them to function.

One of the tools I rely on is something we call "spontaneous gesture," which means watching for choreographic ideas in the natural movement of people's hands as they express themselves. I had never before seen gestures so graceful and lively. As I watched the engineers work to express themselves, I also gleaned a new understanding of another tool—physical metaphor—which describes the many ways in which an idea and its meanings can be translated through movement. This concept would prove to be one of the aesthetic paths we would pursue as the project unfolded. In short, I noticed at this first meeting that while I could continue to depend on a choreographic tool I knew and understood, I was also beginning to discover and utilize another one, one that had emerged from the engineers.

Second, early in the project I had to visit the Rotary Club (an organization of local business and professional leaders with chapters around the world) to explain what we were doing. In previous experiences of these kinds of civic clubs, I had often encountered the most intense skepticism. I knew I would have to make my points clearly, directly and with charm. I was delighted to find that the Portsmouth club was not a men's-only affair. American women had entered these formerly all-male clubs, making the atmosphere decidedly different. I talked for a few minutes, then asked people for images of the shipyard. One woman spoke up immediately to say it wasn't an image, it was a sound. It turned out that she had used the horn signaling the morning shift as her alarm clock all through school; her connection to the yard was completely aural. Then others began talking about the sounds they had heard. It was a moment of swift enthusiasm, with stories told one on top of the other. For me, it opened up a new area of aesthetic representation I had not previously considered for this project. In naming the experience for myself, I named the choreographic structure, enabling myself to begin to imagine a new section of the dance.

Third, after several meetings with an odd mix of individuals interested in the project, it was suggested that we have lunch at the shipyard with the heads of all the departments. This meant a mixture of military and civilian employees, most with administrative responsibility. I was given 10 minutes to talk and take questions and another few minutes for the company to perform. (They ended up doing an improvisation based on the conversation they heard dancing around tables throughout the room.)

What I remember most about this encounter was the amazing quantity of artistic ideas that poured out from the men who had gathered, beginning the moment they were invited to speak. One suggested that the berth where boats were docked for maintenance was a natural amphitheater; in fact, he had privately thought of his work as a kind of performance. Another mentioned the different uniforms connoting different services carried out at the shipyard. Everyone laughed at this, taking enormous pleasure in thinking of the various colors and types of uniforms as costumes (especially those for workers in the nuclear division). Once again, I was taken into new choreographic avenues, given ideas we could take back to the studio and prepare into structures for the community to explore and we could use in our concert work.

Fourth, things moved along in our shipyard project—up to a point, which was the ongoing problem of getting access to what was still a semi-secret government operation. It was decided that I should meet with the commander to negotiate a little more ease in our comings and goings. I was given five minutes of his time.

I spoke very briefly about our project. The commander responded by saying he thought projects like this helpful. When I asked him to explain more, he really began to talk. He said that the shipyard was still cloaked in the secrecy of the Cold War, that the public didn't understand what they were doing, that it all seemed like a great mystery. And that he wanted to change this.

I asked him if he was talking about the shipyard or about modern dance. Except for the Cold War imagery, I said, we could have been discussing

Community participants in the Shipyard Project, 1996, perform with the bridge linking Portsmouth, New Hampshire, with Kittery, Maine, in the background. Photo by George Barker.

either. We both loved that connection. Access was granted, and we launched what we both thought of as a literacy project. I was able to give a new name and new slant to our work by making an analogy to the story I heard from a naval base commander. And he got to see his work and the work of those around him in a new light. The shipyard is a place of immense creativity, collaboration, performance, much a like a small modern dance company. By giving a name to our common ground, we each discovered something new about our disciplines.

IN CONCLUSION

Over the years, as I bustled between concert work and community practice, I often felt I was bringing what I had learned from art making in the studio to my endeavors within the community. The equation seemed more weighted toward sharing concepts and ideas from our studio work with the communities we worked with, to their benefit. But in these last few projects, I have come to see how much my work in the community has emboldened me to make more cutting-edge work for the stage. I see that the freedom to work in so many different ways, with so many invested and excited people, has given me nuance and approaches I would never have discovered had I practiced choreography in isolation from community.

Here is one final example from my work in religious settings, especially synagogues. In the past few years, I have been given the opportunity to build participatory dances within the worship service itself, and I have found this amazing. In my early work in the Jewish community, I spent most of my time in workshop mode, giving people experiences with text and movement in the guise of study groups. Then, as a fledgling member of a local synagogue, I began to experiment with building participatory dance experiences into the service itself. We took it very slowly. I usually did my sessions in 10- or 15-minute segments, often at family services where, out of the desire to involve children, there is high tolerance for experimentation within the framework of tradition. Only in hindsight did I realize that much of this exploration had taken place during a time of deep introspection on the part of religious leaders seeking ways and means to help their congregants make deeper spiritual connections.

I found that many people were seeking new paths within the worship experience. Despite the traditions surrounding typical services, they were even willing to try movement. Over a seven-year period, I was able to discover several ways in which dance could be a valuable part of public prayer. Now when I create a worship experience, I see the "audience" doing so many different things. They will sit and read, sit and listen, sit and sing, sit and talk, sit and dance, stand and do all of the above. The shock was that contrary to my thinking, congregants were willing to try new things in the most traditional of settings. We could stretch the participatory nature of art and religion in many contexts, even within the formality of worship services.

When I noticed the complexity of congregants' experience, I began to compare it to the typical performing-arts audience, which basically sits and watches. That made me wonder: for a long time, I had thought a formal concert was the last place to experiment. We felt free to do many things in strange sites, so long as when it was time for the formal concert in the big theater with the fancy lights and the high ticket prices, we were bound by the expectations that milieu carried.

So now I have begun to try to break that down too. Our most recent project —"Hallelujah"[2]—is for the "audience that won't sit still." I would never have attempted some of what we are doing now if I had not seen first in countless community settings how far people are willing to go to have a real experience. This taught me that even an audience seated in a theater helps to make the art that they watch.

[2] The word is based on the Hebrew for "praise" and "God," an exclamation of praise associated with Jewish and Christian worship, but also used in secular parlance. Conducted in 15 cities throughout the United States, the Hallelujah project created a series of dances "in praise of" topics emerging from the Dance Exchange's community encounters at each site.

As I write this final paragraph I am one week into a four-week residency for the Hallelujah project that is to culminate in a large performance at a beautiful 1200-seat theater at the University of Michigan in Ann Arbor in the Midwest of the United States. The project will include participants from both Detroit (the major urban center sometimes known as "the Motor City" for its role in the auto industry) and Ann Arbor. Some people we have been working with for over a year, and some are new to us and our process. From many years of making art by myself, with my company of professionals and with so many people in communities seeking meaning and enlightenment, I know that making this dance experience valuable will require merging what I know as an artist and what I know as a human being. It is my work in community that has taught me how to do that.

The author wishes to acknowledge John Borstel, Humanities Director of Liz Lerman Dance Exchange, for his contributions to the content and organization of this article.

Protestors stand in
the rising waters of river
Narmada. Photo from
Abhivyakti.

4

Abhivyakti Media for Development
31-A, Survey No. 8, Kalyani Nagar,
Anandwalli Shiwar, Gangapur Road
Nashik 422 013, Maharashtra, India
Telephone and Fax: (91 0253) 346128
E-mail: amdnsk@vsnl.com
Web site: www.abhivyakti.org.in

Nitin Paranjape is the director of Abhivyakti (Expressions), which he co-founded in 1987 in the Indian city of Nashik in Northern Maharashtra, as a vehicle to promote media initiatives for developmental purposes.

It has grown to comprise a staff of 23 and an impressive array of programs. Abhivyakti's main purpose is to "enhance the voice of the voiceless by strengthening the communication resources of developmental actors in the process of empowering the people." It does this through work in four program areas: producing and publishing audio-visual material; disseminating media material and maintaining a resource center; providing training and support for capacity building and media education; and networking and alliance building with other groups.

In sharing his background with the other authors via online dialogue, Nitin expressed the sense of deep connection between personal story and political action. He wrote:

The foremost question before me is not the usual who I am, though I must confess of the struggle to cope with its grip. The question rather is what is the purpose of this existence? It has been uppermost in my life ever since I became conscious of myself in a middle-class family on the move due to compulsion of the job my father had chosen. Being the elder (between two brothers), I was expected to be a role model of sorts, and its pressure perhaps led me to view life differently. Rejecting the normal career paths, I chose social work (now called developmental work) as a profession. … In a way, Abhivyakti has shaped me considerably as I got fully involved in shaping its destiny. The initial dream was to produce people-centered video that portrays the reality from their perspective. Soon, the experiences of using video by the activists led to critical reflections and change in gear. We moved on to a holistic look at communications, and how through our interventions we could strengthen the voices of the voiceless. … My interest is in making communication processes nurturing, open and empowering.

India is a nation of tremendous internal contradictions, with a huge commercial cultural industry and high-tech development driving a modernization that coexists with extremely poor and underdeveloped communities. This essay has something to teach that will be of interest to readers in many regions of the world: even when people have very little in the way of material goods, social imagination can still accomplish a great deal.

Small Media, Big Potential!

by Nitin Paranjape

We all remember much better what we have discovered and said ourselves than what others have told us.

ANNE HOPE AND SALLY TIMMEL, "TRAINING FOR TRANSFORMATION:
A HANDBOOK FOR COMMUNITY WORKERS"

She was bubbly, energetic and vivacious, moving gracefully, carrying herself well without showing the torment she was feeling and had perhaps felt since childhood. She was one of several grassroots activists in India engaged in a process of transforming a community. She was participating in a workshop on team building, and in a voice choked with pain, she shared her anguish: the anguish of being dark-complexioned and not feeling beautiful; of not feeling she belonged; of feeling lonely, incompetent and unloved. These feelings had affected her identity and functioning to such an extent that she did not believe in her own beauty. Low self-worth and self-esteem were natural consequences.

She was not alone. In another instance, an active young man who wanted to experiment on his agricultural land was being forced by his family to migrate from his community roots to a distant city to work in a nondescript government office, sacrificing all for security. The youth, whose heart lay in his farm, was woebegone and confused. His future was rudderless.

Many grassroots activists and local workers suffer from this complex phenomenon of not valuing their own resources, abilities and culture. Its historic roots go back to the colonization process and its value system, which eroded and fragmented the traditional cultural order. In effect, cultural domination by the few marginalized and isolated the majority of the Indian society. Treated as objects and disregarded, those on the margins accepted the attitudes and values of the elite, adopting the imposed system as their own. Inability to enact the cultural standards of the elite was interpreted as lack of capacity.

Constant reinforcement of these ideas by the dominant class led to low self-esteem by the marginalized class. Given this history, it would be too reductive to label the devaluing of local resources and perspectives as exclusively an impact of globalization; globalization has simply taken advantage of this longstanding historical reality. By promoting a consumerist and elitist culture, globalization's forces exacerbate this state of affairs. The spread of this global culture has further devalued local cultures' inherent abilities and strengths, resulting in loss of critical reflection and participation in community life and action. Communities can no longer view their problems from their own perspectives, relying on their own creative methods and viewpoints to generate possible solutions. Instead of cherishing a vibrant and interactive culture that values its own experiences, people have become accustomed to viewing life from the galleries. Unable to distinguish between representations and reality, they accept life passively.

Abhivyakti (Expressions), our media organization in India, was created in 1987 to respond to these conditions through various facets of media. To achieve this, it has not confined itself merely to producing media, but through its various programs has taken the initiative in popularizing media. We work primarily with developmental workers and facilitators, but some of our programs focus on grassroots community members.

Based in Nashik (a fast-growing city north of Mumbai/Bombay, in west central India), Abhivyakti has developmental communication as its main focus, with intervention strategies built around it. In the present climate, where commercial interests dominate space and representation in the mainstream media, it is increasingly unlikely that media policies and programs will be people-oriented. It is in this context that we see a specific role for media and communication. Can media help to strengthen the voice of the voiceless? Is it possible for marginalized people to be heard amidst the turmoil of dominating voices of vested interests?

Our work with media has definitely shown that these things are possible. Our greatest joy is when marginalized people are able to connect with their inner resources and voice their concerns and struggles, when they are able to assert their choice of actions, demanding a life of dignity. It is inspiring to see people break out, creating expressions that spring from their deepest realities. I will always cherish the moment when a group of rural women defied expectations to enact a small role-play demonstrating their woes before bank officials; or when shy girls from a hostel for deprived students banded together to demand from the authorities their right to information. What they wanted was a daily newspaper! Such acts by marginalized communities in the face of adversity and fear kindle our faith in the potential of media to generate a dialogue, stimulating people to facilitate the desired change. Helping to bring about such moments is a challenge, one we have undertaken to fulfill by

Media being tested in a community for its effectiveness. Photo from Abhivyakti.

promoting the right to information, the right to communicate and the right to participate, asserting a community's culture.

Creative use of media in partnership with people helps diverse marginalized voices to be aired and heard within a community. We believe in the power of the media as tools to initiate dialogue between people and developmental actors—activists, facilitators and *animateurs*—on development issues affecting the region. The communication process encourages participation, exchange of perspectives and the creation of an enabling environment that makes it possible for the community to voice its developmental concerns, problems and aspirations. It further enables joint reflection about the historical course of prevalent development practices and about ways to change them through collective action. Media function as tools to bring forth issues of concern, creating platforms for coming together and building long-term relationships. Media can be powerful allies in promoting the empowerment process and popular political consciousness and in creating a base—a launching pad— for governance by the people.

The supporting role of media and communication in development needs to be understood as part of the larger goal of strengthening the voices of the voiceless.

In producing alternative media material that takes cognizance of developmental issues and presents them from a pro-people perspective, in collecting and distributing such alternative forms of expression, in building effective communication capacities of developmental actors and in creating spaces that bring people together and provide opportunities to voice their aspirations, concerns, needs and problems—in all these ways, we see great potential in developmental communication interventions to empower the people.

Developmental media have functions which, if understood and realized, can accelerate the process of social transformation, breaking the shackles of the one-way communication mode of the mass media. They provide means to engage people in a dialogue, creating an atmosphere conducive to participation, action and possible partnership in the future. They ensure that a process of relationship is initiated between the developmental actor and the people— crucial for sustaining interest, motivation and trust, for people to realize their situation, understand its dynamics and feel confident to act from their own perspectives and vision.

What then are the main strategies of developmental media? As described below, the primary strategies of Abhivyakti's interventions are:

- Production and distribution of alternative images;
- Breaking the culture of silence;
- Strengthening communication resources; and
- Partnerships and alliance building.

PRODUCTION AND DISTRIBUTION OF ALTERNATIVE IMAGES

This strategy means taking cognizance of the diverse realities experienced by marginalized and vulnerable sections of society and promoting cross-cultural exchange. The void that exists in mainstream media in terms of developmental images and perspectives needs to be addressed by producing audio-visual materials that promote the perspectives, problems and aspirations of marginalized people on a regular basis. Systematic efforts must be made to circulate such audio-visual materials so that they are much more widely used by developmental actors, becoming part of public consciousness.

Abhivyakti's aims in audio-visual production carry us in two directions. First, we produce images on video on developmental themes and popular struggles that otherwise rarely find space in the mass media; and second, with active participation of the community, we design innovative low-cost, easy-to-use media material on social issues.

Apart from assisting other developmental groups in producing their audio-visual material, we produce and circulate our own quarterly video magazine entitled *Satyachitra* (*True Stories*), featuring stories, struggles, issues, projects and protests of people fighting for their rights. The idea is to produce such images from a pro-people perspective and bring them to the forefront. *Satyachitra* provides an impetus for discussion, creates linkages and often gives evidence straight from protest sites which would otherwise be hard to visualize. It triggers interest and generates enthusiasm for causes, for example, our video on the "Save the Narmada" campaign. It depicts several months of peaceful resistance and agitation launched by activists and villagers in protest against the government's decision to raise the height of the Sardar Sarovar Dam on the river Narmada, thereby submerging many villages, displacing thousands of villagers and destroying the ecosystem.

The *Satyagraha* (a combination of the Hindi words for "truth" and "firmness," coined by Mahatma Gandhi to describe nonviolent resistance) was launched when the monsoons started in 1999 as a protest against this inhumane decision. The video shows the struggle of the villagers of the Narmada valley, who on several occasions defied the swirling waters of the river as it entered their villages to fight for their lives and their environment, standing in the cold rising water as their mark of protest.

The video magazine also serves as a networking device, filling a void in the sharing of information, perspectives and experiences among groups involved in development work. In the hectic pace of work, visual presentations of movements and their action-strategies help developmental actors to reflect on and understand social issues. Resources developed by social organizations— for example a folk play on the issues surrounding a watershed program excerpted in one issue of *Satyachitra*—evoke considerable interest. More important, as in the watershed-program case, it led to profitable exchange, sharing and networking among organizers. Another inspiring story we covered dealt with rural women of Chandwad town (near Nashik) who eagerly came forward to embrace technological know-how, collectively building a water tank on their own in order to overcome the acute water shortage in their village.

Our second aim—designing innovative low-cost media—equips developmental actors with easy-to-carry, -use and -modify material such as puppet kits, flannel story (sometimes called "flannel board"), flip charts and posters. Such modest media materials have great potential to get the message across, but because guidelines are often lacking for effective use, they are not employed as widely as could be. We have learned that if such materials are packaged into kits with instructions and accompanied by demonstrations of their utility, their use increases rapidly. This accessibility also enlarges the motivation of grassroots workers to develop such media on their own. In essence, these activities apply the principles of appropriate technology to communications. We actively encourage this practice of locally produced audio-visual material, providing training and assistance as needed.

However, the idea of people facilitating their expression in concrete forms is not yet widely understood in our region. Toward this end, we made a small beginning that was amply rewarded. While working in the tribal Ashram Schools (residential schools run by the government), we tried out various media forms that would stimulate students' learning in a classroom situation.

We hit on the idea of a "wall paper," inviting students to pen their ideas and illustrations on a theme related to school life. The bimonthly paper, controlled solely by the students themselves, aimed at stimulating the students' thinking and creating a space for their expression in a free and nonthreatening atmosphere. The wall paper opened avenues of expression hitherto untapped or suppressed. Students wrote with feeling and concern about their plight in the school. Their world suddenly opened up with such participation and intensity that their voices carried even to the authorities against whom they were raised, who then became more alert and cautious.

The initiation of the wall paper and the opportunities it presented to students should be seen in context. The tribal students residing in these schools live in fear of authorities and under conditions not conducive to learning. In such government-run schools, communication between students and teachers and among students themselves is restrictive and not very stimulating to creativity. A majority of the students contributed to the wall paper venture. But for some, it seemed at first more like an examination than an independent project; quite a few copied, merely following others. They were either unwilling to try being original or were afraid of the consequences of opening up with their honest views.

Yet on the issue of the quality of food served by the school, many (without disclosing their identities) wrote about corruption, unhygienic food, the inadequate quantity of nourishment provided and other malpractices. It created quite a stir. The nonteaching staff involved in food storage, preparation and distribution were naturally upset. Their union at the district level took up the matter for investigation. The wall paper thus acted as a link between the students and the authorities.

The wall paper is a good example of a medium which carried the often neglected voices of vulnerable children, directly communicating their views and feelings to the external world. The wall paper truly represents a fine example of democratic media by the students, of the students and for the students. It provided tribal children with an opportunity to create their own messages without any pressures from school authorities. It was also a vehicle for exchanging thoughts with other students from different schools, thus binding them together as a cohesive group capable of finding answers to some of their common woes and miseries.

The wall paper also acted like a window to the outside world, creating awareness about the neglected world of the Ashram Schools—not just about their problems, but also about their ways and beliefs that are often ignored and sidelined. In their own language, expressed in their own way, perhaps for the first time, they communicated directly with the external world. The activities involved in producing the wall paper were themselves steps toward empowering the students and enhancing their self-esteem. Finally, one sees in this small example the potential for reversing the trend in the flow of information. Having been mere receivers, as both students and tribal people, this process gave the young people the chance to become creators and also providers of information on various themes of importance to their lives and to the outside world.

The value of alternative media like those we use at Abhivyakti lies in their low cost and ease. Most of these media forms are made from locally available resources and are easy to produce and use, requiring no sophisticated technical knowledge. Puppet shows, a popular medium with any audience, create drama, movement and action commenting on sensitive issues affecting the community. Fabrication requires little more than cloth, plastic balls, socks and other such ordinary items. Flannel story, another effective medium, requires only a length of flannel or even a blanket on which visuals backed with velvet (flocked) paper are displayed. The hairy surface of the flannel and the roughness of the velvet paper create static energy that enables the visuals to be stuck temporarily onto the flannel. To tell a story, the visuals are removed and stuck back in different positions, and this movement, accompanied by the animated voice of the presenter (our grassroots worker!), creates a dynamism that appeals to the multiple senses of the audience. Similarly, a story may be narrated using flip charts made from colored illustrations on chart paper. Innovative methods enhance the flip chart's value. For example, movement is possible in this two-dimensional medium, adding an element of surprise: a slit in the chart paper allows cutout figures to be easily moved across the surface of the paper while the narrator tells the story.

Although posters are commonly used, their effectiveness is often lost when community members with low literacy levels cannot easily understand their message. As posters are simply put in place to be viewed, they cannot be compared to other group media where an organizer makes a presentation to a group interacting with the media. Cultural habits in rural Indian communities are geared toward attending performances more than viewing visuals or written messages. It is essential to learn such culturally relevant information and to keep it in mind while producing and designing media for the community. From our experience of dissemination, it can be said that media and their presenters make a potent combination in catalyzing dialogue with the community. This clearly puts the responsibility on the presenter for making the media relevant.

Alternative media try to follow the approach of Paulo Freire, the Brazilian educator, in developing critical awareness among the audience. Freire called such media "codes" or "problem-posing materials," the aim of which is to

Behind the scenes of a puppet show presentation. Photo from Abhivyakti.

stimulate discussions in community contexts. Such media—puppet shows, flannel stories, flip charts, posters, simple booklets, stories and audio cassettes —are basically tools to reach out to marginalized communities, initiating dialogue with the people. The idea is to choose a local experience and create media around it. People from marginalized communities rarely value their own experiences, let alone their expertise, leaving them as mere spectators instead of actors in their own worlds. Members of one of the tribal communities in Murbad (in Thane District, south of Mumbai) watched the entire rushes—raw footage—of the video shoot of their program for three hours in complete silence without getting bored. The explanation is that it featured their own images and their voices, which they were seeing in this medium for the first time. Rather than using alien experiences, we believe it is essential to depict people's own stories and experiences so that they are valued and valorized.

Another notable characteristic of low-cost media is the ease with which community members can produce such things. We believe that the production process itself is empowering. Both the choice of subject and treatment and the tasks of production create involvement that stimulates participation and use, as was the case with the Ashram Schools wall paper. This lesson has been brought home again and again in our experience working with grassroots groups. We have observed much more spirited enthusiasm for and use of media campaigns in which activists were involved in the design of the material than in those dealing with equally important issues where there was no similar involvement.

Puppet show.
Photo from Abhivyakti.

As the content of these low-cost media forms is local in nature, the issue of their circulation to others is complex. The question is this: do we have to circulate them? Not all media need to be seen merely as products, an assumption that we have internalized unconsciously from the influence of the market on our lives. Low-cost media forms are subjective in nature and deal with a particular context. They exist for a specific purpose: to stimulate dialogue and create opportunities for people to learn about their own reality. Another characteristic is that these media are most effective with small groups, which is why they are also called group media. Yet it is a loss when such media are banished to some obscure corner after their immediate purpose has been accomplished. In giving such media a continuing life, we give them visibility and character rooted in specific cultures, and this recognition is enormously important.

We have tried two things to promote activists' awareness of media in developmental work. First, in order to increase visibility of alternative and group media, we have chosen a few experiences and folk stories which have universal appeal and emotional content. We have produced media kits about these in quantity and have tried to distribute them accompanied by demonstrations and sometimes more intensive training. Second, understanding that such alternative media are seldom preserved, we have begun to collect a variety of these forms, classifying them and establishing a media resource center that stores them, with the aim of acting as a clearinghouse to promote awareness and use. Our attempts have been fairly successful and we hope to accelerate their pace through networking.

Abhivyakti's experience of the past 10 years' collaboration with other groups, nongovernmental organizations (NGOs) and educational institutes has taught us that space for developmental media exists, but it is often obscured. The influence of dominant or mainstream media has overwhelmed alternative or developmental media. Organizers and facilitators—the actual users of such media material—have an uneven relationship with these media due to the absence of permanent network structures and channels for reaching out. The commercial media more than anything else stimulate the consumption needs of the audience, but developmental media propose a much more demanding relationship because their purpose is pedagogic, requiring systematic use. Even though producing media for development doesn't require high technology and vast funds, getting these products used is really the sore point. Efforts have to be taken to organize wider dissemination, screening and exhibition so that vital information can be shared with people who are thus motivated to participate in dialogue.

People are used to the culture of silence. Their inhibition about voicing their views limits their social participation. Alternative and group media attempt to defeat this inhibition. Developmental media must be seen in a context and serve a purpose, a strategy or program, functioning as part of an overall plan or campaign. Such media tools are not effective if used in isolation, but media used by a motivated and skilled developmental actor (whether an activist, facilitator or community animator) builds social awareness, stimulates people to critically examine their realities and inspires a collective spirit for desired action. The advantages of alternative communications media lie in their adaptability, enabling a good communicator to carry audience members to a new awareness of their own environment, stimulate them to perceive their own roles and influence them toward bringing about the desired impact. Further, alternative and group media's effectiveness lies in their two-way communication approach and three-cornered framework: addressing issues of concern to the audience; showing that the answers can be sought and found by audience members themselves; and showing that the audience must control implementation of solutions to ensure the desired results.

Abhivyakti's work stresses the values of participation, dignity, open communication, importance of local resources and equality in decision making, leading toward empowerment. The use of media in this process of empowerment depends largely on the link-person between the media and the people—the development actor—on whose shoulders lies responsibility for initiating the process. A great deal therefore depends on the capabilities and perspectives of these link-people and their organizations. This is an area of weakness that needs to be addressed.

Our experience indicates that not many NGOs or developmental actors are properly oriented toward alternative and group media use. Often they lack faith in their effectiveness. For example, our motivational video on the fight of tribal people against corrupt forest officials was shown one evening in a tribal village. The next day, the village was visited by a petty forest official who demanded his "dues" and got away with it. The tribal people did not protest. Later we discovered that the activist who had shown the video had failed to initiate a discussion after the screening of its relevance to local people's experience with their forest, thus losing an opportunity to strengthen the confidence of the tribal villagers.

As this demonstrates, in order to promote pedagogical use of media for empowerment, strengthening the skills and resources of developmental actors assumes significance. Workshops and other training methods have become the principal tools at our disposal to achieve these aims of shaping and building the perspectives and expanding the capacities of developmental actors.

STRENGTHENING COMMUNICATION RESOURCES

Capacity building involves strengthening the communication and media resources of developmental and grassroots actors. Effective communication is the key to understanding and building relationships with varied constituencies in the process of empowering individuals, collectives and communities.

Along with structured training, our methods also include field-testing, video feedback and group work and opportunities to reflect on experiences. The emphasis is on promoting learning through participation, interaction, sharing and the use of multiple sensory approaches to cater to different learning styles.

For the past five years, since we initiated training programs to expand use of media for development purposes, the experience has been mutually gratifying for both the participating developmental actors and ourselves. The thrust of our program has been in two directions: first, understanding developmental media philosophy and imparting low-cost and alternative media production skills; and second, strengthening the communications perspective and skills of developmental actors.

This second dimension has evolved gradually, guided by our belief that society is characterized by the domination of a powerful few who control vast resources and knowledge and channel the flow of communication in keeping with their interests and to their own benefit. This structure hardly favors those who are vulnerable and marginalized, those with meager or no resources who are largely unorganized. The majority of the marginalized have rich inner resources and knowledge but do not value them, becoming mere receivers of the messages others create. One way we acted on this

understanding was by organizing training programs for developmental actors, parents, teachers and community leaders to learn new skills, attitudes, insights and knowledge. Our educational process creates an opportunity for sharing and interaction, leading to introspection concerning our selves and our behavior and inspiring change. Bringing about social change through alternative development processes entails informing, mobilizing and organizing people to stand up for their rights so that they can identify, articulate and struggle to achieve their fundamental right to lives of dignity and freedom.

Further, given the present market-dominated state favored by globalization, alienation and isolation of the poor are on the rise. Individualism and consumption patterns favoring a materialistic lifestyle are emerging, devaluing local initiatives and efforts. The root of social relations lies in communication practices. The communication process prevalent at present is biased toward the dominant and powerful; this hegemonic approach tends to disempower people. Its impact can be traced in structures and institutions from the family, schools and communities to many NGOs.

The need for an open, just and democratic form of communication that would lead to the lasting ties and relationships needed for pro-people development processes cannot be overemphasized. It becomes imperative, therefore, to put communication on the agenda and give it the attention it deserves.

The role of our training here is to encourage sharing of views and experiences guided by a facilitator in an atmosphere conducive to reflection and learning. Essentially, by focusing on crucial aspects of the communication process, we encourage participants to view themselves not as resourceless, but as sources of information, wisdom and knowledge. This approach values participation and exchange for participants' own learning. Dialogue, interaction and sharing lead to collective learning. Recognizing participants' own contributions and worth to the collective spirit, the process instills or reinforces a sense of empowerment. Feedback from numerous participants has indicated that the training provides much-needed space to reflect upon their resources, their communication styles, their organizations and the steps they have taken to create change in themselves and in their organizations.

However, one palpable countervailing trend has been a decline in confidence, self-belief and critical abilities among activists, a major crisis that needs to be confronted, as it affects their identity and functioning, with impacts upon not only the process but the community as well. One of the major reasons lies in the inability of formal schooling to instill values of self-belief and empower students' expression in their own cultural language and idioms. Communities fed a daily diet of mushy soap operas, stereotypical serials and advertisements need strong local currents to uphold their cultural perspectives. It is difficult to create and defend a belief system that can survive the continuous onslaught of consumerist culture. Promoting alternative modes of production and pro-people values is fraught with immense struggle and demands conviction. It is imperative that the carriers of alternative value systems are able to withstand opposing influences by appreciating their own cause, creativity and commitment. This shift in individual consciousness will in turn motivate and strengthen our collective endeavor to counter the forces of globalization.

But is this possible? Can alternative cultural products that highlight local issues, often emerging from people themselves, be sustainable? Our hope is that such practices motivate people to think of themselves as valuable resources, second to none, and to assert their right to produce their own forms of media, disseminating them for wider appreciation and benefit. If this succeeds, it will point the way for diverse cultures to exist and flourish in the future. Right now, success depends on activists themselves, who are suffering a sort of identity crisis, promoting an enabling and healthy culture that values their own dignity and worth.

PARTNERSHIPS AND ALLIANCE BUILDING

Our efforts to create distribution channels for developmental media are still in the early stages. We have decided to collaborate with a few developmental organizations in our region, where we have been able to undertake a formal networking process among such groups. The networking organizations have come together to work on the issues confronting the region with the aim of facilitating effective collective functioning. The network, built on the foundation of three years' partnership, is based on democratic communication processes, motivating partner organizations to use media in their work, thus enhancing the capacities of their activists in media production and dissemination, and in critical analysis of mass-media influence. As this networking has proceeded, the issues of the region more and more find their way into our productions, particularly our video magazine, *Satyachitra*. As we have featured issues such as scarcity of water and malnutrition and highlighted activists' views and innovative approaches, viewership and circulation have expanded, and regional problems, voices and collective initiative and spirit have found a vehicle. We see this as an alternative to the structural distortions that exist in mass communication systems, an opportunity to present images of the other reality that is experienced by the majority of the populace but which is often ignored and bypassed.

We see the emergence of the network—its opportunities to learn and understand differences, share meaning and perspectives, and the relationships it enables—as creating a force that challenges established exploitative practices. Our aim is to learn from experience, striving to enhance communication processes and strengthen cultural practices that herald a better community life. These are part of the challenge we have accepted: to develop systemic media and communication strategies and interventions, supporting cultural practitioners in becoming more conscious and effective. Through these efforts, we find endless possibilities for reaching people and helping to empower them.

5

Myrtle Cavelho of the Pearls of Wisdom, a group of older adult storytellers organized by Brooklyn, New York's Elders Share the Arts, relates that her father, born into slavery, remembered the day Lincoln was shot. Photo by Dona Ann McAdams.

Oral History Research Office
Columbia University
801 Butler Library, Box 20
535 West 114th Street, MC 1129
New York, New York 10027 U.S.A.
Telephone: (212) 854-2273
E-mail: mmc17@columbia.edu
Web site: www.columbia.edu/cu/lweb/indiv/oral/

"Telling one's own story in one's own words"—to paraphrase Paulo Freire, the author of "Pedagogy of the Oppressed" and a source of inspiration for much liberatory community work —has been a watchword for community cultural development practitioners for decades and a powerful metaphor for the out-pouring of theater, writing, visual artwork, music and movement that results from their work. Instead of the one authoritative voice of history, this approach brings history to life through a patchwork of individual voices. In its pure form—in the collection and archiving of stories per se— oral-history practice has been an inexhaustible seed-stock for community cultural development projects. This essay suggests that as it has developed as a method-ology, oral history has come also to serve as an artistic process.

Mary Marshall Clark is an oral historian—or as she puts it, "I love listening to other people's stories." She is based at Columbia University in New York City, serving as director of the Oral History Research Office, the world's first organized academic oral-history program, founded in 1948, which houses an archive of 8,000 interviews and is a center for teaching oral history.

True to her calling, Mary Marshall explained her professional choice through a personal story.

Here are some excerpts from the biography she provided for her fellow participants in this project:

I was born in North Carolina, in the United States, in the 1950s in a town of 600 people in tobacco country. My mother was a schoolteacher and my father was an insurance agent who mostly gave his money away to pay the premiums of poor farmers whose crops could turn to dirt in violent thunderstorms. While thunderstorms, and even poverty, could be explained to me by adults, there were other realities I was confronted with that had no rational explanation. Among those was racism. When I asked my father when I was four why black people were treated as they were (I am white), he cried. My grandmother had been talking to me about the evils of discrimination (not exactly in those words)—she traveled from house to house in the town nightly to talk to people about how prejudice should end. She set up a summer school for black and white kids to study together in her home, and tried to end segregation single-handedly by

getting herself elected to the school board in the 1940s. My father and mother, when I was a teenager, became very active in the southern desegregation movement and we were shunned by whites for years—except for occasional visits/calls by the KKK.[1]

When I was 12, I bought a tape recorder and began interviewing anyone who would talk to me about their memories and perceptions of life. I was not so much fascinated by history/ genealogy as I was by experience itself. Not just experience, but the way people related their experience in story form. Because of the social movement I grew up in, the stories I was most interested in were stories of liberation. … We listen, if we listen well, with our whole selves (body, spirit, intellect, eye, imagination) and respond, in conversational form, in a way that indicates to the person we are interviewing that we have really heard. If we have not really heard, that is painfully and immediately evident and the interview is a failure.

[1] Ku Klux Klan – a white racist secret society.

Oral History
ART AND PRAXIS

by Mary Marshall Clark

Thus, to speak a true word is to transform the world. —Paulo Freire[2]

[2] Paulo Freire, *Pedagogy of the Oppressed* (New York: Seabury Press, 1970), p. 75.

I was doubly nervous as I made my travel plans to meet my colleagues in Bellagio to discuss our work in relation to community cultural development: nervous about meeting people I would need to get to know so quickly and also about addressing the concept of globalization through artistic practices. I found that others, like me, were uncertain about how to best use our languages of creativity to confront and address the forces of globalization, a social-scientific term describing an increasing imbalance between the rich and the poor (not always to be read as the powerful and the weak).

As we met and talked over the next few days, however, I think we all became aware of the resilience of our methods and of creativity itself in shaping positive human development. While we came from different artistic, cultural and political situations, the languages through which we expressed, demonstrated and explained our creative processes in relation to the philosophy of community cultural development brought us closer together. For me at least, that made addressing the challenges and the problems of globalization seem much more possible. Indeed, oral history, a broad and multifaceted movement with roots in diverse cultural and community practices, is strengthened by an alliance with other forms of artistic practice, particularly theater.

I am grateful to my colleagues for giving me the opportunity to explore the creative uses of oral history to respond to the challenges globalization poses to humanity and to development. However, I remain wary of the term globalization itself: how it is defined, how and in what context it is used and how it defines us or not. Individually and collectively, our resources are dwarfed by the growth of global capitalism in what may be remembered as the era of globalization. Our "best practices" must stay rooted in the soil of our remembered humility, creativity, fragility and pain. Perhaps our most creative response to globalization is to resist it, to continue to live and create despite it and to refuse the embrace of any language that would synthesize and homogenize our efforts to combat it.

THE SOCIAL PURPOSE OF ORAL HISTORY

Oral history, an academic, cultural and artistic practice that has many forms and richly intertwined histories in locations around the world, originated in the attempt by social historians, sociologists, activists and others to recover memories that would otherwise be lost. Motivated by a dynamic and participatory vision of history, oral history originated in the attempt to recover public memories that might not otherwise enter the collective sphere. Paul Thompson, one of the founders of the international oral-history movement, crystallized this view in his 1978 oral-history primer, "The Voice of the Past: Oral History," where he stated, "All history depends ultimately upon its social purpose." [3] While oral history has ultimately evolved as an academic field as well as a tool for social historians, community activists, educators and others, this early statement by Thompson clarifies the central mission of its early decades: to restore the individual human subject to history.

[3] Paul Thompson, *The Voice of the Past: Oral History*, third edition (New York: Oxford University Press, 2000), p. 1.

[4] www.sussex.ac.uk/library/massobs/history.html

Generally defined as the narration, representation and interpretation of history through recorded interviews with eyewitnesses, oral history became systematized as a practice with the popularization of the portable tape recorder in the late 1930s, particularly in northern Europe, England and North America. In England, the movement among historians and others to record the observations of everyday people was inspired by the usefulness of the BBC radio archives to authors and historians, and the creation of the Mass Observation Archive by a group of young historians who aimed to establish "an anthropology of ourselves,"[4] a study of the everyday lives of ordinary people in Britain. This turn toward the person as a source of historical knowledge influenced the value given to first-hand reminiscences, both in England and elsewhere. In the United States, also in the late 1930s, authors hired under the auspices of the Federal Writers Project undertook a series of interviews with ex-slaves which became the first official government-sponsored oral-history project in that country, the first real model of the radical power of oral history. It demonstrated the ability of oral history to record, through individual interviews, collective historical accounts that draw upon traditions of orality and autobiography as a way of understanding the dynamic conflicts of history from within while simultaneously validating individual historical perspectives.

By the late 1940s and early 1950s, the tape recorder was widely used throughout Europe, Latin America, the Middle East, Asia and Africa to document rapid and historical change from individual perspectives. Oral history was used to recover memories of the oppressed in situations of totalitarianism in Russia and Brazil, illustrating its subversive and healing power to address both political oppression and personal suffering. As oral history developed as a movement and an academic discipline in the 1960s and 1970s, there was increasing interest among a wide group of historians, anthropologists, folklorists and others in the rich areas of overlap between oral history and oral tradition. Jan Vansina's "Oral Tradition: A Study in Historical Methodology,"[5] illustrated the central importance accorded to storytelling and the wide uses of oral evidence in indigenous African cultural traditions. This classic text influenced the growing international oral-history movement to embrace the role of storytelling in indigenous and traditional cultures worldwide. Theoretical developments in oral history, intensifying through international meetings and conferences in the 1970s, reflected this fascination with orality itself as a cultural resource, leading to the acceptance of oral history as a form of cultural work.

[5] Jan Vansina, *Oral Tradition: A Study in Historical Methodology*, translated by H. M. Wright (London: Routledge and Kegan Paul, 1965).

[6] Luisa Passerini, "Work Ideology and Consensus Under Italian Fascism," *History Workshop: A Journal of Socialist Historians*, Issue 8, Autumn 1979, p. 84.

The insight that culture was oral history's true source was articulated by the Italian intellectual historian Luisa Passerini in an essay, "Work Ideology and Consensus Under Italian Fascism," that would come to define the significance and broad scope of oral history as an exploratory and multidisciplinary methodology:

> Above all, we should not ignore that the raw material of oral history consists not just in factual statements, but is pre-eminently an expression and representation of culture, and therefore includes not only literal narrations but also the dimensions of memory, ideology and subconscious desires.[6]

Passerini's work, as well as that of her contemporary Alessandro Portelli, stressed the importance of cultivating oral sources to document the impact of fascism on working-class culture. Portelli, one of the most prolific writers of oral-history texts, has written extensively about fieldwork as a forum for the exchange of cultural knowledge and wisdom through the vehicle of the interview. In this vision of fieldwork, the interviewer must enter the cultural and temporal world of the narrator in order to understand the meanings attached to historical events. Community itself is the medium through which knowledge is transmitted. Portelli credits his view of oral history as beginning in community-based cultural work to the teachings of Gianni Bosio, an Italian editor and organizer who described the interview as a politically significant encounter and an "experiment in equality" through which both the interviewer and narrator could be transformed. Contained in this vision is a dynamic view of culture in which the acts of telling and listening are in themselves forms of resistance not unlike the use of songs, popular literature and folklore in social movements.

The growth of oral history as an organized movement, with regular international meetings since 1979, has provided a unique forum for the cross-cultural exchange of stories and of ideas about methods and practices. Organized around broad themes embracing global concerns, these conferences have allowed presenters to explore common concerns and to share indigenous knowledge across geographic and national borders. The vitality and diversity of the oral-history movement, its openness to fieldworkers, artists and academics who hold a common interest in the history and development of culture and community, suggests the significance of storytelling as a form of communication that builds community, both locally and globally. The international forums reveal the rich array of community oral-history projects that exists worldwide.

Oral history is a methodology through which struggle, conflict and development can be recorded, helping to create the conditions for greater mutuality and understanding and a potential source of transformation and dialogue. This is particularly true, as Portelli has pointed out, in situations of war, trauma and genocide, where culture has often been stripped of its inherent power. The importance given to the truth commissions of South Africa and Latin America reveal the enduring power of personal testimony to reshape public understanding, addressing suffering in the public sphere in ways that may allow genuine transformation to occur. They represent one of many models in which personal testimony can be used to support cultural community development, to address issues of justice and reconciliation.

ORAL HISTORY AND COMMUNITY CULTURAL DEVELOPMENT: MODELS AND EXAMPLES

Oral history and cultural community development are linked in four distinctive ways.

1.   Oral history restores the subject to history, documenting the history of communities that may have been excluded from historical accounts and encouraging individuals to see themselves as historical actors. In the most creative of these projects, oral history encourages people to remember as a way of entering and transforming history.

There are many examples of oral-history projects that restore the subject to history, beginning with the collection of the narratives of ex-slaves through the Federal Writers Project in the United States and continuing with many equally important efforts to collect working-class history and women's history. But there are many lesser-known examples of community history projects in which groups have creatively appropriated oral history to record their existence on the margins of society, demonstrating oral history's flexibility and value as a community resource.

One example is the Brighton Ourstory Project in Britain, in which members of the gay male and lesbian community decided to record 40 interviews chronicling gay and lesbian sexual life in Britain from 1950 to 1969. The dedication in the volume of stories published in 1992, "Daring Hearts: Lesbian and Gay Lives of '50s and '60s Brighton," reads, "For all the voices that never will be heard." A section from the preface explaining their approach to oral history reads:

> It's a dislocating experience to visit Brighton Borough Council, Brighton Reference Library, Brighton Museum and find nothing. It's as though lesbians and gay men have not existed, have made no contribution to the culture and economy of the town. Are we all ghosts then, muttering in dark corners and whispering in the wind? In Section 28 Britain, institutions cannot be trusted to tell the stories of our lives. Emergency oral history work is urgently needed. Every lesbian and every gay man is a walking library of information on our life and times.[7]

[7] Peter Dennis, Becci Mannall, Linda Pointing, *Daring Hearts: Lesbian and Gay Lives of '50s and '60s Brighton*, Brighton Ourstory Project, QueenSpark Book 28 (London: QueenSpark Books, 1992).

The Brighton Ourstory Project models the approach in which community members themselves take the initiative to record their own stories, thereby both contributing to the historical record and strengthening their own relationships with each other. The number of similar projects is vast. Many are distinguished by the effort to preserve memory of local groups in the face of historical and social transition and disturbances. A sampling of such projects reveals histories of Brazilian women in the trade-union movement, immigrants to the Czech Republic following the Chernobyl disaster, women's organizing efforts in American steel mills, peasant movements in post-Soviet Russia, Japanese-American citizens' experiences of internment and discrimination during World War II in the United States and many more. They are representative of the uses of oral history worldwide to document the impact of dramatic social change on specific communities that might otherwise not be recorded, and to explore strategies of resistance and survival based upon the stories and conversations that emerge.

One of the most fascinating research themes that has emerged globally through oral history research is the history of women's movements. In parts of India, for example, women are allowed to sing songs of protest even when they are not allowed to gather and demonstrate through direct verbal confrontation. An oral-history project in which these songs of protest were collected, along with stories of the protest movements themselves, has provided a unique resource for community leaders who are training new activists; it demonstrates the vital link between orality in general and oral history in particular.

The goal of community-based oral-history projects is often twofold: to capture history and to transform it. In this genre, traditional methods of interviewing and transcribing tapes for deposit in a paper archive are often too expensive, and are not the most efficient way of disseminating knowledge to a community actively engaged in the process of development and transformation.

One such example is the Audre Lorde Project in Brooklyn, New York, a community center founded in memory of poet and activist Audre Lorde. The project created an oral-history component to begin to document the legacy of Audre Lorde's activism around issues such as racism and homophobia, and to strengthen community participation in its outreach programs. Rather than conducting individual interviews for an archive, the project directors decided to make the oral-history exchange a part of their public programs. Workshops were held to train interviewers in the art of oral history, and interviews were conducted and recorded in private one-to-one settings. After rapport had been established between the interviewer and the narrator, they were invited to perform the interview in a public space before an audience. Community leaders, as well as the general public, were invited to witness the interview, and community activists, scholars and public historians were invited to comment on the progress of the interview, framing questions about content as well as interviewing technique. The narrator was also allowed to comment on the interviewer's technique. The audience not only witnessed the interview and engaged in a lively debate around issues under discussion, but learned something about oral history as a methodology through the comments of panelists and the narrator. The content of the dialogues—stories of resilience in the face of struggle—spread the legacy of Audre Lorde as the project directors intended by providing the occasion for teaching strategies of survival.

A similar strategy was used by the Park West Village Oral History Project, a community-based volunteer project in upper Manhattan, New York, founded to trace the history and legacy of a local neighborhood that was destroyed due to the policies of the developer Robert Moses in the early 1950s. The original community, largely African-American and Latino, was dislocated by new housing-development construction in the late 1940s and early 1950s, which displaced low-income residents throughout the city. The vitality of the community of musicians and artists could not be destroyed by the geographical dispersal of its members, but was kept alive through annual meetings of the 99th Street Block Association. When the community founded an oral-history project in 2001, its first goal was to gather dispersed community members to rebuild the community. Using a methodology similar to the Audre Lorde Project's, public interviews were performed in a community space in the middle-income housing that was constructed 50 years earlier over the ruins of the neighborhood. The interviews were advertised as a part of the public history program of the local public library and attracted architects, lawyers and journalists who were familiar with the contested development. The public interviews, videotaped for the archive, were the stimulus for debate and discussions, also providing opportunities for the displaced residents and their children and grandchildren to discuss the impact of their neighborhood's disruption.

2.   **Oral history is a dialogical encounter** based on rapport between interviewer and narrator. When integrated with other forms of community practice, it can support healing, reconciliation and development.

The clearest example of using oral history to promote well-being and personal growth as a part of the history-telling process is through the "reminiscence workers movement" (alternatively known as the "life history workers movement") in Britain, New Zealand and elsewhere, where social workers practice oral history in a variety of institutional and community settings. Influenced by the recognition of the life-review process as a therapeutic tool in restoring a sense of community through memory in the elderly, reminiscence work is practiced in many institutional settings, including communities of the disabled. The purpose of life review in an institutional setting is to overcome the isolation inherent in hospital-like environments, which may have been a life-long state for the disabled who were shunned from community participation in other settings.

Jan Walmsley and Joanna Bornat, in a presentation at a meeting of oral historians in New York in 1994, argued for the reconceptualization of the term community as a construct rather than an entity, as even the term can imply exclusion to differently abled people.[8] To build a sense of group identity, people are invited to share their life stories with the group. Interviewers record the individual narratives in writing or with tapes which are later transcribed and made into a booklet with photographs and journal entries. An effort is made to ensure that interviewees feel included at every point throughout the process of the interview. A technique used by Bornat and others was the idea of the "Writing Hand," developed by Pecket Well College, founded and run by disabled people. It involves the practice of reading or playing back interviewees' words during the progress of the interview in order to remind narrators that the power of narrative is theirs, as well as to demonstrate their involvement as active listeners, and interested and empathetic interviewers.

Increasingly, community museums are using oral history to explore shifting concepts of community, to build a sense of belonging and simultaneously to reshape public dialogues. An excellent example is the Wing Luke Asian Museum in Seattle, a pan-Asian museum which has used oral history to

[8] Joanna Bornat and Jan Walmsley, draft paper, "Oral History With Vulnerable People: Challenges to Concepts and Practice," presented to the Columbia University International Conference on Oral History, Oct. 18–23, 1994, New York City.

document the conditions Asians and Asian-Americans have faced in the United States. Interviews are drawn from the communities the museum serves, with two examples being Japanese-American citizens who were interned during World War II, and Asian women garment workers who fought to survive economically during the 1950s. Creative multimedia exhibits based on these digitally recorded oral-history projects were mounted, and narrators and other members of the community participated in public dialogues that were stimulated by the use of the oral histories in a public space, featuring a collision of collages of words, images and soundscapes that forces the visitor out of the role of neutral observer. A documentary on Asian garment workers, "If Tired Hands Could Talk," recreates conversational narratives from the interviews. The focus of the work of this dialogical museum is educational, but its impact is far greater as it creates the opportunity for the recovery of human dignity and healing by fusing elements of art and oral history.

Community centers and advocacy groups, with or without a museum or institutional base, use oral history with the arts to stimulate dialogues across generations and cultures. A good example of community-based oral-history work that furthers the goal of integrating oral history with artistic endeavors is that of Elders Share the Arts in New York City.

Elders Share the Arts, a cultural organization offering services to the elderly in immigrant communities, draws upon the skills of playwrights, actors and authors to reshape oral histories taken with elderly citizens into public dramatic readings and plays performed for the narrators. This is an important model in developing individual and group pride by returning the stories to the community from which they come. The interaction between artists and narrators, who are the focus of the performance and the primary audience, is constant throughout the different phases of the production. Stories collected in one community are shared with another through radio and other public programming in institutions, and immigrant experiences are shared across cultures as well as generations.

These are only a few examples of the ways in which oral history stimulates an artistic process that can ultimately foster healing and reconciliation, as well as building historical and cultural knowledge.

3.   **Oral history is an artistic practice** that, when allied with other forms of art and media work, can transform relationships and build new cultural perspectives, opening up new dialogues about the past.

Oral history can take many artistic forms, and can be used in many settings, particularly the theater. But there are certain steps in any oral-history process which define it as an art, whether the focus is on an individual life history, a community or a culture. These steps are not meant to be followed as if they are a list of tasks, but rather as if they are movements in a symphony that improves with practice, the development of a fine ear and, finally, with the real or imagined presence of an audience.

STEP ONE: ESTABLISHING THE FRAME OF THE INTERVIEW

In the beginning of the symphony, the oral historian is the artist, the person who understands what music is and listens for the first expression of musicality, eliciting the first chords and cadences that will determine the shape and tone of the piece that will eventually be performed. As in any practice session, the first interview session may be full of false starts and awkward pauses. It is the responsibility of the interviewer to both wait through these silences, allowing the narrators to find their own point of entry, and at the same time to ask the questions that can open up the conversation.

The first question is always an invitation to participate in what must become a joint venture, the mutual exploration of a life. It is important to let the people you are interviewing understand that you have the time and interest to hear as much of their stories as you can, and that they can make the choices about how and where to start.

In an interview I conducted for a project on the history of women in journalism, my first question indicates that we have met before, and that my interviewee had shared some of her personal diaries with me in advance:

> I am sitting here on the lovely quilt of Harriett Skye, and we are having our first tape-recorded conversation. I would like to start by asking you a little bit about your family life and where you grew up. You can start with whomever you wish. I was very struck by your poem to your mother, because in a way that was a family history as well.[9]

The first paragraph of Skye's answer indicates that she understands that we have begun what might be described as an autobiographical journey in story form, which always has a beginning, a middle and an end:

> Well, I guess the best place to begin is the beginning. I was born in 1931, on the Rosebud Indian Reservation in South Dakota. I'm the oldest of seven children. Two of my brothers were born there. My father is Douglas Joshua Skye, and my mother is Margaret Menz Skye. My father's mother, who I call my Grandma Skye, her name was Annie Murphy, and Annie Murphy was half Sioux and half Irish. Her father's name was Joshua Murphy, and her mother's name was White Mountain.[10]

[9] Reminiscences with Harriett Skye, Washington Press Club Foundation Women in Journalism Project, April 25, 1993, p. 1, in the Columbia University Oral History Research Office Collection, Columbia University.

[10] Ibid.

Eighth-grade students and elders in the Chelsea section of New York City share stories about what life is like during war: their experiences living through World War II and the events surrounding September 11th. Photo by Justine Stehle.

Skye continues to relate her family history, alluding to her cultural history, locating the narrative in both the self and the wider culture, going on to describe how her grandfather was dislocated from his reservation and sent to a boarding school in Virginia, in the southeastern United States:

> It was one of the ways the federal government was going to do away with Indian people. So they took him. It was a form of cultural genocide, because they were taking them away from their parents when they were five years old and sent them from North Dakota to Virginia.[11]

[11] Ibid, pp. 1–2.

Skye's willingness to speak freely about the cultural genocide that she and her family had suffered indicates that the interview is going to be a dialogical encounter, a genuine exchange, in which her responsibility is to tell the truth and mine is to hear it. The tone of the interview is established from the very beginning. That she is Indian and I am white adds to the richness of the cultural exchange. The interview is an experimental educational forum through which important dialogues about the past can be had in part *because* of our difference.

In setting the tone and agenda of the interview, intended in part to educate others (through me) about what life was like for a Native woman in white society, Skye takes the authority in the interview and orchestrates the rhythm, as well as the content, of the interview. My authority becomes that of the interested listener, and I relinquish my role as the director/conductor for the sake of allowing her to perform. She becomes the artist, and I her audience. These roles can be exchanged regularly during the interview, with shifts that respond to the rhythm and pace established by the narrator.

Once the tone and pace of the interview has been established and rapport created, part of the responsibility of the interviewer is to cover the issues that may be difficult to discuss but are critical to extend the interview beyond the biographical frame into wider cultural and historical frames. Dialogue takes form in oral history through the telling and retelling of stories.

This means taking an equal level of authorship in constructing the life narrative, asking questions that shape the interview as a dialogue. In this sense, oral history is an intersection of autobiography, biography and cultural history in which there are multiple authors. The narrator is the first author, but the interviewer's questions also determine the shape and content of the interview. As the narrator reminisces about the important influences in her life, other figures who helped shape her history are brought into the story and figure into the construction of narrative, much like a play in which the dialogue always reflects the intersections of lives rather than a single trajectory. Acknowledging the complexity of identity, its fragmentary and transitional character, is the first step toward using the interview to reconstruct history in all its contradictions.

In my interview with Harriett Skye, the most complex series of exchanges we had were over gender, involving her descriptions of the contradictory roles she played as a woman. She had made it clear to me in conversation that her first identification was as a Native woman and that while we shared the same gender, it didn't mean we shared the same identity. I was careful, therefore, when I asked about her identity as a Native woman to look for ways she had described herself:

> I read somewhere in your notes that you had described part of the Sioux tradition of the "manly-hearted woman." Could you explain that a little?[12]

12 Ibid, April 9, 1994 (session #4), p. 58.

13 Ibid.

Harriett responded:

> Yes, the manly-hearted women were women who were trained much like the men. They went to battle with the men, they rode with the men, and they earned that place, as the men did. They earned their place as warriors, and the women earned that place if that's what they wanted to do and to be. Very much incorporated into the culture—the warrior women, as they were called, or the manly-hearted woman.[13]

But as Harriett entered the narrative herself, in relation to her description of the tradition of the warrior woman, her story became more complex:

I don't know, I'm a Native woman, but I'm more of a woman, too. There's all these parts of us. I mean, I think that's true for all of us. There's a part of me that's Native, that big part of me that's Native. There's that part of me that's woman, there's a part of me that's grandmother, mother and, on occasion, wife. [Laughter] And so I think we somehow incorporate all of this into who we are as human beings, and that was one of the things that I was trying to say in the film I made, in "The Right to Be," that I want to acknowledge that power that's greater than myself as a human being. …[14]

[14] Ibid.

[15] Ibid., p. 71.

As the interview progressed, questions I had about the meaning of being a Native woman journalist, as well as a mother, occasional wife, devoted grandmother and film student at New York University (in her sixties), were addressed through specific stories about her adventures and losses over a lifetime. Embedded in these stories were thick descriptions about the times in which she lived, the pressures she defied and the determination she drew upon to overcome obstacles, which revealed a lot about history.

Oral-history narratives, like history itself, are often unfinished. Harriett's allusion to the power that is greater than herself is really that of history, which she confronts through her own artistic endeavors—her film—as well as her achievements as a journalist. In the end, her biography was a window into a larger world, an occasion for her to speculate on the cultural genocide that she had described earlier in the interview:

> There are many people out there who believe we didn't make it into the twentieth century, that we are part of the past. And that takes us to another issue. That takes us into it's okay to dig up our bones. It's okay to desecrate our graves. It's okay to put us into museums so they can look at us. Do I have to worry about that in two hundred years, are me and my granddaughter going to be in the Smithsonian? Do I have to worry that my sons and my daughter are going to end up in a drawer on the fourth floor of the Smithsonian Institution? I mean, I don't see anyone else worrying about that. I don't see any other group in this country that has to repatriate their funerary remains back to the reservation to be buried 150 years later. …They don't want to give them back to us. They fight us to keep those bones so they can study what we ate and what we drank and how we died. I said, "All you have to do is ask me. I'll tell them what we ate." It's not much different than it was 150 years ago. It's still corn and meat and that kind of thing.[15]

In the conversations that ensued, Harriett allowed me to become the vehicle for her testimony, which she and I both knew would extend the boundaries of our conversation on the "beautiful quilt" of her dorm room at New York University. For one thing, her truthfulness and her courage would have impact on me as a person and an interviewer. For another, the question she implicitly raises, "Why don't you ask me?" is an invitation to participate in this interpersonal and intercultural dialogue on the part of all who read or hear the interview. In asking this question, Harriett is transforming her autobiography into a cultural text, and her life story into testimony.

The move back and forth between personal memories and stories, and social and cultural memories and stories, is a hallmark of oral-history narratives. If the history being told does not contain stories of conflict and reveal contradictions, the interview is not complete and the testimony is not truthful.

STEP THREE: CREATING ART OUT OF DIALOGUE

Harriett Skye was an accomplished filmmaker by the time I met her. She also had been a successful print journalist and had hosted her own television show on Native American affairs during the 1970s. She understood the power and importance of media to create representations that could defy and subvert stereotypes. Due to the budget constraints of our project, the bulk of the interview had been conducted on audiotape. But we were allowed to conduct a final session before a camera.

I thought this might be a burden to Harriett, but she was delighted with the opportunity to present her story to a larger audience. As an experienced maker of visual media, she took the opportunity to create a wall behind her where pictures of most of her relatives, particularly her granddaughter, were directly visible. I had the sense as we began the interview that I was no longer the person she was talking to, that her real audience was the generation of her granddaughter. Adding the dimension of video enlarged the frame of the interview from a biography to a social and cultural history, transforming the subject of the interview from an "I" to a "we."

During the video interview, Harriett took center stage, directing the course of the interview, as an orator or storyteller in another context might draw upon personal experiences to represent the feelings and experiences of a culture or a generation. The stories she chose to illustrate her history and the history of Sioux women were culled from the rich reservoir of testimony that she had given in a more private setting, practiced in preparation for the final symphony. The fact that the story she performed was her own allowed life and art to meet in a way that transformed her dorm room into an amphitheater, her backdrop into a landscape of memory that came alive as snapshots of faded faces representing the forgotten history of a nation.

By the time our work had been completed, Harriett and I had worked together for over a year. I had spent several months reading books, articles and correspondence she had suggested as background research on her life. She had spent time preparing for the last interview session in particular, and we had developed a relationship that would last for her time in New York. Oral history, described by Alessandro Portelli as an exchange of gifts, had left us each with something we needed. For Harriett, it was a completed autobiography, one she claimed could not have been written without first being told.

The gift she carefully and thoughtfully gave me was an entry into her culture. It was one I had to earn. There were many questions I asked in the first session that she did not answer until the last session, until an equality of reciprocity had been achieved.

The art of oral history requires patience, flexibility, vulnerability and mutuality. The development of a relationship in an individual interview is analogous to what must occur in a community oral-history project that is transformed into public art. Like the one-to-one exchange, mutuality and transparency are key.

There are many examples of the ways in which oral history can be transformed into public art, but in each case the element that makes the effort authentic is the degree to which the lived experiences of the narrators and the use of specific languages of gesture and words are the motivating spirit of the performance, as well as the degree to which the audience is involved. Part of the contribution oral history can make to the field of community cultural development is to insist that the dialogical nature of the conversation, which is the occasion for transformation in oral history, be maintained in the public presentation of the art of the interview whether as an exhibit, a live performance or a documentary.

ORAL HISTORY AS THEATER

In a sense, every life history is a performance that is witnessed by two people, and ultimately many more. The same principles and guidelines that allow for the successful completion of a life history or the history of a community can guide the creation of a play in which participatory dialogue, the transfer of knowledge across generations and the transformation of community through artistic encounters are the goals.

This can be accomplished most easily through theater, in which there is a direct and ongoing relationship between the actors and the original or first storytellers, who in oral history are always the individual narrators as well as those present in their stories. An example of a genre of theater work in which the experiences of narrators remain central to the performance throughout —and also of testimony as a form of drama—is "theater of witness." Inspired by the use of testimony in Latin America and developed through work with Chileans in refugee communities in New York, the group Theater Arts Against Political Violence brought artists and survivors of political torture together to explore dramatic uses of testimony. Oral histories were conducted with torture survivors as a way for others to enter into the experiences of remembered torture, but in a broader landscape than one-to-one therapy (or oral history) could provide.

The actors modeled the experience of torture through their bodies, symbolically transferring the words into a lived experience that would be witnessed by the public to break down the conspiracy of silence that often confines the survivor in a world of isolation. According to Karen Malpede, who helped direct the project (cofounded by Jack Saul of the International Trauma Studies Program of New York University, Robert Group, a French theater director and Steven Reisner, a psychoanalyst), the project developed in close collaboration with those who lived through political torture. The project included three testimony sessions held in a group setting to avoid re-creating isolation. In between, the theater company met to develop and rehearse scenes from the stories. The goal of the production was to give the torture survivors the ability to stand outside their own experiences and to witness the transformation of their suffering on stage in the company of friends and fellow survivors. The survivors became the critics, and ultimately the authors, of the transformation.

Similar projects, in which survivors themselves direct and act in productions, have arisen through work with refugee communities of Bosnia, both in the Balkans and in the United States, Italy and elsewhere. A collaboration of psychologists, historians, oral historians and dramatists in Kosovo led to the creation of an Archives of Memory Project, in which theater was used to create a new collective space in which to shape community dialogues, as well as to expose the conditions of oppression which led to the experience of trauma and disruption.

The purpose of these and similar projects is to develop models that allow those who have been deprived of their authority and their rights to restore their voices to history and to reclaim their power, not only as witnesses but as real historical actors.

4. **Oral history is a liberatory practice** which—when practiced in communities where transformation is most needed and where those who understand their needs best can be empowered to speak for themselves and act on their own behalf—is a primary medium for liberation. Stories unleash power, connecting memory and the imagination to the world, and encourage a dynamic organization of forces to combat situations of inequality and justice exacerbated by globalization.

In "Pedagogy of the Oppressed," which many community cultural development workers count as a common bible of sorts, the late Brazilian educator Paulo Freire writes of the importance of language itself as a source of inspiration and action:

> To exist, humanly, is to *name* the world, to change it. Once named, the
> world in its turn reappears to the namers as a problem and requires of them
> a new naming.[16]

People were not created, he suggests, to live in silence, but in work, in "action-reflection." Freire also writes that we live in a state of dialogue, the basic human phenomenon that holds us together as a species, which is only meaningful if we connect it to our actions.

> Within the word we find two dimensions, reflection and action, in such
> radical interaction that if one is sacrificed—even in part—the other imme-
> diately suffers. There is no true word that is not at the same time a praxis
> [the synthesis of action and reflection which leads to the work of transfor-
> mation, or praxis]. Thus, to speak a true word is to transform the world.[17]

For Freire, the process of liberation is a complex one, requiring that the forces of oppression be named, and the relationship between the oppressor and the oppressed be broken before transformation of historical conditions can occur. Oral history can provide the technique through which those who have been silenced can recover their power in history, in both individual and social ways. The power of naming and of telling stories in communities which can themselves become locations for political transformation, is a universal one that has its historic roots in orality itself and in myriad storytelling traditions.

In oral history, the form of the story, the way in which it is told, the audience it is told in front of and the tone through which it is conveyed are as central as its content. Within the specificity of that subjectivity lies the potential for transformation in history through the act of dialogical communication. As Freire suggests, the purpose of dialogue is to release the power of the word in history.

[16]Freire, op. cit. p. 76.

[17]Freire, p. 75.

This has been most powerfully illustrated in communities of the very poor, where the theft of language through depriving people of education has contributed to the success of totalitarianism. In Latin America and South America in particular, a creative response to these conditions that relies upon the power of the word to transform history is the tradition of *testimonio*, in which voices of the oppressed are heard, recorded and read back to survivors in order to build a social movement of liberation. This technique has been used successfully by the Mothers of the Plaza de Mayo in Argentina, the Mothers of the Disappeared in El Salvador and Chile and other groups to create the groundwork for a liberation movement through transforming a consciousness of fear into one of empowerment.

Oral historians working with refugees, exiles and the poor and marginalized in countries around the world have used this technique, and the literary and oral narratives it inspires, to build communities of resistance and resilience in which the spoken word inspires political action in the direct way that Freire imagined.

While there are no universal models for connecting art to praxis in oral history, there are principles and guidelines which can allow for the dynamic exchange among individuals and cultures that can contribute to transformation.

PRINCIPLES AND GUIDELINES

1. In oral history, the ultimate power of interpretation lies with the story-teller. This means, first and foremost, that the narrator takes the ultimate authority in shaping his or her own story and that—just as all cultures are equal—all stories have equal power. In oral history, every narrator is an artist and must become the creator of his or her own narrative.

2. The event of the interview, the preparation that precedes it, the equality that is achieved within it, the insights and actions that result from it, constitute a parable of ways in which the larger processes of liberation and transformation can occur. As a mirror of the past, re-created in the present, the interview can also predict the future and effect the conversion of the word into action.

3. The expansion of the interview into a performance, whether of a single narrator or a group of witnesses, provides the opportunity to challenge the existing order of things and propose a new order. Because the interview is an expression of identity on multiple levels, and the intersection of interviews in a performance reveals the interconnections between personal and cultural forms of expression, the performance can reshape our collective self-understanding in ways that a single performer or one director might not imagine.

If the narratives are reduced to one theme or plot, and the individuality and specificity of memory and experience is lost, the power of the collective voice becomes repressive and the dialogical encounter does not materialize. This means that there must be an active and participatory relationship between the narrators and the designated artists/performers that motivates the production from beginning to end.

4. The creation of an artistic representation of a life, a community story or a cultural legacy based on oral histories must be true to the story as it was lived and shaped through historical and interpersonal encounters. The act of representing history is also the act of reconstructing the possibility of acting in history by understanding how the past influences the present and how relationships can be transformed. In practice, the art of oral history is always rooted in the knowledge of actual historical conditions but attuned to ways in which they can be upturned.

5. Oral history provides a framework in which to reimagine the world, first by remembering it, second by naming it and third by renaming it through the conversion of words into actions.

6. Oral history stimulates the transformation of word into action through this process of naming and renaming, breaking apart silences and finding in them sources of individual and social power. Reframing these stories in artistic performance through theater and other media helps community development to occur.

The art of oral history is to inspire those who have been silenced to speak out and to hear their own stories. The praxis of oral history is building the community from which those stories, told and retold, will transform history.

Judith F. Baca paints
Dust Bowl refugees
coming to California in the
1930s at "The Great Wall
of Los Angeles" mural
in 1979. Photo © Douglas
Kirkland, 1980.

Social and Public Art Resource Center
685 Venice Boulevard
Venice, California 90291 U.S.A.
Telephone: (310) 822-9560
Fax: (310) 827-8717
E-mail: sparc@sparcmurals.org
Web sites: www.sparcmurals.org and www.judybaca.com

Like Liz Lerman, **Judith Francisca Baca** was trained in a conventional artistic path, diverging from it as life challenges impelled. As she explained in the spring 2001 online dialogue:

I stepped out of the university [in the 1960s] unprepared to make art that had a relationship to the people or the communities out of which I had come. I was born in Watts and raised in Pacoima; two [Los Angeles] neighborhoods infamous for racial conflict and race riots between African Americans and Chicanos (Americans of Mexican descent, my own culture).

Today, Judy serves as Artistic Director of the Social and Public Art Resource Center (SPARC) in Venice, California, which she cofounded in 1976. She has also been Professor of Fine Arts for the University of California since 1980, and since 1996 has held two concurrent academic appointments at the University of California at Los Angeles, as a senior member of UCLA's Cesar Chavez Center and as Professor of Art for the World Arts and Cultures department.

Her essay describes an organic process by which SPARC has become the vehicle for collaborative works of art she described in our online dialogue as "sites of public memory":

Through the graffiti on the street produced by young gang members, I learned that the sidewalks and walls were methods of communication that could be used to organize groups in the barrios [Latino neighborhoods] and ghettos of Los Angeles. This led me to the use of public walls/spaces for large-scale organizing projects in which I worked with the people of the neighborhood to envision monumental paintings, parks, metrorail [public transit] stations, billboards, installations that spoke to their shared concerns and imaginings. These works become symbols of a struggle of peoples against borders, cultural differences, and territories defined by racial and class segregation.

Unlike other art forms, such as live performance, which are intrinsically ephemeral and experiential, public art projects have two dimensions: the deeply transformative process of engaging as a direct participant in the creation of a work; and the stimulus provided for others as the work becomes a "site of public memory," a permanent feature of community. This essay embodies the perpetual trajectory of community cultural development—accelerating in the age of globalization—as work that enables voices to be heard from the local to the global, using everything at hand, from the simplest forms to the most sophisticated high-tech tools.

Birth of a Movement

by Judith F. Baca

Perhaps it was the abundance of concrete, or the year-round painting season or the city full of Mexican workers that made Los Angeles the place where murals began to be a predominant art form. Or perhaps it was because an entire population—the majority of the city—had been "disappeared" in textbooks, in the media, in cultural markers of place, and needed to find a way to reclaim a city of Mexican and indigenous roots.

In 1932 a mural was painted on Olvera Street, the birthplace of Los Angeles, by the great maestro David Alfaro Siqueiros, the Mexican muralist/painter. Siqueiros was the last of *Los Tres Grandes* (The Three Great Muralists), who after the 1910 Revolution in Mexico began a cultural revolution that taught the precepts of the revolution and the history of Mexico through murals. Siqueiros, the most revolutionary of the three in materials usage, social intent and content, worked for a period of time in Los Angeles. His 80-foot-long mural "America Tropical" spoke to the exploitation of the Mexican worker. Commissioned by the city fathers for a Bavarian beer garden (owned by a Nazi), the mural was intended to depict a kitchsy Mexican village scene for the benefit of tourists. Instead, Siqueiros made the central image of the mural a crucified figure.

With increasing demand for low-wage immigrant labor and massive migrations of Mexican and Central American workers to Los Angeles over the last 10 or 15 years, this image is even more relevant today than in the '30s. The mural was partially whitewashed shortly after its completion and then fully painted over within its first year on public view, beginning a legacy of

The censored Los Angeles mural "America Tropical" (1932) by David Alfaro Siqueiros, one of the leading Mexican muralists of the 20th century, is now being restored by the Getty Conservation Institute.

censorship that still haunts Los Angeles. In the 1970s, 40 years after it was painted over, the image began to re-emerge from the whitewash. We saw this as a symbol, an *aparicion* (religious apparition) coinciding with the growth of Los Angeles's Mexican population and strength of the Chicano movement. ("Chicano" is a politicized term for "Mexican-Americans.")

Siqueiros prophesied that someday every street corner of Los Angeles would have a mural, brought about by the freeing of the artist from the tyranny of laborious frescos. Siqueiros predicted that a form of muralism would exist somewhere between the moving picture and photography. He did not know of computers, but I would like to think he would have embraced the role they are now playing in mural production at Cesar Chavez Digital Mural Lab of the Social and Public Art Resource Center (SPARC), which I cofounded in 1976, a nonprofit organization dedicated to creating and preserving public art.

Murals in Los Angeles were the first artistic medium to support and then shape a movement toward identity and justice that reached a mass population. This artistic occupation of public space forged a strong visual presence of a people who at that time (late '60s, early '70s) lacked representation in public life, with neither voice in elections nor elected representatives. No person of Latino descent served on the city council or on the school board, despite the fact that in actual numbers we were fast becoming the majority of the population. Parallel to and perhaps growing from this new visual strength, many citizens of emerging Latino communities organized, with very little money and freely given labor, toward the mutual goal of improving the conditions of their communities. While many of the early Chicano muralists were of the first generation in their communities to earn advanced degrees, a racially

Whitewashed view from the
street of "American Tropical."

unsophisticated society tied the Chicano artist to the conditions of the barrios regardless of their educational status. SPARC was born of the spirit of this movement, taking its name from the notion that it takes only a spark to start a prairie fire. The organization has been intent on nurturing this healthy fire within the city as a whole for 25 years.

As the fire of muralism progressed, distinctions began to emerge. Apart from its initial purpose of creating a capacity for the imagery of the people to occupy public space, Los Angeles murals spoke to the cultural demands of previously under-represented peoples. Some works became cultural-affirmation images, asserting only that we exist as distinct cultures; others addressed the hard task of articulating and advocating for resolution of issues affecting the places where our people lived and worked.

This new social power was not limited to immigrant labor nor indigenous people, but spread to the multiplicity of Los Angeles populations. African-American, Thai, Chinese, Jewish and women's murals began to appear on the streets of Los Angeles. Before long, community murals began to attract media attention and documentation. Murals began to tackle larger issues of police brutality, border crossings, drug addiction, gang warfare and other difficulties of a life of poverty and exclusion. Early in the movement, space was freely available and uncontested. If you had the paint and the time, the wall and the message were yours.

In this environment the movement flourished. In the early '70s a visitor could drive from site to site and could have seen Carlos Almaraz, David Botello, Willie Herron and myself all painting simultaneously on the streets of Los Angeles.

As the movement progressed, common themes emerged, variations on those themes developed and our stories began to crystallize. We consciously avoided Western European aesthetics, instead privileging Chicano popular culture, religious iconography, Mexican calendars, tattoos, street writing, whatever could better and more accurately portray our direct life experience. We did not even look closely at Mexico City, an influence far removed from the Diaspora of the Southwest. In this way, we were able to create a unique and specific art form that spoke to our own lived experience in the barrios and inner cities of Los Angeles. This movement spread to the rural communities of the Southwest and developed concurrently, though distinctly, on the East Coast.

In 1970, I began working for the Los Angeles Department of Recreation and Parks, teaching art in Boyle Heights, a neighborhood with the highest number of gangs in the United States. Similar to the neighborhood I grew up in (Pacoima), Boyle Heights had cultural markers—graffiti—with roll calls written on the walls that told you who lived there, what the neighborhood was called and who was from there. But this stylized iconography often triggered destructive conflict, part of the contesting of public space by rival gang members. I began working with gang members from different neighborhoods to establish networks between them to promote peaceful solutions to such conflicts. Redirecting gang members' inclinations toward public expression via my own artistic training as a painter, we began painting murals as a way to create constructive cultural markers.

Our first mural, entitled "Mi Abuelita" ("My Grandmother"), was painted in Hollenbeck Park's three-sided band shell, where the Feria de los Niños (Children's Fair) occurred annually. This work recognized the primary position of the matriarch in Mexican families as a reflection of our indigenous roots. It also marked the first step in the development of a unique collective process that employs art to mediate between rival gang members competing for public space and public identity. Through this work we formulated a group incorporating four rival neighborhoods within the same team, named Las Vistas Nuevas (The New View).

This group, composed of 20 young people 16 to 21 years old, was made up of youth with whom I had developed relationships at several different parks as an arts teacher in the Department of Recreation and Parks' Eastside parks. My teaching assignment had been to move daily from park to park to teach small children's and senior citizens' art classes. To do so I would walk a gauntlet of young men who used the parks as a place to hang out and play dominoes with their homeboys. Over a period of time the shouts of "Hey, art lady!" became friendly exchanges, sharing drawings and tattoo designs of the most talented among them. Soon the young men became collaborators as well as students.

While I could move between the parks, my new friends could not travel even a mile to a neighboring park for fear of reprisals by rival neighborhood gangs. The climate of the time was shaped by the civil rights movement, with events such as the Chicano Moratorium March in East Los Angeles on August 29, 1970. This historical march, catalyzed by organizing of the Brown Berets group, occurred because Chicanos opposed the Vietnam War on the grounds that Chicanos suffered the highest number of casualties in the war proportionate to their number in the population. The Chicanos urged nonviolence on all who participated in this event and agreed to this condition despite their anger toward the war, knowing that senseless hatred would ruin everything—most importantly, their chances of being recognized. Despite this, Ruben Salazar, a reporter for the Los Angeles Times sympathetic to Chicano civil rights activities, was killed by a police tear-gas canister shot blindly into the Silver Dollar Café, where police thought organizers were gathering. Much work was created subsequently around the events of August 29. Manuel Cruz, an early organizer of youth and ex-member of the Macy Street neighborhood, in his mural in the Ramona Gardens low-income housing project of primarily Chicano families, asserted that "Raza killing Raza" (Chicanos or Latinos killing each other) was contributing to their own oppression.

A monumental grandmother image occupies center stage in "Mi Abuelita," painted in Hollenbeck Park band shell, the site of the Feria de los Niños, where children dance in her outstretched arms. This mural celebrates the importance of the elders in traditional Mexican families and was painted by "Las Vistas Nuevas," a group of 20 youth from four neighborhoods in conflict in East Los Angeles, organized by Judy Baca in the 1970s.

While painting "Mi Abuelita" in Hollenbeck Park, the Las Vistas Nuevas group developed a system of lookouts placed in the parks to protect us from those who did not support our efforts to work across defined territories and neighborhoods. The lookouts were to whistle if someone threatened harm to the group. Our plan was that we were to quickly exit the scaffolding of our painting to enter the bandshell's stage doors and wait for an all-clear signal before returning to work.

One day a whistle sounded as we were painting, signaling the approach of plainclothes police officers. The police had been unfriendly to my efforts to bring known gang members into public sites. They said they would arrest my team members if I continued to assemble them in public view. I kept painting and told the 20 others to do the same, thinking that I would try to convince the officers that we should be allowed to continue our work undisturbed. A man's voice called to me from below the scaffolding where I perched. When I heard "Judy Baca?" I expected to see a police officer, but instead came face to face with the general manager of the Department of Recreation and Parks, Sy Greben. He had recently taken that job after having served as the Director of the Peace Corps for President John F. Kennedy's administration. He asked, "Are you being paid to do this work?" Since Mr. Greben was the highest-ranking person in the department, I was afraid to answer for fear that, not having official status as city employees, our painting of park walls would be halted. "No," I said politely, "I am an art teacher in your parks working on my own time."

Mr. Greben understood the power and importance of what he witnessed that day in the cooperative spirit of the young painters. He began a course of action that led to the first City of Los Angeles citywide mural program, making me director of a burgeoning murals program in the predominantly Mexican Eastside of Los Angeles. Freed from my more conventional teaching by the general manager, I began to work full-time with the youth of East Los Angeles at various sites. Three years later, I initiated a proposal to the Los Angeles City Council that became the first citywide mural program. More than 400 mural productions were supported through the Citywide Murals Program under the Department of Recreation and Parks before the program was disbanded. Scaffolding, paints, youth apprentices and stipends were distributed by the small staff of Eastside youth from previous mural crews whom I hired to run the program, supporting hundreds of mural sites in every community of the city.

Within the first year of the Citywide Murals Program, censorship problems arose as communities began to identify issues affecting their lives. Because the program was under the auspices of a city department, local officials tried to exert influence on works that were created within their districts, threatening to withhold funds for the entire citywide program under their purview. One council member, realizing the popularity of the murals, asked to have his own portrait painted on a highly visible public street to help insure his re-election. Controversies continued to arise, of course, and interestingly, the themes that provoked outrage from officials and conservative elements of our city remain controversial today.

Police brutality is perhaps the number-one issue that cannot be painted about freely on a public street in Los Angeles, today as 25 years ago. The irony is that Los Angeles's issues of police brutality have had resounding effects across the United States and the world, with the notorious beatings of Rodney King and a Mexican immigrant woman in Riverside. The devastating 1992 Los Angeles riots were precipitated by the acquittal of police officers responsible for the beating of Rodney King. Today our city is threatened with bankruptcy because of the high-profile Rampart Division police scandal, precipitated by an officer's confession and the resultant indictment of other officers. As a result, a process is underway to acquit and pay damages out of tax dollars to what will prove to be hundreds of so-called gang members unjustly convicted by police via planted evidence and other police crimes. Nevertheless, images on Los Angeles streets that criticize police practices draw instant censorship and guarantee the physical presence of police officers at any mural site where painters attempt to depict such an image.

Additional controversies have arisen over the image of armed men of color, such as gang members (a controversial image even without guns). The image of Huey P. Newton of the Black Panthers in a paramilitary uniform is perhaps the second most controversial depiction in the history of SPARC mural productions.

It was for this reason that the "Friends of the Citywide Mural Program," a group of supporters including attorneys called to defend the often besieged program, decided to form a nonprofit corporation called the Social and Public Art Resource Center, now celebrating its 25th anniversary. In collaboration with members of the city council who felt that freedom of speech was essential for the expanding mural movement, they encouraged the founding of SPARC as an arts organization that could carry out mural programs in such a way as to animate public discourse and free expression of the diverse communities of the city without direct official intervention.

THE GREAT WALL OF LOS ANGELES MODEL

SPARC's first project was "The Great Wall of Los Angeles," a mural. Having worked on murals across the 75-mile expanse of the city through the Citywide Mural Program, I was called to a local site not far from my hometown in Pacoima. The site was a concrete flood-control channel built by the Army Corps of Engineers. Once an arroyo (a dirt ravine cut by river water), the Tujunga Wash flood-control channel was an ugly concrete dividing line within the community with a belt of arid dirt running along either side. The Wash is in Studio City, a few miles north of Hollywood in the San Fernando Valley.

The Army Corps of Engineers first began concreting river bottoms in the Los Angeles basin because of the problem of seasonal flooding associated with the Los Angeles River. This decision to concrete the Los Angeles River would affect the people of the city for generations to come in subsequent planning and development decisions and spiritual discord associated with the land. The concreted rivers divided the land and left ugly eyesores, carrying the water too swiftly to the ocean, bearing pollution from city streets, affecting Santa Monica Bay and depriving the aquifer of water replenishment through normal ground seepage. In a sense the concreting of the river represented the hardening of the arteries of the land. If the river overflowing its banks regularly destroyed opportunities for the real-estate expansion that fast became the chief commodity of the fledgling city of the 1920s, then the river would simply have to be tamed. These first decisions about the river made it easier to displace historic indigenous and Mexican communities in the name of city development.

This development campaign ended in the '70s, when an aesthetic planning division was formed to evaluate how the land surrounding the channels could be better-used and aesthetically improved. I worked with the Army Corps of Engineers' Aesthetic Planning Division to develop a plan for a stretch of the channel running more than a mile alongside two schools and through a neighborhood. A park was proposed for viewing access to the channel walls. I saw an opportunity for a seemingly endless wall, 13½ feet tall and below ground level.

"The Great Wall of Los Angeles," begun in 1976 with 400 participating youth, is the world's longest mural at 13' x 2,740'. Located in the San Fernando Valley flood-control channel, built in the 1930s, it depicts a multi-cultural history of California from prehistory through the 1950s. The Great Wall is currently being restored and extended via Internet participation, with support from the Rockefeller Foundation's PACT program.

The uniqueness of the site provided a safe haven to assemble youth from different neighborhoods of Los Angeles without fear of reprisals from warring gangs, as drive-by shootings, commonplace in Los Angeles, were virtually impossible in the Wash; and the endless wall provided a natural site for a narrative work. Fresh from organizing in the disparate communities of Los Angeles, I was hopeful about a site that necessitated a large team from many places. Unclaimed by any one gang, it was an excellent place to bring youth of varied ethnic backgrounds from all over the city to work on an alternate view of the history of the United States which included people of color who had been left out of American history books.

The concrete river invaded my dreams, its significance becoming clearer to me as the correlation between the scars on a human body and those on the land took shape in my mind. Fernando, a charismatic leader from the original Las Vistas Nuevas team, was brutally stabbed in his own neighborhood's local store the summer of the painting of "Mi Abuelita." He suffered 13 wounds to his torso and one to his face. We were devastated by the attack, but Fernando recovered and returned for the dedication ceremony, continuing his work against violence through the murals for many years until he was killed in his neighborhood park in the 1980s, 12 years after he had abandoned "the life." I asked him after he had healed how he was doing with the psychological scars left by such an attack and he responded, "The worst thing is that every time I remove my shirt my body is a map of violence." It was for this reason that I proposed and designed a series of tattooed images to cover and transform the scars on his body.

Standing at the river on that first day, dreaming of what it could become, I saw the concrete as a scar where the river once ran and our work in the channel producing the narrative mural, as a tattoo on the scar. The defining metaphor of what came to be known as "The Great Wall of Los Angeles" (after a film of the same name by Donna Deitch, film director and cofounder of SPARC) became "a tattoo on the scar where the river once ran."

The "Great Wall of Los Angeles" production began with 80 youth recruited through the juvenile-justice system and paid by a program to employ economically disadvantaged young people. When completed, this project had employed over 400 youth along with 40 historians, 40 artists, hundreds of historical witnesses and thousands of residents involved in the production of a half-mile narrative mural. The work became a monument to interracial harmony as methods were developed to work across the differences of race and class. As a result, relationships were formed that are now 25 years old.

Today, the basic tenets of the early mural movement still hold true. SPARC is dedicated to ensuring the maintenance of a tradition that finds expression through the hands of well-established artists and of young people with spray cans. The beginnings of muralism in Los Angeles are rooted in the need for public space and public expression. In a city where neighborhoods were uprooted through corporatization (as with the Chavez Ravine sports stadium), or the construction of freeways through low-income barrios or ghettos, or the destruction of rivers, the need to create sites of public memory became increasingly important.

From successful mural productions, methodologies were gleaned that laid the foundation for subsequent SPARC projects. During its production, one of the youth assistants suggested making "The Great Wall" global. "We should take what we learned working with different nationalities here in Los Angeles to the world," the 16-year-old said. In 1987, we began work that still continues on "The World Wall," a portable installation of murals by artists from countries around the world offering expressions of world peace.

Through the "World Wall" project, artists were asked to articulate a particular moment, an apex of change for their countries that best described the time in which they live and which could benefit people of other countries and realities. The concept of "from the neighborhood to the global" motivated the development of "The World Wall," a traveling installation mural equal in length to one 350-foot segment of "The Great Wall," which could be assembled indoors or outside in a 100-foot diameter circle as an arena for ritual and dialogue. "The World Wall: A Vision of the Future Without Fear" premièred in the summer of 1990 in Joensuu, Finland, where our Finnish collaborators (Sirka Lisa Lonka and Aero Matinlauri Juha Saaski) added a work called "Alternative Dialogues." That same summer, Alexi Begov of Moscow produced a work during the fall of the Communist Party in the then–Soviet Union called "Waiting for the End of the 20th Century." In 1999, an Israeli/Palestinian collaboration was added: "Inheritance Compromise" by Adi Yukutieli (Israeli Jew), Akmed Bweerat (Israeli Arab) and Suliman Mansour (Palestinian). Each work has represented years of intense dialogue between the artist-collaborators and work with the children of their home villages. The newest addition in 2001 — "Tlazolteotl: The Creative Force of the UnWoven" by Martha Ramirez Oropeza and Patricia Quijano Ferrer — represents the changing role of Mexican urban/indigenous women and Mexico's relation to the Mexican-American border. These works, combined with the four completed by my teams in Los Angeles, create a giant arena for dialogue while encompassing the viewer in a healing circle. The murals function as a visual primer for societal transformation toward balance and peace. This project continues to move internationally adding work as it travels. Works are in planning stages from the First Nation people of Canada, the Australian Bushwomen and prisoners of Brazil.

In 1988, the concept of "The Great Wall" was taken to a citywide level in Los Angeles with the Neighborhood Pride: Great Walls Unlimited program, which has so far sponsored more than 104 murals by artists from different parts of the city reflecting the issues of diverse groups in their own neighborhoods.

Most recently, SPARC has been experimenting with digital mural–making techniques in the SPARC/Cesar Chavez Digital Mural Lab, created in 1996. This new collaboration between SPARC and the University of California, Los Angeles, is experimenting with new methods of producing permanent

"World Wall: A Vision of the Future Without Fear" is shown here in Moscow's Gorky Park in 1990.

Begun in 1986, a new 10' x 30' panel is added by a native artist from each country to which the Wall travels, each exploring the material and spiritual transformation of a society toward peace. The Wall has been displayed at the Smithsonian and other U.S. locations, and in Finland and Russia. A new panel was unveiled by an Israeli-Palestinian team at California State University Monterey Bay in April, 1998, and one by the Mexican team was added in 2001.

murals via computer technologies. Research in the lab is yielding new substrates for murals, methods of expanding community dialogue via the Internet and murals that can be replicated if censored or destroyed. Also, during the summer of 2001, SPARC collaborated with the Human Relations Commission's Shoulder to Shoulder program to develop a project that would bring together youth from different ethnic and class backgrounds from around the city of Los Angeles to discuss issues of race, violence, class and reconciliation. Applying processes developed in mediation between rival neighborhoods in East Los Angeles and "The Great Wall," SPARC created an interdisciplinary arts curriculum that facilitates dialogue between youth about these issues.

In the meantime, SPARC is continuing to invent ways to create new public monuments that reflect marginalized people, such as urban immigrant domestic workers, *campesinos* (farmworkers) in the fields of California and others. While the methodology of the work is consistent from project to project, the outcome always changes. Our approach to art allows for truly democratic processes and critical reflection to facilitate different artistic visions for and about our society.

Of critical importance to our work at SPARC is the distinction between private and public space. Shared public space has steadily eroded throughout urban America within the last 10 to 15 years. In the city of Los Angeles, where SPARC does most of its work, many urban parks have become occupied territories. A park will be described as controlled by gangs such as "Barrio Nuevo" or "Third Street," or the park may be identified with one race such as "the Mexican park" or "the Black park." As defined territories, parks can become among the most dangerous places in our city. Recognition of these

A few of the images from "Witnesses to the History of Los Angeles" commemorate people disappeared from history in the building of the city, displayed at the California Plaza Amphitheatre, with "Toyporina, Gabrielino Nation" in the foreground. These 1996 digital works were produced by the UCLA/SPARC Cesar Chavez Digital Mural Lab, working in collaboration with Cornerstone Theatre, and are housed at the Social and Public Art Resource Center.

relationships of power at a local level is common among residents of all nationalities in our city of nations. If public parks are not accessible to the diversity of all people, then what spaces are? Where can people meet and share the sense that they are citizens of a common land?

In neighborhoods of wealth, people have sometimes taken over public thoroughfares, limiting their use by the outside public. The phenomenon of gated neighborhoods is increasingly common, just as gated cities have grown up around the desire for security from crime and a sense of comfort at not having to deal with those different from oneself.

Under such conditions, where does civic life occur? In the court rooms? In the schools? In the parks? Where do we find places of respite, open places to meet that speak to a shared sensibility about what it means to be a citizen of our city, of our state and country?

The contentiousness of public space has been acted out in the arts in very interesting ways. Legislation to control the production of art in public spaces has multiplied, while rampant proliferation of signage and advertising images has been left unchecked, creating increasing urban blight. Today, for example, it is not possible in many neighborhoods to paint something on the exterior of one's own home without first gaining permission from a municipal authority. While our First Amendment rights guarantee freedom of expression, content cannot be the basis for banning an image. Nevertheless, municipal authorities regularly engage in discussions of content, violating the rights of artists and restricting images they deem offensive or those that tell stories they do not want told. Artists usually lose unless they have the resources to seek legal counsel, increasingly a luxury item to most artists, as pro bono legal services have eroded substantially in recent years. As a result, so-called public meetings are held without challenge by the public on critical issues that erode civil liberties.

Many artists, writers and others have challenged local statutes by painting buildings in forbidden colors. In San Antonio, Texas, for example, writer Sandra Cisneros painted her house in a historic district a bright purple with red trim. She was called to appear before the local historic preservation committee and told to change the colors because they clashed with the Victorian feel of the neighborhood. The commission wanted her to paint her home Pilgrim gray. The irony is that San Antonio (not that far from the U.S.–Mexican border) is Mexican in character, yet historical preservationists there look toward England for inspiration. The United States has enshrined belief in the European notions of gray and white as colors that embody the spirit of ancient Greece and democracy. This is historically inaccurate, as we now know the buildings of ancient Greece and Rome were painted in bright colors and encrusted with jewels. The idea that using gray and white will maintain visual tranquility—a blandness—suggests an association between color and class.

In the 1980s, brightly painted murals on Los Angeles's Harbor Freeway commemorating the 1984 Olympics were criticized for being too bright, and subsequently "too violent." A Los Angeles Times art critic even called for them to be painted over or vandalized by the public. Bright colors have become synonymous with excess, sensuality, the other.

Cafés often extend their tables to the edge of public sidewalks in growing competition for public space. Interestingly enough, homeowners and business owners can be sued for accidents that occur on a sidewalk in front of their property, even though the sidewalk is owned by the city. This clearly indicates the mixed message of public passage.

Unlike European cities, where plazas and promenades exist for communal conviviality, few spaces exist in U.S. cities that allow for meeting those different from ourselves. The growing phenomena of gated cities and sidewalks that roll up at night, of pedestrian walkways owned by corporations so that employees' feet need not touch the real streets—these have created an absence of meeting places.

Nowhere is the struggle for public space more pronounced than in the war against graffiti artists. More clearly than any other, the phenomenon of graffiti art, now a worldwide movement, plays out the power relations involved in public-space usage.

Any discussion of public space requires us to think about the fact that today in California we have some 150,000 homeless people who conduct entire lives that normally are private in public spaces. They sleep in public spaces, they wash in public spaces, they carry out all the life activities that normally would be hidden behind doors in public spaces.

The competition for public space is so extreme that private and public have merged. In many areas of our inner city we've seen front stoops turned into makeshift shops where an elderly woman will sell brooms or a man will sell car parts.

If you ask groups of students in university classes across Los Angeles to define public space, naming a public space in our city, they will most inevitably name a shopping mall: the Galleria, the Beverly Center, the Third Street Promenade. Yet these are corporate spaces where all activities are orchestrated and controlled, and certain people are excluded from participation by virtue of not having (enough) money to purchase goods.

In a recent event near SPARC in Venice Beach, California, the wavering line between public and private became very apparent to those who chose to see it. A hip-hop concert was being held in a picnic pavilion on the beach. Some graffiti artists started to spray-paint images and words on the cement. Police tried to remove the artists, following them deeper into the crowd of dancing young people. In the ensuing confusion—police pursuing graffiti taggers into a throng of hip-hop revelers—the riot squad was called, a fairly frequent occurrence since the 1992 Los Angeles uprising. The police proceeded to sweep the beach, clearing it of thousands of people, whether they were associated with the concert or not. In the process, they asked a young man making a call in a phone booth to hang up and leave the area. The man refused and the cops beat him. A local news crew captured the beating on tape and showed it on the five o'clock news.

By chance, a group of Irish mural artists visiting the area saw the footage and were horrified by what they interpreted as police brutality. They contacted SPARC and expressed interest in creating a mural at the beach showing images of the beating seen on television. We responded by informing them that a mural criticizing the Los Angeles Police Department was not possible, suggesting instead that they paint the mural on canvas and take it to the beach as a temporary expression of their current frustration and helplessness. After finalizing a plan to create a mural using chalk applied directly to the sidewalk as a way to avoid further conflict with the police, the artists called a press conference for the next day. After much negotiation with the police— who immediately appeared as they began making a large and beautifully rendered image of the police beating—they had been assured by the LAPD that they would not disturb the project until it was completed and documented by the media. However when they returned for their scheduled press conference, the mural had been washed away. It turned out the police had hired a homeless man to wash the sidewalk clean.

"Are We Both Americans?" is the question posed on the "Shoulder to Shoulder" banners, hundreds of which were placed on Los Angeles streets to promote dialogue among the city's diverse youth. Images and text were drawn from a series of summer work-shops at SPARC involving 14-year-olds of diverse race and class backgrounds in one-to-one exchange. The young people's own words are superimposed on their drawings and portraits.

On the same beach (the Venice Boardwalk is the number-one tourist spot in Los Angeles, with millions of visitors every year), a graffiti artist painted the silhouette of a nude woman in a cartoonlike image. The image was not sexualized, as details of her body parts were avoided by the pose chosen and the stylized imagery. It was in fact quite an innocent image. The police censored the artwork, destroying it for being sexually inappropriate. The irony is that a few feet away, sexually explicit photos of greased, nude beach beauties, male and female, are on sale on T-shirts, posters and postcards; however, these images were in private space—for sale in a shop—as opposed to public space. Such commercial images are not censored by public authorities, while the images created by the graffiti artists were and are now subject to censorship and are often destroyed by public authorities.

AESTHETICS IN COMMUNITY PARTICIPATORY WORK

Is art work that is participatory and public antithetical to aesthetic practice? Perhaps there is no issue that has consistently plagued community cultural development work and contributed to its secondary status as fine-art work more than the issue of judging its aesthetics. It has long been held that the artist's personal interpretation of a particular moment in time, of an event or experience, is unique. The question we ask ourselves early in the process of creating community-based art is this: is it possible for us as artists to fully integrate the voices of the people that live in the spaces in which our work is being done? The critical element is understanding the process.

Community-based art is not simply one's individual notion of the creation of a masterpiece, but public work that is greatly influenced by the people for whom the work is made. The creation of public art requires a unique sensitivity, the artist's opening to interpretations that are sometimes distant from his or her own. In a sense, a method of compassionate listening is required, followed by a gestation period wherein the artist must take in the often disparate collective vision, then make it the artist's own by establishing central images stemming from the group experience. In no way does this process diminish the capability to create great public art. Sometimes the process connects instantaneously with the artist, or the artist is able to capture a strong image or idea that later has great resonance within the community.

For example, I am not a farmworker, but when I walked the fields of Central California with farmworkers with whom I was working, following close behind a plowing tractor, I was able to feel a sensation and later articulate through the mural medium a way of life of strong physical toil and struggle. Like many, I was until that moment willfully ignorant of the actual expenditure of human energy and activity required to feed the world's population. When I say energy, I mean the countless hours of stooping and bending, cutting and picking fruit and vegetables by hand in miles-long agricultural concerns. By listening to the people who share that experience on a daily basis, I was able to expand my vision to access or integrate their experience, rendering the resulting artwork more authentic, I hope, and certainly more accurate in terms of giving expression to this reality.

When I worked in the Central Valley of California, I invited farmworkers into my studio in Guadalupe, beginning with a simple exchange of images by the taking of Polaroid pictures. Bolstered by people's enthusiasm—many of them Filipino contract-employees who arrived at the studio following a 10-hour workday—I soon found myself examining a myriad of personal data in the form of family photo albums and other intimate documentation, including, oddly enough, the archives of the local police department. It wasn't long before I'd created the region's first-ever archive of the history of their area. Meanwhile the Filipino workers who stayed late were adamant in teaching me the correct way of stooping and cutting vegetables, how to grip the band of the hoe without causing undue back injury. Not only did this exchange greatly improve my vision of their working methods, it added insight, previously unknown or again only naively grasped, into a people for whom this work is commonplace. In an interesting side note to this exchange, I learned of the higher risk of kidney infections and disorders among farmworkers, who do not like to stop to relieve themselves for fear of becoming misaligned with the movement of the tractor, possibly upsetting the necessary brisk pace of work. Through dialogue with the workers, I discovered this psychology firsthand.

Creating community-based art by the process of accumulating a sensibility and history, one must understand the process of paint application more deeply, critically and sequentially than in other forms of art making. The artist must understand the process of applying paint in such a way that it then becomes accessible to any person who may be applying it. This requirement led me to better teaching skills and a greater articulation of how (and why) to arrive at the end product. I was by then able to explain my vision and ideas to others more succinctly and in turn to understand them better myself.

As time went on, I began to see more of the nuance in community-based work, such as the varying capacities of the young hands participating in creating the work, what is intended and what the work can mean to each hand, to each person contributing talents. I began to see the process much as an orchestral composition, how such a composition is achieved and enjoyed in its entirety only when all contributing "voices" meld into one virtuoso effort. The oboe pursuing the clarinet is akin to the hand following hand, hands applying image, color, creating meaning, creating a mural. By moving people through this process, I helped enhance the quality of their work and watched as their work matured, evolving from one end of the project to the other. Hands that were amateur at best became—through a deeper understanding of place, senses, capability and process—more deft, creating a much higher quality of work.

CLOSING THOUGHTS

During the writing of this essay, the tragedy of September 11 occurred. Like most people the world over, I was devastated, heartbroken and in shock. Now, 13 days later, as I worry over the fate of the world, I find my thoughts vacillating from one extreme to another. Either I'm having nightmare visions of a nuclear holocaust, or I'm imagining a world that has learned from this great loss the value of life, the value of peace and the great importance we all must place on cooperating and making compromises to achieve these goals.

Working all these years with people in conflict across race, religion, class, other barriers and defined territorial boundaries, I've learned that the only way to stop violence is for both sides to have the courage not to retaliate. This is easier said than done, of course, but it's the only way. I've seen how one gang member can hurt or offend a member of an opposing gang and how this results in retaliation, provoking further retaliation and so on and on. One fight can start a gang war that lasts for years, far beyond the time anyone even remembers what started the conflict.

Let's hope the gangster mentality doesn't determine the future of the human race. There are a million historical examples of how violence begets violence. But I've seen right here at SPARC how hardened gang members are able to call history-making truces. Collaborations for creative work in the arts has the power to harmonize opposing forces: I've seen it firsthand. We at SPARC will continue to use "The World Wall," "The Great Wall," Neighborhood Pride, Shoulder to Shoulder and everything in our power to help us see that hatred of others and self-hatred are illnesses that can be cured when community and imagination are bridged together.

Dappu musicians from
Andhra Pradesh perform
at the Kala Madhyam
folk *mela*.

7

Madhyam
#1, 10th Cross, 10th Main
Vasanthnagar, Bangalore - 560 052, India
Telephone: (91 80) 2281983, 2259766
Fax: (91 80) 2251707
E-mail: madhyam@giasbg01.vsnl.net.in
Web site: www.madhyam.org

Munira Sen began her work in media when she was 14 years old, scripting and anchoring music shows for All India Radio, going on to work in television and theater. Direct experience with these media prepared her for her role as executive director of Madhyam, a group focusing on the interface of communication, culture, media and development.

Madhyam's work has included producing docudramas and campaigns on violence against women, child sexual abuse, empowerment of women, dowry issues, HIV/AIDS and other issues faced by women, children and other marginalized social groups. The organization has produced films, journals and awareness campaigns and has used street theater and folk-art forms as media for social change. Workshops, seminars and training programs are also an important part of their work. Increasingly, this has meant working in partnership with mainstream media outlets, a challenging development. As Munira explained in our online dialogue:

Being in Madhyam also meant creating partnerships with mainstream media in order to lobby for space for issues related to marginalized peoples like women, children, and tribals. Face-to-face interactions with electronic and print media personnel … was one way of conscientizing mainstream media practitioners on development issues. Actually coordinating two columns on legal and children's issues in the Times of India gave us insights into the marketing compulsions, ethics and changing character of the new globalized media markets.

This essay addresses a dialectical tension in the community cultural development field, pitting questions of market and self-sufficiency against those of preserving tradition. How is cultural tradition kept alive and renewed in a market-driven society? Madhyam is trying to find connections that would return support to indigenous artists, rather than consigning them to a choice between exploitation and starvation. Is there a legitimate role for cultural entrepreneurship that can actually advance cultural development? That is the question taken up in this essay.

Cultural Entrepreneurship

FROM COSMOLOGY TO MARKET

by Munira Sen

India is a pluralistic, multicultural, multiethnic, multi-lingual nation-state housing one-eighth of the world's population. Poverty, modernization, caste and class, illiteracy, economic disparities, the status of women, population pressures and social ferment are only some of the issues which further complicate the complexities already existing within India. Any brief essay runs the risk of inaccuracy in generalizing about the complex nature of this country.

Much of my thinking on globalization has been influenced by the author Thomas Friedman.[1] As he sees it, in the dynamic of globalization we are witnessing the complex interaction between a new system and our old passions and aspirations. We find both the clash of civilizations and the homogenization of civilizations, both environmental disasters and amazing environmental rescues, both the triumph of market capitalism and a backlash against it. It's a complex drama where the final act has not been written.

The faceless phenomenon of globalization is assuming a distinct character in the Indian subcontinent as in every region of the world, further marginalizing already marginalized communities. Innovation replaces tradition. The present or future replaces the past. Nothing matters so much as what will come next, and what will come next can only arrive if what is here now gets overturned. The establishment of large chain supermarkets has caused small provision stores to close down. Reebok, Nike and others have pushed out over 200 leather tanneries in Tamil Nadu. Directly impinging on the folk artists who are the focus of my essay, Chinese goods are threatening our crafts markets.

[1] Thomas L. Friedman, *The Lexus and the Olive Tree* (Anchor Books: New York, 2000).

While the response to globalization is likely to include protesting India's economic "liberalization" policies on street corners, that is not likely to result in sufficient change. The questions uppermost in one's mind are these: What do we do about it? How can we use this system of globalization, which is evidently here to stay, to benefit the most people while inflicting the least pain?

This is the supreme challenge for countries and individuals: to find a healthy balance between preserving a sense of identity, home and community while doing what it takes to survive within the globalization system. This essay deals with some of the questions and dilemmas faced by folk artists, craftspeople and Madhyam, the organization I direct, in addressing these issues in the field of culture and development.

Madhyam is a national development communications organization which uses culture and communication (both mainstream media and alternative folk media) as vehicles of change. In our long and colorful journey of 18 years, Madhyam has been producing communication materials such as films, posters, journals, outdoor publicity media and press campaigns to reinforce messages on children's rights, women's empowerment and HIV/AIDS to effect attitudinal change in urban Bangalore. At the policy level, Madhyam has used an advocacy approach with mainstream media, sensitizing them and lobbying to create more space for development issues related to marginalized communities.

Madhyam's work involves a continuous process of learning and reflection, revisiting—and sometimes reinventing—ourselves at every crossroads in our organization's development. However, at our core, we always remain convinced that the key to addressing social inequity is people's empowerment: giving people access and control over resources, giving people choices and empowering them to make informed choices.

Today, our task is increasingly shaped by what is called globalization, which might best be explained through example.

Perhaps in the old days, reporters, businesspeople or engineers could get away with thinking of local readers, buyers and clients as their "market." But today, Planet Earth has supplanted all local markets through the global integration of technology, finance, trade and information in a way that influences wages, interest rates, living standards, job opportunities, war and culture around the world. This phenomenon called globalization may not explain everything, but its influence on almost everyone grows and spreads continuously. Therefore it is tremendously important for cultural workers to understand the forces that shape globalization.

We need to view the world through the lens of financial markets as well as culture and politics, for the walls between finance, trade, diplomacy and foreign relations are crumbling fast. Relationships between nations can no longer be explained by the quest for power and geopolitical advantage, as if markets don't matter. And economics can no longer be explained solely with reference to markets, as if power and culture don't matter. In the same way, people's behavior cannot be explained just by culture and biology, as if technology doesn't matter. We also need to view the world through the lens of technology —from the Internet to satellite telecommunications—which is reshaping the ways both individuals and nations interact with one another.

As cultural workers, these new conditions call on us to change perspectives— to use these different lenses as different situations require—always understanding that it is the interaction of all of them together that is really defining international relations. Being a globalist is the only way to systematically connect the dots and thereby to find some order amidst the chaos.

Let me offer an instance of one of our first encounters with markets and multinationals. Madhyam was recently approached by an advertising agency with a global presence. We were asked to use our folk performing-art groups to help sell a new brand of tea to the rural market. As an added inducement, the ad agency argued, the tea is fortified with vitamins, which the Indian population direly lacks. When I resisted, they were prepared to negotiate: "You perform street theater focusing on the masses' need for vitamins," they coaxed. "At the end of the play, we'll advertise the tea."

We turned the proposition over in our minds, looking at it every which way. It was backed by a sound health survey on vitamin deficiency conducted by a reputable market-research organization. It would fulfill a health need of our people. It would contribute to Madhyam's financial sustainability, enabling us to continue assisting the field. Viewed in this light, profit is not a dirty word. Still we balked at the proposition.

While in theory we were ready to face markets, in practice we were stretched beyond our comfort zones by this proposition. Though we cannot prevent the "Coca-colaization" of culture, we certainly did not want to be instrumental in bringing it about. If development destroys local culture, then it is development not worth having. So our problem is how to assist in the economic empowerment of communities without exploitation and without complicity in the wrong kind of development.

Similarly, our work has put us in touch with the expanding problem of intellectual-property rights in the field of art and culture, which urgently needs to be addressed.

For example, I recently met Ghazi Khan and his group, who belong to a small village on the outskirts of Jaisalmer in Rajasthan. Their Rajasthani folk song "Nimooda" ("Lemon") was appropriated by the Hindi film industry in Mumbai (Bombay). As a result, the film's music director was much celebrated and the song made the top of the charts. Several agents, recording companies and artists made significant amounts of money. Needless to say, absolutely no royalty of any kind reached Ghazi Khan. Rupayan Sansthan, a local non-governmental organization, is currently working to redress the situation legally, but so far they are not making much headway. In much the same way, Warli and Madhubani tribal art is converted into designs printed onto T-shirts and bric-a-brac and sold for a huge profit, while the artists continue to live in penury, totally unaware of the market appreciation and profits that are going to middlemen. When tribal art is so easy to copy, how does one address the issue of intellectual-property rights?

Madhyam's questions arise from 15 years of collaboration with local folk artists to adapt their work to new conditions. For example, working in the rural areas of Andhra Pradesh, Assam, West Bengal, Tamil Nadu and Karnataka, Madhyam has for some time been using street theater and folk forms such as Therakoothu (traditional and popular theater blending music, dance and dialogue), Chhau (a masked dance form derived from martial arts), Jhummur (a dance associated with tea cultivation), Bihu (song and dance forms traditionally associated with seasonal festivals of Assam) and Burakatha (a form of folk theater incorporating ballads) as media vehicles to effect behavioral change at the grassroots level. We achieve this by weaving social messages into these forms and performing for rural audiences. Using the cultural idiom of the people has a powerful impact, embodying Madhyam's principle that "cultural action is social action." To complement these efforts, by lobbying for performance space on state-owned radio and television, we also organize groups of folk artists to assert their rights to land, housing, public pensions, status and recognition.

As a direct outcome of our work for the social empowerment of performing artists in rural areas, we at Madhyam began to see the potential in the folk paintings and handicrafts of the villages as a possible alternative basis for economic growth in response to the felt need of the people for economic empowerment and livelihood. Excited by the idea of stimulating economic development from within the culture, Madhyam added another dimension to our work, beginning to consider how alternative markets could address globalization's ominous trend of pushing small players out of markets. Our main strategy was to reposition folk paintings as art by organizing traveling exhibitions and executing mural art projects in homes and corporate offices. There is a historical–political dimension to our plan. When the British ruled India, they dismissed folk art, relegating it to the position of craft. As the expression of collective consciousness of the people rather than an individual sensibility, it did not fit into their definition of art. So our economic development scheme also addressed the way indigenous cultures are devalued by colonization.

The "Tree of Life," as depicted by a traditional Warli artisan.

We began by exhibiting the folk art of Bihar (Madhubani, a colorful art form that reflects images from the sacred epics, the Ramayana and Mahabharatha), Maharastra (the work of Warli tribal artists, animists who execute lively scenes of cosmic harmony and village life through stick figures and ritualistic paintings in rice paste), Rajasthan (where Phad-Phad painters depict the epic of their folk hero Pabuji in strong and vibrant vegetable dyes as a large back-drop to a dance drama about Pabuji), West Bengal (the work of Patuas artists, roadside minstrels whose scroll paintings unfold a sacred tale or famous event sung in verse), Karnataka (using Chittara, a dying art form of Karnataka in which geometric motifs are symbolically painted in vegetable dyes) and Gujarat (where Pithora artists take a vow and paint vibrant horses in houses and stairwells to appease their gods).

Positioning folk painting as art was an important aim, but we wanted to go further, taking the next step in our program of presenting diverse elements of culture as a composite whole—folk life—and bringing it into the public domain. More recently, therefore, our work has expanded to include promo-tion and marketing of functional crafts such as metalware, leather, stonecraft, bamboo and cane, hand-looms and other handcrafted products.

In indigenous communities, folk art is passed on from generation to generation, either orally or through imitation. Creations are generally not attributable to an individual painter. The art is continuously utilized and developed within the indigenous community, and it is central to the practice of religion, some-times also serving as a vehicle for recorded history. Madhyam's interventions in this arena are intended to give visibility to folk arts and artists, helping to reclaim space for folk art (as opposed to fine art or craft, two categories to which such work is often consigned); to help city dwellers to rediscover their roots and long forgotten traditions through encountering this work; and to stimulate development from within the culture, by creating income-generating opportunities for artists.

Entering into this project has raised challenges and dilemmas that are linked to globalization. For instance, there are two perspectives on the issue of commercialization of folk arts. One sees it as an assault: marketing strips this art of its sacred meanings, converting it into a product for sale, thereby diminishing indigenous people's identity. Others assert that folk arts, too, are living art forms that must grow, adapting to changing times, and that commercial use of this work can enhance a community's identity as well as its means of livelihood. We have adopted the latter view, seeking to strike a balance between protection and promotion through buyer education and active marketing.

This does not mean embracing all commercial opportunities. Several schools and design establishments have approached us, requesting workshops through which they might learn folk-art forms directly from rural artists. We have strongly resisted such proposals, respecting the folk artists' belief that their skills and knowledge should vest only within their own families and communities. Although our attitude may seem protectionist, given the potentially huge market that exists for folk art, we are convinced that its ownership and ensuing profits should lie with the rightful community of artists.

One initiative seems to strike the proper balance: our project called Rediscover Your Roots. Since folk art originated on the walls of the huts of rural India, Madhyam is currently promoting the same concept for urban areas. Reception rooms of offices, living rooms, columns, pillars and hotels have been our canvas, and corporations, architects and interior designers our patrons. While working with them has been a new and exciting experience, it has also constantly forced us to grapple with new issues the market throws up.

For example, an information-technology (IT) company wanted to commission the depiction of an "IT-village" in Madhubani. We decided to ask the artists how they felt about such a project. Shanti Devi and her son, Vijay Kumar Jha, said this: "Our paintings are thematic. Krishna Ras symbolizes love; Khobar symbolizes marriage. However, there is one festival—namely Dev Uthan Ekdasi—for which we draw pictures of household belongings such as the radio and TV. Even then, we do this as part of our tradition and culture. We won't mind drawing computers because it brings in the money, but our heart is not in such work." One can clearly see that under the conditions of impoverishment afflicting rural folk artists, financial compulsions must often override artists' struggle to retain cultural meanings.

[2] Jaya Jaitly, *Vishwakarma's Children* (Institute of Social Science and Concept Publishing Company: New Delhi, 2001), p. 142.

[3] *Madhyam* journal (Vol. 15, No. 2, Bangalore, India), p. 4.

Consider our experience in handicrafts. Crafts are the clearest reflection of a nation's cultural heritage, but the socioeconomic status and respect accorded to the communities that produce them is not commensurate. A sample study was conducted by Jaya Jaitly[2] with 114 artisans from the hand-loom weaving, pottery, cane and bamboo work, durrie (carpet) weaving, leather, metal casting and woodworking sectors. The survey revealed that 42 percent were members of the backward castes (such as Yadavs, Kurmis and Jats), 24 percent belonged to scheduled castes (castes and tribes associated with the practice of "untouchability" stemming from ritual pollution, now covered by the "Prevention of Atrocities Act") and 34 percent to other castes from the intermediate and upper-caste sectors.

In the craft communities living in rural areas, the assets of a family usually consist of a bicycle, a transistor radio, some cooking vessels and equipment. Another category of artisans may possess a small plot of land and some cows. Twenty percent of the families surveyed owned assets of less than Rs. 25,000 ($500 U.S.); 2 percent had assets valued between Rs. 25,000 and Rs. 49,000 ($1,000 U.S.); 10 percent possessed assets worth Rs. 50,000 to Rs. 75,000 ($1,500 U.S.); 39 percent had assets valued over Rs. 100,000 ($2,000 U.S.). The assets of the others could not be ascertained.

Access to finance, scarcity of raw materials, inability to invest in machinery and better technology and lack of marketing opportunities are some of the main constraints that craftspeople face. Having taken on the challenge of creating economic opportunities through alternative markets, Madhyam must grapple with challenging questions. For example, Jaya Jaitly has described the process of the creation of craft as follows:

> Man's mind creates concepts and his hand creates objects. If one sees a craftsperson at work one can observe the spiritual process of linking the power of the individual inner self to the movements of the hands, to the needs of the community and the larger web of society, to connect with the world and the cosmos. What is unique about craft is the manner in which the craftsperson places the creativity of the entire self into community art performed for community service.[3]

In light of this perspective, certain questions gain added significance: How can the spiritual nature of this creative process be related to economic development? Craftspeople are often seen either as bearers of tradition or as skilled labor that can be tapped for its potential in nation building. But what those of us working in this field need to cultivate is an integrated understanding of heritage and commerce, to comprehend the very real challenges it presents. What is tradition? What can be changed and adapted to markets, and what

Work by traditional artists is offered for sale at the Kala Madhyam folk *mela*.

cannot? Is it feasible to professionalize craft? For example, few craftspeople factor in the cost of their time when calculating the price of their work, yet this is widely acknowledged as a sound marketing principle. Can and should we introduce it? How can we preserve the raw material needed for craft, for example, the bamboo forests which are fast disappearing? What are the bench marks of quality? How do we educate and mold consumers' taste toward crafts?

The danger is that in helping folk arts transform from process to product—from cosmology to the marketplace—their significance can be lost, and mere commodities are presented. How do we as mediators help to preserve the significance of these forms? Contextualizing every craft with background information on craftspeople's socioeconomic conditions and processes of creation is one way we can add value to the consumer's understanding and also boost sales. We find ourselves torn between economic and cultural considerations: these artists need sales income even to subsist, sometimes forcing them into compromises driven by economic necessity. Ways of doing things—marketing crafts and working with craftspeople—will need some rethinking if adequate answers are to be found. The younger consumer whose head is filled with glitzy images of multinational company products must be won over by the charm and potential of craft. If we succeed in reaching a more sophisticated, demanding customer, will craft work need redesigning, new packaging and new forms of promotion?

Notun Dis Gushti, Madhyam's folk group from Assam, performs at a folk *mela*.

These difficulties are further compounded by the fact that the government departments set up for handicraft promotion in India are gradually withdrawing from this sector as the world paradigm shifts from a labor economy to a knowledge society. As a result, 25 million craftspeople need to find alternative models of marketing. One such idea is to create alternative marketing venues based on the village *haat* (village market) concept. A fairly successful Delhi *haat* created by Jaya Jaitly in collaboration with the Delhi state government already exists.

Madhyam, in collaboration with other like-minded institutions, proposes to set up a similar *haat*, an upgraded city version of the traditional rural *haat* which can be seen in myriad forms across the country on any day of the week. Traditional village markets always wear a festive air, naturally and unselfconsciously celebrating cultural diversity. What is innovative about our idea is that it will be a synergistic blend of folk songs, folk dances, folk art, folk food, drama and craft which will showcase folk life and bring it into the public domain. Madhyam has tested this concept through its large annual *mela* (carnival) called Kalamadhyam. We have seen the crowds swell and the earnings of the craftspeople grow substantially with each passing year, leading us to see cultural entrepreneurship as the way forward in a time of revival of folk life and folk art.

Our *haat* will be a meeting place, encouraging face-to-face contact and exchange between urban and rural India. We see it as an opportunity for cultural tourism. It will also empower impoverished artisan groups both financially and socially. It will help urban city slickers to rediscover their roots. And finally it will give visibility to the cultural expressions of *dalit* (marginalized) groups. Here's how it will work:

Producer groups of artisans will exhibit their indigenous art and craft products on a rotating basis. This will enable village artisan-to-consumer direct marketing, thereby eliminating the middleman. Madhyam plans to maintain a plot of land equipped with low-cost, low-technology stalls built along rustic lines. The entire effect would be that of a traditional village. A small multipurpose theater would be built as a venue for marketing workshops for artisans as well as workshops to educate consumers on folk-art products. The walls would function as a folk-art gallery. The center of the *haat* area would be earmarked for folk songs, dance and drama performances.

We expect 1,000 families of artists and craftspeople to gain exposure to the market annually. The results should give them additional resources for raw materials, helping to sustain them for as much as half of each year, during the six months they are not bound to return to their traditional agricultural occupations. This model of cultural entrepreneurship is, we believe, self-sufficient, sustainable and culturally appropriate, as it doesn't change or impose upon the lifestyles of the people. As conceived, its special strengths include involving people's participation at every level, so that the participants are the owners and stakeholders. It supports individual entrepreneurship and yet it is collective in nature.

This is only one model of cultural entrepreneurship as a response to the forces of globalization. The challenges ahead seem Herculean, but every step in the right direction helps to cover the "journey of a thousand miles" toward trade justice and social equity.

8

Trilby Multimedia
148 Poplar Avenue
Edgbaston
Birmingham B17 8ER, United Kingdom
Telephone: (44 121) 420 1482
Fax: (44 121) 429 2943
E-mail: tony@trilby.co.uk
Web site: www.trilby.co.uk

Tony Stanley is founder of Trilby Multimedia, an organization established in 1993 to use new and emerging media formats for the benefit of social and cultural development. Trilby's motto is "Excite and Inspire." The enthusiasm with which he has embraced new media is typical of a community cultural development career that has spanned two decades. As he wrote in the spring 2001 online dialogue with other authors:

My involvement with what we in the U.K. call "Community Arts" began in 1980 when I discovered a whole movement that had been developed in the '70s to use participatory creative activity as a means to empowering local people and presenting alternatives to the dominant culture. Previously I worked in supportive roles in arts and media institutions for 10 years after flunking art college in the mid-'60s. I had returned to higher education as a mature student to do a degree in Visual Communication and began working with Jubilee Theatre and Community Arts Company as a student placement.

At Jubilee, Tony's early work spanned British community arts practice, from posters and banners to large-scale community festivals and fire shows. By the mid-'80s, he and his fellow community artists had begun exploring new technology as a tool for cultural development. By now, he has a depth of experience apparent in the imagination Trilby brings to applying computer-based tools to social empowerment. While most new-media development continues to be driven by commercial and military applications, Tony's essay shows how these same resources can be applied for democratic purposes.

Let's Get Digital

USING MULTIMEDIA AND THE INTERNET IN
COMMUNITY CULTURAL DEVELOPMENT

by Tony Stanley

New technology is providing undreamed of
opportunities to empower people and effect social
change. Responding to this potential, we set up
Trilby Multimedia in 1993 to work in three broad areas: Art, Learning and
Society. This essay uses some of our projects to illustrate how we are attempting to democratize art and media, learning and knowledge and, indeed, to
democratize the world.

Community cultural development takes many forms. My personal journey
as a community *animateur* (organizer/facilitator/artist) began with voluntary
work with a theater and community arts group. My role included driving
variously converted double-decker buses around the inner cities of the
British West Midlands, taking a range of arts and media activities to working-
class housing estates. While never able to compete with mainstream media,
my co-workers and I struggled to pass on the complex skills behind media
production.

I was studying for a university degree when I began working as a volunteer,
becoming obsessed with the principles of community arts as they were then
expressed. As a new graduate (albeit in my 30s by then), I saw a worthwhile
career with some difficult challenges but positive potential outcomes. I felt
compelled to follow this fate rather than take the soft option of becoming
an art-school tutor, passing on middle-class values to middle-class kids.
In community arts there was a clear politics for change, as well as a healthy

skepticism about the way social structures and cultural expressions maintain the status quo. More importantly, we had an agenda of inclusion and fair representation that we later called "cultural democracy."

Since the late 1980s, the primary tools for our community cultural development work have been Apple Mac computers. They revolutionized the ways we work with people and our collective aims. Digital technology has developed to a point where it now provides us with a level playing field where kids in schools and elders in community centers can quickly and effectively have a voice on the worldwide stage, picking up new skills and being empowered to use them.

The same opportunities are available to community arts workers in our cultural development roles. In the early days, we tinkered about at the edges of education and social activism with crumbs of funding from hard-to-please government agencies. Now, as a small independent and self-financing company, Trilby has created a new role: to provide some of the infrastructure, establish networks of opportunity and develop examples of good practice in the use of digital media for social change, helping to move people from a state of passive consumption to become active participants in social communication, thereby growing into dynamic and informed citizens.

In the United Kingdom (U.K.) we are fortunate to have a government that is committed to fully exploiting the potential of digital technology in education and social development. They are creating Learning Centres in every community in order to make the Internet and its potential bounty of learning resources widely available. Wherever the Internet goes, we go, and Learning Centres are set to provide us with new users for our products. The Learning Centres are becoming both local information points and focal points for social action. They may eventually provide as much access to learning as do our outdated colleges of further education, institutions that are well past their sell-by date due to their reliance on text-based learning and academic aptitude. Through new technology, we are all rediscovering the power of learning by doing and learning through play.

We now actively seek out new partners to collaborate in bringing community cultural development products and processes into the wider public domain. Community groups, not-for-profit organizations, trade unions and arts-education organizations are our primary focuses, although currently our main source of income is local-council clients such as education departments and youth services. Ironically, the global push toward privatization of formerly public functions is aiding our independence and our ability to maximize effectiveness: increasingly, we sell or lease our products and services to public agencies that were previously accountable through the local ballot box.

Trilby's small size means we can be flexible and accommodate clients' needs; and our unique approach, fusing arts, science and a politics of progressive development, makes us attractive to managers and decision makers who have social consciences. We often describe ourselves as Social Technology Designers, wanting to clearly label ourselves as a public-interest company motivated by social gain rather than commercial profit. But being a new-media company automatically places us, in many peoples' minds, into the dot.com brigade of techno-pirates. Thus we walk an unusual path that zigzags between techno-logical research and development, artistic creation, media production and social action. We are satisfied only when we can synergize these aspects into practical tools. In contrast to the old days of community arts, when work was subsidized through government grants, we highly prize our financial inde-pendence, which enables us to set our own agenda and engage with partners and clients who share our core beliefs. We have built a formidable set of resources to facilitate the wide range of work that we do: we have all the technical equipment necessary for multimedia production and operate a 2MB Internet connection from our base in Birmingham in the Midlands of the United Kingdom, where we live and work.

This essay documents how we are using multimedia and the Internet for community cultural development, describing some of our products and services. It aims to show how we are using new technology to break down the distinction between spectators and actors, reinstating the equality of dialogue that Augusto Boal describes in "Theater of the Oppressed." Many of the products and services described are available on the Internet. We welcome readers' comments and suggestions about how the work can be made more effective. Please visit our Web site at www.trilby.co.uk, and e-mail comments or tell us about ways that you are using new technology in socially progressive work.

THE AIMS AND SCOPE OF OUR WORK

All of our work has a social dimension. But we sometimes get opportunities to do specific pieces of work that, while having a particular practical (and often local) purpose, also do a job in a wider context. We therefore look for certain integral qualities in all our work, seeking to meet three broad aims:

- **Building social knowledge:** learning about our communities and the wider world, making an analysis and finding ways to make things better.

- **Stimulating social action:** taking ownership of our local community, getting involved, having our say.

- **Supporting social change:** ideas for altering and improving the world, exploring alternatives.

The Ring of Progress for Mankind, a community activity to explore social solutions, offered something for everyone. Here a girl plays a game on one of the iMac® towers. © Trilby Multimedia, 2000

The importance of this work is becoming better understood and appreciated. In the United States, Robert Putnam has identified a growing malaise not unique to that country, a "pulling apart" and a disconnectedness from each other that has grown over the last quarter century or so. In his book "Bowling Alone: The Collapse and Revival of American Community,"[1] Putnam reminds us that interaction enables people to build communities, to commit themselves to each other and to knit the social fabric. For us it is more: creative interaction builds culture. We hope our contribution to people's imaginative lives advances this culturization. Here are two projects that in many ways encapsulate our aims.

[1] Robert Putnam, *Bowling Alone: The Collapse and Revival of American Community* (New York: Simon & Schuster, 2000).

Examples of Projects to Build Social Knowledge and Stimulate Social Action

RPM: Ring of Progress for Mankind—Interactive Exhibition/Workshop

The Ring of Progress for Mankind (RPM) is a social-issue exploration activity consisting of research, playing and making (which also add up to RPM). RPM was originally developed as part of the festivities to celebrate the year 2000. More than 12,000 people came to the three-day festival, and many came through the RPM space, where we had built a stunning set consisting of see-through plastic towers, each containing an iMac for "playing" the game part of the project. Fabric sails tied the towers to the floor and acted as a canvas for the illustrations created in the "making" section. The research was undertaken in several locations: at the introduction panels of our site, on the workshop boards at the back of the set and on see-through plastic tables with more iMacs running multimedia software. The set was brought to life with flashing and pulsed lighting.

As a public event, which was close in feel to a fairground, the RPM set was ideal: it provided something for everyone. Young children could play the game, competing with their parents, then move on to the "making" tables while the grown-ups put their minds to potential resolutions to social problems. It was an opportunity for us to be very visible with the concept of using interactive games and participatory workshops directly related to social action, attempting to raise people's awareness about how they can personally effect change while also challenging their imaginations and creativity. RPM is one of many projects we are involved in, which seek to use play and creativity as learning strategies.

PollCreator e-Voting Software (www.pollcreator.com and www.ypp.org.uk)
The e-voting system used in the Young People's Parliament Web site is based on our proprietary PollCreator software, which allows project organizers to customize an informed electronic vote on particular issues. Project organizers have the choice of channeling prospective voters through an infinite number of information steps where different arguments or aspects of an issue can be presented. These presentations can be in any media format—text, animated graphics, photos, audio or video or a mix of all. The user can be required to go through each and all of the presentation pages before voting, or enabled to vote at any time during the presentations. The vote can be a simple two-way vote, a two-way with a "Don't Know" or "Won't Vote" option or a set of multiple choices. Voters have the ability to specify reasons for their decisions, limited to 25 words. The database structure around which PollCreator is built also lets people use the facility to create online questionnaires whereby opinions can be solicited and consolidated.

We are promoting PollCreator as an empowering strategy in the quest to enable the mass of ordinary people to participate actively in public life. The PollCreator facility will also be at the heart of CitizensMag.net, the "citizenship" section of MagnetSites, a project that aims to widen the scope of Internet usage in schools and explore alternative ways of learning, including learning to be active citizens. In early 2002, the eVoteMag.net project (www.evotemag.net) was our pilot for putting e-democracy into schools through stimulating and supporting student debating groups and classroom voting.

So we employ a number of tactics, from playing to debating, in the process of interaction with participants. New technology provides a bounty of possibilities that we are keen to exploit across the various fields of social interaction, but our focus is on using the arts and we operate mainly in the area of learning. Below, I discuss why these are our primary tools for community cultural development work and describe how we use new media and networks in carrying out the work.

THE ARTS AND LEARNING

Digital technology is affecting all areas of human endeavor, especially the realms of creative production and imaginative communications. We are in the midst of a convergence of media, entertainment, publishing, telecommunications and other industries and activities. For society there is now an obvious need for new skills and for using information as a new commodity.

This convergence is having a massive impact on the arts and education. Its effects on the arts are to create new opportunities for collaborative work and work that crosses traditional mediums, and to provide radically different ways of presenting and distributing artistic endeavor, stimulating a new breed of media makers. In schools, similar opportunities are opening up the ways in which education is delivered and received, with movement toward self-directed and student-centered learning enhanced through digital media and new publishing modes. These changes will affect teachers' roles, providing new opportunities for them to fully exploit education as society's engine of change.

We have difficulty in drawing a clear distinction between creativity and learning; for us, these are limbs of the same creature, the arms and legs of our existence. The following sections on Arts and Media and on Learning have many obvious overlaps. Although the focus is clearly toward one or another area, the social impact is often the same: to nurture and stimulate individual growth and social cohesion, to excite and to inspire. Below, I summarize some of the observations we have made around education, creativity and new technology, then describe examples from our work in these areas.

THE ARTS AND MEDIA

In a 1999 Artform research project on "the potential creative uses of digital media in the arts classroom" commissioned by the Digital Media Project in Dudley (www.artform.org.uk), Trilby argued that there is a close relationship between engaging in creative activity and using information and communication technology (ICT), the term now used in education to add a social dialogue component to information technology (IT). The need for lateral thinking—seeing the bigger picture, bringing order from chaos and imposing structure on a limitless set of possibilities— are skills arguably shared by work in ICT and in other creative activity. Easy to learn and fun to do, ICT also liberates kids from parents and teachers. We are beginning to use this to great advantage in challenging the status quo and empowering groups and individuals.

For example, Peter, who lives on an economically deprived housing estate, was always in trouble with the local police and with school officers. He engaged in petty vandalism, was a fairly good graffiti artist and was too independently minded to conform to the culture of school. Family problems meant he had little direction from parents and skipped school most days. The Youthstart program offered Peter the chance to come into the youth club each day for three months. He soon got excited about the graphic capabilities of computer software and stuck to the course, which helped to normalize his social relationships and gave focus to his life. Now he regularly supports the teaching in other Youthstart projects and is seriously looking for a job that involves working with others, doing graphics and of course using new technology.

The relationship between creative activity and formal education has always been tense. Skills training for economic activity sits uneasily with the free thought, experimentation and potential transgression that the arts encourage, but the arts still provide our best opportunities for human expression. When we work in schools we encourage students to make a video rather than write an essay, or create a computer 3-D landscape rather than paint a bowl of fruit. This poses a dilemma for teachers and examiners, who seldom have the knowledge or experience to handle such demands. Yet these "experts" are increasingly expected by government to fully exploit new technology and support creativity. "You're just another brick in the wall," sang Pink Floyd in their sharp 1979 criticism of a blinkered and reactionary teaching profession. ICT can remove bricks from the walls that enslave young minds.

As cultural development workers, we also see the arts as transformative, able to alter perceptions and build strengths in groups and individuals, letting them take greater control of their lives and build the social fabric we call culture. We strive to promote everyone's right to make art and culture, building mechanisms for creative action and reaction so that human civilization can progress. But due to the nature of the funding system we can't get grants for this, so we have to find other ways of paying for this work. All our projects are in the public sector, where we establish partnerships and alliances to pursue this wider agenda. As informal educators with an interest in general learning, we are keen to explore the many different ways people learn and to seek to devise new ways to stimulate learning. Making learning fun is a way to be paid to offer enhanced arts activities to students; there is growing support for this approach.

Through exposure to artistic expression and the combining of ideas from a variety of sources, many learners become motivated to explore and learn more deeply than would be the case in a sterile, prestructured, "single-subject oriented" learning environment.[2]

[2] Elizabeth Wellburn, "Communications Technologies, Literacy and the Arts," at members .home.net/dhouston1/eliz _bctla.html. This article was originally published in *The Bookmark*, the official journal of the British Columbia Teacher-Librarians' Association, March 1999, Vol. 40, No. 3.

Trilby is also exploring the creative opportunities made available through digital media: interactivity, putting the participant in control of the presentation; the delivery formats of CD-ROM, DVD and the Web; and interactive environments. Exploiting possibilities to broadcast and communicate in the same global territory as anyone else, we are developing an aesthetics of new media—new languages and new forms of production.

Digital technologies are rapidly transforming the process of cultural production and reception. The technologies have made possible a number of new cultural forms such as the computer game and the hyper-linked Web site. They have also fundamentally changed many existing cultural forms, both on the level of aesthetics and of production practices.[3]

Examples of Arts and Media Projects

One project in this area is Digital Dabbling, an arts summer school for the University of the First Age (UFA), an initiative from Birmingham's influential Director of Education, Tim Brighouse. When he launched the UFA, he said, "Giving young people more time, to do more of the same, in the same way, with the same people is not going to raise standards of achievement dramatically upward—we need to seize the opportunity to do something radically different." The University of the First Age is grounded in the philosophy that all young people have the potential to achieve success. UFA seeks ways to maximize people's learning potential. Using strategies that employ theories of multiple intelligences,[4] accelerated learning[5] and associated approaches, the UFA is naturally interested in the arts.

In the Digital Dabbling Summer School, we used a potent mix of traditional art activities, digital media and collective expression to explore ways of illustrating and commenting on our community and ourselves. We used "Figures in a Landscape" as the motif to explore and make statements about our individual and group identities. Using Photoshop, Painter and Poser software, with photography, drawing and model making as our main off-computer activities, we created a range of images and other pieces for Web site publication. We began by looking at figures in landscapes from art history, using this to trigger contemporary commentaries. Composite photo images, 2-D and 3-D animations, issue-based Web pages and video were the end results.

While we were keen for participants to use their local communities as the background to their composite images, the young people preferred to use international iconography such as the HOLLYWOOD hill sign or the Eiffel Tower. We made deals with them, agreeing to their use of such imagery if there was also a degree of subversion of the icon so that the Mount Rushmore image was titled, "We're as important as any President," and Hassan sits astride the BIRMINGHAM hill sign. Some of the animations involved the making of human figures in Plasticine (a colored, nondrying modeling material

[3] Julian Sefton-Green, ed., *Young People, Creativity and New Technologies* (London and New York: Routledge, 1999), p. 2.

[4] Multiple intelligences theory was developed by psychologist Howard Gardner, who suggests there are many different ways that people perceive and make sense of the world. Verbal-linguistic and logical-mathematical intelligences dominate current expectations in schooling to the detriment of the visual-spatial and musical-rhythmic intelligences associated with creativity. Gardner leads the Project Zero team at Harvard, with a mission "to understand and enhance learning, thinking, and creativity in the arts, as well as humanistic and scientific disciplines, at the individual and institutional levels." Their Web site is at pzweb.harvard.edu.

[5] Accelerated Learning, or more correctly Accelerated School, is an approach to school change which aims to improve learning by enriching the school environment through such processes as "unity of purpose," "empowerment and responsibility" and "building on strengths"— solid community cultural development principles. Find out more at www.stanford.edu/group /ASP/brochure3.html.

"We're as important as any President!" is the message of self-esteem and equality from this composite image. The Digital Dabbling project used posed studio shots, as shown on the opposite page, and computer software to create new visual statements about "us" and the things we "own." See more images at www.HandsworthLive.com. © Digital Art School, 2001.

used in the United Kingdom). Alisha was so pleased with her model she said, "This is the best thing I have ever made, she has to come home with me," before going on to animate her creation and put it up on the Web site as a way of sharing her creativity.

The Digital Schools Initiative (www.digitalfilmschool.net)
The Digital Film School was the first of a set of digital schools that Trilby established to support the creative and social uses of digital media. Designed to offer access to professional-level digital-art and media production, the schools have three components: the Mobile Studio, the Online Resource and the Ideas Library. These Digital Schools are aimed at young people in schools and youth settings but are equally valuable in work with adults of all ages and abilities.

New technology makes it easy for anyone to quickly learn how to make movies, design Web sites and make digital art and music. This initiative aims to make these tools available to anyone and in any situation with a power supply and a phone line. Trilby also offers a "Hardware Plus Access" package for around $3,000, which provides all needed hardware, software and support along with a year's access to the Digital School and a space on our servers for each group's Digital Clubs, galleries or cinemas. Martyn, 13, wrote:

> Today we (me, Owen, Laura, Melissa, Emma and Adil) made a movie each about our school. I made one about the school production, Bugsy Malone. I have done interviews, camera, photos and directed all in one day. After this wonderful day I am hoping to get a career in acting. I thank the Digital Film School very much.

Collection Explorer Web Site (www.curiositybox.net)

Designed through a partnership with the New Art Gallery in Walsall, this package aims to connect young people with arts institutions in a dynamic and collaborative way. It is a fully customizable facility that allows users to mix given material such as images from a gallery or museum collection with their own original material, adding text and other details in order to create a new learning resource. The user chooses an artifact from the collection or uses the Personality Test to have an artifact choose the user, who is then invited to do things based on the item or to spring off into related activities. There is a working space where the user can build a collection of related resources, then submit them for inclusion in the catalogue of resources available for others to pick up and use.

This Web site facility stems from the New Art Gallery's Entitlement Project, which promotes the concept of entitlement to Walsall's rich art- and social-history collections by secondary school students (11 to 16 years old), strengthening teachers' awareness of the collections and encouraging their use in teaching. For us community cultural development workers, this is another opportunity to use the arts as a tool for personal and group engagement while also enjoying, exploring and analyzing cultural artifacts and their social context. The Collection Explorer software remains our property so is available for any gallery or museum to use as part of their community-learning and educational-outreach work.

KidsMag.net Web Site (www.kidsmag.net)

This is an Internet club for which students must register to participate. It provides an easy way for them to report about school clubs and other alternative- and extended-learning activities by submitting writing, photos and artwork for publication on the site. Games and other online activities make the site an interesting and stimulating environment for students both at school and at home. A set of Topical Polls and in-depth online questionnaires provide program managers with detailed insights into young peoples' attitudes and opinions.

KidsMag.net uses the Collaborative Authoring Engine that we have developed to encourage collective working. The Internet is a good tool for collaborative working, and we are always looking for ways to simplify the process whereby people can access the facility for creative communication. KidsMag.net grew out of our action-research exploring the potential creative uses of digital media in the arts classroom (detailed in www.artform.org.uk), and the Learning Express Summer School (www.learningexpress.org.uk), a 10-day summer school program for 150 to 200 students. Two 11-year-olds who participated in the program wrote:

> We think Learning Express is a brilliant idea. It helps young people to find out more about using a computer! Jenny and I think that we have learnt more about using a computer just by logging on and seeing what cool stuff we all have done over the past three days. Thanks for making this happen!

The site is complemented by StaffMag.net, a program-management and monitoring facility designed to help project organizers and the management team deliver and report on these new ways of engaging young people in learning. We call the whole package "MagnetSites," and the development is widely seen as an innovation in the use of new technology for social development. EducationExtra, a nongovernmental organization in the U.K. that promotes and supports extracurricular education, has profiled the site as a model of good practice, and government ministers are examining the value of promoting the facility nationally. It is currently used by four city authorities including Birmingham, the largest local authority in the United Kingdom with more than 300 schools. This sort of online resource meets many of the objectives of Prime Minister Tony Blair's target of "empowering the frontline workers" in the U.K. public services. We are adding ArtsMag.net, SportsEdMag.net and YoungCitizensMag.net to the MagnetSites facility during 2002 to provide ideas and support to project organizers. See www.magnetsites.com for more information.

LEARNING

Educators do not act in a value free way. In our view, for something to be called "education," whether it takes place in the classroom or the canteen, it must be informed by certain values—respect for persons, the promotion of well-being, truth, democracy, fairness and equality. These values should inform both the content of conversations and encounters, as well as our behaviour and relationships as educators. Julius Nyerere once summed these concerns up when he talked of the purpose of education as being the liberation of humans from the restraints and limitations of ignorance and dependency. "Nothing else can be properly called education. Teaching which induces a slave mentality or a sense of impotence is not education at all—it is an attack on the minds of men."[6]

Ask teachers, "Where is the worst place to learn?" They will consider a short time before saying, "The classroom!" The Internet offers the possibility of replacing this defunct Victorian concept. The 24-hour school, where you learn as and when you want or need to, is with us now.

Britain's New Labour government understands there is a need for change in the way we organize and deliver education. It has put hundreds of millions of pounds of National Lottery money into "out of school hours learning." This program is designed to provide something different from regular school, actively seeking new and alternative learning settings and approaches.

One of Trilby's motivating ideas is the examination of alternatives to formal education: exploring different learning styles, being aware of multiple intelligences; seeing "operacy"[7]—the ability to do things—as fundamentally more useful than literacy; the notion that "more is caught than taught,"[8] learning through doing; learning through play; and casual learning, where knowledge and understanding happen almost without the learner realizing it—one of the distinguishing characteristics of community arts practice. New media let us create learning settings and experiences that are self-directed on the learner's terms (such as when, where and how often). The learning can be facilitated in an appropriate manner by the use of online tutors or learning mentors, and the collaborative nature of the Internet can help peer-group learning and mutual support. The Web offers access to ways of presenting information that make it relevant to the user. All these new mechanisms and facilities are part of the process of democratizing learning and knowledge.

The U.K. government's interest in supporting this work is providing indirect support to Trilby's operations, especially the products and services we have developed for use in schools. The MagnetSites suite of Web sites is also providing a platform to encourage creative work and stimulate learning by older students and adults in other social arenas such as youth clubs, libraries and community centers. Our new work in Learning Centres is about empowering local people to create their own learning materials, making full use of the new creative, production and distribution possibilities.

[6] Tony Jeffs and Mark K. Smith, *Informal Education: Conversation, Democracy and Learning* (Ticknall: Education Now Books, 1999). Used on the bottom of the "What Is Education?" page at www.infed.org /foundations/f-educ.htm. Also, see www.infed.org /thinkers/et-hist.htm #contemporary for a brief history of thinking about informal education and www.infed.org/thinkers /et-nye.htm for more about Julius Nyerere's vision of education.

[7] "Operacy" is a word coined by Edward deBono, the originator of the term "lateral thinking," and is widely used in *New Thinking for the New Millennium* (London: Penguin Books, 1999); see for example page 4. His Web site is at www.edwarddebono.com.

[8] "More Is Caught Than Taught" (MCTT) is the mantra and a training program of the Federation of Childcare Centers of Alabama (FOCAL). MCTT is a new approach to training and development for all those working with children in the community. More information is at www.playtrn.demon.co.uk /mctt.htm.

The examples below are from our range of work that has a clear education or learning role. Because these projects have a specific and defined purpose, they don't always involve the target groups in production, a process we generally seek to embed in every project. This is always a dilemma for us—being paid by a client to deliver the goods but wanting to "subvert" the funding into community-based workshop activities. Often Trilby personnel act as technology gurus to our clients and partners directing the projects, so the education takes place a couple of strata above street level. A lot of what we do is still very new to many people, so we divert some of our time into evangelizing and explaining the significance of multimedia and the Internet for learning. This has led to our offering training as part of our work and writing a primer on the creative uses of computers and the Internet. We also produce and distribute a small bimonthly newsletter to update community-based arts workers about new possibilities. This can be downloaded as a portable document format (PDF) at www.creativetechnologynews.net.

Examples of Learning Projects

Cultural Roots Multimedia Knowledge Base (CRMKB)—CD-ROM for Young Children
CRMKB is a multimedia resource on the cultural history of the world's population. Volume One contains information on the Ten Sikh Gurus, the Punjabi language, the Black Pioneers and islands of the Caribbean. The general themes of the disk are People, Places, Beliefs and Lifestyles. CRMKB provides a rich overview of some aspects of African-Caribbean and Sikh culture and history, making the most of its multimedia format with music, sounds and animations. We use time lines, games and quizzes to make the learning fun and engaging for young children. Many adults also find the information and activities are an entertaining way of learning about their own and others' cultures.

Got Messed Up—Young People's Health Project CD-ROM
This is an initiative from the Young People's Health Project team in Birmingham, U.K. It is designed as a multipart resource for use in residential settings or other situations where a group of young people will have the time and the focused attention to spend on the issues behind the program. Based around a murder-mystery role-play idea, the CD-ROM contains video scenes from the young murder victim's recent past, as well as other evidence and clues for the detectives to examine.

We worked with the Young People's Health Project, a group of teenagers and the London Workshop Company theater group to make the interactive component of the resource. This murder-mystery game is complemented by role-playing and other activities exploring health issues. We like the way the digital-media element here is only one part of an integrated package, and we are exploring other uses for this multidisciplinary approach.

Also aimed at young people, SkillStationBASIC is an online literacy and numeracy course. SkillStation is a series of online learning packages based on Flash and Shockwave technology, using animation and narration to make it fun to learn important skills. SkillStationBASIC is the first in the series, and we are using the same model to make other online learning resources. Currently in development are SkillStationDIGITAL, to introduce basic computer and multimedia skills; SkillStationCOMMUNITY, to support community organizing; SkillStationBUSINESS for stimulating social enterprises; and SkillStationHEALTH for health and safety awareness. More information is at www.skillstation.net.

We are also working with Learning Centres to design and create online learning resources that are appropriate to their local communities. This ongoing activity is part of our role as community cultural development workers and also an effective response to research findings that indicate the need for such local production. The influential Fabian Society proposes a radical approach to delivering an inclusive information society:

> Bridging the digital divide is about more than simply improving access to new technology. For excluded groups in particular, there is little relevant "content" available on an Internet which is driven by the market and aimed at affluent consumers. The best solution is to let people develop content for themselves. … The case studies show how excluded people can be engaged in using technology on their own terms, and how technology can be used as a tool for social inclusion more generally.[9]

[9]From the publisher's promo for Samantha Hellawell, *Beyond Access: ICT and Social Exclusion* (London: The Fabian Society, 2001) at www.fabian-society.org.uk.

For me there is a sense of déjà vu in this work with Learning Centres, a flashback to 20 years ago where the double-decker bus is now replaced by technology-rich community facilities. We go into communities and facilitate the production of multimedia digital pieces just as we did multiple-media arts events in local communities—involving and empowering with the potential to transform. And of course many of the precepts and core values of 1980s community arts such as inclusion and empowerment are now woven into the mainstream thinking and policymaking of the U.K. government. Today however we have a global distribution network that opens up further possibilities.

GOING GLOBAL

I would like to end with two ideas for global digital projects that put digital media and the Internet at the forefront of international development. We hope readers will agree with the suggestion that new technology offers enormous potential for social progress and for redressing injustice and ignorance. We further hope that you will work with us and other community cultural development agencies to use these new tools to make the world a better place.

The myth of the global village—a utopian world of no borders, free association and equal trade—is rapidly being demonstrated as a convenient sham. Perhaps the only significant exception is the Internet, a global village of information that still has a long way to go in terms of availability and access before the digital divide is bridged. From our point of view it is an opportunity to take aspects of our work around the globe. There are many instances where our community cultural development tools would enhance local action on issues such as gender, as in environmentalist Hazel Henderson's exhortation to "think globally, act locally." And there is an increasing number of examples of new media in action for social change:

> "We didn't see any women on (election) posters, so it meant that men were listed at a higher level," says Kganyago. "Women were shadows in the background." Women'sNet used the Internet to publish and distribute its Election Bulletin newsletter, which contained a wide range of articles on issues relating to women and the elections. The newsletter provided an open window for women from diverse backgrounds, encouraging women to vote and thus have their say in the democratic process.[10]

[10] David Lush and Helliate Rushwaya, eds., *Into or Out of the Digital Divide? Perspectives on ICTs and Development in Southern Africa* (Lusaka: Panos Southern Africa, 2000), from www.panos.org.zm. This quote is one of the Case Studies at www.panos.org.zm /SAwomen.htm.

Examples of Going Global

LiberationTools.com

This project is in development as I write in the autumn of 2001, and the Web site is open for contributions and feedback. The concept came directly from the Community, Culture and Globalization conference, where we agreed on the need to share some simple tactics and ideas for community cultural development. In LiberationTools.com we will use the global broadcasting facility that the Internet provides to share and exchange tools and resources to support our personal growth and development; to help us explore, analyze and challenge the status quo; and to set up alternatives to the dominant social structures that so often oppress and restrict human progress. I see this project as addressing the homogenizing effects of multinationals and the "new world order"—in other words, challenging globalization.

We also hope to use the site to develop some form of international accreditation for community cultural development workers, especially those of us who come from an experiential learning environment rather than academia. Alternative accreditation could promise liberation from the dictates of ivory-towerists and self-serving educational bureaucrats.

RainbowCivilisation.com

RainbowCivilisation.com is a prospective international Web site based on Trilby's multicultural education project here in the United Kingdom (www.positivediversity.com). Its aim will be to celebrate and promote cultural pluralism, serving as a reference point for those working to combat ignorance and prejudice. This is needed more than ever as Europe goes into a protection-ist state of mind, closing its borders to citizens driven from their countries by the forces of globalization as much as by wars, natural disasters and persecution. As the world fractures from reactions to the terrible events of September 11, all of us must develop a worldview that includes all humanity if we are to make headway in preventing injustices that give rise to terrorism.

At Trilby we believe that community cultural development is pre-eminently about building individual and shared agendas for interacting in local, national and global communities in ways that mutually empower all of the actors. To do this we each need to have a basic understanding about the roots of our diverse cultures and gain a feeling for, and empathy with, the emotional importance culture has in guiding our collective action. This is the proposed mission of RainbowCivilisation.com, and it is also the broad agenda that we work on here at Trilby Multimedia.

MC Spex, one of the
Invasion rappers who
emerged from an ADFED
workshop, takes the mike.

9

Institute of International Visual Arts

6-8 Standard Place

Rivington Street

London EC2A 3BE, United Kingdom

Telephone: (44 20) 7729 9616

Fax: (44 20) 7729 9509

E-mail: institute@iniva.org

Web site: www.iniva.org

ADFED

PO Box 23139

London SE1 1ZU, United Kingdom

E-mail: adfed@ukonline.co.uk

Web site: www.asiandubfoundation.com

Gary Stewart's capsule biography, created for the spring 2001 online dialogue among the authors of this anthology, offers a particularly vivid description of the new-media territory he has chosen as the focus for his community cultural development work:

I occupy a fascinating space between cutting-edge, sometimes bleeding-edge technology and direct community action, with many years' experience in electronic media as a tutor, designer and producer with a special interest in the relationship between culture, technology and creativity.

Currently, Gary is Head of Multimedia at the Institute of International Visual Arts (inIVA) in London, a group that offers exhibitions, publications, multimedia, education and research projects designed to bring the work of artists from culturally diverse backgrounds to the widest possible public. He is also a consultant to the European Multicultural Media Agency (EMMA), which promotes youth advocacy, cultural animation and new technologies. Much of the work discussed in this interview was done for ADF Education (ADFED), the educational wing of Asian Dub[1] Foundation, a London-based music group.

The main subject of this interview is Gary's work with young people, exploring technical and cultural issues by creating music and developing computer games. It would be fair to say such work is on the "bleeding edge" of a hot debate for the community cultural development field. Breaking down the one-way relationship between young people and the media seems essential: learning to use these tools for their own ends is obviously a major improvement over the given relationship, based on the much narrower roles as consumers of what is marketed by others. Questions posed by other community artists as they have heard about this work indicate the nature of the debate: Can the same high-tech tools that have advanced globalization be effectively used to advance liberty and democracy? Can the marketplace really support cultural development? How does work created with the techniques and technologies of marketplace media differ from commercial music or commercial computer games?

Beyond these questions, the way that Gary's work is predicated on a mix of cultural influences is very different from some other essays' focus on protecting cultures from alien influences. It asserts a cultural fluidity, a positive dimension to the dynamic interaction of cultures in developed multicultural societies. It is challenging—and to some, a little daunting—to consider that the goals of community cultural development can be advanced by the strategic use of computer games as much as by Forum Theater or community dance, but this interview makes a strong argument to that effect.

The interview with Gary Stewart was conducted by Arlene Goldbard on October 19, 2001. Interspersed with some sections of Gary's interview, readers will find additional material on the ADFED workshops based on an interview Gary himself conducted on November 5, 2001, with Anirudda Das, bass player with ADF, and Lisa Das, who is responsible for running ADFED.

[1] "Dub" describes a studio-based music methodology originating in Jamaica in the 1970s, in which a song's backing tracks are treated with studio effects to create new versions.

Digital Diaspora

YOUNG PEOPLE, TECHNOLOGY
AND CONTESTED SPACES

An Interview With Gary Stewart

We've always believed that the most effective campaigning method is through great art.
If you are making progressive statements, the form has to be progressive too.

CHANDRASONIC, ASIAN DUB FOUNDATION

We began this interview by talking about the Music Technology Workshops that Gary has been involved with for ADFED. Here's how they are described on ADFED's Web site (www.asiandubfoundation.com):

THE MUSIC TECHNOLOGY WORKSHOPS

The major aims of the workshop are:

- To nurture the desire to create music.
- To encourage the creation of original and innovative music.
- To teach the participants skills in Music Technology and, using their own musical experiences as a starting point, develop their music and lyric writing.
- To promote the use of relatively inexpensive, user-friendly equipment that gives high quality sounds.
- To encourage performance, develop performance skills and promote attitudes of mutual support.

Over each ten-week block of workshops the participants will learn about MIDI, Sampling, Sequencing, Programming and Recording, as well as learning to use their own instruments with music technology instruments, developing turntable skills, vocal skills and microphone techniques. The trainees have the opportunity to perform their work in the Showcase Events.

Ongoing assessment is given by our tutors to students and throughout our projects we encourage students to fundraise to buy their own equipment and consider studying further music courses.

Arlene Goldbard: Please start by describing the project.

Gary Stewart: It's going to be quite interesting talking about it, because I'll have to distinguish between two things: we have Asian Dub Foundation, the group, which is an internationally known group who came out of what was known as the Community Music Workshop (www.cmonline.org.uk) in the mid-'90s. Because of the cultural ethos behind that—in other words, because they were a kind of collective group—when Asian Dub Foundation came together, they themselves were passionate and determined to establish an educational wing, and ADFED emerged.

AG: What is the Community Music Workshop?

GS: About 10 years ago, it was founded in London as a sort of improvisation and experimental music group by a jazz drummer; his name was John Stevens. What was really good about it was that he was particularly keen to challenge the way roles were perceived in some bands. He was encouraging all individuals to take responsibility for what they do, so there wasn't your traditional sort of drummer, your lead person or whatever. So that's the starting point. Two members from Asian Dub Foundation used to teach at Community Music, and it informed their methodology for working.

And then we have ADFED, the educational wing of Asian Dub Foundation who, although they embrace technology, embrace what you might call cheaper, obsolete technology. And that is quite deliberate in many respects, because the workshops are orientated in such a way as to try and ensure that people will continue to work with some kind of music making; it would be nonsense to encourage the adoption of so-called latest, greatest technology—I guess you might say "technological masturbation." So it's crucial to understand that when I make references to technology, what I'm really talking about is cheap or obsolete technology and, in particular, sampling[2] technology. That's crucial, because the workshops themselves are orchestrated in such a way as to encourage participants to manipulate samples, quoting from musical found-imagery.

[2]Sampling technology enables musicians to make digital recordings, borrowing portions of existing music to create derivative work with or without further electronic manipulation.

What happens during these workshops, first and foremost, is the term that Asian Dub Foundation came up with: "conscious party mode." It echoes many historical references to celebratory expression. It's a careful balancing act in terms of encouraging these young people's participation, to be able to sustain that participation so that they learn the tools themselves, but also importantly, working with developing their awareness of particular issues of inequality. None of these workshops happen in a vacuum. They don't just come in and start making noises, though we work with that as well, of course.

AG: So in conscious party mode, the emphasis is on *conscious*?

GS: Exactly. Everybody there has a belief that music is the ultimate form of communication because it has life-changing potential, even if they don't say it exactly that way. The workshops are very much about participants defining a public image of themselves.

AG: As committed to changing lives through music?

GS: No. These predominantly Asian young people, the way that they're viewed in this society is really quite dismal, the way that they continually see references to themselves in a distorted way in magazines, on television and in the media. An example might be the uncritical way the music industry talks about what they term "second-generation Asians." They make reference to fusion, a word that is despised by ADFED.

From Gary's interview with Anirudda Das:

Gary: ADF have been described in terms of fusion. What are your thoughts?

Ani: Yeah, a lot of people say that. But to us fusion is more about a deliberate bringing together of disparate elements for the sake of it—the tourist mentality. For us, we have supposedly disparate sounds or things that you are not supposed to put together, but all of it is different sounds that we happen to hear. It's like we always used to say in the early days of community music, there was awful sound-proofing so you would hear someone programming jungle[3] in one room, a percussion workshop in another room and a horn workshop in another, and occasionally you would hear the three of them together and just for an instant it would work, which is really good. Or we would be working on an ADF track and outside, people were doing a vocal workshop in the courtyard, and the next thing you know they had all their faces pressed against the window singing. Or another time I was programming stuff, and people could hear the bass line through the walls, and they were doing an acoustic workshop, and they said their rhythm kept being drawn toward the bass line.

Ours is more about cultural leakage. Because I had been brought up with Indian folk music and classical music and also being exposed to everything else that everybody else hears, it's kind of normal to incorporate those elements. It's as simple as that: it really isn't fusion; it's more like

[3] Urban, nonlinear, poly-rhythmic music at extremely high tempo—160 beats per minute—originating in the United Kingdom in the early 1990s

allowing the different voices. There are certain musical forms which become vehicles, notably hip-hop[4] with its social commentary and to an extent dub and reggae because of the DJ[5] vocals. I've heard of Native American people using hip-hop and also dub as well, but they are incorporating their own sounds, so to me again that is not a fusion; it's more like you are using a musical vehicle but putting your own experience to it. I think we have to turn the question on its head and realize that all music and all culture and language is a consequence of cross-fertilization and a meeting of peoples; that's one of the main things that ADF draws attention to.

GS: You've spoken of the "dynamic interaction of cultures" as a positive thing. In terms of their musical expression, there's a particular definition of second-generation Asians as being a product of cultural fusion, and that's seen as diluting culture. But the point is, culture constantly moves very fast and doesn't have to dilute anything. The kind of music that comes out is a natural consequence of being brought up in this country with all its different influences and diverse elements. It's not part of fusion, it's just normal.

AG: In the century-old discourse of American cultural policy, one idea is the melting pot, which is an old version of fusion, where all cultures melt together into something gray and American. This is put up against other metaphors—a gumbo, a patchwork—things where the ingredients come together, but they remain distinct as well. Is that the contrast that you're talking about?

GS: Yes, that goes down the right road. During the workshops, they talk about how music can be constructed in a way that contains specific references to other pieces of musical composition, so it's a kind of intervention into the surrounding musical culture. What is being encouraged is the process of remaking and reordering, recontextual-izing other materials, so that they can comment on their meaning by changing them—what I said about quoting from musical found-imagery. It isn't the melting pot. A sophisticated yet subtle process energizes the act of audio sampling—it's not merely a shortcut to production. Juxtaposing audio "quotes," which themselves are often fragments and/or abstracted, serves to add irony to the extracted material. The workshop participants also create sonically pleasurable "sound worlds" or environments made up of selected fragments informed by their own cultural history and experiences for their own sake.

MC Swift-E, MC Goldie Bling and Lady Shis-Tee (left to right) from Roundwood Youth Club show off performance skills learned through ADFED, the educational wing of Asian Dub Foundation.

AG: Are you a workshop leader? In a typical workshop, how many kids? How do they learn about it? How do they get there?

GS: I worked with the workshop leader "Spike" (Alan Strochan) with between 12 and 16 participants. Some of these young people are under cultural attack, and they're not actually allowed to go and do extra activities. Their parents or guardians have to be convinced that a safe place for them can be provided so that they can interact with other people without being at risk.

It's worked out as a 10-week block, and so there are specific technical headings that enable them to learn the specifics of music making. But in addition to that, other issues around racism and antideportation campaigns are discussed—they also bring up issues themselves, obviously. There are opportunities for them to talk about issues that affect them personally such as immigration legislation and more global issues, the links between racism and corporate power and Third World countries.

Basically, the music is used as a kind of metaphor. The workshops themselves are about exploring the rhythms of different sounds and exposing participants to connections. It's a bit like an extended metaphor for the connections between people, economics and history.

AG: Boys and girls? Is it free?

GS: Predominantly boys, three quarters at least. There have been specific workshops for girls to encourage their expression. It is absolutely free.

AG: What happens at the end?

GS: At the end, they can get entry to gain a specific certificate as part of Community Music. The whole purpose behind the educational wing of Asian Dub Foundation—it's equipping and training, but it's also genuine empowerment and independence for these students. If they do wish to pursue some kind of role in the industry, they can go on, they've got an insight into it.

AG: Is this supported by income from Asian Dub Foundation's music?

GS: ADFED itself now gets some support from London Arts and the Paul Hamlyn Foundation, so it's getting support as an independent organization.

AG: You said the workshops use "obsolete technologies." What do you mean?

GS: Superseded sampling machines are the core.[6] There are two particular areas: the programming of the sampling machine and composition. The process of composition is really interesting. It isn't just a technical issue, because it carries emotional weight—certain sounds and certain themes and lyrics. A group of young people might be encouraged to sit around with pieces of paper, scribbling down ideas. But even at that point, they're treating scraps of paper in a way that might be manipulated as data within the computer as well. The computer is in effect a sampler itself: it provides a way of looking at sound, the weight and authority of lyrics and words themselves as a compositional tool.

[6] Often the Akia MPC 2000, a portable audio-sampling production studio that is a favorite of hip-hop producers in general.

AG: How do the kids experience this? Do they get the metaphor? Do you follow them to see what impact this has had?

GS: I don't think evaluation happens in a formal way. I think they're critical of each other, but in a kind of peer-to-peer way. The question of how they determine whether it's good or not—that is really an excellent question. They're pretty brutal critics. They are encouraged to analyze in a far more explicit way, rather than just say, "Well, it didn't sound very good," or "The lyrics sucked." As part of the workshops, they're asked to elaborate on their chosen topic, their chosen issue, how the form of presentation relates to the subject matter. But it's fairly hit-or-miss.

I've worked in situations where there's a conscious attempt to introduce a cultural and media studies aspect to the workshops, and I'd say in a group of 10 to 12, maybe two or three get it and extend that to much wider experiences of media, magazines and television.

That's one of the primary aims of the workshops, but there's no way over the course of 10 weeks that you can achieve everything.

From Gary's interview with Lisa Das:

Lisa: We run 20-week courses now, so we have expanded it quite a lot. But if we are working with, say, young people who have been involved in formal music education courses before, we generally start off where our tutor will do an induction session and in that session he will talk to them and find out what music they are into and he will go away and build tracks; so he's basically trying to pull them in by showing them that on the equipment we have here, you can build a track that you really love. We try to work with people who perhaps are ostracized from education, so they wouldn't feel comfortable in a formal setting. So although we try and teach the same quantifiable skills, we try and do it informally, and the tutor is really important to that because he is a musician himself with the same kind of interests.

Then he breaks the track down so they can hear each component, and then they go back to basics and begin to sample and learn how to sequence. It's very simple, but they are drawn into doing something that they really like and endorse in the first place. Most of them are into rap and stuff, so they want to develop their lyric-writing and per-formance skills. So we talk to them about what a track is about, what feeling it has, or pick up on something they might be talking about in the session. They might come in talking about somebody who has been knifed in the street or something. We pick up on that and talk about the wider issues surrounding it. Basically if they start saying, "Big up all the ladies" and stuff, we don't say, "No, don't do that," but we encourage them to talk about it, to discuss what does that mean and why are you saying that, what do you think about the people who say that. So we try and point them, but we can't dictate because we're not there to do that.

GS: Some issues are fairly immediate and their initial responses might be to hit out, or to articulate this in their lyrics as negative ways of moving forward—by that I mean either instigating violence against violence, or retribution. A lot of the battle of these workshops is in trying to find concrete examples of where we believe some differ-ence has been made through nonviolent political action, for instance, or through the life-changing potential of music. It doesn't always work. But that's inevitable and appropriate; at times, I'm quite doubtful myself.

MC Aktarvata, another ADFED workshop participant, performs at Harlsden Community Center.

AG: If you were an advocate of violence, you'd be doubtful about whether that worked. All ways have their questions.

GS: Yes. The workshops are taking a slightly different direction since April, when Asian Dub Foundation went to Brazil and did a workshop there. You can read an account of their experiences at the Web site (www.asiandubfoundation.com).

AG: Is there some way they've brought that experience back to London and integrated it?

GS: The workshops are trying to move a little bit away from the idea that the course is solely about sampling and remixing as the core competency, so to speak. Participants were using it as a kind of shortcut. There's a balance with original authorship. I guess it's like if you're teaching visual literacy, you're trying to teach some of the historical basics such as color, composition and so on—enabling people to then go off and confidently express themselves.

AG: So there's more emphasis now on individual creation?

GS: The current MCs[7]—the Invasian rappers—have come out of one of the earlier workshops: Aktarvata, Spex and Krayzie. It's a group with a big international following, and they continue to be committed to the issues and the politics; but also people are still coming out of the workshop to play a fundamental role in the group itself. On the question of how Asian Dub Foundation is different from a traditional commercial band, that is what makes them absolutely unique.

[7] Derived from Master of Ceremonies, the person who hosts a public event.

This commitment and determination on their part has sometimes led to some anxiety from their recording label. A label first and foremost is motivated by sales, and although the sales are healthy, it's not always a commercially viable recipe for making maximum profit. They have an established audience, particularly in Japan, France and England; but when a record company takes you on, they want to maximize that profit.

Here we have a group that's in a unique position of actually having a distribution network. Certainly in my own experience, each group I've worked with has had a kind of unique and potent combination of authorship and quality of production, but not distribution—certainly not where they could create what you might call critical mass. Asian Dub Foundation are doing this right now, but not without its difficulties. Like all progressive innovation, it's not a stable situation.

AG: It sounds like Asian Dub Foundation is an entity, and different people front it at different times. Is that right? Is the loyalty of the audience there, even though the same guys are not on stage?

GS: That's a constant concern really, about who the audiences are. It's a little bit like gangsta rap: when you look at the majority of the audience, it's really made up of white indie kids.[8] There is an issue about, "Are they actually listening?" This thing about conscious partying: in live situations, sometimes there's little doubt that they're jumping up and down enjoying themselves, but there's no proof they're actually listening to the words. Cynically at times I don't think they are. But what is unique about the whole Asian Dub Foundation/ADFED group itself is that they're working on so many different fronts: the live shows, the workshops, the sound systems,[9] the Web site, the CD-ROM which they've done with the Commission for Racial Equality, the relationship with Campaign Against Racism and Fascism (CARF).

From Gary's interview with Lisa Das:

Gary: What is the working relationship with CARF?

Lisa: We started off thinking that we wanted our students to have a real social agenda in their music. We tried a partnership with CARF for some time, but it became too dictatorial because the students have their own issues and we realized that we wanted them to bring out their own issues rather than saying look at this and look at that. So now we try and do it more organically: we are trying to get them to look at their lyrics and issues that they might have just come in and started talking about, so it's not formalized really. But obviously we are still informed by CARF.

[8] White suburban males, mostly college-aged, who identify with the inner-city urban ghetto.

[9] A highly organized system including self-made high-power portable PA (public address) and disco equipped with sound effects.

GS: There's a certain omnipresence. I remain hopeful, as [the members of ADFED] do, that by one means or another, or through reinforcement, being exposed on so many different fronts with a consistent message, it's going to make some difference.

AG: Yeah. There is this phrase, "multiple reinforcing messages." Advertisers use it. In a way, what you're saying is that they're using approaches that have commercial application—and they have a commercial application, too, but they have a different agenda.

GS: They do have a different agenda. The group had to fulfill a number of different commitments to pay for the Brazil trip. The workshops were paid for and organized by the British Council.[10] There was the contrast between being in the northern part of Rio, a quite moving experience attended by young people, some of them giving an account of the prison uprising and the consequences of that, and then on another occasion performing on a beach with a very different audience.

AG: What you're saying is they're living the contradictions.

GS: They *are* the contradiction, in microcosm. But I'm encouraged in many respects, because ADFED is an integral part of Asian Dub Foundation, and that kernel of contradiction exists, but the workshops provide an opportunity for discussion.

AG: Let's talk about this theme a little bit, because it evokes questions of purity. If you're in the midst of that web of contradictions, then you're going to be constantly tempted and put in situations where it's not going to be clear which is the right road.

GS: My take on it is, I don't see Asian Dub Foundation as being pure and uncontaminated. I don't think there's such a thing. There's a process of contamination, and it's a matter of degree. But I see such tremendous positives, just in terms of the workshops themselves, that I can reconcile it in my own mind. I've accepted a degree of uncertainty.

AG: Some community arts people might feel this involves too much money, too dirty; some might say they'd rather be permanently marginal. I'm sympathetic to the other side of the argument, and what you're saying impresses me, because it sounds like these people are seriously trying to live the other side of the argument. You said that the positives you see justify dealing with the dangers of co-optation.

[10] The British Council has offices in 230 cities in 110 countries and territories that present and support programs in six sectors—arts, literature and design; education and training; English-language teaching; governance and human rights; information exchange and knowledge management; and science, engineering, technology and the environment, aimed at "enhancing the reputation of the United Kingdom in the world as a valued partner" (www.britcoun.org).

GS: I'm happy with it because of ADFED. It all comes down to property as well, doesn't it? Another aspect of this whole initiative has been not just the one workshop, but creating and supporting other workshops that are autonomous and have their own agendas. Spin-offs: I don't want to use the word franchise, because it's not McDonald's. It will be interesting to see what will happen when ADFED buys a building, whether that significantly changes things as well with all the things that come with that. And yet it seems like a natural progression: that they can have a place, an agency, an organization for cultural production that does it on different terms, not because they're motivated just by commercial viability, and how much money they can make, but it actually has a different kind of agenda.

It's close to happening. ADFED fulfills all the criteria for an inner-city conurbation, doesn't it? Deprived area with Asian youth involved in recent disturbances in Bradford and Oldham earlier in the year. It's aimed at young people, it's associated with the whole mentoring and apprenticeship scheme and national vocational qualifications, so it even speaks the speak. It can be submerged in a kind of certified worth if somebody needs to seek approval from their funding body.

AG: How long have the ADFED workshops been going?

GS: They started about three or four years ago. Many young people have gone through. I bump into them all the time. So many have been motivated by a passion to be involved in something that could really change their lives.

AG: And has it changed their lives?

GS: Yeah. It's not just because of Asian Dub Foundation. But had they not been occupied doing something like this, they would have gotten into some serious trouble. Something characteristic about second-generation Asians is that whereas the first generation was perceived to be passive, the second generation is very active. If you do anything to them, or if they think they're under threat in any way, they are less likely to ask questions. That's the kind of backdrop we're working against, trying to ensure that they don't respond in such a trigger-happy fashion. It's unfortunate but true that some of the music that they listen to, the very genre they use as inspiration for their own work, initially emerges from a homophobic, macho, extremely violent lyrical tradition. That's the starting point. If you did a kind of time-lapse photography from the beginning of the workshop, looking at the lyrics that they might have started with and at the end, there's a tremendous difference. I don't know about sustaining that change, but I'm encouraged by it.

AG: Did your daughter, Shakia, take a workshop?

GS: No, she didn't. She was involved in the initial computer games workshop. It's based on the same principle of learning skills in a social context, but they were very different: two very sharp ends of the industry.

AG: So you've done other projects that involve young people with technology and articulating what they have to say for themselves?

GS: The project was called New Player, involving eight to 10 young people between 14 and 18 in partnership with an organization called the "Weekend Arts College" (www.antialiasdesign.com/wac/). It's been going for about 20 years, and provides extracurricular activities for young people on the weekend. So inIVA worked with them over the course of the 1998–99 academic year with the intention of looking at different ways of making computer games, getting young people to author those games for themselves. It was a tremendously exciting project where the participants were given the opportunity to consider games that aren't merely beat-'em-ups, and came up with a number of really interesting scenarios which obviously aren't on the market. It was structured in such a way as to provide a kind of media-studies element with visiting critical commentators. And one of the projects we used as a catalyst for this was a piece of work from the artist Keith Piper called "Caught Like a Nigger in Cyberspace."

That particular piece really is about transgressive acts. You can't proceed in this game unless you're transgressive. It's really great: when young people play, they get to the end really quickly because the "no entry" signs encourage them to proceed. When you get older people—we had it in a gallery installation once—where you have these "no entry" signs, they were reluctant to click it. You get those cross hairs in a rifle, and you have to line it up with black figures and shoot them to proceed. So many people—understandably, actually—are rather uncomfortable; but unless you do that, you can't proceed. The workshop participants came up with a series of fragments; they're not computer games, because it would be difficult in two hours a week to make a full-blown game. But they've got all the elements of interaction and everything else. More importantly, they've created these fragments that look at the historical landscape in cyberspace, looking in particular at the neighborhoods they occupy. This is what they chose to do: reflect that within cyberspace itself with a scenario called Cyber Ai, a game concept that takes place in 2050, where the opening of Robo-Tube, a brand-new Cyber Artificial Intelligence Line, is jeopardized by a group of hackers. This enabled them to consider the moral position of hackers and themselves in relation to society now and in the future.

AG: You mentioned inIVA here, but your work with ADFED: is that inIVA or you?

GS: It is me now, but this is how it worked: the initial work with ADFED, when ADFED started, was with inIVA, because we had initiated a project called Club Mix. It relates to Keith Piper again. In the exhibition that inIVA did with him, called "Relocating the Remains," which was a retrospective of his work, there were two particular comments that stood out: Why did we do it at the gallery in the Royal College? How will people get to see it? That was one comment, which was quite legitimate. The second one was, "This is great material. It has tremendous potential resonance for a much younger audience who do not visit art galleries." And so we put together a project known as the Club Mix, which was about creating music and visuals that had social content, not merely abstracted visuals, to play in clubs.

We did the initial workshop, and I did some workshops independently around the country with other groups, and one of the workshops I did was with the ADFED, using Keith's work as a catalyst. It was tremendous. It was incredibly politically charged. They were just astonished by the quality—it's that classic thing, I've experienced it myself in the early '80s, where you're working with a community group and the process is fine but the product isn't very good at all, and they just don't want to claim ownership of it. But here they had something which they just thought was astonishing. They wanted an opportunity to create their own visuals, which they did in combination with a little agit-prop, slogans and visual sampling. The performance was actually one of the most emotionally moving evenings of my life—all these potent and incredible visuals, some of which were created in the workshops, happening in a club to an absolutely packed house. I don't know that everybody else made the connection: they were probably just dancing to the music.

The ADFED workshops themselves had started about four or five months prior to that, but I think that made a tremendous difference. By itself, the political dimension of the Campaign Against Racism & Fascism might have been perceived as a rather dry entity, unpalatable for young people. But here they had something that was incredibly expressive, vibrant. It wasn't just MTV with content; it was more than the sum of its parts. There was subtlety and a kind of communicative power in those pieces of work that translated well and required very little explanation on our part of what it was about.

AG: There's a thread that runs through all of your work.

GS: What interests me in particular is the history of contemporary youth resistance. That's the underlying common denominator of all the work. It's about how young people—particularly working class, black, female or whatever, those who've grown up under conditions of oppression—how they work with a dominant system of authority. All these projects are articulations of that cultural resistance.

AG: Is that your personal story too?

GS: Yeah, I guess so. It's very much about taking resistance in popular culture as a starting point. It's an extraordinarily powerful dynamic. Yeah, it is my story. I'd forgotten in many respects.

There's empathy happening throughout this, isn't there? It's not like I'm a benign, inert, neutral observer. If anything, I am delighted by the extraordinary expressions from these young people in such an incredibly articulate way, in a way that I was 10 years older than they are before I began to grasp the issues they are dealing with. I find that extraordinarily uplifting. It gives me hope for the future.

AG: You didn't have someone like yourself.

GS: True. It's fantastic to see how their definition of self and cultural identity is so evident and so explicit.

AG: They know who they are way before you did?

GS: Yeah. That's where you want to channel those energies and that vitality in a socially cohesive way, because what happens sometimes is that energy is misguided: you see it in nationalist ideologies being perpetuated, rather than celebrating the diversity of their communities, celebrating the energy in that and how they relate to other people. The workshops are an important means to circumvent that. It's really, really crucial.

10

Flood damage in Latrobe,
one of the coal-mining
communities along
Buffalo Creek that was
completely destroyed in
the February 26, 1972,
disaster in Logan County,
West Virginia. Photo
by Don Stillman.

Center for Rural Strategies
46 East Main Street
Whitesburg, Kentucky 41858 U.S.A.
Telephone: (606) 632-3244
Fax: (606) 632-3243
E-mail: deedavis@aol.com
Web site: www.ruralstrategies.org

The capsule biography **Dee Davis** posted to our online dialogue group began by situating his home region of Appalachia on the world continuum of rich and poor:

I grew up in Hazard, Kentucky, a small town in the coal mining region of the Appalachian Mountains. The region I am from is a place like many others in the world where the culture is rich and the people are poor. It is very rural, and apart from the environmental destruction of the mineral and timber companies, it is quite beautiful.

As a member (and until recently, executive producer) of Appalshop, his work over the last 25 years has involved hands-on cultural production—producing and distributing documentary videos in Appalachia and other rural regions of the United States— but also cultural entrepreneurship and deep thinking about the challenges of cultural development in a relatively isolated, distinct and impoverished region of the wealthiest nation on earth.

Recently, he cofounded a new organization, the Center for Rural Strategies, with the aim of using what he learned at Appalshop to make the case for rural life and culture through the mass media. This essay explores the challenges and opportunities involved.

Full Faith and Credit

by Dee Davis

My home is in the Appalachian Mountains of Kentucky in the southeastern United States, a region known by others for its coal mining, bluegrass music and—since the days of President Lyndon B. Johnson's War on Poverty—for being persistently poor amidst America's abundance. Growing up and making a life here has taught me a good deal of what I know about cultural survival. As the process of globalization imbeds itself throughout the layered framework of local rural life, I have come to imagine how regional messages of cultural resilience and culture's mobilizing power might serve a greater purpose, if they could be made global as well.

It is with this thought that after 25 years as part of Appalshop, a cultural cooperative for our part of the world, I have changed jobs. At Appalshop, I had been working with a group of performers and media producers who used a variety of artistic forms to celebrate local heritage and to address issues of inequity and privation. The work was wonderfully satisfying, but I wanted to see if applying what we had learned working together in the countryside of Appalachia might be useful in other rural regions of the United States and maybe even beyond our borders. The idea is that by describing rural life differently, by framing the stories of rural people differently, new approaches and new ideas will emerge and help reshape a rural policy that now fails on nearly every hand.

In rural regions of the United States, times are noticeably bad. The rates of poverty, illness, drug addiction and educational attainment are measurably worse than in the rest of the country and stack up just as poorly when compared to the rest of the industrialized world. As rural economies based on export agriculture and resource extraction falter, communities seek extraordinary measures to make things better. Many places have opened themselves to interventionist economic strategies that redirect available public money to subsidize private industry, most often hoping to re-create disappearing local jobs by enticing private businesses to leave their current location and move where the wage scale is lower and health and environmental regulations looser.

In this pursuit, small towns and local governments find themselves caught up in a devil's bargain, using the limited capital available to capture some other community's means of support—enticing a factory or other business to relocate —thus injuring that community and participating in a race to the bottom where wages and health and safety standards plummet. This activity among rural American municipalities has its parallels in the developing world where lending institutions like the World Bank provide precious development capital, but then exact commitments for repayment and participation that lead to similarly diminishing standards for workers and communities.

Other communities, more positively, have looked to renewed investment in education, retraining and technology to take advantage of changing opportunities that the new economy presents. These opportunities may include marketing or service-industry jobs that emerging telecommunications technologies have made possible, or they may mean training displaced workers for jobs that they must find in distant metropolitan areas. Nevertheless both responses are attempts to reimagine specific home communities in order to retrofit them into a transforming global economy that seems suddenly to have changed the rules for rural people. Irrespective of which of these paths is chosen, implicit is a willingness to change the work force, the work environment or even the character of the community in order to seek a place at the table. The danger however is that when communities abandon their cultural characteristics in order to save the local economy, they risk assets that could be as serviceable in the long run as the business strategy of the moment. When farms are subdivided, wilderness strip mined or old forests clear-cut, that momentary commerce generates income, but it also undercuts the possibility of more benign and renewable use of the land later and it inalterably changes a culture that has been defined by a relationship to land and earlier land use.

My concern here is that as hard-hit communities seek to make themselves over, attempting to appear more attractive to a world economic system, they not lose track of the values that have kept them together through good times and bad, and that they do not squander opportunities for more meaningful and potentially more beneficial development later.

If an overarching principle of globalization is that an open and competitive global marketplace tends to make the world's products available to the most consumers at the best prices, then the rural corollary is that globalization commodifies rural life, then seeks to obtain those commodities at bargain rates. By and large, rural enterprise produces the raw material and basic products processed by others. As a rule, food leaves rural communities to be processed and packaged elsewhere, wood becomes furniture elsewhere, coal becomes electricity elsewhere, oil becomes fuel elsewhere. Rural communities export their resources raw and value is added further up the economic food chain. The work that has underpinned rural life for the last century— farming and extracting natural resources—has become integrally linked to a world economy that commands the lowest commodity prices, values technology over human power and exploits wilderness for short-term market value. Rural people who previously made a decent livelihood in a less efficient economy are now more likely to be vulnerable to the machinations of a dynamic global market.

For example, in my home region, where coal mining remains the largest economic force, small coal companies have been bought by larger ones that have in turn been bought by energy conglomerates listed on the international stock exchanges. Because a single firm now may be able to supply energy to the market from a multitude of sources—from South African coal mines, Canadian gas fields or Venezuelan oil wells—it can exact pressure to keep labor costs down and health, safety and environmental regulations in check. Such large firms can even afford to bank their resources when the market is soft and build reserves for when trouble breaks out.

Global corporations that have the capacity to shut down production in a community without suffering in the marketplace essentially usurp labor's power to strike and the community's power to resist corporate intention. When the private sector has the ability to shut down and devastate local economies, elected officials who might otherwise attempt to challenge industry's authority are more easily deterred. One miner interviewed for a 1978 Appalshop documentary had a theory that when the industry started calling coal "energy," that's when the local trouble started. One can imagine similar explanations coming from farmers, fishermen, ranchers and hard-rock miners when they discovered that the language had changed for them—that as with coal, their livelihoods had become part of a global marketplace and that their competitors were increasingly likely to be distant corporations speaking a different language and working at a different scale.

As rural economies have struggled, rural communities have similarly been challenged to maintain a critical mass of citizenry and a purposeful direction. In the United States as in much of the world, prevailing economic forces are pushing people away from the countryside and into metropolitan areas where they are more hopeful of finding the means to earn a living. As Thomas Friedman writes in "The Lexus and the Olive Tree," "Globalization also has its own demographic pattern—a rapid acceleration of the movement of people from rural areas and agricultural lifestyles, to urban areas and urban lifestyles."[1]

Wendell Berry puts it more dramatically in his essay "Conservation and Local Economy":

> For a long time, the news from everywhere in rural America has been almost unrelievedly bad: bankruptcy, foreclosure, depression, suicide, the departure of the young, the loneliness of the old, soil loss, soil degradation, chemical pollution, the loss of genetic and specific diversity, the extinction of species, the depletion of aquifers, stream degradation, the loss of wilderness, strip mining, clear cutting, population loss, the loss of supporting economies, the deaths of towns. Rural American communities, economies, and ways of life that in 1945 were thriving and, though imperfect, full of promise for an authentic human settlement of our land are now as effectively destroyed as the Jewish communities of Poland; the means of destruction were not so blatantly evil, but they have proved just as thorough.[2]

Irrespective of how magnificent one may think our cities, or how economically sound our suburbs, rural towns and villages also contribute to our overall well-being. This value may not be immediately recoverable on open markets, but that does not make it insignificant. That people have the necessary skills to grow food, cut trees or make sausage should not have value to a nation only when those people are recognized as low-bidders. Who among us hungers for low-bid sausage?

Put another way, survival of the fittest is a beloved law among the fittest. But within economies as within species, no one remains the fittest forever—indeed, one is seldom the fittest for very long. Cities, nations and continents wax and wane within a world economic framework. As Joel Kotkin and Fred Siegel point out in the *Los Angeles Times*,[3] the history of the world's great cities is intertwined with the real costs of security. The great cities of Mesopotamia in the third millennium B.C., and later Alexandria and Rome, flourished only when they no longer needed walls to ensure security. Similarly, modern cities such as Paris, London and New York could grow only when infrastructure that depended on long-term investment was not threatened by destructive anarchic forces.

[1] Thomas L. Friedman, *The Lexus and the Olive Tree* (New York: Farrar, Straus and Giroux, 1999), p. 11.

[2] Wendell Berry, "Conservation and Local Economy," *Sex, Economy, Freedom, and Community* (New York and Canada: Random House, 1992 and 1993), p. 5.

[3] Joel Kotkin and Fred Siegel, "Attacks Threaten Future of Cities," *Los Angeles Times*, Oct. 14, 2000, M6. Online posting at www.latimes.com.

Globalization depends on reasonably secure markets and safe metropolitan market centers. Economic models assume an acceptable ratio of investment risk to projected reward. In such models, when the costs associated with those risks remain within an acceptable range, there is an accompanying assumption of solid return on investment. But when those costs become unmanageable or when the threats to the marketplace become persistent, capital flees. In our contemporary history we have witnessed conflagration in cities like Belfast, Beirut and Belgrade chase away investment capital. We have seen political corruption in Indonesia and disease across the continent of Africa stem global investment. Now in the wake of the September 11 incidents, the United States, long thought an exemplar of market security, must fundamentally reassess what it will pay to keep its cities secure. Will the country in essence attempt to build walls of security around cities to hold back anarchic forces? And if so, what is the cost to the treasury and to America's concept of an open society? In the week following the World Trade Center terror, the New York stock markets, already enduring recession, lost more than one trillion dollars in equity. A trillion dollars in real wealth belonging to real people and chartered institutions evaporated. Suddenly safe and long-held business assumptions about how the markets would function and where they should be located were called into question.

That for most of American history the countryside has been integral to a strong and fecund economic system should not be forgotten after a half-century of rural decline and metropolitan ascendancy. At the moment the preferred response to a struggling rural sector seems to be laissez-faire abandonment. There is no national rural policy, let alone a plan to preserve rural life, and the scattershot laws and regulations aimed at rural regions are often written by the lobbyists of industries which profit most from the lack of comprehensive policy and planning. That is, the laws are written chiefly by those like corporate farmers who reap the largesse from federal agricultural subsidies, or mineral companies who are given huge tracts of public land to mine or drill. But before global governmental and monetary institutions embrace a de facto policy of economic Darwinism as natural law for rural communities, there is at least the obligation to anticipate the consequences: what is the cost of allowing our rural communities to continue to become dysfunctional and fail?

In a recent video interview with Frank Johnson, an attorney in Carrizo Springs, Texas, we were told the history of a 1920s land scheme there in South Texas where great expanses are populated only by rattlesnakes, cactus and mesquite trees. It had been an unkind string of harvests for Midwestern farmers who were additionally burdened by a succession of terribly hard winters. The land scheme involved chartering trains in the coldest, snowiest, most blustery part of the winter from agricultural states like Illinois and Wisconsin and transporting farmers down to the warmth of Texas to offer them broad acreages of farmland at attractive prices.

One farmer taken by the offer began to quiz the land agent to just see if the
deal was too good to be true. He asked, "Now how do I know if I was to buy
this land and move down here to get away from all the snow, that it wouldn't
turn around and start snowing here too?"

The land agent told the farmer not to take his word for it, but to wait and
he would get independent confirmation. He then called to a young boy
who had come out to see the trainload of visiting farmers.

> The agent asked: "Son, how old are you?"
>
> The boy said, "Eleven years old, sir."
>
> "Son, how long have you lived in these parts?" the agent asked.
>
> "All my life, sir."
>
> "Son, would you tell this nice visitor if any time in your memory you have
> ever seen it snow in these parts."
>
> "No, sir, I ain't never seen it snow," the boy said, then thought for a moment.
> "I did see it rain once."

Like the visiting farmer, perhaps it would not hurt to ask some hard questions
before we abandon any more of the American countryside. Do we really
want a nation without rural infrastructure? Do we honestly feel secure placing
food production and related issues of biodiversity, pesticide use and soil
chemistry in the hands of a few corporate farmers? Are our cities actually
better off when poor country people are forced to leave rural areas and start
over as poor urban people? Who pays the costs of food, shelter, health care
and training to help new urban-dwellers get back on their feet?

I have come to believe that with the decline of our rural populations, something is being lost that is vital to our character as a people—something of value that is discounted at present, but irreplaceable at any cost. Put differently, there is unrealized value in rural life that can contribute to a more thoughtful calculus of global prosperity, well-being and security.

In the coal fields of the Appalachian Mountains some artists and producers have been attempting to use cultural strategies to address such questions of economy and purpose.

APPALSHOP

In my part of the country we are blessed with a rich culture and close proximity to challenge. The land is hilly and unsuitable for commercial farming. It is far from navigable water. Distant corporations with a history of environmental excesses own the abundance of coal, natural gas and timber. Furthermore, the pressures of a global market for natural resources create worldwide competition to keep labor and conservation costs to a minimum. This has meant that the people who live near the exploitable resources become increasingly marginal as new technologies create market efficiencies, reducing available jobs. In contrast with the recent past, only a few laborers are now needed to mine coal or harvest timber. In this environment, corporations have used their power as principal employers as leverage to keep their taxes low and the public sector deferential. As a result, our infrastructure, health care and educational attainment are among the poorest in the industrial world.

In 1973 I went to work for a cultural organization near my home. I had grown up as a child of merchants. As Mark Twain said, "My parents were neither poor, nor conspicuously honest." I spent my youth engaged in political organizing, in community-engagement projects and more prosaically in delivering furniture for my father. At 22, I came to feel that the kind of direct political action in which I was involved was an inadequate response to the pervasive need I saw in my home region. I decided to abandon retail and go to work for an organization then called the Appalachian Film Workshop. Dad asked me to stay and help him out. He said that he knew he hadn't been paying me very much. When I explained that he was paying a good deal more than I was going to get at the film center, a look passed from parent to child that perhaps only a career cultural worker can ever know.

The Appalachian Film Workshop had begun as an outpost of a government-supported program called Community Film Workshop Council of America. That national project was based in New York and modeled after a Canadian Film Board initiative to empower communities by placing motion-picture cameras in the hands of youth. Our program began with 16mm film cameras, but after a few years it opened up to photography, recorded music, theater and literary publication. Eventually it would expand to include documentary television production, broadcast radio, media training for young people and a national cultural festival component.

The other film workshops were located in urban centers, where the idea was to train young people for careers in film and television. What distinguished the program at Appalshop (as it became officially known in 1975) was that from the beginning it sought to build community by recognizing local culture as an asset and seeking a place for that asset in a larger marketplace of ideas and aspirations. The young people who came to Appalshop to learn to be media producers and performing artists began conferring value on cultural practices and community members whose contributions were unrecognized and therefore undervalued. We wanted to document local issues and cultural practices like traditional music, church services, coal mining, herbal healing and quilt making, and then present that work to a broad public. In doing this, we found that in some small ways the value of the culture was raised.

Similarly to the way the value an unknown artist's early work increases as the artist becomes more widely recognized, Appalshop and the handful of national critics and prominent artists who championed the group's work could be said to have initiated a process of recognition and reappraisal of the value of Appalachia as an American place and as a rural culture. For example, motion picture director Arthur Penn ("Bonnie and Clyde," "Little Big Man") said at the time, "Theirs is the most alive use of film I know. The way they make films about the people in their local communities is what writing novels was about in days past."[4] *The Washington Post* wrote, "Appalshop wrote the book on community based filmmaking. And did the film."[5]

[4] Quoted in *Newsweek*, Aug. 12, 1974.

[5] Desson Howe, *The Washington Post*, Nov. 14, 1984.

Appalshop came of age during a moment informed by both the cultural discourse brought forward by the American civil rights movement and the challenging of national assumptions that followed in the wake of the Vietnam War. The country was in a mood to put aside its grander, more nationalistic mythology and for a time examine its component cultural parts. Appalshop, along with a contingent of other cultural and activist institutions like the Highlander Center (a labor and folk school in eastern Tennessee), Broadside Television (an early cable access producer in Johnson City, Tennessee) and the Council of the Southern Mountains (an ecumenical social-justice organization and magazine publisher located most of the time in southwest Virginia) all became "brokers," so to speak. The organizations began to celebrate and promote Appalachian culture in forms like string-band music, handicrafts and storytelling and, through their media, champion the lives of the people living in these impoverished communities as if they were the heroes of their country.

Members of Kentuckians for the Commonwealth rally in the state capitol to support legislation outlawing the Broad Form Deed. From "On Our Own Land," © Appalshop Film & Video, 1988

This recognition and reappraisal began to occur not only within the national discourse, but also to a modest extent within the Appalachian communities that were the focus of Appalshop's work. By illuminating lasting cultural traditions, profiling members of the community who were exemplars of mountain artistic disciplines, such as music and storytelling, and making visible the cultural bonds of community, Appalshop joined what was becoming a larger movement that included regional writers, scholars and journalists who were engaged in the business of making the Appalachian mountain region aware of its assets and its virtues.

Early in the organization's development, this process of community cultural awareness and reflection brought filmmakers, actors, musicians and producers into direct contact with a variety of economic and social issues. When Appalshop began its work, there was virtually no Appalachian study material in any local school curriculum in the region. The idea that those three million or so people who lived within the central Appalachian mountain range shared a common history or purpose was apparent mostly in negative portrayal, reflected in the way that the mass media characterized the region's people as poor, backward and victimized by circumstance. But beginning in the '70s—at first on college campuses and later in public schools—groups of teachers and student organizations began working in loose collaboration to build a cultural awareness movement that would reframe the identity of Appalachian Mountain people. Appalshop's work became available as a tangible classroom representation that could inform the movement first through documentary film, then later in the form of preservationist recordings, publications and Roadside Theater's touring performances of traditional tales.

As this work began to gain acceptance in schools, organizers involved in the political struggles of the region began to employ Appalshop's cultural materials in their community-development work. This cultural material of music, dance, handicraft and folk tales emphasized common bonds across the region, giving organizers a common language with which to speak to communities isolated from each other by terrain or regional borders. In addition to documenting regional culture, Appalshop also had begun early on producing media and performances about social and political issues facing local communities. Films about the destructive practices of strip mining, workplace health and safety, corrupt officials and unionization were shown at rallies and community gatherings. Appalshop's record label issued music to support environmental and labor activists; the theater company performed for union rallies and for benefits; and the literary quarterly published the work of activists alongside that of poets and fiction writers.

As Appalshop worked to use cultural means to address social issues, the organization in turn set out to attempt to influence broad issues that affected the regional economy. A good example can be seen in a range of artistic activity dealing with the coal industry. No one concerned about the future of central Appalachia—certainly no community-based artist—could long ignore the coal industry, the largest employer, the principal repository of the region's stored wealth, the driving force behind the region's politics, and historically the creator of most local infrastructure, such as water systems, medical clinics, retail stores and schools.

How well employees were treated varied from company to company. But economic relations were typically feudal. To understand the extent to which coal companies dominated life in the coal camps, the small towns they built to house the miners, one needs to know that through the 1930s, '40s and into the '50s many of these companies issued their own currency. Miners were paid in company scrip that was only redeemable at the coal company's own retail store and for the prices the company elected to charge. Shopping elsewhere was often grounds for termination. Those coal camps and the mining operations answered to corporate headquarters in far-flung cities. At one time in Letcher County, where Appalshop is located, county residents were living in three different time zones, because the camps were kept on the same time as their parent company headquarters located in distant cities.

Early on Appalshop began working with citizens who wanted to create a more equitable tax on the mineral holdings of large corporations. A region-wide ownership survey had documented that the vast majority of the area's resources were owned by large outside businesses. At that time it was not unusual for a large corporation with thousands of acres of mineral rights and millions of dollars in coal reserves to be paying less in taxes than a local resident might pay on a house trailer or an old pickup truck. A grassroots group, the Kentucky Fair Tax Coalition (KFTC), began mounting direct organizing projects to inform citizens about these inequities. Appalshop artists played a small role in assisting that effort. At the same time, those same artists were able to broker relationships with constitutional rights attorneys who assisted in filing a successful State Supreme Court challenge to the tax code, bringing millions of new dollars to local governments in low-income counties. It changed the base support for education, infrastructure, economic development and other aspects of the common good.

In another example, Appalshop produced "On Our Own Land," a video that detailed the lives of mountain people attempting to protect their land from the abuses of strip mining. This is a controversial and often destructive mining process that removes the earth and trees, and reroutes surface water in order to extract coal from below. Examining deeply held cultural beliefs about the value of a land-based heritage and documenting the cultural cost to the community of losing the very hills that sheltered their way of life, the video showed ordinary citizens standing up to tremendous economic and political power to eradicate an oppressive legal instrument called the broad-form deed. These longstanding deeds, quite often foisted on illiterate landowners in return for token payments, allowed coal companies to destroy surface lands through strip mining without compensating landowners. The video, which won a DuPont Award from the Columbia University College of Journalism, was a major part of the public-awareness campaign and a citizens' movement joined by KFTC and others that led to a Kentucky constitutional amendment outlawing strip mining under the broad-form deed. As a result of this campaign, landowners who wished to preserve their lands now had the legal right to do so.

Thus an intervention in community cultural development played a critical role in realignment of hundreds of millions of dollars' worth of assets. Local landowners took some measure of control of assets that had before been controlled solely by large corporations. Though the value of local culture would have been nearly impossible to assess, before or after the amendment passed, clearly, its influence figured into a massive recalculation of corporate wealth.

The examples of restoring a sense of the value of local culture that I know best are those associated with my home in the Appalachian Mountains and with Appalshop. There, recognition of cultural value is embodied in training programs that encourage youth to remain and contribute in the region, multicultural community education that champions diversity and history projects that chronicle community resistance to industrial plundering. But far beyond the Appalshop and Appalachian experiences, similar initiatives that combine economic development with cultural initiative are growing throughout the rural United States.

For example, development activities at the Llanogrande Cultural Center in Edcouch, Texas, seek to build communities in the *colonias* along the Mexican border by infusing traditional development approaches with Spanish-language education, media broadcast and training, oral history and literary publications. There, school-based programs that started as classroom exercises in culture and creativity have developed into a movement engaging young people to use their culture as the lens for educational attainment and community-building. In the Southern California desert, the Coachella Valley Housing Coalition builds homes for farmworkers, shelters for people with AIDS and survivors of domestic abuse, apartments for the disabled and health-care facilities for rural communities without doctors; yet they also offer mariachi, art and technology classes as key to their development approach. Their purpose is to empower poor people by helping them build communities of civic participation and cultural respect.

In these places, culture in some way informs the price of land and the preparedness of the local community to build homes, produce marketable goods and services and face adversity by pulling together. Nonetheless you won't find cultural life on a list of global economic indicators. Although crafts and regional music may be sold in some form to passing tourists, the principal value of local culture is in personal and community expression. Through such expression, culture reaffirms community values, reinforces identity, undergirds resistance and satisfies the soul. But it nevertheless goes unmeasured by the national and international policymakers who guide development and the corporations.

Traditional crafts that in an earlier time and a less connected world served a utilitarian purpose—hand-stitched quilts, hand-woven baskets, homemade musical instruments, clay crockery—linger in rural societies even though department stores can provide goods that do the same job at a fraction of the cost. Why? Because they retain some sustaining value for the owners that transcends mere usefulness. A community's handcraft can be appreciated as an object of aesthetic beauty, as a representation of a cultural identity and as a repository of shared memory. The current market value of such an item may only be measured in the price a tourist pays today, but the market reality is that underlying cultural values help maintain a modest market for such goods year after year, long beyond the shelf life of most produced goods. Similarly, while a global telecommunications infrastructure measured in stocks, bonds and licensing agreements suffuses the planet with commercial music, drama and 24-hour news programming, throughout small towns and villages, traditional music, dance and storytelling persevere in practice as well as community memory. Why? Because again such practices have real value to please, inform and keep communities together. They may remain unrecognized by the systems created by advertisers to measure audience size and chart brand recognition.

FULL FAITH AND CREDIT

In "The Mystery of Capital," a book subtitled "Why Capitalism Triumphs in the West and Fails Everywhere Else," Hernando de Soto points out that throughout the Western world:

> [E]very parcel of land, every building, every piece of equipment, or store of inventories is represented in a property document that is the visible sign of a vast hidden process that connects all these assets to the rest of the economy. Thanks to this representational process, assets can lead an invisible, parallel life alongside their material existence.[6]

[6]Hernando de Soto, *The Mystery of Capital: Why Capitalism Triumphs in the West and Fails Everywhere Else* (New York: Basic Books, 2000), p. 6.

De Soto goes on to explain that the rest of the world, the vast majority, also have homes, crops and businesses, but without clear title or deeds or articles of incorporation, they lack the essential representations needed for capital formation. For them capitalism fails. He argues that without a way to make the invisible visible, that is without a system for converting intangible assets to real value, the non-Western world cannot succeed as practitioners in a global economy.

Perhaps it is possible to follow this line of thought to make the case that local cultural assets are also intangible but real, that they have estimable value; but like unchartered businesses, they lack the essential representations to make their value manifest. I believe that. However, the fuller value of culture is unlikely to show up on a ledger sheet no matter how enlightened the accountant or how convincing the case. Clearly the rural reality is that until someone can market the immaterial value of local culture—sell it like a used pickup truck—cultural equity will remain largely an abstraction. We know it's there, it does something, we just don't know exactly what.

Perhaps the question then becomes not so much how to calculate the value of local culture, charter it or weigh it, but more pertinently what is the cost of losing it? In the same way an insurance company indemnifies a homeowner for what it costs to rebuild a house lost in a fire, the next step for all citizens is to imagine literally and figuratively what it would cost to rebuild local culture lost because of inattention, poor policy, out-migration or land degradation.

Working backward one can consider prime rural destinations like Tuscany in Italy, the Loire Valley in France or California wine country. Those regions have stayed agricultural and for the most part remained divided into small farms for generations. They are each extremely valuable expanses of rural communities now, because for many years when they weren't doing well, thoughtful policy prevented short-term market development from destroying the fields and the long-term possibilities. In essence no one could come in and strip mine the vineyards. Land-use policy favored the preservation of a cultural way of life that laid the groundwork for later rewards.

In the Appalshop film "Buffalo Creek Revisited," we see a depiction of what happens to a community when its culture is decimated. A coal-waste dam in

Buffalo Creek, West Virginia, failed in February of 1972, releasing a torrent of water, mud and debris. That flood careened down the narrow 17-mile valley without warning. One hundred twenty-five people were killed, 4,000 were left homeless. In the community's despair, government emergency teams came in and condemned much of the creek, disallowing local residents the chance to return to their home site and rebuild. Community survivors were randomly placed in trailers and relocated alongside others they had never met.

In the film Ruth Morris says about the days before the flood:

> Our children was raised together. They wasn't like neighbors: they was family. I've traveled over this old holler many a day with maybe two families in the car to the doctor. My next-door neighbor would take my carburetor and put it on his car. I'd take his tires off and put 'em on mine. That's the kind of neighbors we was. We didn't run and knock on the door and say "Can I do?" We went and opened the door and walked in and did do. We just worked together. I guess you could say we took care of one another. We joined everything. We belonged to the PTA, the scouts, all community affairs, the churches, stuff like that. And every morning to us was a sunny morning, a smile, a "Good morning," "Hi. How are you?" That meant so much to us. We don't get that no more. We don't see it no more. It's a loss. You know, a smile is like a million dollars sometimes and we don't get that no more. We get vacant stares. We get frowns. We get worries. It'll never have another homey atmosphere. That's the only thing I can tell you to define it—it was home.[7]

[7] "Buffalo Creek Revisited," film by Mimi Pickering, copyright Appalshop, Inc., 1985.

To create a different future for rural communities, we need to extend full faith and credit to the value of rural living. Right now, faith in the value of rural life is lacking in part because it has been so consistently devalued in the popular literature, in historical texts, in electronic media and in public policy.

One response that's needed now is a consistent chorus of global voices asserting the importance of rural living and knowledge, helping to create a framework that gives these realities context, respect and a sense that there's a culture there that needs to be examined on its own merits. Some like-minded colleagues and I have formed a new organization, the Center for Rural Strategies, to take a crack at it. Our aim is to take our own experience of addressing these issues in the Appalachian region and apply it in the interests of other rural regions, of rural culture as a whole. In my 30 years in community cultural development, I have observed that most successes are preceded by a string of failures. That's how we all grow and learn. In this endeavor, we expect to make mistakes, understanding that cultural development is an experimental enterprise. Our hope is that by paying attention to the lessons our communities have learned in both hardship and celebration, we can make a difference. The idea is that there is true value in local culture. It comes from a community's understanding of what's come before and faith that if you make an effort, things can be better.

Dajarra, Queensland,
residents Lamar
and Desmond Armstrong,
Thomas Ah-One, Thomas
De Satge and William
Major Junior gather at the
Ardmore Boundary Fence,
an example of some of
the restrictions placed
on Dajarra people.
© Feral Arts and Dajarra
Jimberella Coop, 1997.

11

Feral Arts
P.O. Box 12085
George Street
Brisbane, Queensland 4003, Australia
Telephone: (61 7) 3221 6557
Fax: (61 7) 3221 6995
E-mail: feral@feralarts.com.au
Web site: www.feralarts.com.au

Sarah Moynihan and **Norm Horton** together are the coordinators of Feral Arts, one of Australia's leading community cultural development groups, and one that has evolved since its founding in 1990, shifting focus as needs and conditions change. A primary focus for Feral's current work is Placeworks, a series of projects and partnerships focused on exploring the influence of place on cultural and community identity. One main theme of this essay is Feral's continuing work in the remote community of Dajarra, which is making innovative use of new technologies in community cultural development.

Sarah and Norm have the good fortune to live and work in Australia, which has the best-developed public apparatus for support of community cultural development of any nation on earth. As in all things, success doesn't mean that problems disappear, simply that their character changes: along with continuing to lobby for resources, practitioners in Australia have established debates about community cultural development; for example: Where has the sector come from and where is it headed? Is it becoming rigid or unresponsive? Is it losing its edge or its authenticity as a result of professionalization?

As they pointed out in the online dialogue preceding the spring 2001 conference, their work is shaped by a conscious attempt to influence policy through practice:

Feral Arts is a government funded, community based organisation. We take a long-term approach to work in a small number of communities, both urban and rural.

We work to develop models of practice to influence government policies and inform work by other people in other places.

Thus the other main theme of this essay is the development of Australia's support structure. As they trace its trajectory, the authors suggest how decisions concerning policy and funding have helped to shape practice.

Protest or Participate?

COMMUNITY CULTURAL DEVELOPMENT
AND GLOBALIZATION IN AUSTRALIA

by Sarah Moynihan and
Norm Horton, Feral Arts

It's early September 2001, and the globalization spotlight is heading our way. Brisbane is a modern city with a population of over a million. It is the capital of Queensland, a large, mineral-rich state in northeastern Australia. Next month the biannual Commonwealth Heads of Government Meeting (CHOGM) will bring half the world's leaders to town. Like the G8 summit group[1] and the World Economic Forum, CHOGM has become a target for the anti-globalization protest movement and Brisbane is preparing. A Commonwealth People's Festival with the theme of Connecting Communities is planned to run alongside CHOGM. But rather than connecting communities, the lead-up to CHOGM has brought to the surface differences among community groups, highlighting the complexity of relations between the government, community and corporate sectors and generating debate about the role of community cultural development.

Among the ranks of community groups opposing CHOGM, the e-mails are running hot. There has been much discussion over the aim of the protests and debate as to how to go about it. Loosely aligned factions have developed. The CHOGM Action Network (CAN) has advocated a protest march. The STOP CHOGM Alliance is campaigning for a full blockade of the Brisbane Convention Center where meetings will take place. Some indigenous community leaders working across these divides have sought to reframe anti-globalization protests, refocusing attention on the issue of colonization. Planning meetings have debated whether to accept invitations to meet with government-appointed mediators. Everyone struggles with the challenge of presenting a unified front while respecting the diversity of interests and agendas.

[1] Canada, France, Germany, Italy, Japan, Russia, the United Kingdom, the United States and the European Union.

On the other side of the coin, about 100 community organizations from around the country have decided to participate in CHOGM. They will take up booths in the Brisbane Convention Center to promote their community work and participate in meetings, seminars, forums and conferences running alongside CHOGM as part of the people's festival. Participants include a number of key cultural, political and social-justice lobbyists and advocacy groups, who might just as easily be seen in the front row of the protest organizers' meeting.

The Queensland government finds itself in tricky territory. Having spent 30 of the last 40 years in opposition—sometimes even leading illegal marches—it must be seen to support the right to protest. The government has appointed a team of high-profile mediators in an effort to negotiate and plan for nonviolent actions. Brisbane has a history of large-scale protests over issues including the Vietnam War, apartheid and indigenous land rights. Public interest in the globalization issue is growing, and there is concern over the potential for violent confrontations like those experienced in cities around the world. New police powers have been invoked and big money has gone into security arrangements. The city has witnessed a series of extraordinarily public training exercises: paramilitary teams in helicopters hovering over the city center and rappelling onto rooftops. Protest organizers suggest these displays may have more to do with intimidation than preparing for CHOGM.

This scenario poses questions for the community cultural development (CCD) sector of which our organization, Feral Arts, is a part. Should CCD practitioners protest or participate—or both? Where should our skills and resources be directed? Where are relations between government, community and the corporate sector headed, and what roles should CCD be playing in responding to key issues like globalization?

ON ANOTHER FRONT

Although much of our work is based in South Brisbane, where CHOGM is planned to take place, Feral Arts has prior commitments 2,000 kilometers away in remote northwestern Queensland. Dajarra is a small, isolated and predominantly Aboriginal township near Queensland's border with the Northern Territory. We are starting a four-week community cultural development program focusing on oral and community histories. The work is the latest stage of a 10-year partnership with the community and with the Waluwarra people, the main Aboriginal group living in Dajarra. The program is timed to coincide with annual rodeos in Dajarra and in Urandangie, an even smaller township 150 kilometers farther west on the Georgina River. Urandangie is a traditional meeting place for Waluwarra people. The rodeos have evolved into important contemporary community gatherings, one of the rare opportunities for family and community members to come together.

As in Brisbane the community in Dajarra is gearing up to protest—not about CHOGM but about water. After many years of suffering the consequences of an erratic, inadequate and increasingly saline water supply, they have recently written a letter, signed a petition and sent them to the government and the media. The letter relates:

> We are a small but humble and contented community, living our life on a
> daily basis and coping with the rest of the world's problems, as one needs to
> in order to maintain their own self worth. ... We must stand united and
> strong to fight with one voice so as the many deaf ears can hear our plight
> for a better healthier community and a brighter future for our children.[2]

As we help set up new state-of-the-art digital equipment—a computer, video camera and editing software purchased as part of the project—it seems hard to reconcile the priorities of the community cultural development program with an issue as fundamental as water. In stark contrast to life in Australia's modern cities, conditions in some remote townships and communities are closer to the Third World. Health is a primary concern. Key indicators such as infant-mortality rates and life expectancy, for example, confirm that conditions for Aboriginal people remain well below those enjoyed by other Australians.[3]

But for many in Dajarra, oral- and community-history work is just as central to cultural survival and growth as water. European colonization over the last 200 years has displaced all but the most remote indigenous people from their traditional lands. These processes have been massively destructive to a continent made up of over 300 different cultural and language groups. Responding to the cultural impact of displacement is one of the community's highest priorities and has become a focus of our community cultural development partnership with Dajarra.

DAJARRA

Approximately 85 percent of Dajarra's population is Aboriginal,[4] but it hasn't always been that way. The town grew up around the railway line and was shaped by its role in the cattle industry. For most of the 20th century, it was the westernmost point in the state's rail network. Drovers brought huge herds of cattle thousands of kilometers up and around the great central desert, across the top of Australia and down to Dajarra for transport to the coast. By the 1950s it was a thriving township and one of the biggest cattle-trucking centers in the world, shipping more cattle per year than Texas.[5]

It was not until 1967 that a national referendum granted citizenship rights to Australia's Aboriginal and Torres Strait Islander peoples. Until then, a range of repressive and paternalistic laws tightly managed the indigenous population.

[2] Letter from Barbara Dempsey, Dajarra Maintenance Services, Aug. 20, 2001.

[3] "The Health and Welfare of Australia's Aboriginal and Torres Strait Islander Peoples," Media Release (Cat. 4704.0), Australian Bureau of Statistics Online at www.abs.gov.au.

[4] Paul Memmott and Mark Moran, *Indigenous Settlements of Australia* (Brisbane: University of Queensland Aboriginal Environments Research Centre, 2001).

[5] From Memmott and Moran, *Indigenous Settlements of Australia*, cited on www.ea.gov.au/soe/techpapers/indigenous/population.html.

Emily Marshall, Margaret
Punch, Thomas De Satge,
William Major and
Desmond Armstrong try to
find the goanna lizard
someone spotted from the
car on Urandangie Road
in Dajarra, Queensland.
© Feral Arts and Dajarra
Jimberella Coop, 1997.

The Aborigines Protection and Restriction of Sale of Opium Act of 1897
(commonly known as "The Act") gave local police administrative responsibility and legal authority to control the lives of indigenous Australians.
Most Aboriginal people were moved from their traditional lands to live in
government- and church-run missions. Many in Queensland's northwest
were assigned to work on cattle stations for little more than food and shelter.

Seemingly innocuous changes have had significant impacts on cultural
practices and cultural identities.[6] In 1950, for example, the police station in
Urandangie was closed. Administrative responsibility for Waluwarra people
passed to the Dajarra police, forcing families to move off traditional lands and
into Dajarra. In some respects Waluwarra people fared better than most under
this discriminatory system, if only because many still lived and worked in
their home regions. Thus they were able to maintain important links with
culturally significant places.

[6] Rosalind Kidd's research
provides an overview of the
role of government in the
dispossession of Aboriginal
and Torres Strait Islander
peoples. See especially,
*The Way We Civilise:
Aboriginal Affairs—The
Untold Story* (Brisbane:
University of Queensland
Press, 1997).

By the mid-1970s, massive semitrailers called "road trains" were transporting
most cattle. Dajarra's strategic significance to the industry waned: many of the
white population began to move away; and few station owners continued to
employ Aboriginal people once they were required to pay wages. Smaller
family-owned holdings were systematically amalgamated into larger corporate
properties. In the 1980s, the train line was pulled up and, like Urandangie,
Dajarra slipped into decline, falling through the gaps of government funding
programs and community-development initiatives.

STRAYS

Dajarra people sometimes relate stories about all the dogs that used to roam around town. Back when the railway ran, towns further down the line would put their strays on the returning cattle trains. Dajarra was the end of the line, so that's where the dogs stayed. Feral Arts was a bit like a stray dog when we first came to town in 1992. At that time resources from regionally funded programs were not getting through to Dajarra, and a youth worker from the neighboring town (150 kilometers down the road) had invited us to come up from Brisbane and run arts workshops with young people. We knew very little about the country or the people—so little, in fact, that when we stopped for a swim in a water hole on a deserted back road, we got our four-wheel drive vehicle hopelessly bogged. We wound up walking 25 kilometers in 40-degree heat (104 degrees Fahrenheit) to get help from the nearest cattle station house. We sat embarrassed and exhausted as the 70-year-old station manager dug our car out single-handedly! When we arrived in Dajarra a day late for a community consultation meeting no one seemed too worried, but it wasn't long before the community took us in and looked after us.

Initially, we received funding only to work with young people, but we soon came to understand that the program needed to involve the whole community. First, as suggested in the consultation meetings, we ran an intensive four-week open program in visual arts, music and video. Workshops options included screen printing, batik, painting, leatherwork, songwriting and recording, jewelry making, video clips, interviews and photography. It was standing room only in the old school hall: as more and more people turned up, the workshops spilled outside and into neighboring sheds cleared of snakes and cobwebs. An impromptu boomerang and didgeridoo[7] production line sprang up in the back yard. Workshops ran all day and most of the night; within a few days, pretty much the whole community took part in the program. It was exhausting, but also lots of fun and we quickly developed a productive partnership. The workshop program gave us a platform to build relationships and learn more about the community's cultural needs and interests.

[7] A didgeridoo is a long, hollow branch traditionally used as a musical instrument.

[8] Keith Marshall interview, transcribed from the video "Dajarra" (Dajarra: Feral Arts, 1992).

THE GEORGINA

After the workshops settled down a bit, we were invited to visit some Waluwarra country on the Georgina River about 150 kilometers from town. As community worker and spokesman Keith Marshall explained:

> A lot of the people [living in Dajarra] are from down that way—the Georgina River. The old people used to wander from up near Headingly [cattle station] right down to Roxborough [cattle station], right along the river. A lot of sites where they used to do the corroborees [traditional dances] are down there.[8]

Everyone got a good laugh watching us trying to set up our campsite and light a cooking fire. We went fishing and saw how people hunted and collected a wide range of foods including goanna (large lizards), kangaroo, wild turkey and grubs. We started to learn a little about the country and its rich cultural history and significance to Waluwarra people. More significantly we began to understand that place and cultural identity are inextricably linked. Nancy Ah One explained the crucial role place plays in cultural education:

> With the kids, it is the only way they are going to pick up things [about their culture]—when you take them out bush. In town here, they just want money to go to the shop. But when you take them out bush, they walk around and they go, "What's that on the tree over there?—oh, wild bananas." Or they say, "Let's go and get some grubs out of the tree." There are permanent water holes all along there—Jimberella [a camping place on the Georgina River] has got the big permanent water hole. You can grow anything, as long as you've got a pump to irrigate the water.[9]

The community organized a series of video interviews addressing a range of key cultural and community issues including access to land, hunting, employment and cultural education. From the footage a short documentary was edited together. Community elder Joe Clarke explained:

> Today the policeman stops us from killing the kangaroo. That's our tucker [food]. We used to live on that before the white man come in this country. … Now the station owners stop us. They say, "Don't go on my property." That's not his property, that's black fella's property. Doesn't matter how much he paid for it. That's his money. But it's still our food in there.[10]

By the end of the six-week project we felt much had been achieved. Copies of the video were sent to the government to raise issues and lobby for resources and assistance. The community invited us to come back the next year after summer. We happily accepted, looking forward to what we might do together next time. We had little idea that 10 years later we would still be working with the community on things as fundamental as access to land and the water supply.

LAND AND CULTURE

Over the years we gradually came to learn what the people of Dajarra had known for a long time: the wheels of change turn very slowly in Australia, especially when access to land is involved. The video campaign attracted some attention and generated some new resources for the community. But it failed to resolve the broad cultural and social challenges facing the community. All subsequent efforts to gain access to land for cultural or commercial projects have been blocked. Even a simple application to lease Jimberella for a market garden and cultural and community education projects with young people was rejected. Ironically, the main reason cited was the lack of a water supply!

[9] Nancy Ah One interview, transcribed from the video "Dajarra."

[10] Joe Clarke interview, transcribed from the video "Dajarra."

Longtime Dajarra resident Joe Clark visits a mining project near his birthplace in Bing Bong, Northern Territory, as part of a video oral-history project.
© Feral Arts and Dajarra Jimberella Coop, 1999.

These are local examples of a much bigger struggle. Aboriginal and Torres Strait Islander peoples have fought for justice and land rights since the arrival of the English colonists in Australia in 1788. In 1992, the Australian High Court finally delivered a precedent-setting decision for the Mer (Murray Island) peoples in the Torres Strait, off Queensland's northern coastline. The Mabo case, as it is commonly known, was the first to legally recognize uninterrupted indigenous title to land. The decision overturned *terra nullius*—the legal premise that the Australian continent was uninhabited when the English invaded. But this landmark decision did not result in land ownership being returned to indigenous people. In fact subsequent federal government legislation (The Native Title Act of 1993) upheld existing titles, determining only that limited native title rights would apply to national parks, reserves and areas deemed to be "unallocated" state-owned land.

Even so, reactionary forces conducted a protracted media scare-campaign, claiming "ordinary Australians" would lose their homes and businesses because of the Mabo decision. Some corporate investors, especially in the mining industry, used the uncertainty around native title rights as an excuse to claim government compensation for start-up costs when fluctuations in global commodity prices made projects less viable.

COMPETING INTERESTS

Communities like Dajarra are still feeling the effects of the backlash to the Mabo decision and the broader fight for land rights. Mabo put pressure on governments to deliver certainty to nervous national and international investors, especially in key land-reliant industries such as mining, farming, tourism and property development. In the mid-1990s, at the height of the native title debate, the Queensland government pledged to smooth the way for investment and provide blanket sureties through new state native-title laws. One of its initiatives was to declare the state's northwest (including Dajarra) a mining province, boasting that over 30 billion Australian dollars in minerals would be removed from the area in a 20-year period. But governments failed to balance this initiative by negotiating reciprocal obligations and responsibilities for investors on the behalf of communities. In many instances communities have been left to work out their relations to development projects as best they can.

Queensland Fertilizer Operations at Phosphate Hill, for example, is WMC (formerly Western Mining Corporation) Ltd.'s new mining project and fertilizer production facility. Although 50 kilometers from Dajarra, it is closer than the nearest town and therefore the community's closest neighbor. The Phosphate Hill project has already generated some vital local employment and enterprise opportunities.[11] In reality, corporations like WMC are one of the few potential sources for remote communities like Dajarra to get help with reliable infrastructure such as power, water and communications. Despite repeated efforts to gain government assistance in dealing with the water-supply problem, WMC was the first to put their hands in their pockets to offer assistance. But the Phosphate Hill project is also creating some concerns. The facility draws more than 6,000 megaliters per year[12] of underground water and is facing its own salinity and supply issues. Although all the studies show a separation between the mine's water table and Dajarra's, not everyone is convinced. The production process involves highly toxic substances[13] and WMC has its share of outspoken environmental critics in response to its track record on other projects.[14] Community representatives from Dajarra have been invited to be part of a regional Indigenous Mining Reference Committee. They are excited by the possibilities but also a little nervous about the responsibilities.

Government departments and nongovernmental agencies work hard to support local cultural development and the principles of self-determination through a wide range of policies and programs. Funding community cultural development is an example in itself. But programs like these sometimes find themselves swimming against the tide of a broader economic rationalism. During the 1990s for example, the overarching priority of Australian governments of all persuasions had been to encourage economic growth by attracting

[11] See *Community Development—Local and Indigenous Participation* at www.wmc.com.au /sustain/community /16.html.

[12] Hill, Berry and Forrester, "Water Management for the Phosphate Hill Project," a report by *PPK Environment and Infrastructure*, 2000, p. 6.

[13] The fertilizer-production process involves shipping waste sulphuric acid 150 kilometers from Mount Isa that combines with sulphate rock to produce ammonia phosphate fertilizer. In 2000, the process generated 3,241 tons of sulphur dioxide emissions, 424,469 tons of carbon dioxide and 1.114 million tons of tailings. These and further details from "Industrial Minerals and Fertilizers," the *WMC Business Report*, at www.wmc.com.au /acrobat/busrep00 /busrep00imf.pdf.

[14] See comments on WMC at www.greenpeace.org.au /toxics/archive/dioxin /qld_sources.html.

investment. In northwestern Queensland's case, this meant new mining projects, even though they might clash with the needs and interests of local communities. This is not to argue a conspiratorial line that government-funded initiatives such as community cultural development merely mask the realpolitik of global economic development. Neither is it to suggest that corporate investment through mining and other industry is necessarily a bad thing for local cultural and community interests. Rather, we are suggesting there are complex sets of power relations between governments, communities and corporations through which competing interests are played out. There are opportunities and threats, and community cultural development is part of the equation. But what is its role?

In the context of these complex dynamics, a policy of blanket opposition to globalization makes little sense. Like the CHOGM scenario in Brisbane, the situation in Dajarra presents challenges for local communities and for the community cultural development sector. Global development for many local communities is not just an idea that can be protested or opposed. It is already a reality in their back yards, presenting both threats and opportunities. What are the implications for CCD? We will look at how the community cultural development program in Dajarra has responded to this situation, and through that example build an argument that CCD practitioners should learn more about development processes and globalization, improving our capacity to respond effectively to the opportunities and threats they present.

PLACE, CULTURE AND CCD

Through our experiences in Dajarra we have learned that responding effectively to some of the more fundamental challenges facing cultural and community development—such as access to land and the relationship between place and culture—can be a slow process requiring a long-term approach. Over the last 10 years, the Dajarra community has worked steadily toward long-term objectives in arts and cultural development. Along the way this has included a wide range of activities including numerous oral- and community-history projects, visual-arts projects, music and song-recording projects, video clips, community gardens, and technical training and skills-development projects. Some of the videos and songs produced through the program have won statewide awards, but more typically the outcomes have been locally focused. For a number of years the community has been lobbying for resources for a cultural center to support local arts programs and to care for cultural artifacts and oral and community histories. Applications for this stage of the work are still pending.

But tangible arts and cultural products are not the only significant outcomes from the partnership with Dajarra. The CCD program also provides a platform to engage with some of the more fundamental cultural and social challenges the community faces. At the core of this process is the oral- and community-history program. Even on a local level in Dajarra there is an underlying sensitivity among some of the nonindigenous community to documenting cultural histories: it is seen as linked to native-title and land-claim processes and an unmasking of the colonial history. In reality, however, Dajarra's interest in oral and community history is fundamentally cultural—survival, maintenance and growth. Like many of the world's indigenous peoples, Aboriginal cultures are based on an oral tradition, passing cultural knowledge from generation to generation through song, dance and story-telling. Colonization of Australia significantly disrupted these processes. In terms of survival and maintenance, recording and preserving oral- and community-history material is a stopgap measure, potentially making way for the community to reinvigorate oral traditions in the future.

DIGGING DEEPER

The work in Dajarra has also started to grow in new directions. Community members have begun exploring some of their non-Aboriginal heritage, revealing rich new facets of cultural identity and ways of engaging with other communities around the world. Chinese, Afghan, Scottish, Irish and English people have each had a significant impact on the rich cultural makeup of the Dajarra community, challenging some of the cultural stereotypes.

One example has come from tracing Dajarra's links to Tobermory, a small township on the wind-swept Scottish western Hebrides Island of Mull. You would scarcely find two more geographically different places than Tobermory in Scotland and its namesake on the Georgina River. Yet the displacements of indigenous people parallel each other in so many ways. In the 1850s, Mull was one of the last areas of subsistence farming or crofting. The indigenous population—the Muileach—fought English landowners in the crofting wars. Deciding it was more profitable to run sheep than allow the Muileach to continue to live and work on Mull, the survivors were shipped to far-flung corners of the world including Canada and Australia. Some ended up at Urandangie, eventually setting up a cattle station which they named Tobermory to the south on the Georgina River. Several Waluwarra families lived and worked around Tobermory Station prior to coming into Dajarra. Some of the European family names in Dajarra can be found in Mull genealogies, and several other Mull place names have been taken up by nearby stations. The community is in the planning stages of a series of exchanges with the Mull Museum.

Lloyd Punch hoists the camera while he, Beverley Sam and David Punch do some video work at one of their favorite locations: the Dajarra wrecking yard. © Feral Arts and Dajarra Jimberella Coop, 1997.

Oral- and community-history projects enable communities to explore beneath the surface of cultural stereotypes to get a better understanding of the actual cultural impacts of colonial and global development. These stories uncover many examples of culturally destructive—even genocidal—engagements. But they also reveal stories of partnership and sharing that have led to growth and development. Sharing and exchange through trade is fundamental to cultural development and economic sustainability. There are many examples predating the arrival of Europeans in Australia of trade and cultural exchange between Aboriginal people and other cultures—relationships based on mutual respect and sharing.[15] Colonization on the other hand reflects an expansionist ethic and a fundamental lack of respect for other cultures. Unfortunately, negative colonial values have become synonymous with broader global economic development. In responding to globalization, we need to be careful to remember that cultures are dynamic and evolving, not fixed or static. A significant part of cultural growth derives from sharing and exchange. Does simply opposing globalization run the risk of contributing to social and economic isolation and cultural stagnation?

[15] One example of direct relevance to members of the Dajarra community is the centuries-old relationship of trade and exchange between the Yanyuwa people of northern Australia and the Macassans of Celebes (present day Indonesia). In 1907 the Australian government outlawed these exchanges. See geography.anu.edu.au/people/richard_baker/tek.html.

PLACEWORKS

A significant body of oral- and community-history material has been generated through the community cultural development program in Dajarra. This material includes photos, videos, songs, interviews, paintings, T-shirts, digital images and documents, all of which belong to the Dajarra community. Typically this material might provide the research basis for a documentary video, a photographic exhibit or a publication, as had been the case in some of our earlier work. But in partnership with the Dajarra community we have started looking beyond a research-production-exhibition-distribution model to engage with some other questions. How should this material be managed and utilized to be of the greatest community benefit now and into the future? Where should it be kept? How might it be used and by whom? Who are the audiences for the works produced? What can be shared with other places and people, and what needs to remain as family or community access only? What cultural and community protocols need to be considered?

Over the last few years we have begun to explore the use of new digital technologies in finding new ways of responding to these challenges. Working closely with the Dajarra community we have developed a prototype of a software program—Placeworks—as a new CCD tool. The Placeworks software operates as a digital museum or "keeping place" for personal and community histories. It uses maps of local places to interface with database material gathered through the oral- and community-history program. Placeworks enables users to store and manage cultural- and social-history materials through a computer workstation. The database is initially being developed for use on a local computer network and shared within the Dajarra community. In the next stage, an online version hosted on the Internet will allow the community to share work with other places. Placeworks is being tested and further developed as part of the current CCD program in Dajarra and through a parallel program in South Brisbane.

One of the main uses of the current Placeworks prototype is to scan and catalogue personal and family photographs. Photos are valuable commodities and are greatly treasured. Copying photos is expensive and the CCD program provides community access to digital scanning and printing equipment through a small media studio located in a converted storeroom in the community hall. Through this process people can get copies of their photos, learn new skills and, if they choose, contribute images to the Placeworks database. Another current project, Placestories, involves school children using scanners and digital cameras to work with community elders to involve them in contributing material to the Placeworks database. The project has been designed to combine young people's computer skills with the knowledge and experiences of older members of the community.

CULTURE AND TECHNOLOGY

The Placeworks software initiative continues to throw up a wide range of technical and cultural challenges. The software concentrates on putting control and management of this material firmly in the hands of the local community. Access to material is managed by a system of passwords so that personal material can be either shared or kept private, as required. One of the features being built into the software is the capacity for images of and references to particular individuals to be masked or removed from the database at any time to meet with cultural protocols. There are few precedents for the use of digital media in these contexts and there are lots of mistakes to be made, so we work as carefully as possible. The key to success is ensuring that the local community guides the process.

For many in the Dajarra community, involvement in Placeworks is one of their first experiences of computers and the Internet, so a big part of the CCD program is about skills development and building a resource base. Much of the training is informal as people learn how to use the Placeworks prototype and to scan and print images, use software programs and produce multimedia materials including CD-ROMs, digital videos and digital prints. A local "Placeworker," working as part of the CCD program, runs the studio and access facilities throughout the year. That worker and a number of other community members are scheduled to take part in more focused training and skills development, enabling them to operate equipment and to assist other people in the community. The aim over the next three years of the program is to put in place the skills and resources to enable the program in Dajarra to operate independently of Feral Arts.

Feral Arts' four-week CCD workshop program is structured loosely. People choose when and how they want to be involved. People often work in small groups, sharing new skills and information. As always, the learning process is a two-way street. It is only through developing and trying out new tools like Placeworks that we get to understand what works and what does not—what new features might be useful and which things are less relevant. This information feeds back to the software-development team based in Brisbane to revise and update the prototype.

Beyond its role as a digital museum, Placeworks aims to improve the Dajarra community's capacity to be an active player in cultural and economic development projects. The program provides a mechanism for the local community to engage in the planning and development processes of a project from the outset. The community history being assembled online provides a base of knowledge to inform governments, station owners, mining projects and others about development issues. Over time the history of layers of association will be gathered. The aim is that when projects like Phosphate Hill are on the drawing board, the community will be in a position to play a more effective role in negotiating with the development process to maximize the local benefits and minimize negative cultural, social and environmental impacts. The goal once Placeworks is fully developed is to make the software available to other communities nationally and internationally, developing online networks and information-sharing mechanisms.

The point is that the community cultural development program in Dajarra is not just about cultural survival—it is also about cultural growth and engaging with the complex challenges posed by global development. The community is responding positively to the impact of displacement and building a platform for future partnership and collaboration. Local knowledge is a valuable asset —and if we are not careful, a nonrenewable resource! As Australian governments work to rebuild their economies around the new centerpieces of knowledge and technology, it is important to create opportunities to bring this knowledge to bear on the planning stages of development projects through real partnerships, not just through add-on consultations.

WHAT ABOUT THE WATER?

A couple of weeks into the monthlong 2001 program, the Dajarra community's letter to the media about water-supply problems is starting to get some results. A daylong meeting of key government department representatives has been called to address a long list of issues and do some planning for the future. Big numbers of government workers have made the two-hour trip from their offices in Mt. Isa (the northwest region's main town) to the Dajarra community hall.

At the end of the meeting there are some positive signs. Following their involvement in the meeting, WMC Ltd. is playing a role in a joint government, community and corporate strategy to dig a new bore and fix the community's water supply. They are also involved in another initiative to get a much-needed kidney dialysis machine for the region—a resource the community has been requesting for a long time.

The community's involvement with WMC and the Phosphate Hill Project is still in its early stages. These are small steps, and people still harbor concerns about the mine's environmental impact. No one is taking anything for granted, but they may provide the basis to navigate a strong relationship in the future.

EXPERTS IN GLOBALIZATION?

The challenges facing the small, isolated community of Dajarra are just one example of the complex mix of opportunities and threats facing communities across the planet. Even state and national governments do not always have the political muscle to effectively oppose global development, especially in the prevailing economic rationalist climate. CCD practitioners need to add some new strings to the bow; protesting is important, but by itself it is not enough. We need to be much smarter in our approach—building partnerships, informing change and guiding development. We need to improve our skills as go-betweens and negotiators. Perhaps as well as being expert protesters, CCD practitioners should become experts in development, providing examples to governments and the corporate sector of how development projects can be done better.

CCD IN AUSTRALIA

The program in Dajarra is only one example of community cultural development in Australia. The sector is remarkably diverse: some suggest there are as many types of practice as there are practitioners. So what is the state of the community cultural development sector in Australia? Where has it come from and where is it headed? How ready are we to take up the challenges posed by processes like globalization and to engage more effectively in the complex dynamics generated in the intersection of the government and corporate sectors? Can we become experts in development and play an appropriate role in emerging international CCD networks?

The remainder of this essay will briefly explore these questions from our perspective and experience at Feral Arts. We will draw primarily from the debate at a national community cultural development symposium we ran in 1998. The symposium brought together 40 of the country's leading practitioners to discuss the past, present and future of community cultural development in Australia. Facilitator Anne Dunn described the day in these terms:

> Where have we been, what is our history and, therefore, what can we create
> as a future for the work that we do—to really challenge the notion of
> the place of our work in the world? What are we doing, why do we do it,
> why is it important?[16]

[16] Anne Dunn, "Symposium" PDF, *They Shoot Ferals Don't They?* CD-ROM (Brisbane: Feral Arts, 1999), p. 9. Available at www.feralarts.com.au /home.htm.

The aim was to develop an agenda for broader debate in the sector. A number of the issues raised through those discussions may have general currency.

A NOTE ON TERMINOLOGY

In 1987 the Australian federal government's arts-funding agency undertook a shift from "community arts" to "community cultural development." Although (as we will outline) this was more than a simple name change, in broad terms the people, policies and programs that made up the community arts sector are the same as those in the community cultural development sector.

GOVERNMENT SUPPORT—A SNAPSHOT

Arts and cultural funding in Australia managed somehow to survive the dark years of economic rationalism. One of the big achievements has been the continuity of federal government support for community arts and community cultural development for nearly 30 years. During that time the sector in Australia has come a long way, but it has been a difficult journey. More than once it has had to fight for its survival and contend with attacks— some coming from within the arts industry. Through these experiences the sector has grown stronger, more confident and better able to articulate its expertise and significance to the broader community.

Community cultural development projects involve collaborations with a wide range of government and nongovernment sectors, responding to the cultural needs and interests of diverse communities. The CCD sector has developed unique expertise in partnerships and cross-sector approaches. It is firmly embedded in the infrastructure of the Australian arts industry and has been especially successful at influencing the policy and programs of other sectors of government such as health, social services and social planning, as well as other sectors within the arts and cultural industry. The continuity of support for CCD provides the sector with an opportunity to look at patterns in its development.

Community cultural development now operates in all levels of government (federal, state and local). The federal funding body—the Community Cultural Development Board (CCDB) of the Australia Council (the federal government's arts-funding and advisory body) has been especially important to the sector's development, providing much of the policy- and program-development impetus. Like the other boards of the Australia Council, the CCDB is a committee of industry peers drawn from each state. Its key aim is to enable communities to advance their artistic and social aspirations by working closely with professional artists.[17] It provides operational and project funding to artists and organizations across the country under a number of categories and priority areas, including strategic partnerships, professional development, fellowships, community environment art and design, critical debate, and presentation and promotion. The CCDB also works in partnership with the community cultural development sector to deliver special projects in response to particular needs, for example, national conferences, industry publications, training programs and a national Web site project, currently under development. It provides the sector with a national overview, enabling it to set strategic directions and develop responses to emerging opportunities within the cultural industries and beyond. In the longer term, the CCDB is working toward the full integration of community cultural development into Australia's environmental, economic and social sectors. It promotes the role of the sector in research and development activity, and encourages innovation and experimentation.

[17] *Support for the Arts Handbook* (Sydney: Australia Council, 2001), p. 31.

On a state government level, Arts Queensland (the Queensland government's arts and cultural funding agency) also provides strong support for community cultural development. Feral Arts, for example, receives joint operational support from both Arts Queensland and the CCDB. There is no specific Queensland policy or program relating to community cultural development, but a wide range of CCD work is supported through its existing funding mechanisms. Arts Queensland's Regional Arts Development Fund (RADF) provides arts and cultural funding to communities through partnership with local governments across the state. RADF is a good example of a strategic approach to regional cultural development grounded in the CCD principles of local control and self-determination, with local committees making decisions on how grants are allocated. Community cultural development projects are also supported through a range of non-arts government departments typically working in partnership with arts and cultural funding programs.

Relations between governments and the community and corporate sectors in Australia are on the move. Governments are looking to refocus economies around knowledge, research and information technologies.[18] The community sector (or nongovernment, civil sector) is being heralded as the new lifeblood of experimentation and innovation. Think tanks on both the right and left of politics are promoting the community sector as the core of new approaches to governance and service delivery. These new models aim to use the expertise of nongovernment community agencies in the vital middle ground between government and corporate sectors. They advocate a move away from centralized services toward locally determined models.[19] This situation represents an opportunity for the community cultural development. But how prepared is the sector to take advantage?

[18] A recent example is Labor's Knowledge Nation platform, developed for the 2001 federal election. See www.alp.org.au/kn/.

[19] Mark Latham and Peter Botsman, *The Enabling State* (Sydney: Pluto Press, 2001), pp. 3–5.

[20] Andrea Hull in *Meanjin*, Iss. 3 (Brisbane: University of Queensland Press, 1983), pp. 317–320.

DEFINITIONS

Debates around definitions of community arts and community cultural development have been part of the sector since its inception. In the broadest terms there are two camps: those calling for clearer guidelines and definitions to make it easier to work in partnerships, promote the sector and build its identity; and those advocating broad, inclusive statements of principle to ensure the sector stays flexible, dynamic and relevant. Reflecting on her time as head of Australia Council's Community Arts Committee in the early 1970s (a predecessor to the Community Cultural Development Board), Andrea Hull discussed their refusal to get involved in the "bind of definition":

> The Community Arts Committee agreed that a single definition of community arts could not be sustained, that its program should be influential over a wide spectrum of arts activities. The Board has tried to be open and flexible. It takes the line that it is not the writer of prescriptions for the arts.[20]

The openness and breadth of the earliest funding guidelines meant an extraordinary range of cultural organizations and artists were attracted to the new fund, and accepted as community artists. Lacking the history of other arts-funding categories, the term "community arts" in effect came to describe whatever was funded as community arts. The Community Arts Committee also proved a convenient mechanism for dealing with the bits and pieces that didn't fit anywhere else in the arts-funding structure. This cumulative open-ended approach to policy development set a pattern for the future and the breadth of the sector continued to expand. For three decades the range of practice included under the umbrella of Community Arts and Community Cultural Development has continued to grow.

Has it become too broad? Speaking at a national CCD symposium, Australian practitioner, researcher and theorist Deirdre Williams expressed concerns about the amorphous nature of the practice:

> I think we need to do some work in identifying what it is that our leaders are going to deliver, and with whom. We're talking about "the work"—well I don't know what it is. I don't know whether we're making art or whether we're making happy communities or whether we're making very powerful people who were once powerless or whether we're designing malls? I think that's really, really important if we're talking about community cultural development, because what we produce is going to directly relate to who's going to invest in us. If we don't know what it is that we can deliver, then we don't really know who we can go and sell it to, or even on whose behalf we're selling it.[21]

The diversity, adaptability and individuality of the sector and its practitioners are valuable assets. They ensure the practice stays relevant, flexible and engaged. But does the breadth of the sector come at a price? Does it also present an obstacle to its development, making it harder to promote the work and build our public identity and professional status to enable sustainable and productive partnerships?

In "Creative Community: The Art of Cultural Development" (the predecessor to this volume), Adams and Goldbard identified a number of characteristics of community cultural development in the United States. They describe a field that appears:

> …atomized and dispersed, with no clear identity as a profession. Constantly reinventing arguments to convince funders of the legitimacy of their efforts, constantly reframing their work to fit the guidelines of social service or conventional arts-discipline funders…[22]

Adams and Goldbard attribute this situation to the lack of infrastructure that could legitimate community cultural development as a profession. But despite the Australian sector's more developed infrastructure and continuity of support, remarkably similar concerns are commonly articulated. Introducing the Australia Council's 1997 publication "Not a Puppet," showcasing Australian CCD, former CCDF chair Lex Marinos related:

> What emerges is the question of identity, of defining just exactly what the essence of CCD is. In a field where collaboration is the key and where partnerships are made between all manner of arts and non-arts organizations, it is important to distinguish the role of CCD relative to other organizations. The boundaries of CCD are wide but there are limits; it is only by maintaining focus and direction that the field can continue to deliver.[23]

These experiences suggest that the challenge of definition and building an identity may also be central to the work of emerging international networks.

21 Deirdre Williams, "Symposium" PDF, *They Shoot Ferals Don't They?* CD-ROM, op. cit., p. 17.

22 Adams and Goldbard, *Creative Community*, op. cit., p. 4.

23 Lex Marinos in *Not a Puppet*, Marian Reid, ed. (Sydney: Australia Council, 1997), p. 7.

[24] Eve Stafford, "Symposium" PDF, *They Shoot Ferals Don't They?* CD-ROM, op. cit., p. 8.

[25] Gay Hawkins, *From Nimbin to Mardi Gras* (Sydney: Allen and Unwin, 1993), p. 53.

[26] Community Arts Board 1986 policy statements, quoted in Gay Hawkins, ibid., p. 75.

CCD practitioner Eve Stafford has identified the cyclic nature of the sector's development in Australia. She describes the different phases in the cycle: moments of unity followed by long periods working in disparate settings at the edges of cultural practice.[24] Stafford's analysis suggests that after a time, the sector gets a bit isolated. It needs to come together to catch its breath, compare notes and check its bearings before again heading off in myriad directions. The sector has shown itself to be capable of presenting a strong and unified identity, but those moments of unity have tended to emerge only when the sector is under attack. The 1976 McKinsey Report (the result of a major national inquiry into arts funding) recommended devolution of community arts funding, posing a threat to the sector. A national conference held in early 1977 initiated a major campaign to defend community arts. Gay Hawkins relates:

> The campaign also resulted in new categories. The "community arts movement" was the most significant because it effectively blurred the boundaries between the bureaucrats, whose job it was to administer community arts grants, and the recipients of this money.... This alliance was strategic; it highlighted the complex power relations between the funders and the funded. The illusion that all power lay in the hands of the state or bureaucrats was quickly shattered.[25]

Ten years later another major federal arts-funding inquiry—the McLeay Report (1986)—was released, again challenging the sector. Once again it led to a united campaign and a national conference, heralding a significant refocusing of the sector in the change from community arts to community cultural development. In the broadest terms, this transition reflects a shift from the aim of the democratization of culture (under community arts) to one of cultural democracy (under community cultural development). Policy statements released in the lead-up to the changeover related:

> Community Arts is not a tool for increasing arts appreciation, audiences or purchases of arts products. These may be by-products of a community arts program. But it is a community's active intervention in its own cultural destiny, not a way to increase consumption of other people's cultures.[26]

In the 15 years since the transition to community cultural development, the sector has continued to grow but its status has remained marginal. The powerful alliance between funder and funded, which seems to be a key to the sector's health and vitality, has proved unsustainable beyond times of direct external threat. Outside these moments of crisis, practitioners have demonstrated a clear preference for getting on with their main priority— working with communities. Understandably, policymakers and program managers have been reluctant to intervene. But this leaves the sector vulnerable because the work is hard to categorize, hard to see and hard to quantify.

Descriptions of community cultural development are often grounded in the language of empowerment. There is a pervasive notion that good practice is largely invisible. A successful project is deemed one in which the community "owns" the outcomes. Credit passes to participants and the role of CCD moves into the background. This paternalistic framework dominates depictions of community cultural development practice and is in need of revision. Relationships need to be recast into ones of partnership and exchange, both between practitioner and community and practitioner and funder.

There is a tension between empowerment-based approaches and the sector's own needs to promote its identity and secure its future. If the field is to grow, it needs to become more visible and more accountable. It needs to own its work and the outcomes (good and bad) in a public way. The sector needs to reflect on its failures as much as it promotes its successes. This requires leadership from experienced practitioners and policymakers.

The globalization issue provides the sector with an opportunity to promote its value and build its identity without limiting its scope through prescriptive guidelines and definitions. By sharing expertise and drawing together examples of practice from around the country and around the world, the sector could present a diverse but connected body of work. The CCD sector needs to further develop communication networks and information-sharing mechanisms to ensure that communities are better prepared for engaging with the processes of global development. The sector needs to instill respect for place and indigenous cultures, and to link local knowledge and expertise with models for environmentally and culturally sustainable growth and development.

But before this, the sector may need to rethink its stance on globalization, a stance we feel is limited by its blanket opposition. Sometimes circumstances will require us to protest and march in the streets, but we might just as easily be required to act as a go-between and work in partnership with governments and corporations. Now we need to talk about how this should work: How should community cultural development respond to globalization? What is our role and what principles should guide our responses?

POSTSCRIPT

Following the September 11 terrorist attack on the United States and heightened security concerns, the CHOGM meeting in Brisbane was postponed and rescheduled for 2002. The planned protest actions evolved into a march for peace, dissolving—at least for the time being—many of the factional battles previously in evidence. There is no doubt that this dramatic turn in international relations has made the goal of establishing an international community cultural development network even more vital.

12

The General Assembly
meets in the New York
headquarters of the United
Nations, the focal point
of much international
discussion of cultural
issues and cultural policy.

Culturelink
Ul. Lj. F. Vukotinovica 2
P.O. Box 303
10000 Zagreb, Croatia
Telephone: (385 1) 48-26-522
Fax: (385 1) 48-28-361
E-mail: Culturelink@irmo.hr
Web site: www.culturelink.org

Unlike most of the authors represented here, **Nina Obuljen** is not a community cultural development practitioner or theorist per se, although the biography she shared with fellow participants has something in common with several of the practitioners, describing how her early training as a conventional artist opened out into social concerns:

I graduated both from the Academy of Music (violin) and the Faculty of Arts at the University of Zagreb. When the aggression on my country and particularly on my hometown Dubrovnik started, I left the violin to became active in a student organization that was trying to draw attention of the international community to the war in Croatia... We went on a hunger strike and were involved in many initiatives related to anti-war and humanitarian efforts... anyway, when the war was over, it was too late to go back to playing violin!

Through her past work at UNESCO and her current work with the Culturelink network, along with her post in the Culture and Communication Department of the Institute for International Relations in Zagreb, Nina has been actively involved with international cultural policymakers. She was welcomed to the conference as an ambassador from an international cultural-policy world that has not always been accessible to community cultural development practitioners. In this essay, she analyzes the current state of diplomatic relations between these sectors and suggests some ways to open channels of communication.

Community Cultural Development, Cultural Policy Networks and Culturelink

by Nina Obuljen

The May 2001 Community, Culture and Globalization conference held at the Rockefeller Study and Conference Center in Bellagio, Italy, gathered community cultural development (CCD) practitioners who—despite the fact that they come from different countries and continents, different political systems and different cultural settings, and that they are accustomed to expression through various art forms—all shared an amazing energy and belief in what they do. Their work is much more than merely a way of addressing art, culture or social issues; it is a way of life. It is probably this personal touch that makes community cultural development so intriguing. These practitioners have a visible impact on their communities, and the response to their work is somehow stronger than what is usually received as feedback from any mainstream artistic activity. This personal experience, instead of an adherence to specific literature or methodology, will guide my examination of certain aspects of this field.

I decided to write about community cultural development and networking for two reasons. The first is that I work for Culturelink, a Network of Networks for Research and Cooperation in Cultural Development, so I would like to use Culturelink as a reference point for analyzing the scope of international cooperation and different aspects of cultural policy relevant to community cultural development.

The second reason is the fact that most participants at the recent Bellagio conference expressed their interest both in becoming more involved in networking and influencing cultural policymakers to recognize and support CCD. I would like to explore some of the potentials and constraints that membership in a network can bring to individuals and institutions in the field of community cultural development.

Culturelink was established with the support of the United Nations Educational, Scientific and Cultural Organization (UNESCO) and the Council of Europe in 1989. The focal point of the Culturelink network is in its headquarters at the Institute for International Relations in Zagreb, Croatia. It gathers together about 1,000 networks and institutions from approximately 100 countries in all parts of the world that deal with cultural development, cultural policies and cooperation. The aim of this network is to strengthen communication among its members; to collect, process and disseminate information on worldwide cultural development, cultural life and policies; and to encourage regional, interregional and international joint research projects and cultural cooperation. Besides research, Culturelink network activities include development of the Cultural Development Data Bank and the publication of the *Culturelink* review, Culturelink Directory Series and Culturelink Joint Publication Series. Most Culturelink information, including the contents of the *Culturelink* review, is accessible free of charge through the Culturelink Web site. In effect, the entire space of the Culturelink network is open; this is important, since it means that the network can broaden the fields covered and reach new groups of users and readers without expanding the membership.

CULTURAL POLICES AND COMMUNITY CULTURAL DEVELOPMENT

Comparative cultural-policy research and assistance in the adjustment of cultural policies to the demands of the modern age are goals guiding Culturelink in many ways. It would be impossible to talk about Culturelink without mentioning the Database on Cultural Policies. Work on comparative research in the field of cultural policies started in 1991 when the Culturelink research team, together with UNESCO, carried out the joint project Guide to the Current State and Trends in Cultural Policy and Life in UNESCO Member States, dealing with 160 UNESCO member states. Some country profiles drafted for the purpose of that project have been updated, starting in 1996, and can be found on the Culturelink Web site (www.culturelink.org). Textual, referral and bibliographical data covers national cultural-policy issues, such as administrative structures, financial and legislation schemes, cultural industries, sectoral activities and so on.

It is evident that the position of the community cultural development field within national cultural policies remains ambiguous. In Chapter One of "Creative Community: The Art of Cultural Development," the authors highlighted one of the major problems in approaching this field in the United States: "Because it employs the same art forms as conventional arts disciplines (e.g., dance, painting, film), work in the field has mostly been treated as a marginal manifestation of mainstream arts activities… ."[1] Similar obstacles are sometimes found if we compare the position of community cultural activities within different national cultural policies. In the publication "The Governance of Culture, Approaches to Integrated Cultural Planning and Policies," Anthony Everitt examines new ways of integrating culture into the fabric of public administration in Europe, and offers some observations regarding the perception of culture and social services in the eyes of government policymakers:

[1] Adams and Goldbard, *Creative Community,* op. cit., p. 4.

[2] Anthony Everitt, *The Governance of Culture: Approaches to Integrated Cultural Planning and Policies,* Cultural Policies Research and Development Unit, Policy Note No. 5 (Strasbourg: Council of Europe Publishing, 1999), p. 16.

> In the social services, many public sector institutions and voluntary agencies are making use of the arts to deliver their policies. Thus prisons find that creativity is an effective tool of rehabilitation. Hospitals are beginning to acknowledge that performing arts programs and displays of visual arts in wards and corridors have a good effect on morale and on patient anxiety. Charitable organizations concerned with the care of the old and elderly or with the young devote substantial resources to artistic activity of all kinds. Much of this work is scarcely visible to the outside world and policy makers in government accord it low priority.[2]

Besides this, the fact remains that each country has differing divisions of responsibility in regards to culture, and, in most cases, cultural polices still concentrate more on mainstream art, financing, legislation and cultural budgets, rather than on other forms of artistic expression, intersectoral projects with cultural dimensions and the impact of new trends and technologies on cultural development. Still, it is important to stress that a number of countries have maintained some programs of support focused specifically on community cultural development, especially in the 1970s and '80s, sometimes under the rubrics of "community arts" (as in the United Kingdom) or *animation socio-culturelle* (in Francophone countries). Recent attention to privatization in cultural policymaking circles has caused many of these programs to be cut back, except in countries like Australia, where support continues to flow to a field known explicitly as "community cultural development."

For the past 25 years, at the international level, UNESCO, together with other international organizations, researchers and academics, has made efforts to promote the acknowledgment of culture as a *conditio sine qua non* of endogenous, compatible and balanced development. International conferences in Accra (1975) and Mexico City (1982), followed by "Our Creative Diversity," the 1995 report of the World Decade for Cultural Development, introduced new approaches and mobilized governments in making visible steps to redesign cultural policies through the establishment of links with other sectors. The Intergovernmental Conference on Cultural Polices for Development in Stockholm in 1998 was conceived to address some of these new challenges and help UNESCO member states in designing public policies that recognize the central role of culture in development. The Action Plan on Cultural Policies for Development adopted at this conference recommends that states adopt several policy objectives, including efforts to make cultural policy a key component of development strategy and to promote creativity and participation in cultural life.[3]

But how can the position of community cultural development be improved if it is frequently not even mentioned in cultural policy? As Simon Mundy states, even if a country decides not to have cultural policy, it has already formulated its cultural policy.[4] The same could be said of community cultural development. Although it may not be articulated within state policy, it remains an issue: it exists, and there are some general rules that need to be applied.

One of the first dilemmas is whether there is a way to ensure continuous support from institutions without making community cultural development projects inappropriately institutionalized. Community cultural development organizations share a problem also faced by most nongovernmental organizations (NGOs) when seeking funds from public or private funding bodies. Even when funds are available for their work, filling out the application forms and preparing project documentation requires a great deal of professional time. This is done simply to gain consideration for grants, with no guarantee that the project will receive funding. And even the success of a project does not guarantee continuous financing. As a result, CCD workers are in a state of constant fear that their funding will not be renewed, representing a severe problem in securing the necessary work space and entering into agreements with individuals whose cooperation is required.

Community-based activities, even if designated as cultural, have a much wider scope then conventional forms of cultural expression. It is therefore understandable that their development, and the support offered, must be expanded beyond the usual borders of cultural policy. Community cultural development's content is commonly wider than the simple understanding of culture, regardless of whether it is theater in prisons, dance with the elderly, AIDS-awareness projects or activities for street children. In this sense, support for community cultural development activities reflects the general orientation of cultural policy and is closely connected to the importance of social-inclusion issues. In the introduction to the *Culturelink* dossier "Social Cohesion and Culture: Contrasting Some European and Canadian Approaches and Experiences,"[5] Sanjin Dragojevic argues that there are great differences between Canadian and European cultural policies in their approaches to the position of social

[3] Final Report of the Intergovernmental Conference on Cultural Policies for Development (Paris: UNESCO, 1998).

[4] Simon Mundy, "Requirements for a Sustainable Cultural Policy in Western Europe, North America and Australasia," *European Perspectives on Cultural Policy* (Paris: UNESCO, 2001), p. 61.

[5] *Culturelink*, No. 33. p. 127.

cohesion. The Canadian approach regards these issues as a central part of its cultural policy, whereas for most countries in Europe, this is not considered to be a priority. Repositioning community cultural development in cultural policy could require shifting from supporting exclusively professional art to more cohesion-directed cultural policy. In some places, this would mean asking officials to consider values and projects outside the official, professional cultural sector.

Another important issue where community cultural development workers depend on public policies is the status of the artist working in community-based art institutions. The position of experts in this field differs considerably from one country to another. If the field is not recognized, then policymakers cannot see them as working in that non-existent field. But even without official recognition, CCD practitioners do exist, and they do work. They sometimes teach at universities or schools, they may run NGOs or small businesses, they can be employed by local governments or survive as independent artists. Some are even recognized as artists working for community-based projects. Recognition and status in the community can affect the way an organization operates and the funds that it receives.

One approach that could improve the place community cultural development initiatives occupy among priorities in public policies is to regard culture as a right and not a privilege, as asserted in a UNESCO report:

> Considerable progress has been made in the last few decades in the promotion of cultural democracy and the protection of human rights. Many individuals and communities throughout the world, particularly those belonging to minority groups or who are socially marginalized, are still excluded from the cultural life of their societies. Cultural rights are now recognized as belonging to a more recent generation of human rights. The core cultural right is that of each person to participate fully in cultural life. All such rights still need clearer definition, however. They should naturally be incorporated into the policy framework. Their legal status at the international and national level should be strengthened through participatory negotiation between state agencies and diverse groups (indigenous peoples, minority groups, migrants) so that each group can contribute to the formulation of policies for their understanding, respect and acceptance.[6]

[6] Our Creative Diversity, Report of the World Commission on Culture and Development (Paris: UNESCO, second revised edition, 1996), p. 240.

In this context, community cultural development becomes one of the most important instruments in achieving these rights, because it is more flexible. It mobilizes people and invites them to participate in the creation process.

These are only a few examples of issues that arise from questioning the relationship between cultural policies and community-based activities. Supporters need to establish and lobby through networks to achieve a better position for community cultural development. As will be seen from my findings in the next section, there is obviously a great deal of space for improvement here, requiring continuous international cooperation and communication among those interested in this field. Still, although the strategy of cultural development can be supported through global networks, it will not be successful unless true partnerships between all sectors at national levels become functional. There are many missing elements that need to be recognized and dealt with to support a process of public-policy transformation and the creation of more space for community-based cultural activities.

NETWORKING AND THE ROLE OF CULTURAL NETWORKS

The word network is very widely used in everyday life—there are financial networks, television networks or intellectual networks. It is a modern phenomenon, yet it is difficult to find any segment of human activity that has not been affected by some form of networking.

The cultural community has also responded to these trends, and in Europe alone there are already more than 500 cultural networks.[7] Regardless of their differing aims, structures or means of operation, the role that cultural and artistic networks play in today's world is becoming more important. Networks provide channels for effective and timely cooperation, enable an exchange of information between members, stimulate dialogue and help in setting up joint projects or coproductions. Networks create links between institutions or individuals and, importantly, they respond to the specific needs of their members. Networks also provide opportunities for cooperation across national, disciplinary or sectoral boundaries. In today's world, where there is so much information accessible to so many people, 24 hours a day, networks also serve as channels for transmitting information most useful to specific users in particular fields.

There are at least five principal organizational characteristics of a network.[8] Networks are based on interpersonal relations, informal in character, and are multidirectional rather than hierarchic in their nature. Networks are subject to internal self-regulation and have an evolving and open character. Interestingly, these characteristics are also typical of community-based creative activities.

Networking, as one of the consequences of technological development, influences and transforms traditional methods of communication within communities:

> The network model of communication, and with it the new nature of
> spatial relations, is rapidly changing the locus of learning, leisure and cultural
> activities. It is now possible for many to pursue a wide range of activities
> from home. Without leaving our desk we can browse art collections of
> faraway museums, enjoy the pleasure of vicarious tourism, engage in a

[7] Milena Sesic-Dragievicevic, "Introduction," *European Cultural Networks,* Dimitrije Vujadinovic, ed. (Belgrade: Balkankult, 2001), p. 5.

[8] *La Mise en Réseau des Cultures —Le Rôle des Réseaux Culturels Européens,* Edition du Conseil d'Europe (Strasbourg: Council of Europe, 1999), pp. 29–30.

distance learning course, and conduct business transactions. Conversely, we can easily shop in a museum, have lunch in a bookstore, attend art exhibitions in shopping centers and surf the Internet from the hall of an airport. This disembedding of social networks from geographical and spatial places is transforming the nature of public spaces in contemporary society. With this transformation comes a radical change in the role of traditional urban space, which is acquiring new and diverse functions.[9]

[9]Editorial, "New Media, Urban Spaces & Social Inclusion," *Interchanges*, Newsletter of the Centre for Creative Communities, Iss. 21 (London, March 2000), p. 1.

For this publication, I analyzed the content of the quarterly *Culturelink* review for the past five years to discover the extent to which community cultural development work is present in this network, what kind of information is being shared and to whom this information is aimed. My search was not limited to only the explicit notion of community cultural development, because there are several terms covering similar areas and types of activities, such as "arts and civil society," "arts and education" or "assistance to NGOs." To better understand the context, it is important to remember that in 1989 when it was launched, the idea of a "network of networks" had a much different meaning than today when there are so many individuals and institutions exchanging information through the Internet. The initial goal of Culturelink was to serve as a clearinghouse and a place for exchanging information in the field of culture and development without specializing in any particular segment of research, theory or practice.

CULTURELINK REVIEW

The format of the *Culturelink* review has remained relatively consistent over the years, including information about networking; research and programs; news from UNESCO and the Council of Europe; reports from and announcements of conferences and meetings; information about documentation and new publications; and a dossier dedicated to specific topics related to cultural development.

My overview of the content demonstrated that the network disseminated a great deal of information for those interested in different aspects of cultural development, not only to researchers in the field of cultural policies or mainstream artists and art institutions. In addition to Culturelink members, other sources of information include international organizations, government agencies, research institutions and individual experts. However, the Culturelink membership includes very few institutions or individuals devoted to community-based work, which surely constrains the position of community cultural development projects and activities within the network.

One explanation is that mainstream art institutions, international organizations and research institutions are often able to devote substantial money and human resources to promoting their work, with the result that they are dominant as the most visible actors on the scene. In contrast, information about CCD events or projects—without this type of access to resources—is often less visible within communities as within a broader international context. Another explanation must take into account Culturelink's outreach. While trying to preserve its image as a network of networks, it does not express any preference for certain types of organizations. One of the challenges of the Culturelink network, as stated by the network coordinator Biserka Cvjeticanin,[10] is to maintain a heterogeneous network. Culturelink brings together societies and individuals from diverse cultural backgrounds. It embraces different institutions, universities, research institutions, ministries, cultural centers and NGOs, as well as different professions. Therefore it is difficult for such a network to have higher representation of specific cultural activities, such as community cultural development.

[10]Biserka Cvjeticanin, "La Mise en Réseau des Cultures et les Défis de Culturelink," *Dynamics of Communication and Cultural Exchange*, Proceedings of the First World Culturelink Conference, B.Cvjeticanin, ed. (Zagreb: IRMO, 1996), p. 315.

It is not possible to give a simple answer to the question of whether the presence of community cultural development projects within the Culturelink network was satisfactory. Information exists, it appears regularly and in different formats, but it is surely not dominant when assessing the content of the review. The content of *Culturelink* has always depended more on the contributions received from its members than on some strict concept reflecting the specific interests of its host institution, the Institute for International Relations in Zagreb, or principal partners, such as UNESCO or the Council of Europe. If Culturelink is not doing all it can to reach CCD practitioners, the question remains whether there is interest within the CCD field to be more present in this network and what type of information being shared through the network can be relevant for this field.

The *Culturelink* review has featured a range of national networks or umbrella organizations of use to CCD practitioners. There are numerous organizations that gather NGOs and representatives of civil society where CCD organizations can find support for their work. For instance, in one of its earlier issues (No. 19, p. 13), *Culturelink* presented the Canadian Artists Network: Black Artists in Action, a national multidisciplinary organization of professional artists, cultural workers, curators, art educators and art enthusiasts committed to developing public awareness and appreciation for excellence in "Black art" and promoting African-Canadian artists at home and throughout the world. CCD practitioners might also be interested in some of the networks based on common language—be it between countries with the same official tongue or within communities where a minority uses a specific language. One example (No. 32, p. 8) is ACEP, the Association for Cooperation between Peoples, which gathers Portuguese-speaking NGOs from Portugal, Brazil, Guinea-Bissau, Cape Verde, São Tomé, Angola, Mozambique and East Timor. It offers assistance to organizations that share common objectives in sustainable development, human rights or fighting exclusion.

The search for funds remains one of the most important issues for every organization or community-based association. *Culturelink* has devoted significant space to funding news, for example (No. 33, p. 25), the presentation of national funding bodies such as the National Arts Council of South Africa (NAC), a funding structure for the promotion of South African culture through the arts and free and creative expression. NAC includes a special program, Applying the Arts, with the aim of rekindling and supporting the union of the arts and artists as resources in the continuing process of community cultural development. Or a guide to European Union (EU) funding for NGOs—"Your Way Through the Labyrinth," reviewed in one of the latest issues of *Culturelink* (No. 32, p. 121)—offers practical information on how to draft an application, how to create a budget (the issues of cofunding and voluntary work are important here), how to manage a project and produce financial reports. It also gives information on funding outside the EU.

A special emphasis in Culturelink network activities is the promotion of joint research programs among its members. There is little information about research programs dealing exclusively with community cultural development, but there are many accounts of research projects covering aspects of cultural development and civil society or the position of NGOs and their role in achieving sustainable development. Special Issue 2000 (the most recent), entitled "Culture and Development vs. Cultural Development," presented several practical papers giving best-practice examples and others explaining more theoretical views of culture and development, showing how different concepts that arise in trying to elaborate these issues can be reconciled.

There are two types of training activities aimed at community cultural development workers that have been either described or announced in the review: the first involves practices, methodology and approaches relevant for specific art forms; the second is oriented more toward cultural management and financing.

Issue No. 28 (p. 28) contained information about the MA/Postgraduate Diploma Course on Theater for Development, a one-year program combining theory and practice of making theater with communities, together with a study of some developmental issues. In a recent issue (No. 33, p. 38) was an article about the program activities of the Institute for Culture and Development in South Africa, an interesting initiative to provide training and design curricula for cultural managers, leaders, officials, administrators and policymakers in cultural institutions including community arts centers. Culturelink also tries to publish as much information as possible on workshops and special training and, through its Web site and the Cultural Development Database, provides links to institutions that offer different forms of training.

Reviewed publications and books, articles (most often published in special issues or in dossiers at the end of each regular issue), reports from conferences and announcements of meetings contain critical information of interest to NGOs, community-based organizations and alternative art initiatives. *Culturelink* also publishes information about festivals, exhibitions, fairs or various gatherings of NGOs. The dossier in the latest issue of the review (No. 34, p. 119) presented four papers from a conference on the Role of the Arts in Processes of Social Change, focusing on the contribution of the arts and arts mediation within the processes of social change and on future policy strategies.

Culturelink also regularly presents the work of its members, their publications, projects and activities. For example, the Centre for Creative Communities (the former British-American Arts Association) advocates links between arts practice and cultural policy with the activities of other sectors, and its Web site (www.creativecommunities.org.uk) and *Interchanges* newsletter include information about meetings, conferences, projects and publications in the field of community cultural development. AMARC, the World Association of Community Radio Broadcasters (www.amarc.org), another Culturelink member, is an international organization that seeks to develop and promote community-oriented radio broadcasting as a viable and alternative model of communication and a tool for development, peace, justice and solidarity, and to facilitate cooperation and information exchange among community radio stations.

The Culturelink network embraces many other specialized networks that can use it to transmit information about their work to a more diverse public, as well as to attract new members and look for potential partners.

IN CONCLUSION

To change cultural policy and increase inclusion of the community cultural development field in cultural-policy debates, it is essential for CCD workers to be involved in networking. An interesting observation in relation to community-based creative artists appeared in an editorial in *Interchanges*: "Many such artists are ignorant of each other's work; they may have no affiliation with an arts organization and very often the mainstream arts organizations in their locality are not aware of the work that goes on."[11]

[11] Editorial, "Arts and Human Services," *Interchanges*, newsletter of the International Arts and Education Initiative (London, Nov. 1994), p. 1.

Networking is undeniably important for community cultural development theory and practice. The field needs recognition, but so do the people who are involved in it. Their work has to be appreciated and recognized, and the communities in which they operate have to ensure sustainable support for their work. Public policies, and especially cultural policies, should continue their transformation. Even if major shifts that would neglect mainstream art forms and institutions cannot realistically be expected, it is still important to lobby for the opening of new space and increased visibility and support to community-based activities.

Merely bringing together people who share the same interests and concerns is not enough to create an efficient network. We live in a world where there is so much information floating around and so many possibilities, but very little time. An examination of a day in the life of a person who is fighting for funds, recognition and support, but who also does actual, creative community work, leads to the inevitable question of whether there is any time left for networking.

Even if there is no time, there should be. Simply knowing there are other people doing similar "impossible things" could help overcome crises when an organization or individual is faced with a lack of funding or is denied support from the local community. Sharing information about best-practice examples and innovative ways to seek funding helps others who may be encountering similar problems as they attempt to launch new projects or sustain existing ones. Networking which aims to promote better dialogue with public and private grantmakers can help experts working in the field as well as policymakers.

Culturelink is committed to promoting such partnerships, and I hope that the activities described in this chapter can serve as interesting examples of the possibilities that are offered by this form of networking. Because of its specific nature, Culturelink can not and should not replace specialized networks already established around different themes or art practices used by various CCD organizations. But it can help in bridging gaps between mainstream institutions and community-based organizations, between policymakers and CCD practitioners. Through its information services (Web site, database on cultural development and cultural policy, and Culturelink publications), Culturelink can offer more information about specific challenges of community cultural development and, as described earlier, offer practical information about funding possibilities, research or training programs. One of the main ideas inspiring the Culturelink team during all these years has been *partnership*. In order to be able to dedicate additional space to this field, Culturelink depends on its partners—members as well as other organizations and individuals willing to share their experiences, best-practice examples or research projects.

Culturelink has always been committed to inspiring others in strengthening existing networks and setting up new ones. In that sense, this chapter represents an invitation to the practitioners working in the CCD field to contribute in making community cultural development more present and visible in the Culturelink network.

13

An intervention from
the audience in a Forum
Theater presentation
by prisoners in Presidente
Prudente, State of São
Paulo, Brazil.

Center of the Theatre of the Oppressed
Avenida Rio Branca, 179 / 6º Andar
CEP 20040-007
Centro - Rio de Janeiro, RJ, Brasil
Telephone: (55 21) 2532-5990
Fax: (55 21) 2220-7940
E-mail: ctorio@ctorio.com.br
Web site: www.ctorio.com.br

Bárbara Santos is project coordinator at the Center of the Theatre of the Oppressed (CTO-Rio) in Rio de Janeiro, Brazil. As her essay describes, she came to this work through her job as a public-school teacher, finding Augusto Boal's theatrical approaches to dialogue more effective than the meetings and other conventional methods she'd experienced before.

As noted in the first chapter of "Community, Culture and Globalization," Theater of the Oppressed (T.O.) and related practices inspired by Augusto Boal constitute the most robust sector of the worldwide community cultural development movement. This essay is especially pivotal to the anthology because it explains the core concepts of T.O. and related practices, touched on in many of the essays that follow.

The essay is suffused with a sense of power and possibility that inspires the reader. In contributing to the online dialogue that preceded our meeting at Bellagio, Bárbara described one of the sources of her own inspiration:

Until last January I couldn't see possibilities to change reality together with the international community. After the Fórum Social Mundial— World Social Forum—I changed my view of this. In Porto Alegre (capital of the state of Rio Grande do Sul, in Brasil), I took part in an international movement for change. … Everyone there believed that it is possible to build another world. More than 5,000 people gathered to discuss several issues related to the fight against globalization and the building of other possibilities to live in this world. For me it was a wonderful experience …

Porto Alegre showed me that when we are together we have power. And that when we open our eyes and ears to partners from other fields of work, it is possible to dialogue; maybe not in the exact same language but using a kind of language that includes all of us with our differences, diversities and specificities: the language of good will. When

we can understand that each one of us has specific and necessary tools to build a common project, we can stop our stupid war and identify the real enemy and put our energy to work together against it.

Bárbara's essay is dedicated to Augusto Boal:

… who, as Artistic Director of CTO-Rio, is the one who sets our course. He is both our guide and our supporter on the paths we choose to follow. Boal is our fountain of inspiration and our intellectual challenge. He is the most youthful, the most energetic, creative and dynamic member of CTO-Rio. My humble contribution to this publication is a simple homage to my friend, a great man of the theater, Augusto Boal.

Theater of the Oppressed and Community Cultural Development

by Bárbara Santos

T he purpose of this essay is to present ideas based on my practical experience as a Joker (facilitator/participant) in Theater of the Oppressed. It expresses a personal point of view born of the collective experiences of the CTO-Rio (Centro de Teatro do Oprimido, Center of the Theatre of the Oppressed[1]), of which I am a coordinator.

[1] Augusto Boal's seminal book is *Theater of the Oppressed* (New York: Urizen Books, 1979).

These conclusions were generated through workshops, rehearsals, study groups, theater seminars, administrative meetings, community visits, public presentations and many other activities led by the Jokers of CTO-Rio—Geo Britto, Helen Sarapeck, Olivar Bendelak, Claudete Felix and myself. Whenever I speak about the Theater of the Oppressed, I also speak with their voices. Through them, the voices of the members of grassroots groups, partners in various projects and those of all the people who have provoked and stimulated me with questions and suggestions, helping me learn what I know about this subject, are also represented. One voice, especially, has inspired me, that of Augusto Boal—as a director, as the inventor of various techniques and systems, as a thinker, as a politician and above all as a friend and colleague.

CTO-RIO, FORUM THEATER AND THE JOKER

Since its creation in 1986, CTO-Rio has maintained the same main objectives: democratizing the means of cultural production through the training and diffusion of popular drama groups replicating Theater of the Oppressed (T.O.) methodology throughout Brazil. It is our wish that more and more people use theater as a language, facilitating communication and stimulating ever more varied discussion.

Theater of the Oppressed combines exercises, games and theater techniques that seek to de-mechanize the physical and intellectual practice of drama. Forum Theater is one of the T.O. techniques in which a real-life problem is dramatized: both oppressed and oppressor fight for their respective wishes and interests; but the oppressed, lacking knowledge, are unable to accomplish their desire. The Joker then invites the "spect-actors" (Boal's hybrid term for spectator–actors, those audience members who are willing to participate) to get up on the stage, replace actors playing oppressed characters and, through improvisation, try to modify their original situation.

CTO-Rio's main project is "Legislative Theater," an organization of community groups performing Forum Theater that dramatizes problems they experience, followed by public discussion of these problems. Jokers from CTO-Rio write down the interventions and contributions of audience members. Besides participating as actors onstage, the public can present suggestions in writing. These recorded ideas are analyzed by a team of legal experts who transform them into legal actions and policy initiatives which are then presented to legislators who defend popular causes.

At CTO-Rio we are currently developing several projects aside from Legislative Theater: training of Jokers for the MST (Movimento dos Trabalhadores Rurais Sem Terra, the Landless Workers Movement); popular participation programs in partnership with progressive government agencies; and theater in prisons, where our partner is People's Palace Projects, directed by Paul Heritage (whose own essay also appears in this volume).

Like the Joker in a card game, the Joker in T.O. has multiple functions. The Joker should be able to participate as a performer, rehearse and stage Forum Theater, facilitate workshops and courses in T.O., write and/or coordinate the collective production of theatrical texts, conceive a play's aesthetics and serve as master of ceremonies at a Forum session, stimulating dialogue between spect-actors and the audience.

The Joker in T.O. is an artist with pedagogic and political functions who helps people to understand themselves better, express their ideas and emotions, analyze their problems and seek their own alternatives to change or solve them. The Joker doesn't need to have answers but should be able to formulate questions that stimulate the suggestion of alternatives to each question presented during a Forum Theater play.

The Joker should be an expert in diversity, with a multidisciplinary background and attitude, possessing knowledge of theater, popular culture, pedagogy, psychology, politics and as much else as possible. Beyond that, a Joker must have sensitivity, the ability to communicate with and coordinate groups, heightened perception, common sense, energy and the ability to synthesize. Part of this knowledge can be learned from books; another part can be developed through practical experience. Still other characteristics depend on the personality of each Joker.

Currently, many people fulfill this function throughout the world. They build their own styles from their local cultures, knowledge and personalities. Jokers may have different styles, but they must never forget the humanistic, pedagogic and democratic essence of Theater of the Oppressed.

MY ENCOUNTER WITH THEATER OF THE OPPRESSED

In the late 1980s, I joined a multidisciplinary team whose job was to stimulate and encourage education professionals to experiment with alternative practices. Then and now, these professionals were confronted with uninspiring conditions such as humiliating salaries, disillusionment with the possibility of creating change, organizational apathy and conformity to whatever had already been established. Our team visited schools and classrooms, organized study groups, led support meetings in the schools, participated in class council meetings and put together annual seminars at the beginning of each school year aimed at presenting the educational programs and proposals to be developed over the school year. There were many difficulties, especially with the organization of these seminars.

At the end of 1990, we had no idea how we were going to organize the opening seminar for the 1991 school year, where our main tasks were to organize school–community councils with participation of those responsible for the students within the decision-making bodies of the school; electing directors; and establishing class councils, bimonthly meetings where teachers would discuss students' performance and decide which strategies to adopt for the following semester.

We were aware that these were tough subjects to present to our peers. In fact, we were afraid to tackle them until one of our colleagues came up with the unusual suggestion of using theater to get the message across. Professor Venâncio said that he had participated in a play at a CIEP (Centro Integrado de Educação Pública, Center of Public Education) where director Augusto Boal was coordinating a Forum Theater presentation.

His description was both fascinating and unbelievable. Venâncio's idea was radical; he suggested we organize a play in place of the opening session. He said it would be much more dynamic and effective in introducing difficult themes, whereas we had already encountered resistance at the mere mention of them.

We contacted CTO-Rio, which supported us by sending us a Joker to lead a workshop with our team. She convinced us that the oppressed parties must act out Forum Theater themselves, so that they become the protagonists in their own story.

We produced a Forum Theater play about a young boy who was a failure in school but who, outside of school, had been awarded a prize for the best young percussionist in his samba school. Through the story of this boy, we traced a parallel with the experience of our students within and outside the school system, thus introducing the idea of a school–community council and all the other subjects that were of interest to us.

As in previous years, the teachers were invited to attend the seminar. As they arrived, they were amazed to see a colorful theater set on the stage instead of the usual table with its pompous tablecloth and boringly arranged chairs. The image that greeted them surprised and intrigued them.

Someone made a welcoming speech, announcing that there would be a play by the theater troupe "Virando a Mesa" ("Turning the Table"). To everybody's surprise, the actors who took to the stage were none other than people they were all used to seeing in meetings, study groups, supervisors' visits or at podiums. Yet the cast members had something magical about them. The teachers, surprised by the unusual presentation, were gradually transported by the language of the theater.

The event was a success. Even the more traditional, conservative teachers who usually preferred not to expose their ideas during debates were moved to participate. The theatrical expression magnified our means of communication, allowing us to introduce heavy subjects in a light and dynamic manner. The theater enveloped the audience members, who developed such a rapport with the characters that, before they knew it, they were already onstage defending their ideas. The teachers' participation was intense and controversial. The clash of opposing opinions was facilitated by the use of theater. The teachers all said that they had never participated in such a delightful meeting.

After this event, our group became known as a theater troupe. We promoted a season of shows throughout our school district.

Through Forum Theater, we managed to bring together teachers, public workers, students and the community to generate a dialogue. Until then, we had had no luck in creating events that would unite the different groups involved in the school system. It was not easy to convince education professionals to have discussions with students, workers and the community. In these theater events, the students, the school janitors, the schedule coordinators, the teachers and the principal found a common forum to communicate their ideas. These sessions made the school environment more democratic, symbolizing the content of proposals aimed at democratizing the public-school system. We didn't merely talk about what we believed would make the school a better place: we demonstrated hands-on how a democracy of teachers, students and community members would work.

For me, this was a defining experience: I met Augusto Boal and was enchanted. I started attending all the workshops offered at CTO-Rio, and I accompanied the Jokers to as many external workshops as possible. I did these things in my spare time, of which I had very little; at that time I taught an average of eight hours of classes each day. In 1992, I joined the CTO-Rio team while continuing to teach. In 1993, I left school to become an educator outside the boundaries of the classroom, something I had always wanted to do.

THEATER OF THE OPPRESSED AND
COMMUNITY CULTURAL DEVELOPMENT

In all my work as a Joker in many different communities over the past 10 years, I often hear people saying, "I can't," "I don't know how," "I can't succeed" and "This is not for me." Such beliefs are formed from the time kids begin school, where many, especially the poor, are persuaded that they know nothing and that learning is too difficult. They are taught that the practical knowledge they have gained from life and from their family histories is not knowledge at all. They are taught that their customs and traditions are not culture.

For a community to build its own history, it must exist as a collective community. For a collective community to exist, its members must see themselves as people. The development of a "we" depends on the existence and the strengthening of the individual "I." If each member of a community is seen only as a number, the community will be little more than a dormitory of people who happen to inhabit the same physical space. It will possess a merely geographical identity.

What distinguishes a *number* from a *person*? For me, it is the ability to see oneself as part of a whole, to be able to imagine, dream, envision the possibility of doing things differently.

Theater stimulates and fulfills our need for self-discovery; it enables us to see ourselves as we are and to understand our own potential. Through the language of the theater, individuals learn that their bodies can express much more than they ever thought possible. When people realize that they can get up on stage, that they can sing a song, recite a verse or write down an idea, they discover that their potential is unlimited, that they can change both themselves and the world around them.

In 1993, I worked with a group of street kids aged 14 to 17. Many of them were doing drugs, especially sniffing glue. At first, the partner institution had invited my colleague Olivar Bendelak and myself to use alternative spaces— the street, for example—to conduct the workshops. We decided to make it even more of a challenge by having the workshops at the CTO-Rio head-quarters, located in a public building housing a government-funded theater.

Within the first few days of the project, we realized how important it was for the group to work in a formal setting. It was obvious that they were very proud to be invited into a *proper* space for this activity.

The strategy was to alternate warm-up exercises with visualization and improvisation techniques. After a few weeks, we had done several skits based on their problems and the group started asking what play we were going to put on. We answered that we were already doing it. They laughed and asked what we were talking about. They felt that their stories were not interesting enough to become the subject of a play. They had expected to produce a play using someone else's text, to stage a work that already existed. They said that the play would never materialize because they would never know how to create a *real* story.

It wasn't easy to convince them to be patient, or even to rehearse the same skit over and over again to get it right. We improvised several skits, amalgamated similar ones and then placed the skits into a sequence that told the story of a young boy who ran away from home and became involved in the world of street kids.

Next we told them that we would write down the text of the play. Again, they laughed. The group was full of half-illiterate kids; some of them barely knew how to write their own names. No one believed they could actually write the text of a play. They kept insisting that it wasn't necessary to have a text at all: they already knew how to improvise.

We wrote down the characters' lines, then typed and copied them. The more we worked on the text, the prouder the kids became of their production, becoming aware that they were actually producing something that was truly their own. Even those who were completely illiterate started contributing, suggesting lines for some of the characters. After a while, we had the printed text of a play, entirely created by street kids, most of whom had failed in the public-education system and who were not at all used to reading or writing.

This was one of the most difficult groups I ever worked with; but with them I understood how the reigning ideology, through the public-education system, can destroy a person's self-confidence and how the theater can restore it, by helping people to see, discover and re-create themselves, rather than simply accepting the judgments and labels that society has placed on them. By working in theater, people learn that they are capable of producing a play, something they would never have thought possible. With this experience comes the realization that before saying, "I don't know how," they need to give themselves a chance to try, to investigate their potential and to do what it would take to one day know how.

When people speak about themselves, when they improvise scenes from their own lives, they discover who they are and where they are from. The simple fact of understanding themselves better and discovering that they can do more than they had ever imagined is fundamental for them to start transforming their own lives.

Theater stimulates individuals to discover the "I" at the same time as they discover their power to act, to transform. Theater helps show individuals the vastness of their potential.

Theater of the Oppressed—and more specifically Forum Theater—aside from promoting the discovery of the self, aside from reinforcing an individual's self-esteem and self-confidence, also contributes to the establishment of the collective "we." By "we" I mean not only the specific "we" of the group in which they are working and with whom they share common goals. I also refer to the "we" that comes from becoming a citizen who understands the world as a collective in which events are interdependent, both cause and consequence of social, political, economic and religious occurrences.

In all the groups I have worked with, I have seen significant changes in the participants and in our Jokers who have worked with them. I have seen people return to school, change jobs, join neighborhood and professional associations, divorce and/or remarry, create plays. In sum, I have seen them change their lives.

I have seen changes being initiated and developed collectively as well as individually. In three *favelas* (slums) without basic sewage systems and poor participation in organized community activities located in the neighborhoods of Jacarepaguá and Santa Teresa, across town from each other, theater groups have achieved great influence on electoral processes within their communities' tenants' associations. I've seen a group of black university students organize themselves to participate in a theater festival in Africa. I've seen Forum Theater groups formed under such rubrics as "Ghota" (homosexuals), "Renascer" (senior citizens), "Portadores de Deficiência Física" (people with physical disabilities), "Galera da Levy" (first-grade students) or "Casa das Palmeiras" (mental-health patients) who managed to introduce proposed legislation to City Hall via Augusto Boal, then a town councilor. As I write, "ARTEMANHA" (AIDS-prevention activists) are creating their own social projects.

Every time a citizens' action group presents its play to a new audience, its members gain a better understanding of the problem depicted, discovering new ways of dealing with it through the outsiders' viewpoints of audience members who come onstage to improvise an alternative.

Every new audience that participates in a Forum Theater performance learns through the presentation and goes away with the energy and emotion generated by the event. People do not leave Forum Theater the same as they came in, even if they did not go onstage. The newly learned power to take action stays with everyone present.

Boal often says that "the act of transforming is in itself transforming." For him, the fact that people climb out of their comfort zone, get up on the stage, replace a character and try, through improvisation, to transform the original course of events sets off a process of transformation within those individuals. To take the stage to change something that has been portrayed creates the reality of change.

All kinds of audiences, even those that at first seem resistant, participate actively in Forum Theater sessions, as I have seen in dozens of cities throughout Brazil and in a few other countries.

For these and other reasons, no project intended to promote the development of a community culture should neglect the use of theatrical expression, even if they do not form theatrical troupes or put on plays. In fact, I am convinced that Forum Theater is an essential technique that can make an invaluable contribution to any sociocultural or pedagogic project. Forum Theater generates constant dialogue, brings people together, strengthens them and demystifies their plight.

THE PROCESS OF TRAINING COMMUNITY GROUPS IN FORUM THEATER

Theater of the Oppressed as a whole and Forum Theater in particular have been applied in various forms and with different objectives in hundreds of sociocultural and educational projects in over 70 countries across five continents. Below, I describe the process of training community groups in Forum Theater as used by CTO-Rio. It could be useful to everyone who works in community cultural development. Those interested in learning more about other aspects of Forum Theater can contact me at the address in this volume.

Local Partner

CTO-Rio's work in communities is based on the establishment of local partnerships with groups that have gathered experience in the development of projects in their area. Theater cannot develop in isolation from other community initiatives. For this reason, our initial contact is always mediated by local community associations, church groups, community-based organizations or any partner who can offer us some sort of support in setting up and developing the project.

In some communities, even with local partners, it has not been possible to continue the work due to security reasons. For instance, in 1993, when we worked in Vigário Geral—a community where 21 inhabitants were massacred by the police in revenge for drug-dealers' actions—our van was stolen and the costumes returned with a threatening message.

In Morro da Saudade—another poor community, where a group of women had prepared a lively Forum Theater performance about the situation of local women who live alone and have to confront both police violence and the authoritarian actions of drug dealers—the work was made unsustainable by a curfew decreed by the drug barons.

In Morro do Borel, another *favela*, Jokers had to interrupt rehearsals on several occasions to wait out the end of a gunfight between police and criminals. When the problem is safety, there is little that can be done other than retreat, even when we have partners who are insiders in the community.

To connect the formation of a theater group to other community actions is pivotal in strengthening the initiative and guaranteeing practical results.

Demonstration Workshop
In order to begin a new project, it is necessary to investigate the cultural habits of the community, because theater is not always the chosen option of the group. We have had very good experiences in communities in which we didn't manage to form a theater group, because we discovered that their talents and interests were in music, sport or in some other form of expression to which theater could certainly be associated, but for which it couldn't be substituted. People might be interested in taking part in a few workshops rather than forming a theater group. Sensitivity is a must, as this kind of work should never be an imposition.

In order to have some time for investigation, we use "demonstration workshops," an experimental period in which members of the community and Jokers from CTO-Rio get to know each other. For the group, it is an opportunity to learn techniques and find out if they want to form a theater troupe or only take part in some theater workshops. For the Jokers, it is a time to evaluate if there are appropriate conditions to create a theater group in the neighborhood.

The community of Vigário Geral is an example. We tried several times, before and after the massacre, to form a group there. We never succeeded despite running excellent youth workshops. Today this community boasts one of the most successful music projects in the city: Afro-Reggae, a band that has recorded a CD and is beginning to be successful on the radio.

As a center of theater, however, we are interested in developing projects in this specific language. We use demonstration workshops to identify those communities best suited to develop theater groups.

Definition of the Theme

The first step in the formation of a Forum Theater group is to discover the theme of greatest significance to the group. Not everything that at first emerges in a group is substantial. Frequently, the most important issues are obscured beneath the surfaces of everyday life. The process must allow the emergence, rather than the choice, of a theme.

It's fundamental to the work that the theme should be relevant to the collective expression of the group and that there is a reasonable number of stories about it. If a group insists on a theme that doesn't seem relevant to the Joker, what must prevail is the desire of the group. In the process of improvisation and analysis of the stories, an apparently superficial idea may turn out to be significant and provocative.

When the group's nature is thematic—when people have come together around a specific interest rather than because they live in the same community —the theme is obvious. They work on specific aspects of it, using the theatrical language to develop it further.

If the theme disturbs the Joker's moral principles or political ideas, then Forum Theater work is clearly not possible.

Choice of the Story

In a community group, choosing the story to be presented is part of the strengthening process of the group, so it is best to avoid reaching a decision by voting. The Joker must facilitate an atmosphere of consensus in which the choice of the story can proceed naturally from the stories of group members' lives. For this reason it is essential that the theme expresses the group's reality, as this will allow for the greatest diversity in the improvisations, which will probably have common elements that complement each other. Care must be taken that the story should not be an incoherent collage. The story must express the theme chosen by the group, its lived reality.

A Case Study

In 1998, together with Geo Britto, I began working with a group called Panela de Opressão (Oppressure Cooker), made up of people living in the poor communities of Jacarepaguá, a neighborhood in Rio de Janeiro. Group members said that they wanted to discuss women's health; but in the improvisations, they created scenes about adolescent pregnancy, conflicts between parents and children and racial prejudice.

We did some improvisations and made some Forums from the scenes to help them understand the theatrical method that was being proposed. After some weeks, they admitted that they had wanted the theme of women's health because of the influence of a friendly female doctor who worked in the community.

At that point, part of the group decided to tell us how City Hall was beginning to demolish houses and remove families, negotiating individual offers and deals—and how there had been no community reaction. Group members talked about the problem as if it had nothing to do with themselves, as if these things were not happening to their neighbors, just 300 meters away from their own houses. Why were they so distanced from their problem?

For us as Jokers it was clear that the theme was powerful and that it would be important for them and for hundreds of other people in other communities to deal with this issue. But we couldn't impose the theme on them. We asked them to improvise the story so that we could understand the problem better. As we expected, the scene was very strong and perfect for Forum Theater. What seemed obvious to us had not been so for the group.

The fact that group members did not recognize this problem as something close to them was symptomatic to me of how they had protected themselves from something terrible in their lives. It's as if by not admitting the problem they made it nonexistent. We couldn't force them to face their own lives, but we had a duty to help them notice what was happening. We stimulated more discussion about the subject, suggesting that they should try to gather more information. Two group members offered to go to a community meeting. At the next rehearsal, they told how the community was divided, reporting that residents were fighting for individual benefits, with everyone trying to save their own skin.

In our group's internal discussions, some members began to see that the biggest problem was not with the municipal authorities, but with the lack of unity and cooperation within the neighborhood. Some group members began to attend community meetings on a regular basis; they proposed that the group should put on a play about the subject.

As we were not part of the community, we could not interfere in the discussion about the best option in that situation. But in the improvisations, we showed that it was possible to use Forum Theater to discuss a problem and look for alternatives as part of the solution or the way forward. The group decided to put on a play about the subject. It was a long road to the choice of theme and story, but it was an effective route because group members made the decision fully understanding why they should make it.

The play was very powerful and was presented in dozens of poor communities, schools, public squares and theaters. Through these performances, group members realized the importance of the subject and its relevance to several areas of the city. For group members, as well as for the audiences to whom the play was shown, it was an opportunity to see that their problem was not just local, that in some way it affected the life of a large part of the city's population. It was a rich process of politicization.

The group's process in choosing the subject of their first play is emblematic of work with community groups in Theater of the Oppressed. Frequently the oppressed do not see themselves as oppressed because they are not aware of their real situation. A Joker of T.O. doesn't have the right to tell the group what its theme should be. The Joker must understand how to promote a democratic process that will stimulate group members to formulate the question they will ask their play's audience.

CREATING A FORUM THEATER PERFORMANCE

Improvising the Scenes

Group members begin to discuss their themes and stories long before they start selecting them. From the first exercises, games and techniques, it's already possible to discern what interests and concerns the group. The Joker must be attentive and sensitive to notice what is being shown but not necessarily said: what is being selected and what is being rejected.

In a community theater group there must be time to improvise scenes before choosing the story. In addition to revealing areas of interest, this process is useful to building up an understanding of techniques, because the group will also have to practice Forum Theater in the improvised scenes.

If there is enough time to develop exercises, games, improvised scenes and a diverse range of characters, the definition of the subject matter and of the story to be theatricalized will naturally result from the creative process. The story must have resonance for the group and for the community, as well as provide objectivity and clarity in the chosen conflicts.

Forum Theater performance is a representation rather than a reproduction of reality, and therefore it isn't necessary that all the realistic details of a story should be shown. An excess of scenes should be avoided as should overloading detail so as to transform a story into a saga. It's the Joker's responsibility to help participants understand that images are at once language and message, and that many things can be conveyed without being spoken.

In Panela de Opressão's current performance, a young woman is sexually assaulted by a gang of drug dealers. It was a challenge to find a metaphorical way to show this reality. First we had to discuss what a metaphor is.

We began to research images that represent violence. Everyone showed ideas: a scene with animals during a hunt; another scene with a group of boys pretending they were using knives and forks to eat a girl; another that just waved different pieces of fabric around in a colorful, symbolic choreography. We chose the following: the boys circled round the girl, breaking away at a signal from the boss, one by one lassoing the girl with an imaginary rope as if she were a horse being captured by herdsmen. She matched them with her movements to the sounds of instruments played by other group members. There was no reference to sexual moves, and the girl was never touched.

Scripting the Chosen Scenes

The group's story could come from a variety of scenes that refer to the same type of conflict. To script is to organize the performance into a sequence of scenes with a coherent logic. Once the script is ready, it's necessary to reimprovise and adapt the scenes.

Once a script is created, the group has its story ready, with a beginning, a middle and an end. A story can also be told in an improvised way, without text. Many groups don't have time to elaborate a text for performance and therefore define only certain phrases and cues, so that the cast knows how to organize the dialogue from improvised lines based on the logic of each character. If there is no time to write a script, a well-structured narrative is enough to organize the performance so that actors will not get lost during the presentation.

This process allows people to discover that they can create a story, open their mouths and sing, be on stage and act, and change the reality of an image.

If there's time, the group should write a text. It's fundamental for community-based groups to discover that they are able to write, create texts and master written language, to be dramatists of their own life stories as well as their protagonists.

The Collective Text

Having the script as a base, each scene is reimprovised using rehearsal techniques. Those group members who are not performing in a scene write down the dialogues. I prefer each person to be responsible for the notation of only one character. When there are more people outside the scene than characters onstage, I ask more than one person to write down the speeches of each character, especially for the protagonists and those who have the most speeches. As a Joker, I remain attentive to see that the most interesting phrases don't get lost. This is what I call the elaboration of a "hot text": we note down what is said in the heat of the action. This text comes without much thought to the right word or concerns of dramaturgy: therein lies its richness.

I collect this mountain of paper from each rehearsal and type it all up in time for the next rehearsal. In addition, the people who are in the scenes are responsible for rewriting them at home, trying in the cold light of day to rewrite the dialogue from their own scene, choosing the phrases that have the most impact, getting rid of the waste material and introducing new ideas. With this work we create various versions of each scene, with each person writing the script for their own scenes.

When working with a community group made up of poor people with limited formal education, you have to stimulate the participants to write and make sure that no one feels unable to do the job. That's why the Joker should never behave like a writing teacher. The idea is that people should express their vision of the world and their ideas about the story through written language. It doesn't matter if the text has spelling mistakes. I never scrawl things on people's writings, correcting words or phrases. Instead, I correct while I am typing. When people receive the typed text, they can see where there are changes without feeling humiliated or exposed. Everyone else has the same typed and corrected script.

The written texts from the rehearsal improvisations and from each member's solitary work at home are typed up and handed out. All must then read, cut and edit according to what they think most appropriate. Each person becomes a playwright, with total freedom of creation.

I prefer that everyone experience doing this job individually, but this doesn't stop people from helping each other, especially those who appear together in the same scene. At this stage, all are free to produce texts for all the scenes without limiting themselves to the ones in which they appear.

At the end of 2000, together with the Joker Geo Britto, I had one of my best experiences in producing a text, with Panela de Opressão. The group is made up of 11 people between the ages of 12 and 40. They all participated: jotting down improvisations, rewriting them at home, reading and editing the typed material and writing dialogue for scenes in which they would not take part. Even the youngest members who didn't enjoy writing at school brought several contributions, including musical ones. The play had six musical interventions, all played live by the cast. Only one song wasn't original; all the rest were composed by the cast or CTO-Rio's musical director Richard Coelho. We had 11 versions of each scene. We prioritized what was most frequently chosen and used, systematized the different compositions and produced one version of the show. As far as possible, we tried to maintain the group's style while creating a dramatic text that was strong and interesting.

The text was reworked by the Jokers and Boal in CTO-Rio's Dramaturgy Seminar, leaving its essential features intact. The text was then reanalyzed by the group. Sometimes we thought it better that a character said this and not that; but if the group defended an opposite position, we sought a solution that reflected the group's wishes while preserving the dramatic qualities of the text.

At CTO-Rio we set out to make THEATER, to produce ART, with capital letters. When we pass the means of theatrical production on to community groups, we stimulate them to create shows that have heart and soul, that speak of human passion, that put conflicts on stage. We do not want plays that are only intellectual debates: we want people to see, feel and understand things beyond spoken words. We want the silence also to carry a message. All the things we put onstage and all the images we create must say something. We want audience members to come onstage because of what they hear, what they see and especially what they feel.

This happened in the city of Presidente Prudente (in São Paulo, August 2001), where I accompanied a group of inmates from the city's semiopen prison in presenting their play in the town square. They were participating in the project Staging Human Rights, an examination of human rights in the penal system through Forum Theater. CTO-Rio is in charge of training the 52 Jokers who implement theater workshops in 37 prisons in the state of São Paulo.

The play was performed in a square full of people who had stopped to watch and ended up discussing injustices within the system, especially those that persist when a former prisoner tries to reintegrate himself into society. The people who participated in the Forum session seemed perplexed by the theme. Many admitted that they had never stopped to think about the subject before.

Would those people have gone to a debate about human rights in the prison system if it were not for theater? Would they have participated with the open and willing disposition they showed if it had been a conventional debate? Would there even be a debate in the town square about such a subject?

One of the interventions came from a young woman who acted opposite a prisoner in the plain light of day, under the attentive gaze and with the approval of all those sections of society represented in that square. If it were not for theater, how would this meeting and dialogue be played out? Would the black, poor prisoner be able to talk to the young, white, middle-class woman in a public square?

The young woman was very moved by the story. She came onstage to show what she thought. She didn't need to say anything, because her action was more revealing than any word: she left her role as spectator, took her place onstage to stand side-by-side with the prisoner, spoke with him without fear and touched the man as if he were a normal person. In shock, he accepted her action. This meeting in a public square—in a sunlit theater in the round, witnessed by all present—was not a theatrical meeting, but a real human encounter.

On their return to prison, the 15 men who made up the cast spoke of how surprised they had been that people participated. They expected fear rather than participation. Through theater, through an aesthetic language, we touched people and stimulated them to react. The action was theatrical, but it was also real and caused real reactions and emotions. The theater interfered with the reality of the public space. This happened because it was theater, rather than merely a debate.

Learning the Text

The process of producing a collective text is both pedagogic and political. In making theater we explore our working theme and learn more about theater and dramaturgy. In addition, it helps to clarify the question we want to ask the audience.

When community-based Forum Theater players produce a written text of their play, they reappropriate their own stories. I love promoting read-throughs of the text as in conventional theater as a means of valorizing the production of the play. Also, read-throughs help the group memorize the text.

Casting the Play

Although the Joker is the artistic director of the group—and the person with the most experience on which to base artistic decisions guaranteeing the best performance from each one—the Joker doesn't have the autocratic power to determine casting. A community group is not a professional group, and the Joker must be open and transparent throughout the process. Directing nonactors, it is important to avoid negative feelings that could hinder the development of the work and inhibit the bonds of friendship and fellowship which must be fostered in the group.

In staging Panela de Opressão's latest show, we first did improvisations with volunteers. Then all the actors experimented with all the roles, male and female. We used a rehearsal technique that rotated the characters, so that actors could see each role's possibilities and discover their preferences, capabilities and limitations. We listed all the characters, and each group member said who they thought most appropriate to play which parts. Then everyone revealed who they would like to play. The casting was thus a combination of the group's suggestions, individual wishes and the Jokers' opinions.

As we had been engaged in a process of experimentation since beginning improvisations, and we had encouraged people to take on the roles for which they were most appropriate, we had few problems in defining the cast. The only disagreement was with a young woman whom we had chosen for a character that she didn't think herself capable of playing. We managed to overcome this through discussion and encouragement.

Despite having defined the cast, we encouraged exchanges of roles within the play's season. In Panela de Opressão there are three young women who can play the protagonist; also, several characters are played by more than one actor. This is good for the training of the cast and enables substitutions, as we cannot always be certain that everyone will be available for all presentations. Flexibility of cast, scenery and staging is one of our work's essential features.

Rehearsal Techniques

In the improvisations, rehearsal techniques help with the creation of characters, the discovery of their traits, the stimulation of dialogues, experimentation with styles and the reworking of the story.

With a written text, rehearsal techniques must be used after the text has been memorized, as there is no more interest in creating new improvisations at this stage. The objective here is to strengthen understanding of the text and the depth of the characters.

There will probably be changes in the text during rehearsals, as T.O. techniques are always revelatory and creative. But the text shouldn't be altered too much, so as not to make the cast insecure. The text must be an instrument to facilitate the work. It should ensure that the cast knows what is going to happen, guaranteeing that everything the group wants to say is said.

Rehearsal techniques help cast members de-mechanize the memorized text, making it possible for them to reappropriate the text. In the beginning, the improvised text belonged to the group: coming from the soul of each actor, it was alive. When it was systematized and structured as a written text, it acquired a reality of its own, just as children are born and have their own lives. Rehearsal techniques are instrumental in helping the group reinternalize the text.

Scenery and Costumes

We want to involve the public with the magical language of the theater, so we dedicate the same attention to the look of the play as we do to the creation of the text. The image is the message. Everything that goes onstage has a meaning and a reason for being there. The image of a play must also be the collective creation of the group and the Joker.

From the first improvisations, when characters and locations begin to be defined, up until rehearsals with the text, the group must be stimulated to imagine and create the elements that make up the context lived by the characters. At CTO-Rio, visual artists help our groups put their ideas into practice. In this process, we prioritize the use of recyclable material. The same is done for the costumes.

Open Rehearsals

Final rehearsals should always be open to partners and friends. At this stage of the work, we are no longer capable of seeing what is obvious and of criticizing ourselves. The presence of people who understand what we are trying to do and who have an artistic sensibility is essential in helping us to make final adjustments and alerting us to anything that might be missing.

At CTO-Rio, Jokers come frequently to each other's final rehearsals to give support and help with the theatricality of the play and its suitability for Forum Theater. Before a group has its first performance for the community, we do a preview at CTO-Rio for Boal, the other Jokers and other T.O. community groups. Open rehearsals also provide practice for the Forum sessions.

First Community Performance, Dialogues Between Groups and Touring the Play

Open rehearsals give the group strength to begin its series of performances. Usually after a few performances, contact with different audiences reveals new possibilities and options so that the group can include new speeches and change certain scenes.

The opening performance of a group must be on their own territory in order to strengthen links to the community, ensure support for the work and make the cast feel more secure about beginning to tour.

We are used to promoting "Dialogues" between community Forum Theater groups. This happens when one group invites another to perform and do a Forum session in their community. Afterward, there is a meeting to exchange ideas about the themes and shows.

Final Considerations

If there were more space, I would have liked to talk about the process of training the Joker and about how to hold a good Forum Theater session. There was also no space to discuss CTO-Rio's exciting projects in progress. But anyone who is interested can write to us at ctorio@domain.com.br or to me, Bárbara Santos, at beta@domain.com.br. On December 3, 2001, we launched both *METAXIS*, an international magazine about Theater of the Oppressed, and CTO-Rio's Web site, at www.ctorio.com.br.

Do keep in touch!

14

Primary Health Care
Forum Theater in
Mulangali, Malawi, 1986,
in a play based on a local
folk narrative.

David Kerr
Fine and Performing Arts Department
Chancellor College, University of Malawi
P.O. Box 280
Zomba, Malawi
Telephone and Fax: (265) 622349
E-mail: kerrdavid42@yahoo.co.uk

David Kerr's life embodies the transnational character of community cultural development work. As part of our online dialogue, he shared with fellow participants an account of involvements leading up to the projects discussed in his essay:

I'm a British citizen, but have spent most of my life in Africa working, from a University base in theatre (and to a much lesser extent media) for community renewal purposes. 1969–73 I was in Malawi where I was one of a team which helped found the University Writers Workshop and Traveling Theatre. From 1974 to 1980 I was Artistic Director of Chikwakwa Theatre in Zambia, where I became involved in Traveling Theatre and "Theatre for Development" projects in rural areas, as well as in some TV drama work in Lusaka. 1980–1992 I was in Malawi again (my wife's native country). I helped set up the University's Fine and Performing Arts Department and was coordinator of the Traveling Theatre. I became heavily involved in using theatre for communication purposes in delivery of Primary Health Care in Liwonde District through Village Health Committees. I also did some video and theatre work for Mozambican refugees, and did unofficial research work on human rights for Amnesty International (Amnesty was a banned organisation in Malawi at the time). 1992–2000 I was in Botswana working with a University-based group called UBE423, which created plays mostly around human rights issues for such women's or children's organisations as Emang Basadi, Women & Law in Southern Africa, Metlhaetsile and Childline. I also worked closely with a community theatre group, Ghetto Artists, on AIDS issues.

David's essay treats an important question for the community cultural development field: how it is possible for community artists' work to perform its most important work of conscientization—stimulating people to take action in behalf of freedom—when the work is so often supported by governments and nongovernmental organizations (NGOs) for its instrumental effects, advancing a particular social goal or policy. He raised a related question in the preconference dialogue:

Many of us have been closely attached to NGOs, and as I mentioned in my piece on conditions, etc., this can sometimes cause problems. If it's an indigenous NGO like PETA [the Philippines Educational Theater Association] I think it is less problematic. But in Africa there are few, powerful indigenous NGOs. I have worked in partnership with GTZ (Germany), AIDS Action Trust (USA), ZOA Refugee Care (Holland), etc. All of the people I worked with were very idealistic and hard-working. However, there is quite a lot of analysis from political economists which suggests that NGOs in Africa contribute, probably unwittingly, to local dependency on donor funding and to the erosion of national governments—in other words to the recolonisation of Africa. I'm sure all of us have been in situations where we've had conflicts between what WE wanted to do and what the NGO partners funding the project wanted us to do, and we felt frustrated, maybe even guilty about it.

The observations and analysis in this essay will be useful to anyone wishing to make community cultural development work deeper and more effective.

The Challenge of Global Perspectives on Community Theater in Malawi and Botswana

by David Kerr

This is a very personal account of my own experiences in Malawi and Botswana facilitating the creation of theater pieces by various groups. To some extent it traces the evolution of my own political and theatrical commitments, concerns and doubts. In particular I try to show some of the difficulties in making cultural representations and mediations of local African society, while satisfying two apparently contradictory demands: the search for a theater sufficiently concrete to be accurate and useful to specific communities, and yet sufficiently complex to capture the communities' links with and responses to the imperatives of a wider global economy.

I start with Malawi. We are in a fairly small village called Mwima in the low-lying swampy district of Liwonde in 1985. My colleague from the University of Malawi, Chris Kamlongera, is playing the part of a village headman in a company-created play in the local language, Chinyanja. Other villagers are played by drama students doing their fieldwork for a course entitled "Theater for Development," who are helped by Mrs. Banda, a community-health nurse from Liwonde. The real village headman is a member of an audience comprising about 40 adults (mostly women) and 20 children. Also in the audience is Dr. Schmidt, the director of the Primary Health Care Unit (PHCU) at Liwonde District Hospital, who along with Mrs. Banda is employed by Gesellschaft fur Zusannenherbeit (GTZ), the German development agency funding this program. Our improvised play is about the problems of cementing the surroundings of village wells so they don't become contaminated.

This is a vital issue. Diarrhea and malaria are major problems, and in villages not far away people have recently died from an outbreak of cholera. Chris, in his role as headman, is hearing evidence from the pretend villagers about why the wells are not maintained properly. He throws questions out to audience members, both onstage and real. At first only the audience of actors responds, but soon people from the real audience give answers, explaining how lazy herd boys allow cows and goats to go too close to the well and how some women wash their children's nappies nearby. When the play eventually comes to an inconclusive end, the whole audience (including the until-now silent real headman) joins in the discussion. While praising the accuracy of some of the play's observations, they criticize some inaccuracies. Eventually, a few young villagers agree to do another version of the play showing problems about wells, pit latrines and other key sanitation issues.

The second version reveals human issues about which the PHCU knew nothing, particularly social problems concerning conflict over the best-located well in the village, close to a village store. The store owner built the well himself, but only allows the villagers to use it if they shop at his store. The university and PHCU teams learn one of their most important lessons, that problems concerning primary health care are rarely confined to the clinical or administrative fields, but involve social relations within the community and between the community and the outside world.

This experiment in Mwima village marked the beginning of a campaign using theater as a communication strategy to support the efforts of the Liwonde PHCU in tackling water-borne diseases. Over the next five years, participatory theater acted as a combination of stimulus, social lubricant and safety net in the sometimes conflicted process of building and maintaining safe, hygienic pit latrines and wells throughout the Liwonde district. Examples of some of the social tensions the plays addressed are: (1) conflicts between indigenous villagers and fish traders in Mphonde; (2) conflicts between government bureaucrats and villagers in Mbela; (3) conflicts between petit bourgeois elites and villagers in Mwima; and (4) conflicts between men and women almost everywhere.

The whole process was powered by a network of Village Health Committees (VHCs) run mostly by women, which provided essential health monitoring and even basic diagnosis and medicines for such ailments as diarrhea and malaria. They were also important communication vehicles for the early AIDS-awareness campaigns. Since Malawi was at that time a one-party dictatorship with no meaningful elections, the whole democratic process of running elections for the VHCs and using them to criticize some aspects of local government health policies was a major innovation.

[1] E. Kalipeni and C. Kamlongera, *Popular Theatre and Health Care* (University of Malawi, Zomba, 1987).

According to a survey sponsored by GTZ, the Primary Health Care campaign in Liwonde in the late 1980s was very successful, with various indicators showing improvements in health standards with respect to water-borne diseases and with much improved health-communication systems.[1] In 1990, however, the Malawi government curtailed the GTZ PHC scheme. The reasons for this are not clear, but probably it was owing to its very success, compared with PHC programs in other districts; success created tensions within the Byzantine system of furtive patronage and entitlements dispensed by President Banda's office. The political atmosphere of paranoia that dominated the last years of the Malawi Congress Party (MCP) regime in the 1980s, prior to the referendum on multiparty democracy in 1993, had a strongly detrimental effect on the implementation of socioeconomic policies.

This was only one of several factors relating to political economy that gave me misgivings about my Theater for Development work with Liwonde PHCU. Of course, I was well aware of its achievements. Compared with earlier Theater for Development projects in which I'd been involved, the Liwonde PHCU work was much more genuinely participatory. This was not only because the villagers took control of the play-devising process, but also because indigenous cultural forms from the local community—*nyimbo* (songs), *nthano* (stories) and *miyambo* (didactic messages)—were incorporated into the performances. Some of the earlier plays, where we simply sought community participation at any cost, were little more than static role-plays, and thus aesthetically very crude. Some of the later plays, however, especially those created at a major workshop in Mulangali (1987), were much more successful aesthetically because we took pains to research not only the health problems of the community, but also its cultural traditions. These cultural forms became the basis of the plays' structure, thus giving the community a much greater sense of their "ownership." Another major achievement was that the whole Theater for Primary Health Care process was sustained over a long period and integrated into carefully thought-out and well-managed health-communication campaigns linked to democratically elected local institutions. It was not just a one-off workshop, which made token gestures toward "follow-up."

Nevertheless, I couldn't help feeling frustrated at the limitations of the Theater for Primary Health Care process. The main problem was that the one-party MCP dictatorship at the time made honest developmental communication virtually impossible. It's true that in the Forum Theater presentations there was some unexpectedly frank criticism made of local party bureaucrats (for example, of area party officials at a performance in Mwima in 1986), but this always happened when there were non-Malawian witnesses to the occasion. The Village Health Committee actors were much more circumspect when they did not have the protection of outside witnesses. Even when GTZ or university observers were present, there were clear limits to the amount of confrontation that was possible, even though government polices were often major obstacles.

One of the fundamental problems of Theater for Development is that if it is to make any genuine changes in people's lives, it is bound to offend some stakeholders in the status quo. The clearest African example of that is in Kenya in the late 1970s and early '80s with Kamiriithu Community Educational and Cultural Centre. The issues of teenage pregnancy raised by Ngugi wa Thiong'o and Ngugi wa Mirii in the play "Ngaahika Ndeenda," created with the Kamiriithu community, were extremely offensive to the ruling Kenya African Nationalist Union Party, especially since these issues were linked to an attack on religious, social and political elites as well as on global capitalism. The play was banned and Ngugi wa Thiong'o was imprisoned for a year without trial. In 1980, after Ngugi's release, another play—"Maitu Njugira" —was also banned, and the open-air theater built by the Kamiriithu community was razed to the ground. Ngugi wa Thiong'o, Ngugi wa Mirii and most of the other facilitators fled into exile.

The Kamiriithu experience was a heroic inspiration to community theater activists, but it also marked the limits of what was possible in a dictatorship. The Theater for Primary Health Care facilitators in Liwonde had no intention of pushing communities into open confrontation with the Malawi government, not least because the villagers would be the ones who would suffer most. It is never legitimate for a theater facilitator to opt for other people's martyrdom. At that time it was normal practice for agents of the Malawi government to harass perceived opponents by seizing their property, beating them, putting them in detention without trial or even killing them extrajudicially. In that context, Theater for Development campaigns could never push their collaborative analyses too far into the realm of the political. This is probably the main difference between Theater for Development, with its concern for conscientization, and Theater of the Oppressed, with its greater commitment to radical transformation.

I expressed my frustration at these limitations in two ways—one professional, another personal.

At the theatrical level, my duties at the university were not restricted to Theater for Development. I had a third-year course of more mainstream practical drama, and I was coordinator of a student club, the Chancellor College Traveling Theatre. Both had repertoires that mixed English-language and Chinyanja plays, some scripted, some company-created, and performed mostly in urban areas at schools and community halls. The disadvantage of these plays was that it was difficult to avoid the elitism that comes from academic artists taking their prepackaged products to the wider world. The advantage was that the theater was not restricted to the agenda of any nongovernmental organization (NGO), and the students were aware of the dangers involved in pushing criticism of the political regime beyond certain limits. A few plays created in this way did manage, through techniques of allegory, allusion and association (easily decoded by audiences) to go beyond the stage of proximate social observation; they sometimes achieved complex and devastating criticism of both the Malawian political system and its linkages to global power mechanisms.

This was particularly true of the company-created plays of the third-year Practical Drama course, which were intended to teach students skills in acting, directing, playwriting, design and stagecraft. The 1985 play "Ulemu Unlimited" uses a story of two brothers struggling to improve their economic status as an allegory for recent events in Malawi, including the assassination of four prominent politicians who had run afoul of the president's inner circle of power. "Willing Spirits" (1987) is set in an imaginary East African country, Ngambika, a very thinly disguised Malawi. The play deals with a psychologically disturbed Ngambikan, Aggrey, who describes in flashback his betrayal of friends in Ngambika, speaking to an almost equally disturbed British psychiatrist. The unofficial drug trade in Malawi/Ngambika is used as a metaphor for Aggrey's obsession with consumerism and, more widely, for Third World dependency on Western cultural values. "They Call It Africa" (1990) uses the dramatic frame of aliens visiting earth to rescue it from ecological destruction; this allows the play to attack Malawi's exploitative tobacco estate system and the global tobacco industry with which it is linked.

All of these plays pushed near or beyond the limits of the state's tolerance. "Ulemu Unlimited" had one scene cut by the Censorship Board. Police questioned some of the actors and myself about "Willing Spirits," while the Censorship Board banned "They Call It Africa" after one tumultuous performance to an audience of about 1500 people. In the absence of democratic political debate in Malawi, theater of this kind assumed a significant role as a focus for and expression of popular dissent.

The other outlet for my frustration at Malawi's dictatorship was personal, in the field of human rights. Over the years I had made contacts with Amnesty International (A.I.) concerning human rights abuses involving people I knew, particularly the cases of four students, two of whom were prominent members of the University Traveling Theatre, detained without trial for a year (1983–84). When my close friend and colleague, the internationally renowned poet Jack Mapanje, was detained without trial in 1987, he was eventually able to set up a furtive communication system (through a sympathetic prison guard) with an Irish priest, Patrick O'Malley, and myself. Jack and later some of his fellow prisoners were able to smuggle out very detailed accounts of conditions in the notorious Mikuyu Detention Prison. The Malawi desk officer at Amnesty International asked me to become a volunteer researcher on a clandestine basis (since A.I. was a banned organization in Malawi at the time). My human rights activism blended into the movement for multiparty democracy, especially after the release of Mapanje and most other political prisoners in 1991 came about as a result of international pressure. The Malawian secret police in turn put pressure on me (through threats to me and my family) to leave the country, which we did in 1992, seeking work and schooling in different countries.

I took up a post teaching drama and English at the University of Botswana. Botswana had a totally different political history from Malawi's. It was relatively wealthy, owing to its prudent stewardship of revenue derived from the diamond-mining industry. It had a vibrant and well-resourced educational system and a healthy multiparty democracy with a strong tradition of civil liberties, including free cultural expression.

As in Malawi, I became involved in two different types of theater. My duties with regard to a drama course (called E423) led me into a tradition of devising company-created plays with my students in a mixture of English and Setswana. During vacations, I worked with some students on a voluntary basis in support of government- and NGO-sponsored Theater for Development HIV/AIDS-awareness campaigns.

My hope was that Botswana's cultural freedom would provide a context in which Forum Theater would be able to push beyond domestic relations, family breakdown, promiscuity and the need for condoms to larger issues. But in Botswana, too, I did not feel that the Theater for Development work in which I was involved progressed much beyond the parochially instrumental.

The project was part of a partnership between volunteer students and myself from the university and two organizations, the Ministry of Health's AIDS/STD Unit and a fairly small NGO, AIDS Action Trust (ACT). In the first campaign, I trained the student volunteers in Forum Theater techniques related to AIDS awareness, then helped them train a theater troupe in Mochudi, a large village (almost a small town) 35 kilometers from the capital, Gaborone. The theater group consisted of unemployed young men and women, most of whom had dropped out of school. First the university group members created their own play, using the Mochudi group as an audience and teaching them Forum techniques. Then the Mochudi group did their own participatory research into attitudes about sexuality and HIV infection in the village. On this basis they created their own play, with cut-off points for opening up the discussion to the audience. This play was performed at the village *kgotla* (assembly), in schools and in the main street outside the post office.

The strategy of the government and NGO facilitators, working in close cooperation with each other and with the university group, was to use Theater for Development as a tool both for community awareness and for research into attitudes about sexuality and AIDS, especially among young people. The AIDS facilitators had their own system of monitoring the impact of the campaign through psychometric tests on participants and audience samples. Testing during the 1993 campaign in Mochudi showed that the main attitude change—accepting the link between unprotected promiscuous sex and HIV infection—was found not in the audiences but in the group of young men and women who formed the drama group.

At the evaluation session the communication officers at the AIDS/STD Unit and ACT felt the best way to capitalize on their findings was to try to establish AIDS-awareness drama groups in secondary schools, so that they could form the nucleus of a peer-education process. In the following year, during the long vacation, the university drama team, after further intensive training, undertook the much larger task of training interested secondary-school students in AIDS-awareness drama techniques in Gaborone and the nearby villages of Lobatse, Ramotswa and Molepolole. Although the campaign seemed successful according to follow-up research conducted by the sponsors, it was difficult to sustain once the university leaders had returned to college, owing to lack of interest and support shown by teachers at the school.

I had some of my own doubts about the effectiveness of both the 1993 and '94 campaigns, despite their obvious achievement. One point related to the Forum technique. I was expecting the freedom that existed in Botswana to make Forum Theater an even more useful tool of conscientization than in Malawi. Certainly, audiences were quicker to participate in discussions during performances, no matter who was present, sometimes almost destroying the whole frame of the play in the process. The biggest problem, however, was that the large size of the audiences (rarely below 200) made opening-up techniques counterproductive, since peer pressure often encouraged the participants to reproduce social prejudices toward sexuality rather than to challenge them. More productive and franker discussions took place within smaller groups after performances.

I also became aware of a broader set of misgivings that paralleled my earlier doubts about the political boundaries placed on the Primary Health Care work in Malawi. I became increasingly aware of audience cynicism toward AIDS messages. One reason was that the almost missionary zeal of the facilitators sometimes made the audience feel they were being preached at, no matter how assiduous the participation techniques were. This was compounded by audiences' perception that the whole AIDS-awareness campaign, even when conducted by Batswana, was being orchestrated by shadowy agencies from industrialized countries with dubious agendas. This impression was in turn reinforced by the unremitting instrumentality of the plays, particularly when condom-wielding members of Population Services International, an American NGO that promotes contraception, accompanied the performances.

I felt that the plays did not push the inquiry into the causes of AIDS far enough beyond the proximate issues of marital infidelity and prostitution. I wanted to address the wider issues of poverty, urban anomie and cultural imperialism which come into play as the fabric of Botswana's society becomes enmeshed, through its recent industrialization into global markets, with the forces of global capitalism.

I would like to illustrate my doubts about both the Malawian and Botswana Theater for Development programs by showing in graphic form the possible problems NGOs have tried to address through theater, and the series of analyses which the theater process did make, as well as the more complex ones it failed to make.

Problem	Unhygienic Wells	HIV Infection
1st why?	Villages lack information and communal activism	Promiscuity Nonuse of condoms
2nd why?	Insufficient schools Lack of local democracy Private ownership of wells	Marriage breakups "Skin" sex preferred Teenage affairs Ignorance about HIV Prostitution Rape
3rd why?	Rural underdevelopment Dictatorship and corruption Capitalism attacks communalism Patronage replaces self-help	Migrant labor and adoption of urban values Poverty, urbanization, social anomie Male distortion of tradition—machismo Peer pressure and lack of sex education
4th why?	Malawi's conservatism supported by industrial-nation powers Poverty and dependency syndrome	Global capitalism and cultural imperialism Scapegoat syndrome and machismo

I have stopped after four iterations, but obviously it is possible to go much further.

The process of using Theater of the Oppressed requires constantly asking the question "Why?" to reveal the causes of social problems that sometimes lie quite far in the past. The analysis starts with proximate personal issues, but

The arrest of Robert Sobukwe is portrayed in "The Death and Life of Bessie Head" in Gaborone, Botswana, 1996. This E423 play about the South African/Botswana writer Bessie Head examines the political and psychological roots of racism in Southern Africa.

keeps pushing participants to probe more deeply until fundamental structural causes are revealed. In this way, apparently disparate local issues connect to each other through their common linkages to more complex, global problems, for example, the last two "Why's" in the above chart. In Theater for Development, it is rare for the analysis to go beyond the first two "Why's."

The reasons for this are not difficult to find. The main sponsors for Theater for Development projects are NGOs with specific missions of their own. They are part of a global aid industry, which is subject to some of the same disciplines of accountability as global corporations. The project directors can only guarantee continued budgets from their donors if they provide fairly concrete indicators of success, normally within a system of annual audits. In such a system, success can only be easily audited through concrete achievements—wells surrounded by cement protective guards, or condoms distributed, and so on. Attitudes are notoriously difficult to measure, and there is no managerial incentive to engage with complex, global relationships underlying the development problems of different sectors. Nor is there any incentive to analyze historical causes of problems; the "developmentalist present" proves just as restrictive as the rightly maligned "ethnographic present."

It is this neglect of deeper global imperatives that caused my misgivings about Theater for Development in both Malawi and Botswana, so I don't wish to neglect them here.

A simple way of looking at globalization is to see it as an extension of imperialism. Multinational corporations, global currency markets and the domination of developing economies by the G8 countries[2] through organizations like the General Agreement on Tariffs and Trade (GATT) and the International Monetary Fund (IMF) perform in the early 21st century a similar role of surplus extraction, market manipulation and political control that the imperialist European nations played in the late 19th and early 20th centuries. At the cultural level, the glamour of commercial mass media (especially from the United States)—popular music, film, television and advertising, backed up by the prestige of the English language—provides a lubricant for the industrialized world's economic hegemony.

Such an analysis might suggest it would be easy to recognize the injustice of the system of global economic and communication networks, leading cultural workers simply to identify with nations outside the G8 block, particularly those in the Southern Hemisphere. Unfortunately, the struggle against global domination is more complicated than that. Although global capitalism has its heartland in the United States and the other G8 countries of the Northern Hemisphere, it manifests in every nation and continent, either directly through multinational corporations or indirectly through trade, finance and communications arrangements which articulate Third World economies with those of the Northern powers. A network of economic and political treaties, understandings, influences and pressures create allies, partners, accomplices or sympathizers in Third World nations, whether in governments, the private sector or aid agencies.

The struggle, therefore, although global in scale, is not purely geographical; it is between a richly endowed, subtle, evanescent, multipenetrative system of domination and commodification on one side and on the other, a variegated, sometimes confused set of social, industrial, cultural, ecological and gender alliances emerging from the ruins of communism's collapse and the failure of modernization schemes in the Third World. The diversity and scope of this struggle is therefore very complex and constantly shifting. Agencies within nation-states frequently clothe themselves in the language of liberation to disguise their fundamentally oppressive nature, while others may fight globalization with one limb while supporting it with another. Cultural workers' main task, therefore, is to unmask false images and map the shifting maze of options and strategies.

One major source of contradiction is fundamentalism, whether based on religion, ethnicity or culture. A very natural reaction to Northern cultural domination of indigenous Southern cultures is an almost knee-jerk recoil into essentialism—a desire to affirm one's individual and group identity by participating in an emotionally supportive meta-community that posits an ersatz ethnic, religious or cultural purity as an escape from the confusing morass of multinational, postmodern commercial images and sounds with which capitalism floods local communities. Fundamentalism and essentialism

[2] Canada, France, Germany, Italy, Japan, Russia, the United Kingdom, the United States and the European Union.

nearly always have their roots in appeals to history or to a sense of community tradition arising from ancient practices. Very often these "histories" and "traditions" are actually myths, supporting elites with a stake in a specific cultural ideology.

One problem is that such fundamentalism may give rise to new inequalities with powers based on aggressive nationalist or religious influences or a cultural atavism that scapegoats such marginalized groups as women, teenagers, gays or those suffering from disabilities (including HIV infection). At certain historical periods, a tactical resort to essentialism might support a progressive resistance to global forces; but more often fundamentalism masks local oppression, undermining the cultural and institutional alliances necessary to combat Northern global hegemony.

In short, compared with the anti-colonial struggle of the 1950s or the anti-apartheid struggle of the 1970s and '80s, there are no easily identified barricades in the early 21st century behind which African cultural combatants can muster their weapons. The constantly shifting battle lines created by a massively resourceful, fluid, global communications industry require flexible, well-informed and vigilant local cultural workers, able to adapt their practices to new strategies. Also required is play making which is not restricted to the accessibly concrete and local, even though that would normally be the drama's starting point.

It is within this context of a search for a theater methodology capable of linking local problems to global issues that I began to put most of my energy into the E423 practical drama course I taught. E423 was rather similar to the third-year course I taught in Malawi, except that these students had even less experience of drama. They hoped that the course would provide them with basic skills in playwriting, direction, acting and design, so that they could become patrons of drama as teachers in Botswana's rapidly expanding secondary-school system. The course was built around the creation of a company-created production centering on controversial and usually topical issues in Botswana society.

[3]For further information on some of the E423 plays, see David Kerr, "Drama as a Form of Action Research: The Experience of UBE423 at the University of Botswana," *Southern African Theatre Journal*, 11/1 and 2, 1997, pp. 133–153; and Kerr, "Sexual Abuse and Gender Conflict: The Experience of a Play Creation Process at the University of Botswana," *Journal of Dramatic Criticism*, 15/1, 2000, pp. 121–136.

Although the structure of E423 was very similar to the third-year course I taught in Malawi, I tried to base the Botswana group more on student-led research into the problems raised by the play. This research element gave the process some similarities to Theater for Development, but the play was created over a period of about 10 weeks rather than a few days. Even more importantly, NGOs did not give the topics to E423. Instead the students chose the topics of the plays, and then sought out appropriate NGOs or institutions for research and sometimes for cooperation in development campaigns. As the course attracted more women than men, there was a tendency to deal with women's issues and human rights. I shall summarize a few of these plays and explain one in a little more detail.[3]

In 1992–93 the students created a play eventually entitled "You Are Not Dead" with assistance from two women's support groups, Women in Law in Southern Africa (WLSA) and Emang Basadi (Women Stand Up). The starting point was to look at the problem of women abandoned by their husbands or partners and receiving no maintenance for the upkeep of their children. This was an issue on which WLSA and Emang Basadi were vigorously lobbying the Botswana government, and also one faced personally by more than one woman enrolled in the course. Through research with the two women's organizations and their own primary research, the students started pushing the issues beyond the immediate problem of broken marriages to broader questions of sexism in society in general and in Botswana's legal system. The protagonist, Mmabontle, is abandoned with three children, and her sister, Daisy, with one child. When they take their men to court, the male-dominated legal system is unsympathetic, dismissing one case and providing a risible maintenance charge in the other. The title of the play is a line spoken by the ghost of Mmabontle's grandmother during a possession ritual. In her possessed state, Mmabontle has a vision of a utopian future where the courts are dominated by women rather than by men.

E423 created another play about women's issues in 1994–95, working in partnership with women's rights NGOs, Emang Basadi and Metlaetsile. The executive director of the latter organization, human rights lawyer Unity Dow, gave considerable help to the students in researching the play and in the final script-writing. Even the title of the play—"I Love My Country But…" —was based on a bumper sticker adorning her car (I Love My Country But I Fear My Government). The project started when a young female student (who at the time had a relationship with an American) proposed the topic of intercultural marriages for the group's play. When the students started their research, with Unity's help, they became very concerned with a topic currently causing great controversy: Botswana's Citizenship Act. This act discriminated against Botswana women who married foreigners, effectively making their children stateless. Unity, a victim of the law, took the Botswana government to the High Court and won her case, but still the government refused to change the law. "I Love My Country But…" took up this cause. The play used flashbacks into Botswana's history to show some of the events that contributed to the cultural fundamentalism fueling the sexism at the basis of the law. It also drew upon transcripts of Unity Dow's case as dialogue in the play. The total campaign, of which the play was a small part, was successful: a few months later, the government changed the discriminatory clauses in the Immigration Act.

In 1996–97, E423 took up another topical issue, the outbreak of cattle lung disease in Ngamiland, the home district of some of the students in the group. Although the students began by researching the disease and its social impact on affected farmers, they eventually realized that those issues could only be understood by analyzing events in Botswana's past and linking the cattle problem to broader issues of land ownership, ethnic tensions, class exploitation, politics and global ecology. The story deals with three Ngami farmers who consult a San spirit medium after an outbreak of cattle lung disease and are induced to perform a trance dance. In their visions (hence the play's title, "Vision in a Dance") they see the roots of Botswana's land and cattle problems in the history of colonialism and neocolonialism, which has led to the gradual privatization of land in Botswana.

The 1998–99 production "Murdering the Soul" returned to more domestic issues as its starting point. The play's main topic was the sexual abuse of children, and the students' research efforts received considerable help from the university's Social Work Department and from Botswana's human rights NGO, Ditshwanelo. However, the main partner in the creation of the play was the children's rights NGO, Childline, especially its local executive director, Malecha Monthe, who helped ensure that the information about referral of abused children for psychiatric help was accurate. The play, based on real case histories, dealt with two 13-year-old girls, one sexually abused by her stepfather, the other by both her teacher and a pedophile tourist. The play links these case histories with broader issues of poverty, religion and machismo in Botswana society, the international tourism industry, prostitution and the psychosocial causes of pathological violence.

The play I want to deal with in a little more detail is the 1999–2000 production of "The Ghosts Return." That year there were two conflicting lobbies in the very large student group. One wanted to create a play that commemorated the 15th anniversary of the 1985 raid by apartheid commandos on various targets in Gaborone, killing 11 people, injuring others and destroying much property. Another group wanted a play on the topic of Botswana Television (BTV), which was to be launched within two months of E423's target date for the first performance. In the end we satisfied both lobbies by creating a play about a Botswana TV crew making a documentary on the 1985 raids.

Information gathering for the play had to be extensive. There was archival research into the raids, especially old newspaper accounts, fleshed out by interviews with witnesses and survivors. On the television side, some of the newly trained recruits to BTV, including one very enthusiastic graduate of the 1997–98 E423 course, gave considerable information about the structure, atmosphere, issues and working practices at the new station. This was supported by readings in the theory and practice of African media.

The main issue to emerge was that of media freedom. Botswana has a very good reputation for tolerance, with a lively independent press that is usually successful in resisting government attempts to muzzle it. Even the government-backed station Radio Botswana attempts to cover opposition politics as well as those of the ruling Botswana Democratic Party. However, we found that the newly trained BTV technicians, journalists and artists were concerned that television's much stronger emotional appeal, owing to its use of visuals, might tempt government into trying to control it. The whole issue was made more complicated by the fact that white expatriates held the senior managerial and technical positions in the new station.

"The Ghosts Return" centers on the conflict between a young Motswana documentary producer, Refilwe, and her boss, Bernard. Refilwe is an idealistic woman who wants to make a documentary that not only shows the atrocity of the commando raids on Gaborone, but also draws attention to the danger of allowing the Botswana Defense Force (BDF) to use the excuse of the 1985 raid to expand its powers in the year 2000. Bernard, concerned for his own job, is worried that the topic is too sensitive. The following dialogue gives some feeling of the clash of interests:

> *Bernard:* This documentary as it stands will cause havoc. How many times do I have to remind you that this is a government TV station?
>
> *Refilwe:* Correction. It's a *public* TV station.
>
> *Bernard:* A public TV station almost fully funded by government.
>
> *Refilwe:* There's a difference.
>
> *Bernard:* You cannot criticize the government and its departments on its own TV station. That's a simple fact of life.
>
> *Refilwe:* Why not, if it's in the public interest?
>
> *Bernard:* Because I run this TV station, not you.

At a later stage, in a more conciliatory mood, Bernard explains how the media in Europe and America are also controlled, not necessarily directly but by what he calls "an unwritten rule…an understanding between so-called gentlemen." This media system, governed by global corporations, is inherently racist because it values Western lives far more than African lives. As he puts it to Refilwe, "The political and commercial lobbies, the advertisers, the invisible strings. This is the new imperialism. Indirectly the Turners and Murdochs will tell you what to think. At least your government claims to have the interests of the Botswana people at heart. Do you think private enterprise has any interests? It's just the bottom line, and don't rock the boat for them."

The documentary made by Refilwe raises some of the issues of racism, neo-colonialism, struggle and commitment that she faces in her conflict with Bernard. Some of the victims, like the young Christian Batswana women, Eugenia and Gladys in the play, had no interest in politics and were killed by the South African commandos in error. Others were exiled members of the African National Congress, though not necessarily serving any military function. The most famous of these was Thami Mnyele, a renowned artist;

the commandos not only killed him, but also shot round after round of bullets into his paintings and posters.

While Refilwe is trying to make up her mind whether to resist Bernard or not, the ghosts of Eugenia and Thami appear on the studio monitor to haunt her. Eugenia urges submission to Bernard, while Thami urges continued resistance, saying that it is a continuation of his own struggle. At the end of the play the ghosts present two endings for the audience to choose: Eugenia's ending, in which Refilwe hands over the master tape of the contentious documentary to Bernard; and Thami's ending, in which Refilwe organizes a demonstration of workers against Bernard.

"The Ghosts Return" was performed several times in Gaborone, including a major performance at the Maitisong Festival. It received considerable attention in newspaper articles and gave rise to some public debate about the new TV station, which sent a camera crew to film one performance and interviewed members of the cast about the issues. The production was very timely in that it coincided with major debates about the BDF and about media freedom. A year later, an expatriate senior news editor whose opinions were obviously closer to Refilwe's than to Bernard's resigned because of what he perceived as government interference into BTV's news and documentary practices. At about the same time, two newspapers, The Guardian and the Midweek Sun, were in legal conflict with the government over attempts to muzzle their criticism of BDF.

I have described "The Ghosts Return" in detail because it well illustrates some of the qualities of a committed theater which I was able to explore in most of the E423 plays, but found missing in my Theater for Development work. The E423 plays were able to show how current problems facing society have deep historical roots that are connected to wider social and political forces affecting the region, the continent and even the whole world. Of course, they were not able to address immediately accessible problems; no cement bags or condoms were distributed at the end of performances. Instead, the plays challenged audiences on major issues facing the nation of Botswana and allowed them to make links with progressive institutions that were struggling to solve those problems.

Since E423 was university-based, I may have given the impression that only well-educated theater groups are capable of this type of analytical, research-based theater. That is certainly not my contention. University groups have the advantage of access to research channels, but they have the disadvantage of tight academic calendars. Several institutions (Emang Basadi with "I Love My Country But…" and Childline with "Murdering the Soul") wanted E423 to travel around the country with the plays as part of specific campaigns concerning women's and children's rights. The university group could not fulfill these requests, owing to their commitments to exams and other academic programs. I am quite convinced it is possible for theater groups which are not based at an educational institution—and the bulk of whose members may not be well-educated—to create the kind of theater I am advocating. Some southern African groups such as the Sibikwa Players in South Africa and Zambuko/Izibuko in Zimbabwe have already achieved it.

I may have also given the impression that I am opposed to Theater for Development and to NGO promotion of that theater mode. This too is not true. NGO's promotion of theater can be extremely useful as a communication tool. Most NGOs are committed to progressive change; their problem is that the constraints of project-oriented funding policies, their lack of long-term planning and the high turnover of field officers make it difficult for them to address the fundamental problems that lie beneath the obvious obstacles to development. My main concern is that in southern Africa at present, NGO-funded Theater for Development has become so dominant as a form of patronage for small-scale, resource-poor theater troupes that it is difficult for artists to explore the full range of issues facing Africa, particularly those with roots in the past or those which cast light on global issues.

The solution is for African theater workers to build strong local institutions and networks that reflect indigenous concerns, rather than agendas chosen for them by NGOs or government agencies. One model for such a southern African institution is Amakhosi, a theater group from Zimbabwe. Through a shrewd mixture of NGO funding and private enterprise, it has built its own cultural center in Makokoba, a high-density location in Bulawayo, where it attracts considerable support from local residents. Likewise, the Southern African Theatre Initiative (SATI), operating from the Market Theatre Laboratory in Johannesburg, South Africa, may provide the basis for regional networking. If such institutions could be developed, it might be possible to negotiate with funding agencies from a position of greater strength, so that drama can be created that genuinely reflects local interests in the struggle to understand the rapid transformations society faces from globalization. It might also be possible to begin the process of making the grassroots linkages and alliances necessary to combat globalization's worst excesses. These alternative channels of communication would be able to contribute to the growing counter-globalization movement, which uses global media not to destroy but to sustain and strengthen local cultures.

Students from the
University of Lesotho
perform a skit in the street
to get audience reaction
and gather data to create
the play "Moiketsi."

15

Masitha Hoeane
Dean of Student Affairs
Technikon Witwatersrand
Student Affairs, House 5, Louisa Street (on campus)
37 Nind Street
Doornfontein 2094
Johannesburg, South Africa
Telephone: (27 11) 406 2401
E-mail: mhoeane@twrinet.twr.ac.za

Masitha Hoeane is Dean of Students at Technikon Witwatersrand, a 12,000-student university in Johannesburg, South Africa. In introducing himself through the online dialogue with his fellow conference participants, he stressed his background in theater and development:

I am a South African living and working in South Africa. But I spent most of my life in Lesotho where my parents chose to live in harder times.

I studied at the Universities of Lesotho, Nairobi and Leeds, the latter as researcher into theatre and development. I have been involved in various projects which dealt with development communication through the theatre. In the '80s I was teaching at the University of Lesotho, where the Marotholi Traveling Theatre under Zakes Mda was also quite active. I directed the the NUL [National University of Lesotho] Theatre Group which dealt primarily with commissioned work from government departments as well as parastatals like the LPPA, UNICEF, etc.

It took up issues such as family planning, HIV/AIDS awareness, etc. But I became more interested in working independently with communities as animateur in which regard I formed two community theatre groups.

His collection of participatory theater pieces, "Let My People Play!"[1] was published in 1994. As described in this interview, conducted by Arlene Goldbard in November 2001, Masitha's work has in recent years focused more on institutional change than on grassroots theater in villages. But whether one works with villagers confronting problems in local infrastructure or South African students facing the dilemma of creating a dynamic and authentic culture that can serve the needs of a nation emerging from apartheid, he has found that the same core questions pertain: how is it possible to protect, nourish and extend indigenous cultures against the pressures of globalized community culture?

[1] Masitha Hoeane,
*Let My People Play!
Participatory Theatre Plays*
(Johannesburg: Institute
of Southern African
Studies/NUL, 1994).

Culture as the Basis for Development

An Interview With Masitha Hoeane

Arlene Goldbard: Please start by telling a little about your own work, so that people understand where you're coming from in discussing these topics.

Masitha Hoeane: I started working in theater when I was working at the University of Lesotho. At that time, I was working with a theater group based at the university, and most of the work we were doing was Theater for Development, commissioned by government ministries and so on and so forth. We took up various themes, for instance, the Department of Health asked us to do something on HIV/AIDS or family planning, and we would take these themes and turn them into theater and take them out to the rural areas and villages and perform them out there, basically taking certain messages to the community as an educational campaign.

For instance, with the National University of Lesotho (NUL) theater group, we were given a brief to do a play on what is called family-life education—family planning—to promote its adoption by women in the country. There were many problems in relation to attitudes, especially of the men, who mostly worked in the South African mines and thought it would lead to promiscuity, especially during their absence. The NUL theater group took this particular brief and tried to work around it. They expected us to go out there and tell these people what to do. But we found that rather untenable, so we decided to do a little bit of research, if you like, within the community itself in order to get a sense of what people feel and create the play around it. What we did is to go to the bus terminal, where people are congregated in large numbers. We had a short skit. We took two nurses along, because we knew we weren't professionals in family planning, and if questions came, we wanted to handle them professionally. At the same time, we were running an experiment, because we wanted the public to react. And right in the street, we staged the play right there. The reactions of the public—some of them were quite angry, some were critical: "You're bringing these things here, you're corrupting our women!" We took that as data collection, and out of that, we started creating the play.

The final end product was actually a video, an educational video, which this LPPA—Lesotho Planned Parenthood Association— was going to use in educational campaigns. Even now they still use it in their campaigns. They were quite happy about it. It's entitled "Moiketsi." It's part of a proverb. There is this communications shorthand in Sesotho. This proverb would be well known. It says, "*Moiketsi ha a lleloe*," meaning something like, "He who brings misfortune upon himself, we do weep for such a person." Like if you go out and provoke people and you get hit, you've brought that upon yourself. But in Sesotho you don't say the whole proverb, you simply mention the first word, "*Moiketsi*," and the rest of it falls into place; people know what you are saying.

Like all Theater for Development in Africa, we saw some constrictions in working to a brief. Sometimes in the process of presenting them, we would find that they are not really priorities, and that was a bit disappointing. We began to work a little independently because that allowed us to address more relevant themes than coming into a community with prescribed things. We would go there to talk about health, or immunization, and find that the people wanted to talk about unemployment; that was uppermost in their minds. Or they were more concerned about the political situation. So it sort of gave us a feeling of irrelevance, and in the end we moved away from that and started working differently.

AG: In what way?

MH: We understood you could go out into a community without any specific agenda and then begin to commune with the village. We would carry out theater exercises to find out what people are talking about and listen when they expressed themselves. So you begin to explore together, and that made it relevant, in the sense that you picked the point of the theater from what they are saying. Then what the theater addresses would be what is raised by themselves.

AG: This was possible for you because people worked at the university? They were supported by the university?

MH: In Theater for Development, I did one big project which was part of my research. We worked with people from the university who were acting as *animateurs*, but in the end we handed over the project to the community, including its performing.

AG: When was this?

MH: We started in the '80s, up to '91, and then I left Lesotho. I came back in '95 and just worked briefly, and then left again.

AG: Since '95, have you been doing any popular theater work?

MH: After '95, I haven't been doing anything outside institutions. I've been working inside institutions with students.

AG: Why is that?

MH: Because of the conditions for Theater for Development in Africa. Working in Theater for Development can be quite frustrating.

One is that invariably you lack sponsorship. There are very few sponsors around, and that can hamper the quality of the work you do and the extent to which you can do it, and that can be quite demoralizing. When you work in communities, you definitely need some resources; and the people in the community also need things, because it costs money to run theaters, to move people around and so forth. So that's one problem we ran into. Occasionally you get a sponsor: UNICEF in this case sponsored "Moiketsi." But such sponsors are quite scarce, so you go without sponsorship. That's one problem.

The second one is that you cannot work on this thing full time. You can only give it partial attention because, again, there are no funders. Nobody works in Theater for Development full time, so you've got to get another job and do it part time. So there's a sense in which it encroaches upon your work. You don't give it sufficient attention. You can have a passion for it, you want to do it; but [there isn't] enough time, there isn't enough money. And also experience has shown elsewhere in Africa that it can actually be a thankless job. Theater for Development is people-oriented, it tries to uplift people in society; but the people who do it often run into problems with authority, as opposed to [authorities'] appreciating their doing the work of developing people.

AG: Why isn't this kind of work being supported?

MH: It's a kind of general problem we have in Africa, where there is a general absence of democracy. People get into power through the barrel of the gun, with tyrants in power. There are all kinds of tendencies, such as the oppression of women. In the very nature of Theater for Development, you are thinking of democratization, you are anti-tyranny, you are trying to liberate people, you are trying to raise their awareness. You are talking about their rights, making them feel they are important. They matter. Which is exactly what oppressive situations don't want.

AG: Did this suggest to you that a different context would be more successful?

MH: Yes. It's either that or you abandon it because sometimes you are gripped by despair. It's not the kind of despair in which you lose faith in Theater for Development; it's simply because the conditions under which you are doing it become very, very difficult. So it has been my decision, like many other practitioners, to function within an educational institution. You need to have some primary source of income which will allow you to do other things; so you do it as a hobby of a kind, and you do it for love. You don't expect to get anything in return. You need something to sustain you while you do it. It's an act of self-sacrifice, if you like. And also, it's important for you to function within an institution in the sense that when you work within an institution, then you can relate it to your work, then you can feed off your work, even in terms of resources. Also, I think African universities are the most protected environments in Africa. Otherwise the general situation is insecure.

AG: Why is that?

MH: I think the reason is simply that African tyrants are afraid of universities. Universities always have expatriates, people that are international, and if you do anything overt, you'll draw the attention of the world. Remember, these countries rely on foreign aid, so it's absolutely critical for them to pretend to the rest of the world. That's why they won't touch Westerners. It's not that they love them, but they fear exposure. So the universities are like islands, a certain measure of protection. I'm not saying total.

AG: How has globalization overall affected Theater for Development in Africa?

MH: Perhaps I will begin broadly in terms of globalization, because I feel globalization is not necessarily something new. When I talk about globalization, I am talking about a context of the way Africa has experienced the broader West. I'm talking about whatever theories of development have been brought to Africa, the attempts to emulate the Western world as a strategy of development in African countries. In the long run, that proved ineffective as a model of development, and people began to move toward alternatives, talking about the cultural dimension of development and so forth. That is the broader background.

Theater for Development as I see it is something that was started by the elite in Africa. By that I mean Western-educated people, and they started off in the traveling theaters. They started off by wanting to commune with communities, wanting to reach out. But they were reaching out in the wrong way—for instance by taking English plays to the villages. All of this presupposes an enlightened center, and some periphery out there which has to be enlightened. And in the process they ignore language issues, they ignore issues of culture and so on. A lot of mistakes were made. Over time, especially after independence, they retained the concept of the traveling theater, but began to undergo a certain transformation in the kinds of plays they were taking. The evolution I am talking about is a gradual realization over a long period of time: first, to change the language; and second, the performance modes; and third, it was not to make assumptions about the culture, but to go there by way of learning as much as teaching. In other words, the traveling theaters evolved into *animateurs* who were prepared to work on an equal footing with the community, and really that changes their content, their issues. That changes their performance modes, the language and everything.

AG: Do you feel that this transformation had been accomplished? Has everybody gotten this point, or are there still people out there trying to bring elite theater from the villages to the center?

MH: It has been a general development in that direction, although you could say that theater in Africa is not exactly the same in different places. But in general, there are very few people if any now who still do that kind of theater. The broad majority of practitioners of Theater for Development wouldn't do that anymore.

AG: In David Kerr's essay [in this volume], he talks about all foreign-aid NGOs commissioning or sponsoring traveling theater projects, describing how their agenda comes with the money. He raises the question of how popular theaters can be supported so they don't come with NGO strings attached. How do you see that?

MH: That has been a problem that I have encountered personally— because you have to have money from somewhere. As a practitioner of Theater for Development, you have to provide what you might call a courier service for the ideas, to have some way for them to reach rural areas. And in the process of doing that, you find yourself compromised, because you are like somebody who is employed to do something that sometimes is not what you believe in yourself. When you go out to the village, if you're a genuine community worker, you begin to commune with people. You might find that the conclusions you reach might be different from the ones you've been given the brief to do. But if you are working to a brief, if these are your sponsors, then you must see the message through, because that's what they paid you for. The practitioners of the theater —when they are not themselves the generators of the message, when it is generated elsewhere—I think it is not appropriate for the theater and for the village as well.

In other words, for it to develop properly and genuinely, for it to remain relevant and authentic, it needs to break that link with the current sponsor, or to get a sponsor in a different mode, who thinks differently, who can say, "Go to your community. I want to help that community." Then I didn't come with an agenda: there's no self-interest in any way, and I respect the integrity of that community to be able to identify what is desired and help it along—because it *is* possible to get sponsors like that.

AG: Who are they, for instance?

MH: I have never actually encountered one. Unfortunately, within the context of Africa, you will find that it is government that's the sponsor, and they are not in that mode. The NGOs I know operating here are also not in that mode. But some people say, "I'm doing my own work, I'm doing my own research into the field." Nobody is saying, "I should look into this or that; people are supporting me to do what I do." Do you see that kind of thing?

AG: Not a lot. It's been interesting to get everybody's essays, because we're building up a sort of composite picture of the field, and very much these same problems are coming up in a lot of different places.

MH: Well, theoretically at least, there will be a breakthrough if theater practitioners could get that kind of funding to facilitate their work rather than determine it.

AG: Yes, absolutely.

MH: And unfortunately, we are trapped in a situation where the former is the case.

AG: In essence, you're saying the practitioners are ahead of the funding sources in understanding what's really needed.

MH: Exactly. The practitioners are far ahead, and the practitioners are also, you might say, closer to the community, more receptive. They know what is going on on the ground. And I think a lot of them, the more progressive ones, are well disposed toward communities and how they develop. They're more in touch with what's going on down there. They wouldn't go and parachute something into a community. They would more likely start to say, "Let's work with the community: this community has got integrity, there are things I can learn from as well." And then work from inside there and try to get somewhere. But NGOs simply come with the attitude, that "No, no: most communities don't know what they want. They need an external person to show them where to go. We know the agenda. We know what's good for them. They can't help themselves." And it's simply because [community people] don't have the money. [NGOs] don't realize that's the difference between the two: some have money, and those that do not are incapacitated in that sense.

What we are talking about here is culture as the basis for development. Every culture should be able to have the resources to say what it needs for development. That development must really be inside that culture rather than [imposed] externally. That may sound controversial, I know.

AG: Well, not in this company. I think you'll find a lot of like minds. Because you've lived inside and outside South Africa at this important point in its history, I'm wondering if you have observations to share on this question in relation to South Africa. When you say every culture should have the resources to say what it needs to develop, there you have a particular kind of problem which we've seen in other places like in Czechoslovakia, the former Yugoslavia, where a nation has been liberated and has to develop a new culture.

MH: Within South Africa, I suppose that's about the hottest thing that's going around here. But fortunately, I think the context now in South Africa, despite whatever other problems may be there, is that South Africa is coming out of a history of conflict and, I think, extreme backwardness—racism, racial intolerance and so on—the context, guided by the constitution, explicitly promotes multiculturalism. Everywhere, everybody talks about it. The institutions here are talking about diversity and how to handle diversity, so that even the funding for these things considers the fact that people are sponsored across the spectrum. There's a lot of sensitivity for culture. Yet there is still some inequality and a great bias, I think—perhaps unwitting a lot—toward Western culture. What I see on a large scale is black people are mimicking white cultures. This is a very strong thing here. You see it on TV especially: the so-called celebrities, they mimic things that are from outside of here.

AG: So what do you feel from your perspective in cultural development: when you look at that society as it's growing, what do you feel is needed to balance that?

MH: In South Africa, in the long run, cultural activities are going to be very expensive to fund because there are so many cultures. Talking of a common South African culture is a big problem. You know, we see ourselves as the rainbow nation. We need to see ourselves in that context because I don't think there's what you can call a South African culture. We have a spectrum. It is a nation of several cultures, which…come from a history of antagonism. So what should be developed is some kind of peaceful coexistence between those cultures. In some cases, you do get a true kind of coming together. Let me say Johannesburg. If you ask the people here what language they talk, you won't get one answer. In Johannesburg, you just speak many tongues, and yet you communicate, they understand each other. In the taxi, in the public places, people get by that way. Nobody's controlling that; it's happening spontaneously. A lot of the people here in Johannesburg are really detribalized over a long process of living around here. Even their names: a person with a Zulu surname will have a Sesotho name. Intermarriages, what have you, I think they are quite integrated, and they get by quite well. Johannesburg is not a bad example of culture in South Africa.

This is also associated with the mines. I think that's where it first started. The mines brought together several tribes, and they met with the Afrikaners and the Europeans and so on, and they had to take instructions and get by somehow. They spoke something called

Fanakalo, a South African form of pidgin, a conglomeration of a little bit of Afrikaans, a little bit of Zulu, a fantastic jumble. But in the mines, they speak it and they understand it.

AG: Gary Stewart's interview [in this volume] describes work he's doing with Asian kids from London, second-generation, their parents emigrated from India or Pakistan mostly. He was saying something new is being created by the mixing of these cultures, and there's a tendency to say it should be a sort of melting pot, that it should all come together to be one British thing; but the way he looks at it and the way he's working with the kids, it's more like a constant quoting and mixing without diluting. He said, "We don't want to call it fusion, we just want to say it's normal for the conditions of our lives." Sounds a little like what you're saying.

MH: That's interesting, because when I was in Leeds I did a project like that addressing racism, so we were dealing with young people from different backgrounds, but mostly they were British and Asian and a few black ones. We decided to create a dance theater because we realized with hip-hop, that music was a sort of common ground where they meet. They aspire to the same things, the same dances; that was the one really common thing, so we played around with that. It was quite interesting.

AG: As Dean of Students, you are now seeing the younger generation in great numbers.

MH: Yes. We deal with several problems that are current: HIV/AIDS, we address that through theater as well; we deal with diversity issues. We've run some campaigns. This year, we set some goals. We were going to launch a wellness office, where originally we thought of an HIV/AIDS office, but we did not want to stigmatize it in that way, so we just called it the wellness office so we can deal with other issues that the young people want to talk about. We trained peer helpers, because we want student-to-student communication, which is better than when adults talk to them. So they were trained by counselors to be AIDS educators and peer helpers. We also ran other campaigns, like what we call the "Talk to 10" campaign, where in a particular period you are asking each student to talk to 10 other students to get them to take ownership of their own issues. So it's talking to 10 other people, asking them a question or expressing an opinion about HIV or any aspect of it. We are hoping that if each student talks to 10, and it goes like that, it will spread and embrace the whole student community. And it worked quite well. We took a survey to find out how many people were talked to in that kind of elementary way, and we found that over 80 percent of the students had participated.

AG: I can't resist asking you a question now that relates back to your original point about work that's driven by an agenda. Did the students find out things their fellow students cared about that you hadn't known, that weren't part of your agenda?

MH: That was our concern immediately. We said that it might not be giving information; it might also involve asking a question, expressing an opinion, so that it doesn't just become didactic in a very narrow way. There should be communication, but we should leave it open to a range of possibilities. By the very nature of an intervention, you must be careful. Sometimes you come with a bias, even unwittingly. Sometimes there is an attitude you bring.

In South Africa, here on the campus, we just had a discussion the other day where we said, "You know, we are so preoccupied with race because we come from that kind of background; we think that's the thing that we've got to get right. But there are so many issues between students. Some of them are not even thinking about it anymore. I'm not saying it will fade altogether, but there are other issues now—abuse of girls, other issues that belong to the world of students—that we may lose sight of, because we are emphasizing that concern, because race has always been a problem for our generation.

AG: It's ironic in a way, isn't it? Because race was the preoccupation before liberation, and now for the healing of that, it's still a preoccupation, which can have unintended consequences as you point out. You mentioned, for instance, this need to have a culture that's not based on mimicking people from the West. How do you see it as possible to affect that, to replace it with something that feels more South African?

MH: The culture is emerging and has been for some time now in the townships, where it was a conglomeration of languages. It's got, for example, songs from different cultures that people have heard and seen as their own, because they grew up hearing them. That's an alternative source of culture, although it goes back to the question of money: Who controls the money? What will TV stations buy? I think people behave like that (mimicking the West) not only because they want to be like that, but also because that's what sells.

AG: When we talk about globalization, that's a big part of it, that all these commercial cultural products are coming out primarily from America and flooding the globe.

MH: Flooding the globe. One example: only yesterday, Manchester United, the football team, was playing against a team from somewhere in Europe. They showed it here, and there was a good local match but they didn't show it. That's a small thing, but in the morning, you listen to the news, they tell you the scores of the European Cup. They can show you the goals that were scored in Europe, but they cannot show you how the goals were scored in this country. There is more coverage of European subjects than you can get for something of local interest.

AG: It creates the message that what is happening here is inferior somehow?

MH: What is happening here is inferior, and I think it is doing a lot of damage to our children, to their self-image, self-esteem. I think it does something to their morale. Even when they grow up, they grow up with a disrespect for that which is local, because it doesn't seem to matter. I think that causes tremendous social problems. Values, respect, attitudes—they together create a system. When that system falls apart, the culture becomes confused. When you lose an identity, the identity that remains is reflected in the values I see in the young people here. I think some of them just fall apart, and I don't think they know what they are doing, whether they are coming or going, because they have lost what they had, and they have not fully grasped that which they want to change.

AG: If you were in a position to do whatever is needed to change this, what would you do?

MH: If I had the power, I would start with the media, because the media are a very powerful force that are stimulating this process and pushing it. The media ought to change priorities, to try to engage the local situation. They should become more reflective of where we are and more promotional of what goes on locally. The media would have to go back to research in the communities and reflect that on the screen. At the same time I suppose you'd have to change the educational system to begin to reconstruct wrong attitudes about culture, because I think that's where it begins. You would also have to go back and invest in developing local culture, because the media cannot promote local culture if there is nothing coming from local culture.

AG: Is that happening now? Is there funding for local cultural development in South Africa? Are people able to get resources to do things like reconstruct traditional languages or practices?

MH: There is something in that direction, but I'm not sure whether it has been strong enough. Neither do I think enough resources have been put there. There is already an entrenched inequality. My suspicion is that it becomes easier to go on with established things than to go back and try to create new foundations. As an example, let me talk about the university when South Africa became free. There were so many black universities and so many white universities. Many of the white universities were very well-resourced in terms of the level of the institution, the equipment there, everything, whereas many of the black universities were really the opposite. Some of them were almost bankrupt.

When the government changed, there were discussions of differential funding, so that we could pick up the poor universities to the level of the others. But I think that scheme was practically abandoned, because it is easier to say, "Why don't we close down the bad ones and run the already successful ones, except making sure that they have equal access?" And it becomes a very emotional matter, because those that are historically black, there's a lot of sentiment around them; but to bring them up from where they are to this level is almost impossible, because of money. So the easy way out is just to abandon them, and that is the reality. That is the writing one sees on the wall.

AG: In the American South, in the Deep South, in the places that held on the longest to segregation in this country, they also had black schools and white schools. They were both public—that is, government-funded—schools, and the white schools had a lot more money and better books and classrooms, but the black schools had a respect for black culture. They had black principals and teachers, so there was more of a feeling of autonomy, even though they were not as good in terms of resources, there was a feeling that the culture could be preserved and advanced somehow through them. Don [Adams] and I did some work down there. We talked to several people who had been principals or head teachers at black schools, and when they ended segregation, the black schools were closed down. In effect, everything that had been built up just disappeared. There are a lot of people there who say they paid a high price for the end of segregation, because it also meant the end of these community institutions.

There's an underlying theme in a lot of what you've been saying which has to do with, on the one hand, what should be happening, and on the other hand, what is happening because of how the money flows, or expediency, or what seems possible. Seems like there's a big gap between those two things.

MH: I think there's a really, really big gap, and that gap is very difficult to negotiate, because there are all sorts of things that are emotive issues. For instance, the situation is that you find that black teachers actually send their children to white schools in the post-'94 period. This is a general trend in the public, but I think it's very telling that the black teachers do it as well. This is a matter of public debate, when the public can say, "Even the teachers…" That to me is a very serious signal in a negative sense, when people have lost entire faith in their own institutions, in the things they do. They feel they would rather surrender their children elsewhere. With the coming of independence here, we see rising expectations among the black people who also happen to be the destitute majority. And their rising expectations— which are rising fast—I think really they cannot be met.

So you sort of enter a period of depression. You start with euphoria, you perhaps have unrealistic expectations, but certain things haven't happened that people thought would happen, and nobody ever thought clearly about how they could be done. So there is that period you enter into now of uncertainty, disillusionment, cynicism. It's hard for people to do anything in that kind of period.

AG: That's a frightening time for any society.

MH: I think so too. Because some of the people you see in Johannesburg here, you just don't know what happened to them. There is a big, big confusion in terms of what is happening.

I see a microcosm of this within the institution. This was a white institution not so long ago. Then it transformed very rapidly. The student population is now about 80 percent black, but the staff is still as it was. A few people have come in, just like myself. But a lot of the time you find that this is an institution that requires healing. Black students have formerly spent their time fighting authority. Schools were seen as legitimate spaces to fight the system because also they were extensions of the system. Now the whole thing has to change, and we are supposed to lead the change in that culture, so we become the shock absorbers, if you like. At the same time, I think the white lecturers have certainly been traumatized by the coming of black students. The caliber of students that they are teaching is no longer the same, and I think some of them get annoyed with that; and then the failure rate is very high, and the students complain that they are being failed, and you get that kind of tension. Also, black students don't have the means to pay. It is so difficult. You have to bring these groups together to have some kind of dialogue that's a healing process toward the normalization of the institution, to bring it more in line with what an institution should be, so that the lecturers feel much more adjusted. The lecturers say the caliber of students is no longer the same, but their duties are the same: to bring them up. We suspect they need retraining because of all that happened, and there was no preparation for it.

AG: How has your work in the university been informed by what you've learned from your Theater for Development experience?

MH: In many ways, fundamental ways. I actually transferred the work into that environment and the entire approach is informed by that. Let us take some concrete examples. When first you meet students—the potential cast, the potential group of people you're going to work with—you'll work with them in a certain way, the methodology of preparing them with theatrical games and exercises, making them bond, building a sense of team, that interdependence that is so critical to the functioning of a cast. Then all those techniques you use to advance your goals and to communicate with these people. So that's one way. Then of course, people learn in certain ways. You can lecture to people endlessly; that's one way of teaching. But in the theater, we believe differently, because it's all about participation and involvement: transformation of people and enhancement and change of their consciousness through direct involvement and participation rather than through being told. As a matter of fact, I think my effectiveness, to the degree I've been effective, is directly dependent on my early involvement in Theater for Development.

AG: Is there a specific project you've worked on at the university that addresses these cultural concerns you've brought up?

MH: We had what we called the Diversity Project, which we did in the second half of 2001, up to October. We looked at the multicultural situation. We have different racial and cultural groups within the institution, but somehow they seem not to connect well, which we thought was denying students a very important experience in terms of their development. So that's how the project was born: find ways of getting students to bond, to communicate, to reach across these barriers.

The Diversity Project was meant to do that, and the way it functioned was as follows: identify categories—racial, ethnic and so on, including also disabled students, international students, various groupings—and bring them together in a two-day workshop. They would sleep out and have sessions together, a mixture of formal workshop sessions and entertainment to maintain the human context between them. And then you talk to them about diversity issues, and they would come back with shared feelings together. And we thought that maybe this would create an alternative world for the students, give them an experience which their society denies them, which would make education very life changing for them. When the students come back, we had sessions with them to find out how they felt. It was just wonderful listening to them, some of them telling us how this impacted their lives.

AG: What kinds of things did they say?

MH: One said, "I have been fearful of the campus. I have not been mixing with the other students. But now that we've been out there, I understand their cultures better. I feel more adjusted. I felt part of it. I even have a few friends, and I can tolerate other cultures better." And he was saying the project was most useful to him.

AG: You're starting with a core of people in the workshops?

MH: In the workshops, you actually recruit people quite explicitly. You tell them what the purpose is, what you hope to achieve and what is going to happen, so that people know that they're not going to be forced to do anything they don't want to do, and so on. And then they come forward, and you accept them on the basis of first-come, first-served, but there's a quota for each category. Then the whole idea is that once you have groups like that, you take them out and you train them. When they come back, they will be used as growth points for other groups, to spread this influence. If you train 30 and each one of them forms a diversity group of 30, you can see how many people you'll have. When it spreads like that, we just hope at the end of the day people will be part of it. And the students showed a lot of interest. Once the first group had come back, when we called for the second one, we couldn't handle them all.

AG: In a way, you're using the university as a laboratory for cultural transformation.

MH: Precisely, especially if you consider the kind of society in which we live—that all these racial attitudes, prejudices, conflicts continue to linger in the outside society—and we must address that. We must give our students a different experience. A university is a community of young people, and also young intellectuals, the cream if you like of society, the future of society. So one idea is that in that space, you must create people who can lead. It isn't just a space where you replicate the problems in the larger society and where they are played out. To the contrary, it's where you reverse issues. As you said, it's a laboratory, an experiment in showing new possibilities, new directions. We are hoping to lead society, rather than follow its vices. Yes, the wider society does impinge, because these students come from somewhere, with backgrounds, influences and teachings and fears, anxieties, some of which are very difficult for them to handle as young people in this time of change in particular. If they're just left to their own devices without some strong intervention to reverse those trends, the students will just go on and become like the generations before them.

AG: It sounds as if the transition to the new system after the fall of apartheid was abrupt for the university. People just came to school one day and it was all different?

MH: Yeah. And I think everybody has hoped that things would be fine. And yet I don't think things happen that way. I think some people have to go to workshops to prepare them for the transition, so they can cope with it. You can't just wait there and hope. The students just stand there and say, "They don't like us. That's why we are failing." The white lecturers feel like, "We are not wanted here." They blame that for everything. But you need to bring those groups together because if you don't, education can't happen. And when you talk to them in smaller groups and separately, there's so much good will. But someone's got to come and take the initiative to be the catalyst, try to do that healing.

AG: Is that you? Are you in that position?

MH: Yes, we are driving that process right now. It's amazing what we are doing, one person at a time. A lecturer said, "Yeah, people don't listen to us here, nobody cares. Now for the first time I can stand up and say what I think." Because otherwise they stand up there and think, "Do you even care what I'm saying?" Now we want to know how people feel, for them to express what they feel—their frustrations, their anxieties—openly. We say, "Don't feel guilty about it, just say what you feel." It's not a question of who blames who; it's that we need some kind of articulation of what we have all felt, the students too. After that, the feeling was quite different.

AG: But it's hard to be in your position with that. You're absorbing a lot that you may sometimes wish you didn't have to absorb.

MH: Yeah. I've felt that myself, that one might need counseling, too, because you see these people and you stand in the middle. Being a dean of students, people have these expectations. You're concerned for young people and the need for education, and you know that fighting doesn't help. So you have to dialogue with them on a congenial basis, you have to be their role model, their friend. But at the same time, you might have to tell them off quite frankly one day; and to do that, you must carry some credibility as well. Sometimes they are in a fight, and you have to call them and tell them, "No, you can't do that."

AG: On the university Web site, I saw you giving a talk to the students about drinking too much at parties.

MH: You see, those are the kinds of things we talk about. To explain why students are failing, we have to look at the whole range of issues—just dialogue with the institution, so people respond with their views, saying this is what I've observed, this is what I feel. Talk about everything: teaching methods, what have you. There is also the question of students coming from disadvantaged backgrounds, so people don't drive themselves. We are talking about all the policies, including drinking.

Early in 2001, Masitha authored a provocative discussion paper about the nature of education at Technikon Witwatersrand, challenging his colleagues to put students first, rather than blindly following a syllabus that produces failure rates as high as 80 percent. This excerpt seems to sum up his philosophy:

> Academic disadvantage is not an original condition; neither is it permanent. Disadvantage should vanish like vapour against the advancing light of education. It can be thrown off like an unwanted coat. The question is what it consists in and what the relevant variables are. It is our observation, for instance, that a large section of our students do not have enough language resources to study in the English language. It is common for them to ask to revert to the vernacular in communication. Are we approachable enough for our students to communicate their problems? Our approachability becomes crucial because the learners are already removed from the situation by the language barrier. In the circumstances, they need more than just a dispenser of knowledge but a person who is a friend and ally, a leader, a role model and a teacher all rolled into one to guide and reassure them. Indifference might prove to be the last straw in the already difficult circumstances. The social dimensions of education are brought to the fore and trust becomes a major factor in learning. Those who have had to operate in a language different from their mother tongue will readily identify with the present line of argument.[2]

[2] Masitha Hoeane, "TWR Student Affairs: Some Thoughts on the Support Function," unpublished internal document, Technikon Witwatersrand, January 2001.

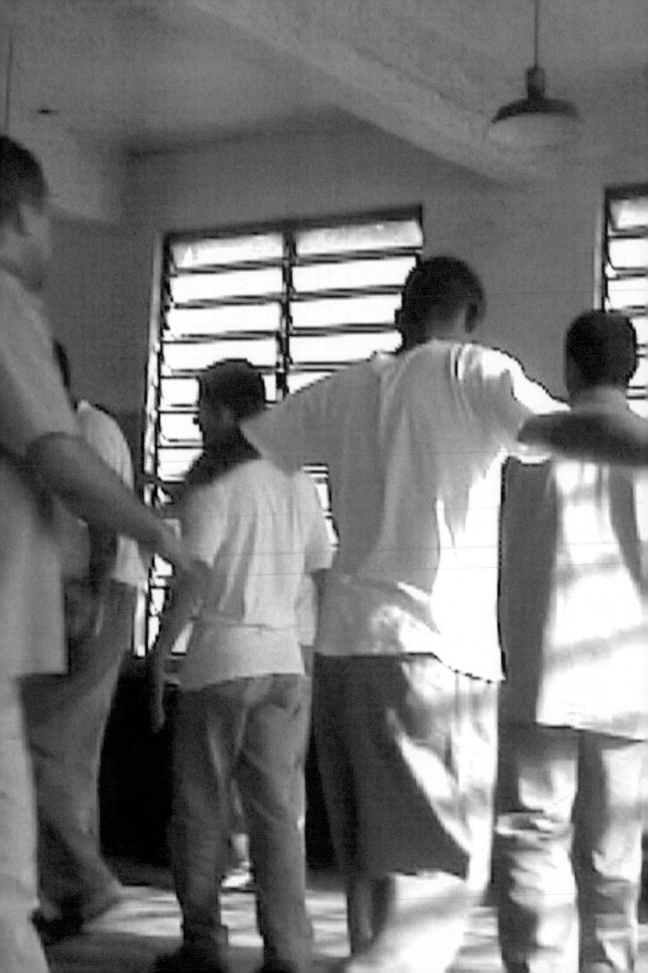

16

Prisoners take part in a drama workshop in the Penitenciary Doutor Sebastião Martins Silveira in Araraquara, State of São Paulo, as part of the Staging Human Rights program, 2001. Clip from a video by Paul Heritage.

People's Palace Projects
Queen Mary, University of London
Mile End Road
London E1 4NS, United Kingdom
Telephone: (44 20) 7882 3195
E-mail: p.heritage@qmul.ac.uk
Web site: www.peoplespalace.org

Paul Heritage's essay describes theater projects conducted with prisoners in the Brazilian penal system; he has collaborated in some of this work with Bárbara Santos from the Center of the Theatre of the Oppressed in Rio de Janeiro, whose essay is also featured in this anthology.

Prison is certainly the most extreme of the social institutions in which community cultural development projects take place, but it is by no means the only one: other authors in this anthology describe projects undertaken with senior centers, health-care programs, educational systems and so on. The prison environment, more starkly than any other, highlights the contradictions between community cultural development's liberatory intentions and the forces of social control. As Paul's essay points out, the work is badly needed there, and its powerful effects in such contexts

have been amply demonstrated, leading to expansion of programs and support. There is some irony in the fact that in certain places, it is easier to get support for community cultural development projects in prison than in "free" society.

Participating in our online dialogue, Paul described the history of his involvement in this work:

I started working in prisons in Brazil because I was invited there to lecture on Shakespeare, to accompany the world tour of Cheek by Jowl's all-male "As You Like It" in 1991. I started to work in prisons in the U.K. in 1986, because I was invited to give workshops on Safer Sex. This led to various commissions to establish drama-based programmes for use in prisons and probation. In 1992, with James

Thompson, I established the Theatre in Prisons and Probation Centre at Manchester University, which is still running. I left Manchester in 1996 to take over the Drama Department at Queen Mary, University of London. We offer a range of courses, including what I believe is the U.K.'s first undergraduate degree in Applied Drama.

His essay describes a course of work that has pointed toward expansion and replication of projects. For a field that stresses the local and specific, he raises essential questions about scale and offers some surprising answers.

Real Social Ties?

THE INS AND OUTS OF MAKING
THEATER IN PRISONS

by Paul Heritage

AN ENTRANCE

At the American Embassy in London last year, I was translating for my partner as he applied for a visa to accompany me on a visit to give a series of lectures at New York University. On the grounds that he has "no real social ties" in the United Kingdom, the visa application was rejected. Our relationship, the house we own, the joint bank account we have, his studies in Britain were not enough to convince this official that my partner —a Brazilian—would not want to remain permanently in the United States. Indeed, the official perception of the fragility of our relationship was made all too apparent when I was asked if I insisted on taking all my boyfriends to New York. How could our weak and inconstant ties compete with all that the U.S.A. would offer to entice him away from the seeming impermanence of what we have created together in London?

The incident forced me to contemplate what these "real social ties" are, that mean so much to the American government that they should be used as factors in determining who shall enter their country. In trying to escape from all that was negative, abusive and degrading in that incident, I began to wonder about the social ties this official so rigorously invoked and the means by which we know if they are real or not. The incident has helped me to think about the social ties that I have been engaged in during the making of theater that crosses social and community boundaries, in particular the boundaries between where I am in my own social, sexual and national cultures and where I go as an artist. This article will look at those border crossings, with particular reference to my recent work making theater in Brazilian prisons.

I suspect that anyone who engages in art work linked to issues of social development has met a version of that embassy official over the years. The borders we have to cross to make the sort of theater we believe in will always be policed and guarded in some fashion: because of the way in which this work is usually conceived and constructed, there will always be a point of entry made by someone from outside. As the official at the embassy made all too clear, permission to enter is dependent on intention to leave. At the American Embassy, my partner and I were naively honest about the social ties that justified our travel together: the reasons for both our entry and our exit. In reflecting on my theater work, I wonder how honest I have been in my declarations to those other border guards? I wonder what promises I have made about the time that I would spend across these different borders? What social ties have I created and how real were they? Above all, has it been harder to enter or to exit? In this essay I look at my comings and my goings: the ins and outs of making theater in Brazilian prisons.

AS A POINT OF DEPARTURE, I BEGIN WITH AN EXIT...

There is often a moment at the end of a drama workshop when you try to take the temperature of a project. In those fleeting moments while the group is dispersing, you can often discover the most important things in the casual question and the overheard comment. This is particularly true in prison, as different realities crash into each other with the movement out of the physical and metaphysical space of the drama workshop and back to the prison.

Last year I was watching a workshop in a São Paulo prison which formed part of Projeto Drama (1999/2000), an education project implemented in 43 prisons across the state. The program, which was part of my work in Brazil for over three years, involved a succession of four-day drama-based workshops on AIDS/HIV. As they were leaving, I talked informally with the men about the impact of the drama workshops. When asked if he thought that the project would change his behavior in the future, one of the young men exploded with emotion. "I have just taken part in a workshop where I have cried, hugged, laughed, played in ways that I have never done in the past. I have changed totally. Perhaps next week I will have unsafe sex. I don't know. Why are you so obsessed with the future? What has happened now is most important."

That prisoner's comment brought a sharp realization of how far I have come in looking to make theater that is tied to other social realities. The justification for making this work—the application for my visa to enter this world—has often been made in terms of the way in which theater has a social impact beyond the moment of performance. It is not in the now that this work is tested, but in some indeterminate future: it will reduce risk, increase safety, construct citizenship in some other world that is not the one in which the performance or the dramatic activity has taken place. Performance work is thus established that is in some way not bound by time or space, but becomes boundless. Is this what we want? Is this what we are promising?

SECURING THE BOUNDARIES

Prison drama is constructed before we as artists seek to remake it. Played out first as social realism and then as romantic melodrama (or is it the other way round?), life in prison is always seen through the peepholes of our cultural imagination. Latin American prisons are places that inhabit our nightmares. Whether these images come from Hollywood or international human rights agencies, the story is of torture and a denial of human rights. Brazil is a country which is framed by clichés that come as much from stories of crime and street kids as from beaches and Bossa Nova. But since 1993 I have been trying to make theater with prisoners in Brasília, São Paulo, Recife and Rio de Janeiro.

To experience a city such as Rio de Janeiro or São Paulo is of course a negotiation with its borders and its margins. The shape and form of these cities, like so many others in Brazil and beyond, is one of the key conse- quences of the modernist revolution. As rural immigrants arrived they were pushed to the margins of the cities, which might paradoxically be close to the center. Networks of friends and family who followed them were crucial to a sense of survival within an unknown social reality, and thus the survival strategies of the poor were recognized as cultural. The reaction of the state was an inaction that was legitimized by maintaining the illegality of these areas and their assumed peripheral position in relation to the economic life of the city. The reaction of the middle classes? A constant assertion of their difference and superiority, often configured in terms of European or North American cultural values, and articulating a predominate sense of danger at these borders. The reaction of those who live on the other side of the border is experienced as victimization to a violence that is as likely to be perpetrated by the state as by the criminal forces that have filled the vacuum of civic power and order. But such territories are also subject to a fierce romanticism which variously colors the regional past or the present community, and at times even seeks to tint the crime that devastates all these borderlands.

Luiz Eduardo Soares was, until March 17, 2000, responsible for the political and operational strategies of public security in the state of Rio de Janeiro. He has written of life in the *favelas*[1] as being reminiscent of feudal warfare:

> The masculine hegemony is affirmed in the supremacy of courage and
> loyalty, which has always been restricted to the arts of war, and to a
> hierarchized environment exclusive to the group itself which enforces
> an explosive situation of fratricidal factionalism.[2]

[1] Shantytowns. I use the Brazilian word, as any translation evokes the settlements found in English-speaking countries such as India and South Africa. The use of the Portuguese word evokes the cultural specificity of these improvised communities.

[2] Luiz Eduardo Soares, *Meu Casaco de General* (Rio de Janeiro: Companhia de Letras, 2000), p. 271.

Bidding farewell to a prisoner participating in the 2001 Staging Human Rights program in São Paulo. Photo by Paul Heritage.

These values are precisely those that modern society has supposedly abandoned in favor of a world which recognizes at a certain level the equality of human beings, subject only to the laws of their gods (in the religious version) or the laws of their society. It is a development that has allowed the rise of the individual and the citizen, of a world in which politics, civic administration and psychology govern lives. Even when violent reaction is brought to the fore, such as in the postmillennium demonstrations against globalization in London, Montreal and Genoa, the rule of law is supposedly superior to the law of force. In the *favelas*, this cannot be assumed. Lest there be any doubt how far these borderlands are removed in fact and imagination from contemporary notions of society, we can look to the system implemented by the administration of a previous governor of Rio de Janeiro. From 1994 to '98, Marcello Alencar authorized payments to individual police officers that were involved in acts of "bravery." The police were encouraged to enter into armed conflicts with bandits, and received a reward for the number of fatal victims they claimed. The system was referred to by press and politicians as the *Premiação Faroeste*—the Far West Prize.

The culture of the prison reflects and further exaggerates the lawlessness that we associate with all borderlands. Of course, that is not what we expect of prisons. They are meant to be the place where the law is most rigorously in force, but that is rarely the case. We in Britain should not be surprised or complacent when we remember that it was John Major as prime minister who, in claiming that prison works, remarked that at least when a man is in prison he cannot commit any more crimes. The idea that a prison is so far outside of our social world that it is a place where crime cannot be committed finds its logical and terrifying conclusion in the 1994 massacre of 111 prisoners in less than two hours in the São Paulo prison complex of

Carandiru, and in the daily assassinations that produce an annual massacre of unimaginable and often unrecorded levels in the prison systems of Rio de Janeiro and São Paulo.

The walls that divide the prison from the rest of society are not the only boundaries that separate those within from those without. Social, economic and racial factors determine global prison populations as much as legal and judicial agencies. In São Paulo, where 70 percent of the population is white, the incarceration rate per 100,000 is 76.8 for whites and 280.5 for blacks. Black people account for 66 percent of the homicide victims, and the lethality index (number of people killed by the police divided by the number of people wounded in such encounters) is 37 percent to 100 percent higher for blacks as compared to whites.[3] In Rio de Janeiro, 60 percent of the population is white, while black people make up 70 percent of those killed by the police and 60 percent of those killed in prison. Thus black people are over-represented both in the prisons and the morgues. Penal policy reveals itself as a means of social exclusion, and the boundaries of the prison wall can be seen to be as much social and cultural as bricks and mortar, but in every way real.

[3] All statistics from Julita Lemgruber, *Racial Bias in the Brazilian Criminal Justice System*, Presentation to the World Conference against Racism, Racial Discrimination, Xenophobia and Related Intolerance, Durban, South Africa, Aug. 2001.

If the incarceration of the prison population can be seen as based on factors that go beyond the physical and judicial, then the means by which such boundaries are crossed must also go beyond the concrete and the legal. To talk of cultural action in the face of such barbarities is not to underestimate the forces that conserve such a status quo, but to recognize that there are multiple ways in which liberty, justice and human rights can be achieved. All of us working in the cultural development field are faced with questions about the realities of our work in comparison to that of well diggers and AIDS nurses. But the complexity and interconnection of issues such as social exclusion, the environment and health care open a space for our interventions.

OPENING AND CLOSING DOORS

The prison gate is a transitional space marked by rituals that seek to distance the world that is left behind from the world that is entered. Visitors, guards and prisoners each in their way are subject to the rites of this particular passage, which operate on both exit and entrance. Drauzio Varella has worked for 10 years as a doctor in Carandiru, Brazil's largest prison. Perhaps in his words we can see how the entrance to prison life is controlled as much by ideology as by vigilance:

> No need to knock to go in; as your head approaches the window of the
> small door, the shadowy face of the porter appears telepathically from inside.
> The opening of the door follows the oldest routine of all prisons, which
> dictates that a door can only open when the last door and the following one
> have been closed. It's a good lesson that helps you learn to wait without
> showing any signs of impatience. It won't help. I hear the tapping of the

door being unlocked and I'm in the Ratoeira—the mousetrap—an atrium with bars and on the left two ample windows for the visitor to identify himself. Between these windows is a corridor that leads to the Director-General's office, large and full of light. The table is old. On the wall behind is a photograph of the State Governor. But underneath it, one of the directors, a man who has spent his life in the prison, has put up a brass plaque: "It is easier for a camel to pass through the eye of a needle than for a rich man to be a prisoner in Carandiru."

I return to the Ratoeira. I wait for the internal gate to open and stand in front of the wall that circles the prison, watched over by military police armed with machine guns. I pass into the Divinéia, a large yard that is shaped like a funnel. At its neck lies the room reserved for body searches, obligatory for everyone who enters, except for directors, lawyers, and doctors. Before gaining access to the pavilions, you have to enter this room and raise your arms in front of one of the guards, who will give you a quick frisk at the waist and a pat on the outside of the thighs.

It's another prison ritual.[4]

[4] Drauzio Varella, *Estação Carandiru* (São Paulo: Companhia das Letras, 1998), p. 9.

Like the directors, lawyers and doctors, I am rarely searched as I enter Brazilian prisons, which only serves to increase my anxieties. If security is compromised by prejudice, then it is unlikely to be effective. But I wonder, what would the guards be looking for if they were they to search me? And what should I declare? My foreignness is obvious, and my gender and age are reasonably apparent. Class and sexuality are both confused, as gestures, intonations and dress codes that might mean certain things to a British guard are regarded as a part of my nationality in Brazil. My status is in contradiction: I am university professor, theater director and Englishman. These play out in different ways for me in Brazil and Britain, but my comings and goings bear a curious relationship to the power of all these factors. I have a large wooden key made for me by prisoners in Brasília. It reminds me that the real keys of prison are only half as effective as the cultural and social means by which the doors are locked and unlocked.

I can still remember the first time that I entered a Brazilian prison. It was through the same small door that Dr. Varella describes above. There, in a prison that holds over 9,000, I was taken to see a samba competition. Of all the images I could have expected, this was the least likely for me to have conjured in advance and the one that vividly remains after the physical horrors have become part of an accustomed—if not familiar—world. The greatest shock was to see how the inmates were organizing cultural activities in a self-sufficient way that I had never seen possible in the British prison system. It was as difficult to interpret such activity as it was for me to judge the sambas, which I was asked to do in the middle of my visit. Perhaps we should not read such manifestations with quite the naive enthusiasm of my first encounter. Today, I might temper my wonder with the thought that such practices are a means of survival, expected and incorporated into the system. My work in prison inevitably owes a debt to the participatory traditions that are associated with such cultural forms, and is permissible only because the authorities open the doors. But within my work, I have attempted to ask if it is possible to break the ways in which spaces and lives in prison are circumscribed and imagined within constrained possibilities.

In making theater in prison, we engage in a marginal activity in a marginal space. What is it that performance can offer as it declares its arrival at these different borders of marginalization? When writing previously on a theater company based in one of Rio de Janeiro's *favelas*, I commented that theater can operate as a register of individual and collective social histories.[5] It is common for Brazil to be called a country without memory, and the lack of official structures within such a marginalized community as a *favela* makes the act of registering histories all the more difficult and all the more necessary:

> Individual stories of violence or of resistance start to gain a wider resonance in the collective story telling and remembering that forms a part of this process. Without it, individual acts of barbarism are experienced as terrible and chaotic incidents that are out of control because they are a part of no pattern. The physical fabric of the *favela* is in itself provisional and subject to constant disruption and destruction, unlike the official urban environment which is generally experienced as stable and permanent. While modern and historic cities are integral parts of the national patrimony, the *favela* is that part which must be removed if all that is deemed wholesome and healthy is to survive. The survival of the lives of the residents in any form of cultural registration is thus at odds with the very environment in which those lives are lived.[6]

This is all the more apparent when theater is made in prison, a site that arbitrarily *re*structures the subject's experience of place and time. Theater, in contrast, *de*structures our perceptions of where and when. In its very liveness, theatrical performance adheres to spatial and temporal boundaries that declare it is only ever here and now. It has no past and demands no future. It asks only that it exists at this moment, while it simultaneously offers the possibility that all time can be present in that one instant. Augusto Boal, the Brazilian theater director, reflecting on his incarceration during the military dictatorship, offers a prisoner's perspective on the reconstitution of the boundaries of time and space which resound with an echo of the power of performance:

> In prison, I had a certain kind of freedom. We, who are free in space, are prisoners of time. Those who are prisoners of space, of time become free. Outside, in the daily routine of life, the day to day tasks would not allow me to see myself—I was always in a hurry, always doing, going to do, seeing it done: in my cell, I was obliged to look at myself and see. Outside, schedules, tasks, smiles—the rituals of life gave me no time to reflect. To say "good

[5] Heritage, "The Promise of Performance," *Theatre Matters: Performance and Culture on the World Stage*, R. Boon and J. Plastow, eds. (Cambridge University Press, 1998), pp. 154–176.

[6] Ibid., p. 145.

morning" to myself in the mirror. We hardly spoke, myself and I. In the huge space, I had no time. Now that I had time, I had no space. In the diffuse disintegration of time in prison—that time in which now was permanent, no before or afterwards: just the eternal moment existed—and in the concentrated scantiness of the dense space, I thought of myself. There, I heard the sound of silence.[7]

[7]Boal keynote speech at *Mundança de Cena II: Teatro Construindo Cidadania*, Recife, Sept. 2000.

[8]Soares, op. cit., p. 47.

FINDING THE EXITS

Theater offers a live and immediate experience in a place where so often the past is unthinkable and the future unimaginable, and thus brings something essential through the very act of performance. On another level, theater finds its place in prisons in the very real possibilities that it offers of new civic relationships that are prohibited by the construction of our system of criminal justice. Despite the geographic centrality of many of our Victorian prisons in Britain, they seemingly occupy the Renaissance position of being outside our city walls. Throughout his book on his 500 days at the forefront of public security in Rio de Janeiro, Luiz Eduardo Soares emphasizes that what is most decisive in the successful policing of any society is the direct involvement of its citizens in the processes of administering the law. "Above all," he writes, "in this field that is so complex and so delicate, the objective and the subjective superimpose themselves in a way that is almost inextricable."[8] Thus, demands for vengeance and for mercy mingle with technical and economic considerations about how a person can most effectively be processed, incarcerated and subsequently liberated.

Perhaps that is where theater finds its function. The special relationship between private and public, individual and collective, psychological and social that is contained in the very act of performance means that it crosses the borders that normally keep such worlds apart. Perhaps these are the social ties that theater can offer to a world where so much has been ripped asunder. At the very least, theater offers the possibility that prisoners who are the objects of the system's vigilance and society's denunciations can begin to look and to speak as subjects in their own lives.

FINDING THE ENTRANCES

Thus it has often been the making of theater that has attracted me within the prison context, a search for the means by which performance-based activities can be sustained. In order to find ways in which theater could become a language and an action that could be incorporated into the daily life of the prison, I have worked closely with the techniques of Theater of the Oppressed. In recent years Boal and members of his Center for the Theater of the Oppressed have become involved in the development

A Staging Human Rights drama workshop takes place in 2001 with prisoners in the Penitenciary Doutor Geraldo de Andrade Vieira in São Vicente, State of São Paulo. Photo by Paul Heritage.

of these projects. The basis of Projeto Drama and another of my projects, Staging Human Rights (2001–02), has been to train prison teachers in the use of theatrical games and exercises that can be used most effectively by nonactors. I have written elsewhere about other approaches, including the use of Shakespeare with juvenile prisoners in Brazil.[9] However, the methodologies of Theater of the Oppressed offer the possibility that after the artist has left, the theatrical activity will remain. In Staging Human Rights, teachers are running cycles of workshops and Forum Theater performances across 37 prisons. No amount of coming and going by artists could match the depth and structural impact of this project. Even if it were possible to hire theater artists to implement a project on such a scale—even if the aesthetic possibilities might thus be enhanced—no visiting artist could achieve what these prison teachers are doing. They are part of the commitment by the prison system to a way of thinking, talking and doing.

While we hope that the value of the project lies in the insights and discoveries it makes about human rights in prisons, its impact may be most profoundly felt in other ways. Perhaps the strength of the project lies not in what it enables people to say, but rather in the actuality of what they are doing. It is in the staging of human rights that the most fundamental rights are guaranteed. This is not an abdication of the responsibility of content: the location of the project and the nature of the participants determine that the subject matter of these dramas will release visions and explore territories that are absent from the main stages of Brazilian culture. But these projects reach beyond content to make other connections.

[9] "Stolen Kisses" in Maria Delgado and Caridad Svich, *Theatre in Crisis? Performance Manifestos for a New Century* (Manchester University Press, 2002).

A DIFFERENT EXIT

August 2001, and I am with a group of 20 prisoners rehearsing their contribution to the Staging Human Rights project. It is a Forum Theater play about the amorous relationship between an ex-prisoner and his lawyer, and I watch as the new connections we seek are being tentatively forged. I am in a small town, eight hours' drive from the city of São Paulo, and the prisoners have been invited to perform their Forum Theater play in the town square the following week. The rehearsal falters. Members of the all-male cast are uncertain about which of them should play the female lawyer; they are tense about rehearsing in front of the guards; they are nervous about how they will be received when they present the play to the general public. The guards shift and smoke, enter and exit unannounced. They too are nervous. Is security the issue here? And if so, whose? We are rehearsing in a space away from the prison, so the guards could be here to protect society from any possible threat by a prisoner. Or perhaps they are here to defend me as a foreigner among high-risk prisoners. Or perhaps the prisoners need defending from each other. Or perhaps it is the guards' own security that is at risk. If so, is that a physical risk, or is it something that is happening through the theater?

As the rehearsal progresses and the prisoners become more comfortable, the guards seem increasingly restless. By now, the prisoner playing the female lawyer is giving a real show, and there is a sense of enjoyment and achievement in the room. Thoughts of the public who will see the performance have now become an incentive to the group to tell the story as clearly and passionately as possible. They work hard, repeating and refining their original ideas, throwing away, editing, creating as the play grows and the conflict becomes more tightly focused. They accept my directions and enjoy the discipline of rehearsal. When I miss something or cut out something essential, they show me once again that oppression always exists in the detail. A samba is added, making the scene both simpler and more profound. Having found what they were looking for, the rehearsal comes to a close with laughter, dancing and the eager anticipation of seven more days of rehearsal and the performance to come.

Forum Theater directly tests its connections with an audience. On the day of this presentation, the town of Presidente Prudente made a connection with its maximum-security prison in ways that would usually be unthinkable. Would the audience enter the stage to substitute for the protagonist and seek alternatives to the problem presented? In this rather unconventional version of the Forum model, they could choose to substitute for either the ex-prisoner or the female lawyer. In the event, all the interventions were made on the side of the lawyer. I worried that the prisoners might be upset that no one had wanted to substitute for the ex-prisoner. But they watched in delight while a lineup of valiant audience members fought for the right to love someone regardless of criminal record.

It is not the sort of content that we imagined when we created the project. Indeed, when I arrived for the rehearsal I was uncertain if it was really an appropriate subject for the project. Other workshops during the Staging Human Rights program have covered issues of access to health care and education, conjugal visits, giving birth in handcuffs and the inevitable but nonetheless shocking instances of violence and torture. Was this story of forbidden love really about human rights in prisons? And then I remembered what one of the men had said to me in another prison, about another situation: "I want the right to serve my sentence as it stands." Perhaps that is what this scene was about: the right to serve a sentence and finish it, not to carry it with you forever. And perhaps that is what made the guards so nervous when they watched the men rehearsing. The role the guard has come to play in the prison is to extend the boundaries of punishment beyond that of the sentence. To do so they must sever the human connections the men have with each other, with themselves as guards and with society beyond the prison. The theater we are trying to create seeks to do the opposite.

A DIFFERENT ENTRANCE

In the scene described above, we can already see theater's failures emerging along with its successes. Those guards, nervously making comments at the back of the hall, are the same ones who will take the men back to their cells. They are the same ones who will tell the prisoners what fools they made of themselves during the rehearsal, the same ones who will look for the merest hint of a smile or insubordination to make sure that João, Giovanni or Johnny doesn't make it to tomorrow's rehearsal. And they are the same ones who might also take part in their own drama workshops as part of the Staging Human Rights program. Indeed, the guards' program is the most significant advance on the current project and, wherever possible, takes place away from the prison environment, to remove the guards from the environment and culture of the prison. Based on the same techniques of theater games and exercises used to work toward Forum Theater presentation, the only direct connection to the work produced by prisoners comes in the final Legislative Forum Theater presentation at the end of the project.

Never having worked with guards before, I had no means of predicting the results. I expected resistance, which we were given in abundance. What I could not have predicted was the level of emotion and anger toward the society that discriminates against them for where they work. As one of them said in an early workshop, the three worst jobs in São Paulo are street cleaner, grave digger and prison guard, but the prison guard is the worst because it combines the work of the other two. Nor could I have expected to hear a guard say at the end of one of the workshops that he loved the chance to do the drama games because for the two hours of the workshop he forgot he was in prison. This was most remarkable, as at that moment he was about four hours' drive from his prison, off-duty, out of uniform and in a school building. The guards as much as the prisoners live 24 hours a day in their prisons.

Staging Human Rights is not remarkable for anything other than such moments when it unfixes the world and makes new connections and new crossings possible. It draws attention for its scale: 37 prisons across a state the size of Spain, with the involvement of over 5,000 prisoners, guards, prison staff and families. Before we embarked on the May 2001 Community, Culture and Globalization conference at the Rockefeller Conference and Study Center in Bellagio, Italy, Don Adams posed a question to our group: "Can we preserve our decentralization and still effectively oppose the huge global corporations and quasi-governmental agencies thus far calling the shots? What would it take for this balance to shift?" Reflecting on my own practice, it seemed that I had spent nearly a decade engaged in a process of globalizing my work so that it could grow to the proportions of Staging Human Rights. How had this come about, and what are the implications?

MY FIRST ENTRANCE

When I finished my first theater project in a Brazilian prison in 1993, I felt an elation that was rare even within the pleasure zones of this sort of work. At the outset, the guards wouldn't even let me have a room for the workshops, so I was forced to work in whatever outside space was available. We spent the initial weeks exposed to airless heat and the gaze of the entire prison population, as 20 Brazilian prisoners and one English academic began to make images of their worlds on the baked red earth of the exercise yard. Over the eight months of the first project in Brasília, I not only managed to conquer a regular meeting space inside the prison, but those 20 inmates were also able to take their play to the Ministry of Justice head-quarters for a performance to judges, journalists and politicians. As I took my leave of Colonel Flávio Souto, the prison director, I was taken aback by his response, which recognized the benefits of the project while totally demean-ing the scale on which it had taken place. He found my energies laudable but laughable. At the end of his day, there is so much that needs to be done for the prison population as a whole that a project which prioritized so much time and money for 20 prisoners was an irrelevance.

Colonel Souto made me more determined than ever to find ways in which I could increase the impact of the work I do. I expanded the project in Brasília so that by 1996 there were five theater workshops running on a regular basis and the work was seen to benefit those beyond the immediate participants. Some of the original group left the prison and formed a theater company which in 2001 is still touring schools and colleges in the federal district of

Brasília. With each performance they make their own response to the colonel. Then in 1996, I began working in São Paulo, which holds 25 percent of the total prison population of Brazil in only 12 percent of the prisons. The problems there are on a scale that would make a drama workshop with 20 prisoners seem very small indeed.

My work evolved to try to meet this challenge. I started looking at ways in which it might be possible to train existing prison staff to use cultural means to engage prisoners with their lives. That process culminated in Projeto Drama, mentioned above. This was followed by Staging Human Rights, which is funded by the UK Community Fund and brings together the Center for the Theater of the Oppressed with FUNAP, the State Agency for Education and Work in São Paulo. British participating organizations include People's Palace Projects (based at Queen Mary, University of London) and the Center for Applied Theatre (based at the University of Manchester).

It seems as if I have been working toward a "globalizing" of cultural work within the warped world of the prison. In São Paulo for the launch of the human rights project in March 2001, I addressed the directors of the 40 prisons where the project was due to take place. Standing beside the Secretary of State for Justice, I reflected on how far I had come since the dusty patio to which the workshops were banished in 1993. These directors had recently to cope with prison rebellions that had captured world headlines. While the state can rarely organize anything coherent within the system, the prisoners had managed to take 5,000 hostages across a series of prisons on the same day. Neither human rights nor theater can have seemed a major priority for many of the people in the room on that Thursday morning, who looked as if they had become hostages to a process that they did not understand.

UNCERTAIN EXITS

But I too was confused. And my confusion grows with the projects. While Staging Human Rights goes forward, we are now raising the funds for a three-year youth project with juvenile prisoners in Rio de Janeiro. Meanwhile, I am discussing with the Ministry of Justice the details for an implementation of Staging Human Rights in a further six states across Brazil during 2002. Of course, I hope that every participant will continue to "write their own page of the story,"[10] however big the project becomes. But my focus has been on the ways in which cultural-development work can be multiplied, and its impact extended, rather than on those small and particular experiences which I think we all believe initiate and incite the creative and political process.

And that is why I find in the fabric of my current project echoes of Don Adams' question about how we preserve the decentralization of our own work against the drive toward globalization. How big should we go? What is

[10] This phrase comes from Azril Bacal during the e-mail group discussion prior to the authors' meeting at the Rockefeller Study Center in Bellagio, May 2001.

our responsibility as cultural activists when faced with the need to justify the impact of our work? It surely cannot be a numbers game. What is the balance between quality and quantity? The program I describe above will not be equally good for 5,000 people. Does that matter? The original drama project in Brasília did not have an equal effect on the 20 people who took part. But is my desire to replicate a theater project across 40 prisons caught up in the imperatives of a capitalist model that gives value only to that which can be reproduced? Is the theatrical experience worth more when it can be packaged in such a way that it can be repeated? That way Disney lies.

I have no answers to these multiplying questions. I know that my fascination with performance is rooted in its unique existence at its moment of utterance, in the impossibility of its reproduction. Yet here I am trying to build ways in which it can be structured and repeated. Perhaps it has something to do with the prison itself. As I have written on another occasion:

> A prison is a world where survival is tested at its limits. Performance is normally thought of as that which does not survive, thus in seeking to ensure a continuity of theater in the prisons, I seem to have been engaged in a bizarre act of negation: denying something essential in both the institution of prison and the activity of theater. The survival of performance in prisons has for me become a form of resistance and negation of the system itself. And perhaps that is why replication and reproduction have become important.[11]

[11] Delgado and Svich, "Stolen Kisses," op. cit.

Making theater in prisons is a means of staging impossible encounters. All the greatest plays seem to be initiated by a meeting that should not or cannot happen: Oedipus with his father; Romeo with Juliet; Estragon and Vladimir with Godot. My memories of the last 10 years of making theater in Brazilian prisons are full of just such impossible encounters. The aim is for prisoners and guards to find new ways of engaging with each other and their world, seeking to restage the seemingly impossible meeting between prisons and society.

On each of my visits to see the work as it progresses, it is as difficult as ever to match the individual experiences of the participants with the conditions in which they are working. The power of a simple theater game to transform the dehumanized spaces and relationships of a prison never fails to move and excite me, even after 15 years of making theater within the criminal justice system in Britain and abroad. As one prisoner reaches across to touch another, you know that a contact is being made that only happens because of this activity we call theater, and it is in direct contradiction to the ways in which people are meant to relate within that space. Prisoners, teachers and guards have all given moving personal testimony to the impact of the work, reminding me of all that has been achieved in these years.

12 Paul Heritage, "Theatre, Prisons and Citizenship: A South American Way," *Prison Theatre: Perspectives and Practices*, James Thompson, ed. (London: Jessica Kingsley, 1998), pp. 31–41.

13 Ibid.

Of course, if such work is allowed to continue and grow, it probably doesn't represent much of a threat to a system that is in need of a complete revolution. I have written elsewhere about the relationship between prison theater projects and rebellions,[12] and it is as important in Brazil as it is in Britain to question at all times the acceptance of cultural projects by a system that is based on such degrading and inhuman conditions. Projeto Drama, dealing with AIDS/HIV and therefore with sex and drugs in prisons, was never likely to trouble the prison authorities. It raised subjects that the authorities would prefer to remain unspoken, but like the prison itself, the program appeared to address the security of the inmate. However, in announcing the new program on human rights, I was aware that in both form and content we threatened to challenge the boundaries that hold the prison and the prisoner in place.

For all the quantitative data that has been gathered about the projects—how many workshops run, how many prisoners attended, how many condoms distributed—there remain doubts haunting their qualitative impact. Does it work? As a result of these programs will we really be able to say that there is less risk of AIDS/HIV in the São Paulo prison system? Will human rights abuses really be prevented? What is the relationship between the reality of the prisons and the image of them that has been remade through this work? The answers to these questions don't seem to get any closer as the project expands. Indeed, the proof that is required of the efficacy of the work seems to become more elusive as the demand for it becomes that much more empirical. The Department of Preventative Medicine at the University of São Paulo undertook an independent evaluation of our AIDS/HIV program that included interviews with 400 prisoners before and after the project. They concluded that there was a significant change in the level of knowledge and attitudes concerning AIDS by those who participated in the program and that all the objectives were achieved.

Despite that apparent success, as I have noted elsewhere,[13] I have chosen to look for indicators of success away from the notion of individual change. Of course we hope that as a result of the AIDS/HIV project people will make individual choices that do not place themselves at risk. But we cannot show that. What we can show is how the presence of this drama work in the prison changes the institution, and how new relationships come about as a result of the project. This in turn may lead to an environment of respect for self and for the other, and that might make some of the necessary individual changes more possible.

Although successes are important to note, failures are too. For every successful workshop, there is the one that didn't happen because a guard wouldn't open a door or a fight in the yard meant that all activities were stopped for a week.

If I remember what theater has been able to achieve, then I must also remember the young man who wrote the poem on which we based the first play I produced in a Brazilian prison in 1993. Two months later he died of meningitis in the prison because none of the public hospitals would take him. His name was Moisés, and his poem still serves as a reminder of the question that must stand behind all our work in prisons: "Why, Brasil?"[14] It is in the questions and not the answers that these projects seek to make their interventions through encounters that might otherwise be impossible.

[14] Ibid., p. 41.

I have been a privileged spectator in Brazilian prisons for nearly 10 years. My visa to enter this world has been the theater skills that I teach, and I hope that by passing these on throughout the system, crossings can be made both ways. Our visits to the other worlds that performance offers are by their very nature limited, yet we are constantly embarking on journeys within such projects that seem to offer something more than the transience of the performance itself.

Staging Human Rights is intended to offer a means by which supposedly human connections can stand against the social discord that separates. The ties that currently bind prisoner and guard will be tested, as much as the ones that bind both of them with the society that has placed them inside the prison. As prisoners and guards begin to talk about the hidden worlds they inhabit, they can start to participate in public and urgent debates about crime, violence and prisons in ways that challenge the dominant discourses that condemn us all to live in the ever-increasing shadows of the borderlands we have created.

17

After asking permission to go out with her friends, a Vietnamese-Australian girl is lectured by her father in a 1998 professional production in Sydney of "Chay Vong Vong," written and directed by Tony Le Nguyen. Photo by Heidrun Lohr.

Vietnamese Youth Media
45 Moreland Street
P.O. Box 479, Footscray
Victoria, 3011, Australia
Telephone: (61 3) 9689 5677
Fax: (61 3) 9689 7886
E-mail: vym@fcarts.org.au
Web site: www.vnet.org/vym

By any criterion—medium, method, aesthetic aims, social goals—the community cultural development field is diverse. Just as projects can be strung like beads at every point on the continuum from process to product, community artists are varied in their relationship to the "mainstream" art world and its practices. Some community artists entered the field through the gateways of community organizing or social services; and for others, the entry point was frustration with the restricted roles the art world offered. Some artists are entirely engaged in collaborative, participatory work, simultaneously satisfying their social aims and their individual desires for creative expression and exploration, while others maintain an individual art practice apart from their community work, finding they need self-directed expression and aesthetic innovation to stretch and nurture their gifts.

On this continuum, **Tony Le Nguyen**, the founder of Vietnamese Youth Media, is hard to place. His community cultural development work stems equally from several motives. He did indeed begin work as a conventional film and theater artist, racking up a long string of credits in movies, television and on the stage. (He is probably best-known for his role as Tiger in the film "Romper Stomper.") And he did indeed experience the constraints of the commercial cultural industries:

My family and I arrived in Australia in 1978 as refugees from Vietnam. In 1985, 1 got my first taste of the arts by playing a Viet Cong Boy in an Australian miniseries, "The Sword of Honour," about the Vietnam War. Since then, I have had many exciting parts, playing many different Vietnamese Boys: Minh, Dinh, Thanh, Phan, Nam and Loc. I also got to play a Vietnamese Gang Leader in "Romper Stomper." Then moving from there I got to play a Chinese in "Paradise Beach," and a Japanese in "Fast Forward." Then one sunny day, I was asked to play "George." Wow, I thought, this was going to be exciting, a non-stereotyped character for a change. As it turns out, "George" is a Vietnamese criminal, but because the show was "Australia's Most Wanted,"

they weren't allowed to use his Vietnamese name, so they used George instead. So to sum up my acting experience in Australia, I am a Vietnamese/Asian/ Criminal character expert.[1]

But he understood the obstacles he faced were not merely personal, but indicative of social conditions facing the entire Vietnamese diaspora, and ought to be addressed systemically. In 1994, he founded Vietnamese Youth Media (VYM) with the support of the Footscray Community Arts Centre in Melbourne. As Tony describes it:

This was to be our own company, a place where young Vietnamese-Australians can come and make art, tell their own stories and create their own characters. The work that we do ranges from theatre to documentary-making, from music production to karaoke performance nights. We make our own work, because we don't

[1] From an address to the Globalization and the Live Performing Arts Conference, June 2000 in Melbourne, Australia.

[2]Ibid.

want to wait for Anglo writers and directors to give us work; too often the work is offered because they feel sorry for us or because they think it's the most politically correct thing to do.[2]

VYM's 1995 production, "Chay Vong Vong" ("Running in Circles"), was the first contemporary Vietnamese-Australian play in Australia, focusing on the vicious cycle of poverty, discrimination, unemployment and social isolation in which many Vietnamese-Australians were caught up. This first production was a community project, with nonprofessionals participating fully at every stage of conception, production and performance. The following year, VYM received Australia Council for the Arts funding to mount a professional production of the play, reworked for a smaller cast, in South Melbourne's Napier Street Theatre. Tony has followed this pattern several times since: organizing a community cultural development project that culminates in a participatory production within the Vietnamese community; then using that production as the basis for a smaller professional production in a mainstream Australian theatrical venue for a wider different audience.

As the following interview makes plain, the concept of bridging— between generations, ethnic groups and countries—figures importantly in his practice. With VYM as a base, Tony has extended his work beyond Melbourne to the farthest reaches of the Vietnamese diaspora. In 2000, he received a Community Cultural Development Fellowship from the Australia Council for the Arts to visit Vietnamese communities around the world, including the United States, Canada, France and the United Kingdom.

Today his work embraces the dialectic of local and global, as local community members collaborate on projects that are performed first for community audiences and then reframed as professional productions; as young artists learn community cultural development practice along with theater skills and use them both in community arts work and in mainstream professional theater; and as exchange and travel are used to discover commonalities and potential connections among the two million Vietnamese currently dispersed around the globe. His work seeks to address problems that also bridge the local and global: those of an artist thwarted by a racist society; of a minority cultural community subject to discrimination and its insidious effects; and of an entire culture displaced and dispersed by war and hardship.

Consequently, his work has multiple aims: to facilitate individual expression, understanding within the community and cross-cultural communication; and to champion an entire people's right to culture.

This interview was conducted by Arlene Goldbard on June 18, 2001, when Tony was producing a new community theater project titled "Aussie Bia Om," about the experience of young people who are forced into the sex industry, where they are exposed to extreme hardship, violence, abuse and the premature loss of innocence. The play explores prostitution from a historical Vietnamese context, in contrast with the current *Bia Om* (literally "hugging beer/hugging bar") situation in Vietnam and the illegal sex trade in Australia. The production takes as its framework the 17th century "Story of Kieu" by the poet Nguyen Du, Vietnam's equivalent to Shakespeare, and incorporates Vietnamese and English text, poetry, music (including Vietnamese lullaby and opera) and Buddhist rituals.

Sweet Honey Kill Fly

VIETNAMESE YOUTH MEDIA

An Interview With Tony Le Nguyen

Arlene Goldbard: I want to talk to you about your travels around the world in the Vietnamese diaspora, what you've learned, and then go back and pick up your work in Australia.

Tony Le Nguyen: I first went back to Vietnam in 1995. I was very much interested to learn about Vietnam as a country: where's it at socially, culturally and politically? I was not going anywhere with my work in Australia. I needed to find out about my roots, my origin and my past to come to some sense of reality, so that I could continue to move on.

AG: What were you able to see?

TLN: A lot of my understanding of Vietnamese culture and Vietnamese history was through whatever I'd picked up: oral history from my parents, or from the Western writers or journalists, or documentaries made by either French or Americans. There was another version written inside Vietnam as a form of propaganda for the government. Most histories of Vietnamese culture are much distorted. Personally, I feel that the real Vietnamese history and culture are somewhere between all those conflicting views and opinions of what Vietnamese people are about.

I wanted to see where Vietnam is at the moment: that is, where they live, how they sleep, how they eat, how they work, how they think, how they deal with government, how they deal with bureaucracy… If I hadn't gone to Vietnam, the only thing I could do is live inside my Dad's anger of the past, not understanding why I was angry.

Maybe I could try to understand some of his anger or the anger of refugees who've been dispersed all over the world. That was important to me; I needed to do that for myself.

AG: So what did you recognize in yourself that felt at home, and what did you recognize that felt like, "I'm not from here"?

TLN: I realized that I'm not Vietnamese. I'm not as Vietnamese as the Vietnamese in Vietnam. But being in Australia, I thought that I was very Vietnamese, due to what this society tells me. Everything that I do here makes me feel so Vietnamese; but the more I go back to Vietnam, the more I realize I'm very Westernized. My whole concept of Vietnamese is very Westernized. I also realized I'm not alone in this: I'm part of the 1.5 generation. I grew up here since I was 10, so I have taken on a lot of these things that I didn't even realize I've taken on.

The longer I was gone, the more I realized that Australia feels more like home. But coming back to Australia, I also felt very depressed, feeling that I don't really belong anywhere, not Vietnam nor Australia. That's a huge thing to come to terms with, that you don't really belong anywhere. I don't feel totally comfortable with being part of Western society. I live with them, I work with them, I'm an artist. I hang out with a lot of Western artists. But the humor, the joy, the pain and the way we think about politics and religion and everything—I think very differently. Even the whole thing about equality, human rights and compassion—I'm very strongly influenced by Buddhism, Vietnamese Buddhism.

I applied for a fellowship so that I could spend more time meeting with different Vietnamese people, to see the differences between the Vietnamese people living in all parts of the world. We all left Vietnam for different reasons. For instance, the Vietnamese in France have been there for a long time, during the French colonization. And then there are those who went overseas to study during the Colombo Plan.[3] Then you have the large number who fled Vietnam after '75, a large population of former public servants and teachers like my Dad. Then there were people who left Vietnam for economic reasons. In America, I realized the Vietnamese in America are very different from Vietnamese in Australia, partly due to the sort of people they accepted, a very large number of former South Vietnamese government officials and soldiers, angry because they lost the war, and they also have a larger group of half-American Eurasian kids, from Americans who left little babies in Vietnam. Now there's another whole new group: children of high-ranking party members who can send their kids off overseas to study. Some have a lot more

[3] The Colombo Plan was an aid plan established by the Commonwealth countries to develop Asian countries, aiming to slow the spread of communism by providing capital aid, student education and technical help to the poorer countries of Southeast Asia. Australia was one of the most active donors. Thousands of Asian students were trained in Australian universities.

money to spend than we have. Some of that money is funded through corruption in Vietnam, which is really crazy.

So we are trying to find the dialogue, the language and understanding —trying to find the common values to connect the Vietnamese people. That is maybe my lifelong mission, to do that through the arts.

AG: You mentioned yourself as a member of the 1.5 generation. Is that the focal point of what you wanted to look at, the people who like yourself are not Vietnamese in the way of those who live in Vietnam and not French or American or Australian in the way of someone who feels at home there?

TLN: No, not quite. I'm more interested in understanding the diversity within the Vietnamese people: political diversity, cultural diversity, religious diversity and generational diversity. What kind of influence or impact has the foreign culture had on them? That will help me define a dialogue to make art.

In Vietnam, 80 percent live in country towns; it's almost like opposite to the West. In the West, 80 percent live in the city, and maybe 20 percent live in rural areas. The Vietnamese in the West live almost like Westerners: they're educated, they live in cities, but at the same time, there's very little understanding of or appreciation for the arts. There's no cultural democracy within the arts in Vietnamese society, because there's still segregation between literature and the sort of things that I do, performing arts. Literature is considered to be high art. If you can speak, if you can write, you're considered to be an important person; you're part of the intellectuals. Performing artists are considered to be the other end of the scale, closer to being considered a prostitute than anything else. To them what we do is like a kids' game, all just for fun. Now they realize it's actually a lot more complex, so they start having a bit of a fear because we use a lot of words they don't want to know, like the four-letter words.

AG: Do you see yourself as having a role in creating with these Vietnamese communities around the world, or is it more a question of meeting, learning whatever you can and bringing that back to Australia?

TLN: My dream has always been to be part of the global Vietnamese community, and then part of the global world. To me it is very important that we are all human beings. But I feel that the work that I do is so rare on this planet, especially focusing on the Vietnamese community. You know, we are only about two million people. There's not many of us working in this area at all, especially in between community cultural development and youth theater.

In a nightmare sequence from "Chay Vong Vong," written and directed by Tony Le Nguyen, a young Vietnamese man is tortured by the army in this rehearsal for the play's first production at Footscray Community Arts Centre in Melbourne in 1995. Photo by Andrew Locks.

AG: Let me ask you about this process of translating something from the community-level production, which is very much people telling their own stories, to a production that you want to tour. Explain why you feel that's important.

TLN: The work I do is modeled pretty much on the community cultural development process, where the content evolves through the community, where the outcome and the process are equally important. Sometimes I think maybe the outcome is almost like a bonus.

The model that Vietnamese Youth Media operates on is a cross between youth theater, community cultural development work and professional work. So one project would start out as a community-theater project, and then the following year, we reapply and rework the script and get a full budget, hopefully even pay people. The third phase, which we haven't got yet, is to tour the show. The difficulty is we started with a community show with a large cast. You'll not be able to tour a show with more than six members, or maybe eight if you're lucky, which dramatically changes the whole thing. And that also creates problems for me. Immediately, when you turn professional, you kind of lose essence—that community voice and all that power. All of that is very important to me.

Community theater can sometimes be preaching to the converted. You are telling your story to the same people who've already heard it hundreds of times. So it's really important to take your story beyond your own community. That's really important because that other community is part of the dominant culture oppressing your community. Unless they are aware, unless they know about it, nothing's going to change. It's good that we can sit together and cry, but, hey, sometimes it's equally important to educate and inform those outside our community. We need to let them know that the things they do are hurting us.

How do you take that message out from your community and still keep the essence of the authenticity? That's tricky, because now you're at another stage, and when you do a professional show, you will be judged as a professional production, rather than a community production. People come to see a community production partly because they want to support your content or the participants, to say, "Yes, oh great, you've got the courage to go tell a story which I really want to talk about." But now it's a different ball game.

I am still struggling with that. I'm still searching for an answer. At the end of the day, when I'm producing a show, I have to deal with reality, which is the budget, the costs. When we do a show in the community we can use a church hall, use this space or that space. We can find someone to help out with sound. If you haven't got money to pay for a professional lighting designer, one of you can operate that. But when you're in a theater it's a very different story. Where do cast and crew eat, where are you going to perform, how do you generate audience, publicity, all of that? What you have to do is exactly same as any professional show; otherwise you won't get an audience.

AG: And you have had this experience?

TLN: "Chay Vong Vong" started out as a community show, then it went professional, and then it's gone back into another version of a community show in a different city, in Sydney. Using the ideas and issues and themes from the show, we developed a whole new show with the same name.

AG: You talked about the importance of sharing your story with other communities, especially people whose actions oppress the Vietnamese community. So what happened? Did you get mixed audiences?

TLN: All our work attracts a mixed audience, because I think that's the challenge ahead. The first thing I have to do is ask, what kind of story do I tell, what kind of theater do I make to enable Vietnamese people to like to come see the show. The second thing is within the Vietnamese people, there is diversity. The old people tend to like something they can more relate to, like Vietnamese traditional opera and theater, and the young people like something a bit more hip, a bit more modern, a bit more challenging and confronting. And then I have got the challenge of dealing with the traditional theatergoers: What do they want? How do I make theater that challenges and excites them and that they want to see? That's the challenge of every single project I make, because I'm very interested in generating new audiences to see my work.

Of course, when we actually reproduced the professional show the following year, one of the issues we had to deal with was do I do the show in a Vietnamese community area or do I take the show and perform it in a traditional theater space not in a Vietnamese area? Because I'd done the community show in a Vietnamese area already, I decided, let's do it in a traditional theater space, because I really feel that I need to bring Vietnamese people to a new space. They have a right to go and experience different things. I know there's a chance that my Vietnamese audience will be reduced, but at the end of the day, I'm not upset by that, because I know I am doing something very important, bringing Vietnamese to a nontraditional space. I'm constantly questioning, do I build a bridge from the Australians into the Vietnamese community or do I build from Vietnamese community into Australia? I do one project in one way, the next in the other.

AG: Do you find there's a different character to the experience or impact if you're doing it in a mainstream theater or a community-based place?

TLN: If I do it in a Vietnamese area, we probably won't have a theater—but if I do a show in a Vietnamese area, I know that there will be a chance that I will lose a bit of the traditional theatergoing audience, because they're not used to going to a place like Footscray to see theater. And then when I do my play in a traditional theater space, the Vietnamese people kind of feel very strange. But I have to do a bit of give and take, to try to increase my audience number with every show.

AG: Let's explore your reasons a little bit. What is it you hope for from that exchange?

TLN: First I want to make a political statement about the right to be in a particular place. Even though the Vietnamese have been here over 25 years, there are a lot of spaces where they have never set foot. A lot of Vietnamese tell me that they don't feel comfortable in these spaces, that they don't feel they belong or have a right to be there.

Members of Vietnamese
Youth Media perform
in a Dem Lieu Mang
performance night
directed by Tony Le
Nguyen and Huu Tran
at Melbourne's Footscray
Community Arts Centre
in 1997. Photo by Yen Le.

On the other hand, there is a wider theater audience who are used to a theater district, complete with bars and cafés. When we choose to perform in a nontraditional space—no bar, no café, no champagne—I know that I risk losing part of this audience. My solution is to create a theatrical experience that explores aspects of contemporary Vietnamese society as truthfully as possible.

AG: Do you feel you've had an impact?

TLN: I think so. If people talk about theater in Australia, they'll probably mention my name. I have made a huge impact in this country and I want to continue to do so. But while I'm doing it, it's really important to bring other people along with me, especially young people. With their energy and their ideas, I will be able to transfer some of my experience to them.

AG: When you say "bring them along," what do you mean?

TLN: The project I'm back in Australia to produce is "Aussie Bia Om." The director is a young guy, Huu Tran, who's worked with me for about seven years. He graduated from drama and media two years ago; this is his directing debut. My job is also to be a mentor for him and other young emerging artists such as the costume designer Yen Le. This is her first costume design job: she's a young Vietnamese-Australian; she's designed other stuff, but she's never really designed a theater show before. My composer's the same: Anh Dzung Nguyen is a multitalented musician who plays nine traditional instruments. He's currently completing his Bachelor of Music, majoring in jazz and blues at Monash University. As composer of "Aussie Bia Om," he has to work with non-Vietnamese kids, creating new music which has elements of traditional Vietnamese and a bit of jazz and blues. We're really interested in crossing over and challenging each culture, to challenge and reinterpret Vietnamese culture as much as to challenge and reinterpret Australian culture.

AG: With the younger artists you're mentoring, it sounds like what they're learning to do is be more involved in professional theater. Are you also doing training for community artists, community cultural development workers?

TLN: Funding bodies in Australia require that a professional artist is employed to work on any cultural development project. Such a person must have a proven track record as a paid worker on community projects. If we are to have community artists working on our project we have to provide an opportunity for some young people to build a professional career in the arts. Out of maybe a thousand young Vietnamese with whom I have worked, only a few will continue on and do further training, some of them coming back to work with me. For example, Huu started out in my youth theater group and continued on and got his degree. Now I'm able to say to him: "Okay, it's your turn to do it."

Despite Huu's experience, I do not think that our role at Vietnamese Youth Media is to turn Vietnamese kids into artists. I want to be very realistic. I want them to know that life in the arts is very tough, and I tell them that a majority of artists are very poor, but I also say that the arts are a very powerful place to be. Many young people often fantasize about the arts. They think it's very glamorous, and they think there's a lot of money out there. All they see is MTV and Hollywood and dream that one day they all can be rich and famous. I'm not saying that's impossible—nothing is impossible—but understand the reality, that a majority of artists are not rich.

My job isn't to brainwash anyone or to convert anybody into an artist. All we're doing is using the arts as a way to help people, to give them an outlet to express themselves: their anger, frustration and sadness, whatever is inside of them. If they don't express themselves artistically, they will do it physically. They'll hurt someone else, or they'll hurt themselves. We all need some outlet, and often, if you're a young Vietnamese person, you're very limited, because your culture does not allow you to do that: it's a hierarchical culture, and you have to learn to be top-down.

AG: When you talk about challenging and reinterpreting Vietnamese culture—you've mentioned these hierarchical elements several times—what's your goal?

TLN: I believe that there's a middle ground. One extreme is the very strictly ordered hierarchical system that exists in conservative Asian culture, and then you've got the other, "Who gives a shit?" kind of Western young people's attitude. I'm very sad when I see on the news stories about kids attacking older people in the street. I realize that somehow this whole notion of having respect for older people is not as strong here as within Asian culture. I don't want to feel that you totally disregard people who've been there before you. Of course they often have a fixed way of doing and thinking, but you don't have to treat them like shit.

I'm hoping that my work can inspire and excite the next generation of artists—whether they are American-Vietnamese, French-Vietnamese, Vietnamese-Canadians or Vietnamese-Australians or Vietnamese in Vietnam—to see the possibilities that we have in this life. All they need to start is just a bit of imagination and hard work. I hope to inspire people to go out there and do it and take bigger risks and make mistakes.

I've learned a lot by making mistakes. Four years ago I thought I knew everything I needed to about community cultural development or community arts or whatever you want to call it. When I first started making "Chay Vong Vong," it was a very angry project. Then three years later, I realized that if I continued to do that kind of work, my work would become predictable, and those who don't want to be confronted will stay away from my work. But maybe those who choose to stay away are also those I really want to see my work. So how do I get them to see it without offending them—and also without losing my integrity—and still be able to deliver my message?

AG: So you are looking both at what is worth preserving in traditional Vietnamese culture, like respect for elders, and what might need to change as well.

TLN: Yeah, the nice part is what we need to respect and honor. If other things are part of Vietnamese culture, like encouragement to bash up a woman, or pouring fish sauce down the kid's nose—these are things that I'm totally against, so I said, "No, I'm sorry, but I don't think that's Vietnamese culture." Yet I like this whole thing about having respect for elders. They did look after you when you were younger; maybe when they get older, we should look after them.

After working for seven years with young people, I realize one thing: young people seem to be easy to work with, but they're very difficult; and old people seem to be hard to work with, but they're very easy. Old people have a fixed way of thinking, because they stop taking risks; they cannot deal with the diversity and complexity of society, so it's better for them to have a stable way of thinking and living. With young people, the challenge is to find unpredictable stuff, new, exciting stuff, so that their minds change all the time. The biggest difference is that an old person is more likely to have more discipline than a younger person. They can accept things more easily.

When I first started, I found it very difficult to work with old people because I was scared of them, but I've realized that both old people and young people are extremely vulnerable. Adults tend to be angry because they feel they are losing respect and power. What my work is really trying to do is to allow the young people to see their parents, and the adults to see the young people—that could be their children. Theater is a way to see and learn about yourself, and to learn about things indirectly.

AG: Some of the issues you talked about—in passing, you mentioned men beating their wives, or conflicts between old and young—it made me wonder if your community work connects with other forms of community organization or political movements. Have you been hooked up with groups working on the issues you address?

TLN: Yeah. We often work with schools, juvenile justice centers or health agencies on issues that are relevant to our work. We like to get non-theater people involved in our work so that they can support us both with the content and, if issues arise during the process, offer advice.

We also want to work closely with the Vietnamese organizations and groups to let them know about what we're doing. Sometime it's hard to explain to them how can we do a 50-thousand dollar play and it doesn't make any money. They are not used to working this way. Most of the Vietnamese cultural events are organized by commercial producers.

AG: How do you work with partners? How do you get them involved?

TLN: When I start a project, I go and talk to people about our ideas to see whether they would be interested in being involved. One of the most important things is to see whether we can work together, so that it's their project as much as my project.

On top of that, I do a two-level negotiation: first it's with the workers and the community; the second level of negotiation involves the artists. I am always interested in finding artists who want to work on a particular issue or have an interest in working with the community. Then we put a package together, and then we just wait. A larger project might take a couple of years in the planning.

But with a small project, because we're lucky to be based at Footscray Arts Centre, we have access to reasonable resources: rehearsal space, performance space and lighting and sound, photocopy and Internet—stuff like that. We're kind of the adopted child of this center. They didn't actually bear us, but they kind of liked us, so they adopted us.

AG: How about your relationship with the community cultural development field in Australia in general? Do you participate in those debates and conferences and dialogues and so forth?

TLN: Yes, I attend a lot of conferences and I often speak about our work. We are always looking for new partners to develop projects with, so those conferences are really important. I'm also at a stage where I like to send some of the young artists to work with different companies so I'm looking at developing a kind of exchange project within this country with companies that haven't had much exposure to Vietnamese artists yet.

AG: Where does the support for your work come from?

TLN: Government and some private foundations, like the Sidney Myer Foundation and the Lance Reichstein Foundation, they have been very supportive of our work. My biggest problem at the moment is I don't have enough people who have the ability to manage huge projects. I think it's really important we do larger projects as well as little ones, because I can also use these projects as a way of training people into different positions and responsibilities. This helps them to build credibility and a track record that allows them to move on to other companies, if they so wish.

AG: So are you training people to manage the various projects that you're doing?

TLN: Training is an important part of every project. The composer, the music director, everyone has to learn about working on a community project: the decision-making process and protocols; how to negotiate and work with the community as well as with each other. Sometimes we do things very Vietnamese and sometimes we do things very Australian.

AG: Could you give me a snapshot? Like when you say that sometimes you work in a way that's very Vietnamese, what would an example of that be?

TLN: First of all, I don't know whether it's Vietnamese or not. I say it's Vietnamese. First we have to ask what's the difference between Western culture and Vietnamese culture? Vietnamese culture is family-orientated. The way that we address each other is "brother" and "sister." We don't have this nine-to-five system.

And sometimes when I'm working with kids, I operate very much like a gang, a Vietnamese gang. So I am not afraid of telling them directly what I think of their work. I don't constantly go and pat them on the back and tell them, "This is great already." There are many little subtleties. It's kind of hard to explain, because trying to explain something from another culture is difficult unless you have a cultural reference point.

One thing I'm doing at the moment is just being conscious that we constantly want to work together, like on the current project. Half the people involved are not Vietnamese, and then you've got half Vietnamese, some who don't speak good English at all. And I want to have that range of people, people with different levels of experience, some who are only good at performing in the Vietnamese style and professional actors who are used to working in a particular way. So by creating such an environment, I'm forcing people to change their way of working.

A lot of adults in the Vietnamese community tell me they feel threatened by my work, and I realize that's not what I want to do. I want to be effective. I want them to understand the pain of young people; but at the same time, I realize that adults also have a lot of pain. When we have a lot of pain, we ignore other people's pain, so I really want to connect; I want to make young people see and feel the pain of the adults, and I also want the adults to see the pain of these young people. The only way I'm going to make some real change is if they both come to see my work. The work has to be relevant to each of them and have their voice in it, or else there's no reason for them to come and see it.

That is something that I'm pushing within the Australian theater industry all the time because they are complaining about lack of audiences. The only way they're going to be able to generate new audiences is to make their theater relevant to their community. And if that community is black, or Vietnamese and whatever, then they have to deal with the complexity, because at the moment, they're not dealing with it at all.

AG: Talking about the material your work is based on, you've mentioned feelings of anger and pain and sadness. Do you feel like that's the story that needs to be told above all others, or are there other stories that may be more celebrations or stories of empowerment?

TLN: The only thing I want as an artist is for my audiences to think; I want them to take something away to think about. Of course what you do has to affect people to enable them to think. You want them to come in, and then you leave something inside them. At first my work used to be very confronting. Now, my agenda is not about confronting, but to be effective instead. Huu and I talk about making seductive theater, where we actually seduce our audience. We base this on a Vietnamese concept. There's a saying: "Sweet honey kill fly." So don't be fooled by the sweet honey, because that might kill you. The sweet honey will attract people to the theater, but just be careful, okay? That puts people slightly on edge already. But they want to come and see it, because they've been seduced.

Of course, some people say we're not being very fair; are we trying to trick our audience? It's a very fine line. I said somewhere at one of the conferences, "Youth theater is sometimes like a drug, because you make these kids feel good and after the performance they all got high and then it's all over. And then they all get depressed. Now, what are you doing? You are as bad as a drug pusher."

AG: So what's the solution?

TLN: Mine is that there has to be continuity. We'll develop the next work together. Let's keep doing it, and we'll do it with or without funding. If the kids want to do it, we'll do it. If they want to do stuff on karaoke or martial arts or whatever. If they're used to doing karaoke, how can you make karaoke interesting? Start with karaoke as a base, as a starting point. If they're used to watching Chinese martial-arts movies, Jacky Chan stuff, and they all want to hit each other, how do I turn it into performance? We take cartoons, game shows and video games; then we add a story to it—that's what makes performance. I'm really interested in starting with what people feel comfortable with and then slowly stretching them.

AG: What about criticism and evaluation? How do you know if what you're doing is working? Who do you listen to about whether it's good?

TLN: Criticism in youth and community theater can be very interesting. Traditionally many theater critics are of Anglo backgrounds. They are still struggling to understand anything beyond "English-language fourth-wall theater." So how do we expect them to understand theater from cultural and diverse backgrounds, being created by young Vietnamese-Australians who have complex cultural experience? In the past, I liked the idea of people writing nice things about me. But now the more I've been around, more people know me, even good things that people write, like praise, I don't always believe them. There's not many Vietnamese who do what I'm doing. The critics used to write things that I'd get upset about; now I'm struggling to see something which really upsets me. In community theater, I look at the process and outcome as equally important. So if they only focus on the outcome, and not on the process, then it doesn't bother me that much, because they don't really know what my process is.

AG: How do you get response from your participants?

TLN: If the community and young people don't like what we do, we won't be around too long, because they won't come and see the show or work with us. There's not many of us; if they don't want us, then we're in trouble. So, yeah, we do have to work very closely with them, and we have to monitor ourselves. Our process has been really great, totally and fully involving from start to finish. I keep begging people, "Please come in." But the reality is they have school, they have work, or they're looking for work, or whatever. I often tell people it's up to them how involved they want to be. If they want to be really involved, then we give them more responsibility. If they want to be involved a little bit, then they can have a bit of responsibility. I like to know whether people are going to be there or not on the day when we're performing. It's not fair on the others if they don't turn up for rehearsal.

If people cannot come, I really want to know why and whether it's a transport issue, financial issue, or if there's anything that we can do to help, like organizing car pooling or whatever. Closer to the performance time, we also try to feed people, we'll create a community kitchen. We try to do as much together as possible. I encourage people to come and work with me constantly.

AG: When we were talking together about globalization earlier this spring, many of the things that people described have already happened to the Vietnamese: to be forced to be refugees, to have to go elsewhere to look for security, economic or personal security and to be leaving behind cultural traditions in favor of new cultural products of the country you go to. What insight does this give you into what's happening around the world now on a larger scale? How do you see the Vietnamese experience relating to the whole question of globalization?

TLN: I think like all minority cultures of the world, the Vietnamese culture will eventually be swallowed by the dominant culture. That might sound too harsh, but I think there are many signs of this happening already. Every year when I go back to Vietnam I see these changes, from the music people listen to, to the food that they eat and the clothing that they wear.

This sad reality is because Vietnam is so far behind the rest of the world. The Vietnamese leaders are too busy trying to make quick money at the expense of arts, culture and education. The Chinese film industry from Hong Kong, Taiwan and Singapore has also exploited this opportunity by flooding the Vietnamese market with low-budget Chinese films with Vietnamese voice-overs, all over the world. In America, even with the largest Vietnamese community outside of Vietnam, they are still not doing very much apart from reproducing American and Chinese music with Vietnamese lyrics.

The future for Vietnamese culture and other minority cultures of the world is looking very bleak. I'm very much saddened by the thought of the day I can wake up in Saigon, have McDonald's for breakfast and KFC for lunch and have dinner at Jack in the Box while watching CNN and drinking Coke.

18

"Abu Shaker's Affairs '99"
Ashtar Forum Theater
production, Ramallah,
Palestine, spring 1999.

Ashtar Theatre
P.O. Box 17170
East Jerusalem 91171, via Israel
or
P.O. Box 2127
Ramallah, Palestine
Telephone: (972 2) 2980037
Fax: (972 2) 2960326
E-mail: ashtar@p-ol.com
Web site: www.ashtar-theatre.org

With her husband, Edward Muallem, **Iman Aoun** is Co-Artistic Director of Ashtar Theatre, the company they cofounded in 1991, as well as its Public Relations Manager and a performer. As she described in her contributions to the online dialogue among the authors in this volume, her career has followed a trajectory typical of those who have not come to community cultural development work through academic training —that is, total immersion in on-the-job training:

I started my career in theatre back in 1984 with the internationally known Palestinian theatre company El-Hakawati. At that time I did not have any theatre training or education—how would I, when Palestine has not one theatre school up till now? With Hakawati I participated in all its productions: acting, improvising, sewing, sweeping, dancing, traveling, assisting the administration—basically everything that was needed. The group was my home, my school, and theatre was and still is my lifestyle.

Woven through Iman's essay are the problems of a community under siege, struggling with identity and autonomy:

In Palestine even the baby in its mother's womb is politicized, this is our destiny. So as we say here, we breathe politics and eat politics with our daily bread— but wait a minute, social politics aren't the same. Our society has many taboos and prohibitions especially when it comes to women's issues. This is why we started in 1997 our Forum Theatre productions.

The latter part of this essay describes an annual Forum Theatre series, "Abu Shaker's Affairs," that has allowed the theater to raise troubling questions for Palestinian society in a safe forum—a project received with great enthusiasm, and one that has enabled Ashtar to reach remote areas and rural villages where inhabitants had never before seen theater.

Interspersed with the essay are excerpts from an interview with Iman conducted by Arlene Goldbard on November 27, 2001.

Different Art Forms, Mutual Concerns

by Iman Aoun
Translated by Fatin Farhat and
Antoine D. Nesnas

Since An-Nakba (Arabic for "catastrophe," used in reference to the Israeli occupation of Palestine in 1948) and the subsequent creation of the State of Israel, Palestinian culture has played a prominent and significant role in the preservation and crystallization of a Palestinian identity in the face of the occupation. Through folklore, art, poetry and literature, culture has been essential in expressing an attachment to the roots of popular culture and helping to rebuild confidence.

Ashtar, our Palestinian nonprofit organization for theater production and training, was founded in Jerusalem in 1991. When Ashtar was established, theater in Palestine suffered from an acute shortage of professionals in all fields. At the same time, a great need for creativity and self-expression among young people in Palestinian schools was identified. Ashtar's founders wanted to offer these youth, growing up in the wake of the first Intifada (uprising), a voice, a chance to express their feelings of frustration and to search for opportunities for growth and development in a very restrictive period of our history. In this essay, I want to show how different cultural domains played significant roles in shaping the sociopolitical awareness of our community, and treat the particular dilemmas and challenges of community cultural development under conditions of occupation, exploring some of the ideas, influences and approaches that shape our work in particular and other such work in Palestine. To begin, it is necessary to set the context.

Prior to An-Nakba, major Palestinian cities served as a nucleus for Arab culture. For example, the creation and multiplication of publishing houses and literary journals reached its apex in 1929. The reality of pre-1948 cultural institutions refutes claims that Palestine was a land without a people to a people without a land, used by Zionists to attract Jewish immigration. In the aftermath of An-Nakba and the forced emigration of Palestinians in 1948, the city as an entity and the city culture disappeared from Palestinian society. Consequently, culture began to revolve around rural society, which in turn introduced its own folkloric elements which came to predominate, although they did not represent the true original Palestinian culture.

Palestinians were dispossessed and forced to emigrate to numerous host countries. Those of rural background settled in Palestinian refugee camps in the Arab world. The camp dwellers stressed the revival of their cultural heritage both as a group survival strategy and as an obstacle to attempts to assimilate them into host countries. As a result, the homeland became a cultural project manifested through literature, other arts and creativity, formed according to the collective dream of the dispossessed.

CREATIVE LANGUAGE IN THE FACE OF SUBJUGATION

Palestinian culture—the infant of the catastrophe—was constructed by authors and artists over a half-century of forced emigration, exile and occupation. This culture continues to be the most sensitive and controversial issue with the Other (Israel in relation to Palestine). The struggle centered on the land in myth and actuality. The Other enacted its myth on the Palestinian land, spreading it all over the world while the Palestinian reality was reduced in both history and geography to mythic confines defined by its author. As a location, Palestine has become divided between a new politico-geographical reality with a unified cultural history and the place of exile in which the homeland was packed and transported in a suitcase.

Many poets, authors and artists broached the subject of this homeland struggle in their writings and artistic works. They articulated national concepts and feelings of the Palestinian public. Their creative works centered on the formation and structuring of national symbols, so that Palestinian literature often used symbols to epitomize the lost homeland. The most important of these symbols was that of the Palestinian hero, a substitute for defeat and conquest which befell the people as a result of An-Nakba and the loss of the homeland.

Palestinian poets and poetry were instrumental in developing the thinking and approach of the Palestinian public in all its sectors and locations, crystallizing popular political aspirations. The famous Palestinian poet Mahmoud Darwish played a significant role in this context, going beyond the Palestinian horizon to gain international acknowledgement. Consider this description of the impact of Darwish's writing by Jordanian poet Muhammad Abeid Allah, former professor of Arabic literature at Philadelphia University:

> Mahmoud Darwish caused me surprise and amazement...he occupied me and filled up my spirit as he did to my colleagues and to my entire generation. Darwish formed a distinguished mark in our consciousness from childhood. We grew up with his poems and memorized many of them...dictated them in our notebooks, planted them in our spirits, to dream of flourishing in a more beautiful and noble world similar to the one whose features are drawn through the poems that enchanted me. Mahmoud Darwish's poetry backed us and preserved our souls from defeats. Chanting and poetry lifted up our souls and supported them. Darwish, significant fabricator of our mood, taught us the rituals of Palestine. His poems that were transformed into melodies of lyrics have become a part of our daily rituals that point toward him and toward an unknown Palestine to those born in the Diaspora. Palestine's image remains alive within us through the poetry that was planted in our souls strongly and vitally. Darwish inherited the land of language, and recognized that "land is inherited as language" and "language is inherited as land." Thus, through Darwish we have acquired the alphabetic rhyme of homeland and language.[1]

[1] Muhammad Abeid Allah, "Poets," *House of Poetry Magazine*, Edition 4–5, Summer 1999, p. 259.

Similar to other Arab societies, Palestinian culture takes immense pride in its Arabic language, which due to its ties to Islam and the Quran's linguistic miracle is considered sacred. Eloquence and rhetoric are the strongest and most prominent creative productions in the entirety of the Arab civilization, and language has played a significant role in Palestinian popular culture.

Thus language in Palestinian culture plays a significant role in shaping the minds of the people. For Ashtar, language is a collective proposition for self-affirmation; it's a voice, an emotion and an act of the body. Ashtar's production "Of Soil and Crimson," for instance, focused on the history and the origins of the cultural conflict with the Other. We delved into the original mythology of our ancestors the Canaanites and the way that the Hebrews, arriving centuries later, mixed facts and fiction in their accounts of the Canaanites. Thus, competing mythologies about the land underpin conflicts over the contemporary history of Palestine.

Another inspiration to the community was Naji Al Ali, a Palestinian caricaturist whose first drawing came to light in the Ein El-Halweh refugee camp in Lebanon in 1963. Naji Al Ali voiced the concerns of the poor and the oppressed, expressing their anger and sorrows, declaring he had lost faith in rotten Arabic regimes and economic elites, thus gaining numerous enemies. Over the quarter-century of Naji Al Ali's visual commentaries on the daily news of Arab politics—particularly the Palestinian problem—people got accustomed to reading the daily papers backward, starting with the last page featuring his caricature that accurately, honestly, realistically and scandalously depicted the political reality of each day.

Naji was simple, popular and direct. This is why people have memorized his words, chanted his slogans and personified his drawings into theater. He was considered a mentor to Ashtar, especially for his critical thinking. His example guides us in raising a generation of young actors to have a critical eye and voice and a strong social and political awareness.

Handala (from *handal*, a bitter plant) is one of Naji's main characters, exemplifying his people's suffering and defining the meaning of exile. This miserable, poorly dressed, barefooted child observes each new event from a distance. He is seldom actively involved. He captures childhood's innocence, allowing him to express his views and anger openly and freely. Here's how Naji Al Ali defined Handala:

> Handala was born at ten years of age and will always remain ten. At ten, he was forced out of his homeland and he will remain ten until he returns. Then he will start growing. Nature's laws do not apply to Handala. He is an exception since a homeland's loss is an exception. Matters will revert to normalcy when he returns home. I introduced him to the reader and named him Handala, the symbol of bitterness. At the beginning, I introduced him as a Palestinian child. However with the development of consciousness, he acquired a national integrity and a universal human horizon. He is the witness of this undying age, who entered life forcefully and will never leave it. He is the legendary witness and this character is immortal. It was born to live and challenged to survive and go on.[2]

[2]Daod Ibahim, *Naji Al Ali: An Artist Not for Display* (Ramallah: Al Yarmouk Organization for Culture and Media, 1989), p. 61.

Akin to Handala, the child who never ceases scrutinizing the world around him, Ashtar Theatre keeps faith with Naji Al Ali by breaking all social and political taboos and raising all suppressed issues in our society, breaking the silence and raising the voice of the poor, the oppressed and the marginalized.

Arlene Goldbard: Ashtar feels it needs to be critical of problems in Palestinian society, and from what you've said at the conference, some Palestinians don't like that. Could you tell a little bit about your experience?

Iman Aoun: Since we started our public awareness program with Forum Theater in 1997, we've been raising difficult topics that the society hesitates to reveal. Earlier, we always touched on sociopolitical problems, and society viewed our approach positively except when we criticized Palestinian politics.

When we criticize the occupation, we receive the public's approval. But when we talk about our own problems, the public gets irritated.

As we started using Forum Theater to criticize the social order, some groups were aggravated. Some influential social figures denounced our work as we have broached sexual harassment and incest.

Sometimes when people are watching these plays, they would stop us and protest: "This is not right! You are exaggerating!" As Forum demands, we turn their rage to the advantage of the play. Even if they were negative, at some point they would still receive us with respect at subsequent performances. So it's not really a hostile relationship; but when they do not like something we present, they do say that out loud.

AG: So it takes courage for you to continue to persevere against this opposition.

IA: Of course it takes courage, but somehow it also needs diplomacy. We're not trying to offend our society. What we're trying to do is to open up discussions and to say that although we are the same people we might be different, we have different opinions and what we perform and the way we work is only to say that we need tolerance along with the different attitudes. This is the message that we are trying to convey.

Our own organization, Ashtar, developed without the continuity that could have been a natural process in other places. The Palestinian theater, which started during the rise of Arab theater in Lebanon and Egypt, was unable to sustain what should have been its natural growth and development due to the various political catastrophes that befell it. Its roots started in Christian missionary schools built during the 1850s, then spread through the fertile fields of the Jerusalem, Jaffa, Bethlehem and Haifa schools, and also through YMCA and Moslem Brotherhood clubs and into legitimate theaters.

During An-Nakba of 1948, thousands of innocent civilians fled to safety. The Palestinian Diaspora began, with people displaced all over the world. The literary leaders and cultural icons in Palestinian society emigrated from their homeland, and the theater movement, which had reached a peak of its prosperity in 1948, was unable to regroup until the 1970s, when theater in the West Bank and Gaza Strip began to revive.

Ashtar was the first Palestinian theater program geared toward theater development and training. We are actively engaged in research and experimentation with artistic elements, tools and techniques, continuously developing ideas and methods, cultivating a critical soul. We understand our work as part of the march for transformation and evolution of the Palestinian nation.

Ashtar's main activities can be summarized into two categories: first, providing drama-training courses to those who wish to engage in the world of theater either as drama teachers or as actors. We are gradually increasing our role in

Palestinian schools, giving children the chance to discover new horizons through drama lessons. We recognize that drama is a valuable tool in developing the students' capability of using and expanding their imaginations, creating stories to help them express their hidden talents and portray personal experiences.

Second, Ashtar is engaged in producing plays that are either performed by its students or by its professional actors. One of our aims is to promote and present these plays both locally and internationally, reaching all the sectors of Palestinian society in their own places. Toward this end, we produce three types of theater: school theater is primarily directed toward the students; professional theater is directed to theatergoers and produced in cooperation with local, Arab and/or international theater groups; and finally, for the past five years we have been working on Forum Theater with community groups and organizations in Palestine, particularly producing and performing an annual serial entitled "Abu Shaker's Affairs."

WHY THEATER? ASHTAR'S SOCIOPOLITICAL ROLE

Forum Theater, based on Augusto Boal's Theater of the Oppressed, is an alternative form of theater that allows the audience to influence the outcome of the play. The audience views the play once without any interruptions, then the play is re-performed and audience members are given the chance to participate in the direction of the story by stepping in and providing alternate behaviors, choices, actions and wording. The productions provide an open forum for those voices that are usually overlooked or ignored by the community to express their views through developing alternate strategies to combat oppression.

This type of interactive theater works as a continuous awareness campaign and an alternative discussion forum. In general, a Forum Theater performance is based on social and cultural particularities of the region, spoken in Palestinian dialect and performed anywhere: at the village meeting place, in a hall or even in a classroom. It reaches out to all levels of society all over the country. Spectators are asked to step on-stage to act out their own suggestions directly. They can even suggest additional scenes and characters to be played by themselves or other members of the audience, with the aim of changing the sequence of the original play in service of the protagonist.

The dynamics that arise from the audience are considered important elements of the Forum experience. Indirectly, while focusing on the objective of directing characters on stage, the audience is going through certain democratic processes—listening to each other without interruption, observing someone else's suggestions performed on stage and proposing other active and effective suggestions. Armed with strategies that were enacted on the stage, audience members begin to acquire new coping mechanisms to use in daily life and new keys to problem solving.

This Forum Theater series has a strong impact on the Palestinian community, helping to foster the skills necessary for active and democratic participation in shaping society. Given the opportunity to intervene in the outcome of the performance, audiences respond eagerly to this challenge and express their satisfaction in the presentation. Ashtar's Forum Theater is an example of community cultural work where action toward social change takes the lead.

Increasingly, we consider Forum Theater one of the essential pillars of Ashtar's work. In particular, the annual series of "Abu Shaker's Affairs" plays an important role in fulfilling Ashtar's aim of making theater reach all sectors of the Palestinian society, giving life to theater in areas where theater has never reached before. "Abu Shaker's Affairs" is a community-based project using theater as a vehicle to engage diverse groups in a form of conflict resolution and teamwork, raising awareness of contemporary issues such as democracy, human rights and the environment. Each annual production in the series acts as a mirror, providing Palestinians with a reflection of their community's changing needs, problems and realities.

The series is set within the context of a Palestinian family—Abu Shaker's— presenting critical issues through the lives and experiences of his family members.

Subjects that Ashtar Theatre has tackled through the five "Abu Shaker's Affairs" series were family violence, early marriage, child labor, water shortages, trading with rotten food, land confiscation, collaborators (Palestinians who work with the Israeli intelligence agency) and even taboos such as incest.

The reaction to "Abu Shaker's Affairs" has been overwhelmingly positive, with the show increasing in popularity each year. Over the past four years, demand has grown steadily from groups wishing to have their issues tackled in the play, as well as from grassroots organizations prompting us to raise some of the problems they confront.

Given that Ashtar is a group of theater makers and not development workers or actual victims of a social problem, Ashtar's team enlists the assistance of both local organizations and international experts in Forum Theater to develop each year's episode of "Abu Shaker's Affairs." We work closely with community groups and organizations to research and develop the issues and present them in a realistic and responsible manner, thereby distinguishing our work from the other Forum Theater work in the region, which is seldom grounded in community collaboration.

Ashtar conducts three stages of formative research in the development of each "Abu Shaker's Affairs" script. The first stage is a review of any existing relevant literature; this is followed by focus-group discussions with social workers, counselors or other knowledgeable sources; finally we interview people to obtain case studies—for example, victims of incest, child laborers and so on. In developing each play, Ashtar seeks true-life stories that provide insight into the nature of the problem and its plausible solutions.

In the theatrical lab, the team explores and shapes the ideas and the material collected from various sources. The artistic team is then ready to develop the skeleton of the production through discussions and dramaturgical work. Improvisation helps to create the text and build up the show.

Rehearsing, the group uses a number of exercises that are essential to the creation of the work:

1. Exercises exploring concepts of power, leadership, dominance, submission, status and oppression. Working in pairs or in groups, participants find postures associated with chosen themes.

2. Image theater techniques: the director offers a topic, and the group improvises a still image around it, exploring power positions and ways of breaking or supporting this power. The image changes slightly every time the group assesses the strengths and weaknesses it embodies.

3. Exercises to explore personal life-journeys of the characters, train Jokers (facilitators between the actors on stage and the spectators) in the skills necessary to lead the "spect-actors" (spectator/actors who rise from the audience to play a role) in democratic interventions as they seek change.

4. Character development work, creating a life story for each persona, based on the material collected in the field.

5. Re-improvisations of scenes and text.

6. Rehearsing the specific roles of actors, the Joker and the spect-actors.

The following synopsis is an example of one of the "Abu Shaker's Affairs" Forum productions in 1999:

> Abu Shaker oppresses everyone around him. He mocks Shaker, his handi-
> capped son, exploits his nephew and harasses his sister-in-law, all in addition
> to having sexually abused Mashael, his niece, when she was a child. He
> bought his sister-in-law Katmeh's silence over his incestuous affair. Now, Abu
> Shaker proclaims that Mashael is disgracing the family's honor by studying
> at the University and wanting to work. He forbids his son Shukri to have a
> relationship with her.

Shukri confronts Mashael with his father's accusation, and Mashael confesses to her cousin that she is indeed not a virgin, but that she loves him and has no one else in her life. Yet she challenges him to have the courage to ask his father about his allegations.

In response, Abu Shaker urges his son to kill Mashael, using her younger brother Hafeez, who is at a loss about what to do.

Faced with these circumstances, Katmeh, Mashael's mother, finally raises her voice to request the killing of Abu Shaker, which should have been done eight years ago for his disgraceful action.

The annual "Abu Shaker's Affairs" series is key to Ashtar's work, because it enables us to reach groups that are not otherwise very accessible due to social, cultural, economic, political and, at times, psychological barriers—for instance, women, youth, the elderly, the disabled and the poor. We also involve actors who would not otherwise have an outlet to use their talents. These efforts express our policy of making Ashtar's services accessible to all members of Palestinian society regardless of economic or social status, particularly those who are on the lowest rung of the economic ladder. We believe that the poor, who struggle to fulfill their basic needs such as food and shelter, are entitled to a place to discuss their own social problems. In this light, Ashtar reaches them and motivates them.

The "Abu Shaker's Affairs" series usually targets youth—students in private, public and UNRWA (United Nations Relief and Works Agency for Palestine refugees in the Near East) schools, universities and summer camps. Young people are not so fixed in their attitudes, values and behavioral patterns as older people and are therefore easier to influence. Other target groups are women in villages, rural areas and refugee camps all over the Palestinian territories.

As the performance depends fundamentally upon the intermingling of audience members, Ashtar insists, whenever possible, on performing for mixed-gender audiences. An audience member once commented, "Men may not realize that they are oppressors. They as well as the oppressed need to have their consciousness raised." However in some villages, due to social restrictions, separate performances are organized for males and females.

Ashtar has become a model of Forum Theater in Palestine. In Nablus, for instance, some young women aged 17 to 21 who had seen "Abu Shaker's Affairs" and who normally do not have a chance to learn acting used the form and the themes to develop their own play along the lines of Ashtar. The Women's Affairs Technical Committee, a national women's rights organization that has been a supporter of Ashtar Forum Theater, then rented a public hall for them in Nablus on International Women's Day, and the play was performed in front of a large audience. Another group of young women, from Dehesha refugee camp in Bethlehem, copied a production of "Abu Shaker's Affairs" and performed it at the camp. The impact of Ashtar's Forum productions is growing by the year.

With every year's new production, Ashtar is able to see increased involvement of audience members, especially those who have seen a previous "Abu Shaker's Affairs" episode and speak of the impact that the previous performance has left on their lives. Indeed, the behavioral changes promoted by Ashtar are subject to centuries-old traditions, restrictions and social boundaries. Yet the spect-actors' involvement in scenes provides them with a strong embodied memory that will be evoked when they face similar real-life situations. For Ashtar to have this impact, people need to have a follow-up, something beyond viewing one single performance. We therefore try to return to the same groups to perform subsequent versions of "Abu Shaker's Affairs," presenting a new episode every year.

In this year's "Abu Shaker's Affairs 2001," Ashtar focuses on problems that cropped up during the current Intifada: poverty caused by the continuous closure of the Palestinian territories, the expansion of child labor and the escalating risk of increased numbers of collaborators. This production is aimed at students 13 years and older. Daily performances were given at schools for the last few months to immense reactions from the spect-actors.

> Shaker, the protagonist, is 13 years old, the oldest son of a family of six kids. His father lost his job as a construction worker in Israel due to the recent Intifada and is unable to find an alternative job. His mother is a passive woman who cares for him but does nothing to protect him. Shaker had to quit school in order to sell chewing gum to feed his family. His only friend, Anwar, whose father is a national activist, is a spoiled child who refuses to lend him money, boasting instead of having to move residence for security reasons, because his father is wanted by the Israelis. In great need of money, Shaker, convinced by two gang members, steals a radio from a car. He is caught red-handed, as he did not know that this was a setup. At prison the Israeli investigator treats him gently, showing him sympathy, and succeeds in turning him into a mole (collaborator). The deal is that he should provide information about wanted persons in his neighborhood in exchange for payment. The first piece of information Shaker gives is the new address of Anwar's family, receiving a large sum of money in return. A few days later, a rocket hits Anwar's house, not killing his father but Anwar himself. Shaker is confused, in pain, and sorry for his action. He asks for the help of the audience.

AG: Ashtar started after the first Intifada, and you've been there through the entirety of the second Intifada so far. How have the uprising and the response to it affected the theater? What's it like to be there?

IA: It is very difficult on all levels; but for theater, if we weren't working with children at schools, we would have been forced to close the theater long ago, because people cannot move from one city to another, including Ashtar's team.

On the other hand, usually when we do a Forum play, we travel a lot with it to other urban and rural areas, to places where usually they don't go to theater, or theater doesn't reach them. We are not able to do this, these days, because we're literally stuck in one place. We have our theater in Ramallah, and actually we cannot leave Ramallah. Except when one has to travel abroad, then we have a special permission to leave one's own city and the country. Some months ago a group of theater people from Gaza had to be in Hebron for a theater workshop with Dutch directors; to be able to attend the workshop they had to travel to Egypt then to Jordan and get through the Jordan River into the West Bank to Hebron. That was the only way to reach from Gaza to Hebron, which is less than 50 miles. What an absurdity!

Besides, whenever there is an Israeli military incursion, everything closes down, so we sit at home. If we have performances, we can not perform. The last time the Israeli tanks invaded Ramallah, soldiers were occupying our apartment and tanks were just in front of our house and theater. We weren't able to reach the theater at all, we were stuck. Students were not able to go to schools either. Life was just one stalemate.

Due to the Intifada, we had also to modify our production's planned themes. Our Forum Theater topics for this year should have been tackling drug addiction, yet we had to deal with collaborators, a topic that poses a great threat to our society. Current conditions have their own dictates on what we can and should do.

ASHTAR AND SOCIOCULTURAL CHANGE

In an attempt to trace the effectiveness of Forum Theater on Palestinian society, an evaluation was conducted in February 2001 by Dr. Edward Green at the request of Care International, a partner organization of Ashtar Theatre in the Forum Theater program. It focused on the "Abu Shaker's Affairs" series, and the following results were found:

From the evidence gathered in the evaluation, those exposed to an Abu Shaker performance of the past three years almost always liked the method, and found it far preferable to traditional, didactic pedagogic methods, such as the active-teacher/passive-student model. As one teacher commented spontaneously, "This play is equal to a month of classes using regular teaching methods; students learn much more by participating, rather than just listening, and the Forum Theater method gives the audience a sense of power."

A woman, after seeing the performance of "Abu Shaker's Affairs 2000," declared that none of her own daughters would be forced into early marriage.

Another woman told how she resisted a man who touched her on the bus; in fact she slapped him in the face. She would not have done that kind of thing before. "Abu Shaker's Affairs '99" gave her the courage to stand up for her rights.

A refugee woman in Jordan commented, "Seeing 'Abu Shaker '99' helped me not accept sexual abuse as normal, as 'just the way things are.'"

Another told of a man in her neighborhood who used to make obscene gestures to local women. He even exposed himself. She got together with her neighbors and armed herself with a stick and began to look for this man. The exhibitionist was never seen again.

One woman stayed at the home of a female friend for a whole week in order to help her with an abusive husband. She commented, "We as women can act differently now, and we can help each other." Seeing "Abu Shaker's Affairs" gave her the motivation to act like a "volunteer social worker" at these times.

Corroborative evidence of changed behavior was also found. For example, a lawyer who runs a legal service for refugee women in Jordan reported that significantly more women came for counseling after they saw "Abu Shaker's Affairs '99," and she had evidence that the Ashtar performance motivated them to use legal services. Moreover she observed changes in attitude and behavior in the direction taught by Ashtar. This lawyer now uses stories from Abu Shaker in her legal service work and even in court.

In another example, "Abu Shaker's Affairs '99" was shown to a group of disabled people, in cooperation with an NGO that works with the disabled. This audience picked up on the play's sub-theme that the disabled have a right to, and ought to, find and hold employment. The head of this NGO testified that many more handicapped people associated with his NGO actually got employment after viewing "Abu Shaker's Affairs '99."

In still another example, members of a labor union were represented in one of the "Abu Shaker's Affairs '99" audiences, one theme of which was illegal child labor. Viewing this play empowered union members to confront an employer's association with threats that they would send letters of warning, and eventually take legal action, if employers continued to hire illegal child labor.

From the above one could tell that giving a platform, a voice and a chance for the marginalized and the oppressed to express themselves and actively take part in the formation of their destinies help [shape] a more democratic, free and productive society.[3]

[3] Dr. Edward Green, "Evaluation of Popular Theatre in Palestine" (Jerusalem: Care International, May 2001), printed document.

After 10 years of continuous and dedicated work toward social, psychological and political development and change in our community, educators and officials are now seeking the cooperation of Ashtar Theatre in setting future national strategies for theater education and drama training in Palestinian schools.

The second major program of Ashtar's work, as mentioned earlier, is drama in the schools. This adds a new dimension to our involvement in the community and highlights the role we play in creating public awareness within Palestinian society. Ashtar works with students in rural areas, in public, private and refugee-camp schools, using drama techniques to stimulate the students' creativity and to help them explore themselves through verbal and nonverbal communication. Young boys and girls manage by the end of a workshop to reach a stage of free exploration of their senses, utmost use of their bodies and spontaneous response, entering into free-association and creative improvisations that reveal stories and subjects from their daily lives and concerns, such as the impact of occupation and Israeli settlements on the day-to-day functioning of the Palestinian community, including the loss of land, house demolitions, water pollution and hindering access to free movement through sieges and check-points. Ashtar uses Forum Theater techniques such as image theater and improvisational skills in working with these children.

Our current major problem stems from the continuous closure of the towns and villages in the Palestinian territories which restricts all movement between them, thus severing communication with our urban and rural audiences. This has left us with a limited number of schools to work with in our immediate vicinity.

Thus, the conditions under which we work are dire. As of the end of 2001, and since June 1967, Israeli occupation authorities have expropriated 79 percent of the West Bank and the Gaza Strip territory. Of these areas, 44 percent were taken for "military purposes," 20 percent for "security" reasons, 12 percent for "public use" and 12 percent because the owners were "absent." Notwithstanding the Oslo Accords of 1993, Israel has continued to expand settlements; since the signing of the Declaration of Peace in September 1993, the settler population in the West Bank and the Gaza Strip has doubled to 200,000 and over 280,000 dunums of land have been confiscated, in addition to 282,000 trees that have been uprooted in the West Bank alone.[4]

[4]"Agenda," *PASSIA-Diary 2001* (Jerusalem: Palestinian Academic Society for the Study of International Affairs, 2001), p. 257.

[5]Michael Naima, *Joubran Khalil Joubran: The Complete Work* (Beirut: Sader Publishing House), p. 416.

AG: What is Ashtar's vision of the Palestinian society you hope to be working toward, the relationship with your neighbors you hope to be working toward? Is there a sense of the cultural reality you would like to help bring about?

IA: We are striving for a free and a democratic society where pluralism, in the different domains of life, is accepted and practiced.

Because we have lived for years in a cultural ghetto under the Israeli occupation, and were cut off from the natural cultural flow with the Arab world, we are trying now to establish our presence on the theatrical arena of the Arab countries. Therefore we are stimulating coproductions and cooperative projects with various Arab theater companies in Jordan, Tunisia and Morocco, though these projects have been seriously affected, due to the new ghettos imposed on us by the Israeli government.

We always cooperated with those who share our vision and working methodology. We work a lot with Europeans, and we have also worked with Americans. With Israelis, we haven't worked, and we don't think the time has come to do so. First, we have to accept the existence of one another. As cultural people, we have a very powerful impact on our societies, as expressed throughout my essay. We just have to be sincere with our public, as we are continuously under the spotlight. ...

"Life without freedom ... is like a body without soul, and freedom without thought ... is like a disturbed soul; life, freedom and thought are three hypostases in one self that never perishes."[5]

September 5, 2000,
parade around Infanta
town. Photo by PETA.

19

Philippine Educational Theater Association
61 Lantana Street
Cubao, Quezon City 1111, Philippines
Telephone: (632) 7249637 or (632) 4100821-22
Fax: (632) 7226911
E-mail: peta@drama.com.ph
Web site: www.petatheater.org

Maribel Legarda grew up in the Philippine Educational Theater Association (PETA), the group she now serves as artistic director. Here's how she described this history to fellow participants in the online dialogue:

Munira Sen wrote in her bio, "I don't know where the 'I' begins and where 'Madhyam' [the organization she directs] ends." I feel exactly the same way. It's hard to separate who I am from what PETA is and how the work has evolved me. I started my "love affair" with theater and PETA as a young primary-school student who had a PETA children's theater teacher. I loved going to her classes because it was there that I felt free and able to express who I was and what I thought. One day, she took us to a place called Fort Santiago, a part of the Walled City, which was the first settlement built by the Spaniards. Inside was a beautiful open-air theater nestled within walls of red brick and piedra china, at the center of which was a T-stage

which in those days seemed such an unusually shaped performance area. This was PETA's home, and as I stood there I made a vow that I would one day be part of that place, that theater called Rajah Sulayman. Ten years later, I took a six-week PETA Summer Theater Arts Workshop and I haven't left since. Twenty-two years have passed and I can say that PETA became the place where I "grew up." It has become my second home, or you can also say, my community.

PETA is a flagship group of the community cultural development field: ambitious, adaptable and enduring, creating powerful work even when it was essentially outlawed by the Marcos regime. As this essay describes, PETA's challenge is to find effective ways to work with groups that are among the most marginalized

in a country that is one of the poorest and has felt globalization's damaging effects more intensely than most:

We are not prepared for the onslaught of globalization, so what we sell are our human resources. We need to send our women as domestic helpers and our men as laborers abroad, and in exchange, we have more young people growing up in extended households and generating social problems because there have been little efforts to create a support system to cope with this shift from the nuclear family to extended households.

Imagined Communities
PETA'S COMMUNITY, CULTURE AND DEVELOPMENT EXPERIENCE

by Maribel Legarda

A 7-year-old girl stands in the middle of a classroom, listening intently as she goes through the motions of the story her drama teacher is narrating. She feels free, she feels confident, she feels at ease. Here in her drama class, she can express herself. She does not feel the same way inside her classroom.

This is my own story—not unique, not isolated, but still mine. It could be the story of a child sex-worker, a child laborer, an out-of-school youth, a battered woman, a peasant farmer, a fisherman or a poor urban mother. It could belong to countless other marginalized people who, through an opportunity to participate in an intensive community theater workshop, have found a safe space to break silence, discover a voice to speak, think and feel from the wellsprings of their own beliefs and ideas.

In this essay I have attempted to share the work of PETA—the Philippine Educational Theater Association, where I serve as artistic director—in community theater, focusing on three groups: women, children and young people. How does PETA wield theater arts as tools to contribute to a community's development? What are our strategies? What philosophy drives the strategy? How does PETA sustain the work? How does the work contribute to the larger reimagining of a society under constant political and economic challenges? To address these questions, I draw from my own stories and from stories of fellow artist–teachers who have been conducting workshops with women, children and young people all over the Philippines.

The impetus for organizing the Philippine Educational Theater Association in the late '60s was the need to create a theater practice that was Filipino in both language and content and national and international in scope. PETA's founders also wished to introduce theater to both formal and community settings. At the time, there was a clear dichotomy between formal theater as practiced in schools and universities, presenting theater in English, and the practice of community-based groups performing traditional theater in the local dialects.

The wish to bridge this gap informed the vision of PETA's founder Cecile Guidote in creating a prospectus for a national theater movement, then using two major strategies to realize this vision. The first was creating a company known as the Kalinangan Ensemble that would develop into a highly skilled group of theater artists doing original plays in Filipino as well as translations and adaptations of world classics. The second was the introduction of theater arts in schools, while disseminating theater skills to the communities all over the Philippines. In short, PETA's aim was to develop a new and liberating theater pedagogy that would lead to the creation of original Filipino dramaturgy at both professional and community levels. The synergy of these two initiatives led to the birth of the national theater movement Cecile Guidote envisaged.

PETA was founded during the Marcos dictatorship. This experience of making theater under such conditions sharpened the group's stance: it was no longer enough to assert the importance of cultural identity, asserting the right to a Filipino national theater; the theater also had an obligation to oppose dictatorship. The content and form of both its aesthetic and pedagogical work were shaped by the conditions of the time.

PETA's founders believed that theater is a mirror of society: it was necessary to hold up this mirror to our audiences so they could reflect on social realities and, it was hoped, act for social change. PETA created performances tackling major social issues such as the plight of the landless farmers, workers' struggles, the rights of indigenous people and also questions of nationalism and identity. Alongside these performances, PETA also recognized the need to decentralize theater from the city center and democratize it so that anyone could create theater, whether professionally or in a community setting. Our "artist–teacher" concept was developed at this time. This meant that it was not enough to hone one's skills as an artist. The artist must be able to go into communities to share these skills, then bring these experiences back into PETA's repertory work. The need to link to communities created the impetus to network with many sectors and groups, and this became a key strategy to delivering PETA's services to our various partners. The skills that members of these communities learned were then used in organizing and in designing creative processes to enable participation and use theater in dealing with community issues.

Once this national theater movement was formed, its dependence on the capital region gradually diminished until local participants were able to organize and train their own communities. The existence of this network then enabled PETA to further develop its own aesthetics and pedagogy, but now in partnership with the regions. From the '70s to the mid-'80s, this movement swelled. During the same period, a great deal of international funding was given to the Philippines because of international support of the movement against the Marcos dictatorship. PETA responded in three ways: by developing curriculum with the objective of conscientizing various sectors in Philippine society; by doing street theater as part of the people's protest movement; and by simultaneously developing its repertory aesthetics through the Kalinangan Ensemble.

After 20 years of plunder and violence, the Marcos regime was brought down by the combined forces of the EDSA Revolution[1] or "People Power," as it is commonly known, the result of the relentless organizing and education by progressive forces in those 20 years.

[1] The February 1986 uprising, named after Epifanio de los Santos, a ring road around Manila that was the site of confrontation between pro- and anti-Marcos forces.

The Cory Aquino—and later, Fidel Ramos—administration brought back democratic institutions that created conditions for investment and what seemed to be budding prosperity. To the rest of the world we appeared to be progressing. The Philippines moved out of Third World status into the developing nation category, wanting to follow the path taken by the so-called newly industrialized countries, including the Asian tigers such as Thailand. But the "tigers" fell, revealing that economic recovery had been founded on quicksand, not solid ground. Though what was called democratic space had been established, real issues such as the equitable distribution of land and resources remained unaddressed, and genuine democratic and social reforms were never implemented. Cronyism and corruption were present in every aspect of our political institutions.

Early in 2001, we went through what is now called "EDSA 2." Inspired by the People Power Revolution of 1986, Filipinos took to the streets once more, bringing down President Joseph Estrada, whose administration had been rocked by charges of gross corruption and blatant misuse of power. In his two years in power, his administration further increased poverty in the country and left the current administration with problems of bankruptcy, terrorism and banditry, and factions within the military, all on top of the serious problems we suffer as effects of globalization.

Being ill-prepared for the onslaught of globalization, the Philippines has resorted to exporting its human resources. Overseas migrant workers have continued to swell in number since the early '80s. In 1996 alone an estimated $7 billion U.S. was remitted to the Philippine economy, making this sector the Philippines' largest dollar earner. There are at least seven million migrant

Filipinos all over the world, a socially costly situation. The increasing number of broken homes can be traced to the continuous absence of one or both parents. Children are left without strong role models in their formative years. This then translates into youth problems with drugs and/or the law. The values of these young people are also affected as their standard of living increases due to the dollars that are sent home by parents working abroad: their spending patterns change; consumerism creates the urgent need to buy branded clothes such as Nike and Levi's. These tendencies are exacerbated by the global culture of commercial film, music and television.

It is in this context that PETA and other Filipino cultural workers now operate. Also within this context lies our next set of challenges. I will illustrate PETA's response by narrating our experience of partnership with three groups we've been working with for several years: Dulaang Smokey Mountain, a children's and youth theater group based in a poor urban area of Metro Manila; the Pukot Festival, a community youth theater festival held in the Prelature of Infanta, Quezon, a province in Southern Tagalog; and Teatro Kabbule, a community-based theater group in Ifugao province in the northern part of the Philippines, the Cordillera region.

DULAANG SMOKEY MOUNTAIN

Smokey Mountain sits on a mountain of garbage at the outskirts of Manila. Most of the children who live there work as scavengers, often rather than going to school. In this project, 20 children were gathered for a two-month workshop introducing theater performance skills through games, movement, action songs, storytelling and improvisation. Its aim was to build the child-participants' sense of self and community. PETA artist–teachers guided the children toward mounting a production about what it is like to be a child at Smokey Mountain.

The challenge was increased by the circumstances surrounding these children. Firstly, they had uneven educational backgrounds. Some were full-time students, others went to school on a part-time basis because of their scavenging work, while others dropped out of school to become full-time scavengers in order to increase their contribution to family income. Their lack of education was exacerbated by the fact that the children lived under the shadow of malnutrition, breathing the poisonous fumes that decomposing garbage emits. Even simple instructions such as stepping right and stepping left were difficult for children to execute after years of exposure to this social and physical decay.

Playful use of what PETA calls the "Basic Integrated Arts Approach" to theater transformed the workshop venue into a virtual play space. The Integrated Arts Workshop is a systematic and cumulative weaving together of creative drama, creative sound and music, body movement, creative writing, visual arts and group dynamics. In essence, it is creative drama experienced and understood through various art disciplines. Exercises focusing on these different components are geared toward stimulating the participants to discover their creative potential for self- and collective expression. The process of creation and discovery is experiential and improvisational. The key to creation is spontaneity and the belief that we each contain a gold mine of riches, waiting to be discovered, brought into the light, polished and honed.

After months of challenging workshops and rehearsals, it was amazing to watch the children sing and dance and move and laugh as other children do. For that one moment, they were able not only to reclaim themselves but to reclaim their space. The children of Smokey Mountain realized a most fervent wish—to have a playground. For me, this is what the pedagogy of PETA's children's theater is all about: to create playgrounds in seemingly impossible environments—if not playgrounds in physical spaces, then those that grow out of the imagination.

Through the workshop, the children had become more confident, articulate and expressive, especially among their peers. They created a play which toured to other Metro Manila venues, reaching out to other children's communities and educating them on children's rights. Three years later, Smokey Mountain was leveled to the ground. The children's group, with the help of PETA playwrights, reworked their script to include the issue of relocation and its attendant problems, including related issues like child prostitution and drug abuse.

The Smokey Mountain experience illustrates how PETA continually adapts its strategies in theater-in-education to situations where formal educational systems are virtually nonexistent. In the Smokey Mountain case, theater was education. This reality requires the PETA artist–teacher to step out of the artistic confines of a conventional theater ensemble into the arena of development work, where one reinvents theater not only as a means of self-expression but as a venue for imagining, proposing and actualizing change.

The story does not end here. Ten years later, at least eight of the children who originally participated are now young adults between the ages of 17 and 21. They have sustained this group, calling themselves Dulaang Smokey Mountain (Smokey Mountain Theater). They run their small theater group themselves, performing plays that tackle different social issues. They have gone on to perform not only stories about members' own social conditions, but also issues of AIDS, child prostitution and other relevant themes. They work in consultation with PETA's children's and youth program, but can proudly say that they have produced these short pieces using their own internal resources.

These young people's skills have now evolved to a point where they are capable of analyzing the social and economic conditions that surround their poverty. They are conscious of such institutions as the World Bank and of government corruption. This deeper understanding makes it possible for them to find constructive solutions to their challenged lives. They now have a driving need to finish their educations. They realize that the power to make the changes they want in their lives rests in their creative hands.

THE PUKOT FESTIVAL

The Pukot Youth Theatre Festival is conducted in the Prelature of Infanta, a province in the Southern Tagalog Region of the Philippines. This province is rich in natural resources. It has the Pacific Ocean on one side and the Central Plains of Luzon on the other. Quezon has abundant fishing resources and coconut farms. The island is split by the great mountain chain called the Sierra Madre Mountains, home to an indigenous tribe, the Agtas. This geography enriches the perspective of the population of fisherfolk, peasant farmers and indigenous peoples. The Roman Catholic Church has been a major influence in Philippine society and culture since the days of Spanish colonization, and this influence has not diminished through time. In the Philippines, the Catholic Church has played both an oppressive and liberating role in people's lives. It has burdened us with traditional church dogma as well as supporting our struggles against oppression. Quezon has been traditionally known as an outspoken region with progressive clergy. In this province, the Church has championed the establishment of Basic Christian Communities, a concept inspired by theology of liberation. In the Philippine context, this has been expressed as the "preferential option" for the poor.

Pukot is a manner of fishing using a net, which serves as a metaphor for the gathering of experiences in the prelature. This project was one element in a consistent partnership with the Prelature of Infanta begun in the 1980s, so the success of the Pukot Festival owes something to prior working relationships and collaborations with these communities.

This particular project's objective was to create different performances to commemorate and reflect on the past 50 years of missionary work and its effects on the community. The first step was to apply the Basic Integrated Arts Approach, beginning with research on the traditional cultural practices of their communities. The young people also went through a workshop intended not only to hone their skills as performers but also to train them for other major aspects of theatrical performance such as design, choreography and the technical aspects of production. They also created the initial improvisations and scenarios for their performance. Upon completion of this phase, PETA facilitators left the young people to work toward finalizing their pieces. The facilitators returned only three days before the festival to offer their final critique and to work on points needing improvement.

The five-day festival brought together 200 young people, six communities and at least 200 adult community leaders. The six major productions addressed local community issues ranging from their experience of the Catholic Church, development aggression as illustrated by the government's plan to build airports, commercial seaports and golf courses, turning agricultural land into industrial complexes, creating major shifts from local to export crops (e.g., from rice to potatoes) and so on. These moves will have a marked effect on their environment, as well as current youth problems such as drugs and family relationships. The use of several Tagalog dialects still alive in their communities is important to note. The performances mixed stylized forms using music, dance, short realistic scenes and magical characters. A beautiful dance was developed using a lamp inspired by the lamps that fisherfolk in their villages use for night fishing. The festival began with a parade for which the young people created masks and dances exploring their theme of the rainbow: in their island, a rainbow can always be seen as one arrives or departs; for them this means that God is always present in their island.

The festival allowed a collective experience of the varied histories, issues and cultural practices of diverse local communities. This enabled people to connect the problems happening in each parish to the larger problems of the province. They were able to experience simultaneously the unique expressions of each community as well as shared and collective manifestations.

This is where the PETA paradigm of the O-A-O proved most useful. O-A-O stands for the interplay of the aspects of Orientation, Artistry and Organization. Orientation deepens a project's thematic directions; Artistry opens choices for expression; and Organization emphasizes the spirit of group cohesion and cooperation. The three-pronged O-A-O paradigm evolved over the course of years, expressing PETA's commitment to developing not only theater as an artistic expression but also theater as a pedagogical or educational process. The paradigm also emphasizes the development of leadership that can be sustained in the community.

For example, to complement the theater festival, a leadership seminar was also conducted, bringing together the youth of the Infanta community to discuss their role and their visions of society. The young people were also being prepared to conduct and manage the festival, with intervention from adult leaders only when clearly necessary. This concept of youth participation is currently one of PETA's chief thrusts in its work with young people.

This experience produced an action plan by the young people, declaring their determination to continue to come together as youth theater groups and share their learning in their schools and communities. They also recognized the power of theater to bring messages across with creativity and impact.

Bishop Julio Xavier Labayen, Head of the Prelature, has this to say of the work: "The impact on people's consciousness of our youth's theatrical presentation is indisputable. Our people enjoy the youth's entertaining presentation and, at the same time, imbibe the message in their consciousness of the ongoing story of our world today and our responsibility to save the world."

TEATRO KABBULE

I would like to further illustrate the O-A-O paradigm by discussing the PETA Women's Theater Program's work with Teatro Kabbule, a community-based theater group in Ifugao Province, located in the Cordillera Region.

The PETA Women's Theater Program facilitated the formation of Teatro Kabbule through a three-day workshop conducted in 1998. The group is composed of 25 adults and young people (students, NGO workers, government employees, etc.) from various *barangays* (communities) in Ifugao. It advocates for women, raising issues of violence against women. PETA supports the group's advocacy and education work through skills training workshops, repertory theater guidance and organizational development.

Kabbule is a local indigenous term for ghost or monster. It is also a traditional chant (like a children's rhyme) used by participants in the workshop as a group dynamics game. Traditionally, this chant is used to scare children about ghosts and monsters to make them sleepy and go to bed early. The chant talks about roaming ghosts moving from one house to the other. The idea of using the game as a metaphor for the group's presentation came out of initial brain-storming during the workshop and eventually became the title of their own informational performance, and later the name of their own theater group.

In Ifugao Province, the orientation problem was how to evoke from the community an assessment of a situation that was clearly traumatic and deemed taboo by indigenous society and culture. How does one surface stories that are deeply repressed by the culture? And how does one translate frameworks of feminism and empowerment while remaining equally sensitive to highly regarded customs and traditions? Artistically, how does one tap into the rich performance traditions often undervalued by the participants themselves out of a desire to please what they perceive as artist–teachers' urban sensibilities? Organizationally, how does one ensure that the experience doesn't become a one-shot deal?

Using the chant as the organizing structure, the group was able to come up with a 30-minute play depicting actual cases of abuse of women and children in their community. The play was performed before local government officials and to several towns in Ifugao in a bid to raise public awareness, advocate and lobby for local mechanisms (e.g., laws, social services, welfare programs for women, etc.) and establish institutions such as a women's desk and crisis center in their own community.

The play narrates three true stories of family violence in Ifugao, touching on physical abuse of children, incestuous abuse and wife battering, woven together and using the Kabbule character as an image and metaphor mirror-ing the acts of the perpetrators of this violence. The chant became the basis for a discussion of fear and aggression. With the sensitive guidance of the artist–teachers, the young women gradually put a face to the monster: that of the grandfather who continually abused his own granddaughter, the drunken father who burned his own child in a fit of fury, the enraged husband who banged his wife's head on the house post.

Toward the end of the play, the Kabbule character says:

> In our lives, there are ghosts and monsters created by our minds and there
> are also real ghosts and monsters that actually exist. They are people we
> know, people we love. They are near to us, and more often we live with
> them. And we must be able to know and deal with these ghosts in our lives.

The group did not merely perform the play; it also held discussion groups on domestic violence and abuse. Debriefing workshops were conducted during advocacy performances. The community audiences were able to identify and relate to the issues presented because the stories were based on cases in their own community and province that were shared during the workshops. It was also obvious during these debriefing workshops that people were still

uncomfortable in confronting these issues. But people were beginning to
question why such things happen.

> Yes, they want to preserve their names, they don't want dirty things to get
> out of their houses. They would rather keep the secret within the family.
> —A MEMBER OF A LOCAL AUDIENCE IN IFUGAO

I shall backtrack a little to further detail the process by which Teatro Kabbule
came into being. In 1998, PETA launched a project entitled "Tumawag Kay
Libby Manaoag" ("Call Libby Manaoag"). This production was part of a
larger campaign, the National Family Violence Prevention Program (NFVPP).[2]
"Libby Manaoag" is the story of a radio-show host; many women call her
program to talk about their issues. Three women who are experiencing
different forms of domestic violence—physical, emotional and sexual—
become the main voices that shape the stories. We hear advice from experts
such as lawyers, psychiatrists and social workers. The scenes are woven
together with songs and dances, and the characters are all performed in a
broad acting style with much humor.

[2] A nationwide partnership of more than 20 NGOs, government agencies, civic groups and academic institutions initiated by the Women's Civic Center to advocate for the prevention and elimination of violence against women within the family.

An "informance" like this is a performance that carefully works information,
issues and debates into a play's structure. Its objectives are clearly developmental
in nature, but artistic elements are not sacrificed in favor of these developmental
aims. Unlike Boal's Forum Theater, it does not ask audiences to take over
actors' roles or offer possible courses of action or decisions that the characters
in the story can take. It is a complete story, yet not prescriptive. Instead, after
the performance, a debriefing workshop is conducted where the issue is
discussed and understanding deepens.

Another crucial activity employed for this informance was the organization of action teams in each area where we performed. A team of PETA artist–teachers would return to conduct from three to five theater workshops with local women. Each workshop would focus on domestic violence as they experienced or perceived it. With this foundation, the groups would create their own performances. Some were even able to tour theirs in their towns and provinces. Teatro Kabbule is a product of this project.

Other communities opted to create other types of actions such as forums and discussions, but the Cordillera Region really focused on developing theater groups that carried issues of domestic violence through their performances. Though these groups have limited funds and resources, they are committed to sustaining their performance and training activities because they have seen how effective the process of theater can be not only for themselves—how these women have found their voices to articulate their own ideas on issues concerning their lives—but also how their performances translate within their community. Local government officials support their efforts and value their work. They have moved on to tackle other issues such as reproductive health and the need to recover and preserve their own indigenous culture. They are now moving from analyzing their domestic situations to larger issues such as globalization that have affected their lives, destroying their environment through mining and driving their young people overseas in search of contract work.

The groups, some of whom have not even finished secondary school, not only run their theater groups but have also led in the formation of other groups in their province. Through theater, they have become women's rights activists in their communities.

Theater work has become a popular medium for information dissemination in Ifugao. Other groups, especially government agencies like the Philippine Information Agency and the Provincial Social Work and Development Agency, are now beginning to organize their own groups for women's issue advocacy, inspired by what Teatro Kabbule has initiated.

The Teatro Kabbule group continues to experience its own unique processes of integration, consolidation and organizational dynamics—a necessary stage and a test for them. Group transformation happens alongside personal transformation within members who mirror individual experience in the stories they present: their play echoes their own reality as individuals. The experience has become a process of healing and support. Its members now consider the group a sanctuary or community whose support they miss in periods of inactivity.

Just recently, the mover and organizer of Teatro Kabbule received a regional award as an outstanding government employee in Cordillera for all her work in running the organization. The group has been conducting independent workshops within Ifugao, which in turn facilitated the formation of a children's theater group advocating for reproductive rights, now receiving support from UNICEF. They have also organized and conducted their own art camp with the strong support of the provincial government.

NEW CHALLENGES

It has been 34 years since PETA was founded, so we have an unlimited stock of stories to share. I hope these three stories will suffice to give the reader a general picture of PETA's community cultural development work, which is always evolving, never static.

PETA's vision has not altered. We continue to work toward a vision of full actualization of the human person, a free society, a liberating culture and a clean, healthy and rich environment. But changes in our context have made it necessary for PETA to re-evaluate our strategies in working toward these visions.

More than ever, these last two decades have been a time for reflection and shifting paradigms. We have been affected and challenged by changing political, economic and social conditions in our country and by rifts in the progressive movement that have disrupted the basis for organized action in solidarity with other groups.

In 1986, Filipinos toppled a dictator in what is now called EDSA 1. In the succeeding decade, we once again challenged government, enduring a difficult trial leading to the downfall of a corrupt president: this historical moment was given the title of EDSA 2. However, a few months later, the EDSA 3 phenomenon unfolded as at least a million poor and disadvantaged Filipinos took to the street in support of the corrupt ex-president. The political tension seems to be turning into a class war. Yet at the core of this protest lay the issue of basic rights and participation for the majority of the disenfranchised poor.

The Philippines is a nation of paradoxes. In some ways, it exemplifies best practices in democratic participation. But haves and have-nots alike succumb to a long tradition of patriarchy and patronage. Growing poverty and the widening income gap are social bombs that ignite human rights abuses, crime and rebellion. Basic services have not reached many of the poor. Among the poorest Filipinos, participation in community development is very low. Poor access to services and lack of participation are the result of structural policies that continue to marginalize the disadvantaged sector of society. Lack of public funds, bureaucracy and lack of political will are other factors. The Asian crisis and globalization have worsened our national dilemma.

The EDSA 3 phenomena shook the intelligentsia and NGO and development workers, impelling deep reflection of the underlying causes of the Philippines' political and economic ills. One cannot address these issues without confronting the culture of poverty that has taken root in our society. We cannot ignore the long historical disempowerment that has shaped the Filipino psyche. We cannot forge lasting change if we do not penetrate the center of citizens' being, their hearts and minds. What are the deepest values by which they live? Are they based on a constitution inherited from the West, which talks of democracy, liberty and equality? Or are they traditional Filipino concepts of *tao* (person), *loob* (inner self), *labas* (outer reality), *kapwa* (other person)— of knowledge of self, acceptance of the other and the great value placed on *pakikipag-kapwa ta* (personal relationships and interactions)?

As cultural workers, these inquiries have led us to focus our work, recognizing that our work in culture is crucial to any real social change. In recognition of the realities of poverty in the Philippines, we have chosen to work with women, children and young people—those hardest hit under these conditions. We work with these sectors through several programs:

1. Theater for Development
PETA intersects with development agendas through its participation in various human rights advocacy campaigns for women, children or young people. Our participation is expressed through the development of performances and informances that tackle these concerns and through the development of a curriculum that integrates the study of these issues within a theater process.

2. Theater in Education
The role that education plays in nation building is unquestionable. But the educational system for Filipino children does not function at an optimal level for two major reasons: (1) insufficient resources from the national budget because primary importance is given to such items as infrastructure building and debt servicing; and (2) an archaic system of education which still operates on rote learning and the "banking" system of education that treats students as empty vessels to be filled with educational materials that have yet to be fully adapted to Filipino culture. Even the government recognizes these deficiencies as it tries to implement its Ten-Year Master Plan for basic education. Its objectives are: (1) enhancing relevance of the school curriculum; (2) enriching the learning experience; (3) empowering the front-line managers; (4) enhancing teachers' competence in facilitating and evaluating learning; and (5) enhancing partnership with stakeholders.

PETA involves itself in the educational system by networking with schools and conducting teachers' training, introducing the use of theater methods in the classroom and curriculum. It also coordinates with school-based drama groups and clubs, indirectly training their students. These trainings cover not only the study of Philippine culture and theater arts but also have leadership and consciousness-raising as major objectives.

3. Developing Filipino Aesthetics

For 34 years, PETA has unceasingly devoted itself to the development of Philippine theater by the creation of original Filipino plays and experimentation with traditional and contemporary Filipino theater forms as well as translations and adaptations of foreign materials. Our quest is to develop Philippine theater and ultimately Philippine culture. In a highly globalized world threatened by homogenization, erasing cultural diversity, this becomes even more crucial.

Our colonial experience—described as "300 years in the convent and 50 years in Hollywood"—has left our cultural identity confused and fractured. We were taught disdain for what is ours and admiration for what comes from the West. We have been cut off from the wealth of our cultural legacy. No nation can survive without a clear understanding and respect for its culture. Therefore PETA provides a process by which communities can reflect on their own cultural traditions and practices which in turn become the source of their performance. PETA seeks not only to rediscover what is inherent in Filipino traditions but also to revitalize it and keep it continuously evolving.

To illustrate this, let me share briefly the process of one of our most successful productions, "Macli-ing Dulag." Macli-ing was one of the leaders of the Kalinga tribe, one of the indigenous groups in the Cordillera region. Their ancestral land was threatened by a proposed dam that would destroy sacred burial ground. He took the initiative in organizing the first intertribal *bodong* (peace pact) against the projected Chico Dam. They were eventually able to stop the construction of the Chico Dam by the National Power Corporation. Shortly after this triumph, Macli-ing was brutally murdered on April 24, 1980. His death served to unify the Kalinga tribe to oppose the military and the development aggression being carried out in their lands. Macli-ing became a hero not only to his people but even to the lowlanders, who were inspired by his integrity and commitment.

In April of 1988, PETA produced the play "Macli-ing Dulag," inspired by this heroic story. It recognized the powerful metaphor that a life and death could inspire in the time of the dictatorship.

A group of artists including a director, designer, choreographer and musician traveled to Lubuagan, a small Kalinga town, staying there to carry out research and interact with a well-respected community leader, Cirilio Bawer. Songs, dances, rituals and philosophical visions were shared by him and the rest of the community. This process of integration and research set the tone of the whole artistic process, embodying the inspiration so generously shared by the community.

A rice terrace was built on the old brick walls of the open-air theater with bamboo pipes that allowed water to flow down as in the town of Lubuagan. The dramatic structure was woven into the rituals of the Kalinga, using their songs and dances effectively in the storytelling.

This artistic concept was inspired by the Kalinga's belief in the interconnectedness of life with land and in respect for the gifts of nature. The audience was made to experience being there through the re-creation of sights, sounds, colors, smells and textures. The theatrical fourth wall between audience and performer was broken, allowing them to interact and be part of the play, as was the traditional way. The audience would not merely watch but experience a man's life, struggle and culture; in so doing, they would involve themselves with a journey of heroism and love.

Every available space in the theater was used as the audience moved through it. The play proved to be one of PETA's most successful productions, not only bringing its message across, but artistically commended as one of PETA's most powerful productions. The standing-room-only audiences it generated every night covered a cross-section of Philippine society, from working class to the monied class.

In "Macli-ing Dulag," the fusion of elements of indigenous culture, theater aesthetics and social issues melded into a powerful experience that affected audiences not only in heart and mind, but to the inner core of their being.

Together with our educational and development theater agendas, PETA stresses the development of Filipino theatrical aesthetics. In fact, this is the spine of our educational theater work. This commitment is embodied by members who as artist–teachers become the main implementers of PETA's vision. We therefore recognize the importance of our own internal training to prepare artist–teachers to meet complex demands. The constant balance required to effectively pursue our educational, developmental and aesthetic objectives has challenged us to continuously seek effective methodology and processes, perpetually exploring new ways of delivering our services.

In our interaction with Filipino communities, sectors and institutions, the search for a Filipino cultural aesthetic is constant. After all is said and done, our greatest contribution is having been part of the journey that is constantly discovering the Filipino's true identity.

4.   Cultural Networking

We also recognize the need for networking far beyond our region, not only within the sphere of cultural work, but also with institutions in many fields that share our visions, and not only locally but internationally. This strategy is practical, promoting the exchange of information and resources; and more broadly, it helps to strengthen the movement for social change.

Under the specter of globalization, this strategy becomes even more imperative: community cultural development cannot succeed in isolation. Our creative process opens a space for individual discovery of power and ability; this is then linked to the immediate community; and through the experiences that emerge, the individual consciousness opens to the larger imaginings of the country and the world. Awareness must always expand in an ever-enlarging spiral.

In the final analysis, community cultural development battles globalization by creating every possible opportunity to shape a creative mind and spirit. Every individual offered this opportunity could chart a course, claiming with certainty their own uniqueness. The destructive effects of globalization cannot prevail in a world populated by those who take pride in their own culture, having no need for validation in someone else's eyes.

20

Asian People's Theatre Festival Society
c/o 15A Block 2, Parkview Garden
8 Pik Tin Street, Taiwai, Hong Kong
Telephone: (852) 9800-7169
Fax: (852) 2601-4897
E-mail: hkaptfs@netvigator.com

Mok Chiu Yu is Executive Secretary of the Arts with the Disabled Association Hong Kong and a veteran popular theater activist with the Asian People's Theatre Festival Society. His personal story is one of activism leading to theater, as he related to fellow participants in the online dialogue preceding this publication:

I was born and bred up in Hong Kong and attended university in Australia. I was a student radical in the '60s ... at the University of Adelaide. I got involved in the peace movement of the '60s in Australia and the aboriginal land rights movement, etc. On my return to Hong Kong I became involved with the youth move-ment here in the '70s, and I was involved in publishing an alter-native youth paper called '70s Biweekly, *which had a readership of more than 10,000. Hong Kong was then a British colony — we, the youth movement, were critical of British colonial rule and the capitalist system, which we saw as exploitative, alienating, turn-ing people one-dimensional, etc.,*

etc. That made us attracted to socialist ideas. We were to split, not unlike the radical youth movement everywhere else in the world, with some believing in the Beijing Maoist propaganda hook, line and sinker, some turning to Marxism–Leninism, libertarian socialism, liberal democrats, etc. I was more a libertarian socialist, being influenced by ex–Red Guards (the whole nation of Chinese youths were Red Guards) who fled to Hong Kong. They believed that China was ruled by authoritarian bureaucrats and Mao was the biggest bureaucrat of them all. My political stance has since been anti-colonial, anti-capitalist and anti-bureaucrats, identifying myself with movements fighting against imperialist control and domination in the underdevel-oped countries.

In this essay, he describes both transnational collaborations of Asian popular theater workers and a series of projects aimed at creating theater with a group that is a particular target—and some would say, casualty—of globalization: migrant workers in Hong Kong. His encompassing vision suggests a different type of globalization, the expansion of community cultural development projects beyond national bound-aries, creating common cause where social trends have sown fragmentation.

The author would like to acknowledge the substantial and valuable assistance of Charito de la Cruz in preparing this article.

Theater, Migrant Workers and Globalization

THE HONG KONG EXPERIENCE

by Mok Chiu Yu

Born and schooled in Hong Kong, I always felt the oppressiveness of the British colonial education system: studying all subjects in English (with the exception of Chinese language in high school) and having to sing "God Save the Queen" at school assemblies. But I was radicalized at university. My parents, being part of the lower middle class, slaved to send me to Adelaide, Australia, to further my education. There I began my activist involvement in various causes: demonstrating in the streets in opposition to the Vietnam War, to the Russian invasion of Czechoslovakia, support for the Aboriginal land rights movement.

When I left Australia in the late '60s to return home with an economics degree, I joked to my Australian friends that I was going home to fight against British colonialism and all the evils of Hong Kong society. Sure enough, soon after I returned to Hong Kong, I became part of a youth movement that tried to articulate an alternative to the colonial, undemocratic and exploitative system; we also saw ourselves as internationalists and our fight as linked to the radical youth movements of the rest of the world. We published alternative papers and held political rallies and demonstrations. While some of us experimented with filmmaking, theater and other artistic media, I was more a "politico." The movement in Hong Kong really lacked a cultural or artistic dimension.

I did not get involved in theater and music until the late '70s, after an encounter with Julian Beck and Judith Malina of the Living Theatre, in Milan to perform "Seven Meditations on Political Sado-Masochism." I was on a European speaking tour in support of the Chinese Democracy Wall movement. I was inspired by the Living Theatre; so when I returned home, with like-minded comrades, I created the Hong Kong People's Theatre group. We began doing street theater and theater in the communities. Our models were Western theater groups including the San Francisco Mime Troupe and the Bread and Puppet Theater.

While we called ourselves a people's theater, we did not grasp that a real people's theater entails people doing their own theater to articulate their own voices. It was when we came to know groups like the Black Tent Theater of Tokyo and the Philippine Education Theater Association (PETA) that we discovered the methodologies that offered systematic participatory training to unleash tremendous creative power to make theater, to "voice out." These encounters led us to a network of people's theater groups in Asia (and subsequently in the Pacific region and beyond). We believed we could learn from one another and share our common concerns politically, socially and aesthetically. Cross-cultural collaborations would be our search for artistic excellence, for a theater which is Asian, and a way to manifest our commitment to common goals for a better Asia, a better world.

As the pace of globalization gallops, countervailing international exchange activities have become even more meaningful, although local community cultural development continues to be a prime task for any concerned artist. But alas, in the present global system, the local and the global are so tightly linked, as is easily understood by examining the case of migrant workers, as I do in the latter part of this essay.

Over the last two decades, I have come to understand the power of culture to effect social and individual transformation. One of the clearest impacts of globalization has been the perpetual migration of workers from impoverished countries to rich ones, a never-ending search for livelihood under conditions that barely acknowledge migrants' humanity—let alone their rich cultural heritages and the contributions they might make to people's empowerment and cross-cultural understanding. In this essay, I describe several projects of the Hong Kong–based Asian People's Theatre Festival Society (APTFS) that show how cross-cultural and local/migrant cultural collaborations might help build the basis for a strong and deep anti-globalization movement.

GLOBALIZATION: STAGE 1

[In 1405 A.D.] Cheng Ho led his great fleet and sailed across the seas.
In 27 years, they visited South and Southeast Asia, the Arab lands and East
Africa. Cheng Ho simply represented the Chinese Emperor to go and
declare nominal sovereignty of these places. No economic interests. And
when Cheng Ho's fleet no longer roamed the seven seas, four little ships
led by Vasco Da Gama began the great exploration and exploitation which
was to follow. Looking for spices and riches, the Western nations fought to
be the master of the oceans.

—FROM "MACAU 123," A PLAY ON THE STORIES OF THE
    CHINESE, PORTUGUESE AND MACANESE IN MACAU

Asian People's Theater Workers Unite Against Globalization

The plays quoted above and between major sections of this essay were
produced in 1999, 1997 and 1994–95 by the Asian People's Theatre Festival
Society, founded in the early '90s and based in Hong Kong. The APTFS
is a group of Chinese people's theater activists whose concern with
global exploitation and inequalities has propelled them into cross-cultural
collaborations with people's theater workers in other parts of Asia. These
collaborative theater productions have invariably toured a number of Asian
cities: "Big Wind," for example, was rehearsed in Patan, Nepal, premièred in
Bhubanesawar, India, and then moved on to Calcutta, Dhaka in Bangladesh,
Kathmandu in Nepal, Bangkok in Thailand, Hong Kong and Taipei and
Xingang in Taiwan. Casts are always multinational, and the plays take as
their themes issues of common concern to the participants.

Many of these productions have touched on issues of migration, migrant
workers and other topics related to globalization. "Big Wind" is about the
plight of workers who migrate from South and Southeast Asia to Hong
Kong and the international movement of capital. "Yours Most Obediently"
deals with Indian migration to Hong Kong; "I Came From the Himalayas" is
the story of the Nepali Gurkhas; "Hairy Monkeys at Chung King Mansion"
reveals the lives of the Pakistani migrants in Hong Kong; "Black Sky" tells
the stories of South Asian migrants in Hong Kong, Taipei and Tokyo; and
"Macau 123" is about Portuguese migrants to the Orient. (Only one collaboration—"A Tale of Two Cities: Beijing 1989/Dhaka 1990"—was an exception,
focusing on the democracy movements in China and Bangladesh.)

Other groups have staged international and cross-cultural exchanges during
the past decade, such as the series "Cry of Asia 1, 2, 3, 4" staged by the
Philippines-based Asian Council for People's Culture; and many binational
and multinational theater projects by Taiwan's Assignment Theatre, collaborating with groups like Kaliwat from Mindanao, PETA from Manila and
Japanese artists including Nakayama and Sakura Daizo. Taken together, I see
them as a collaborative effort by people's theater workers to raise a collective
voice against the onslaught of globalization, asserting the commonly held

principle "people before profits." In carrying out these projects, the participating groups have also sought to establish links, to network, to support one another, to learn from one another and to explore the aesthetics of an Asian people's theater.

To what extent are these multinational theater projects effective in combating globalization? Obviously, we cannot depend on one piece of theater to change the world. But as part of a wider movement, we see such international theater activities as meaningful responses to the globalization process. Through our practice over the past decade, it is evident that such multinational collaborations are fruitful and should be continued.

The cross-cultural product arising from the interaction of artists well-versed in traditional and contemporary performing arts skills has been an antidote to the Western popular culture which has otherwise begun to dominate the leisure and recreational life of Asian urbanites. The fusion of traditional and folk gestural vocabularies from different parts of Asia has generated visually and aesthetically exciting forms and movements. Each multicultural encounter creates a theater product that is uniquely Asian. The themes of our performances are critiques of what is and portrayals of what ought to be, asserting our opposition to something that we clearly cannot want. Such theater pieces can also be regarded as rehearsals for change and for life. Through them, people—including the participants—are informed, educated and empowered. They may spark action beyond the theater.

There is value in both the actual performance and the process of creation, which can be a confrontation of conscience, fraternal dialogue, exchange of skills, mutual learning opportunity and a means to collective strength and creativity. To realize this full potential requires sufficient resources; good translation and interpretation as well as effective communication; democratic decision-making processes; and participants who are mature, selfless, tolerant, excellent artists and highly politically aware. Some projects have failed or functioned merely as artistic experiments because some of these conditions were not met.

With respect to audiences, different people respond and participate differently. When we play to those who are already aware of what the movement against globalization is all about, we generate solidarity. To others, we represent a challenge, an alternative view, an alternative source of information, even an inspiration or enlightenment. Ideally, we should be able to engage our audiences emotionally, aesthetically and intellectually: this is what makes a good performance. We cannot necessarily change the way people think or behave by a single act of performance, but a performance can be so bad that the audience disengages. In the end, to judge success we must ask each audience if our performances are empowering.

GLOBALIZATION: STAGE 2

Chorus: Who are they?

People, Indian people.

People who have come over as soldiers.

People who have come over as policemen.

People who have come over as businessmen.

Chorus: And the deprived wretches who have come over as domestic helpers.

The famous divide-and-rule policy for governing Hong Kong.

An Indian army and an Indian police force.

You don't have to fear.

An Indian army and an Indian police force.

They were the ones entrusted with guns. The right to kill people.

Some Chinese were also recruited as cops. They got swords.

The very sight of the strong bearded young men from Punjab drives people
      inside in terror.

The terror exists till today. Bearded Indians are terrible men.

Stay away from them. Stay away!

I hate Indians.

Why?

1899, just a year after the lease treaty for the New Territories had been signed.

The British mobilized Indian soldiers to suppress the resistance in the
      New Territories.

But it wasn't that easy. The fire of resistance was burning. Tai Po, Yuen Long,
      Kam Tin. The people were transformed in the corpses.

Hey Indian, kill him.

But why? Why do I have to kill him for no reason?

Because your job is to obey me. That's why you're paid.

But he also has a family. Dependent parents. And familial responsibilities.

— FROM "YOURS MOST OBEDIENTLY," A PLAY ON THE STORIES
  OF INDIAN MIGRATION TO HONG KONG, 1841–1997

Migrant Workers and People's Theater

While many of the collaborations discussed above dealt with globalization
and migrant issues, the direct participants were people's theater artists. Migrant
workers (for example, those in Hong Kong or Taipei) were involved only as
sources of information and stories and as audience members. At most, they
were invited to participate in workshops facilitated by visiting artists.

In the year 2000, APTFS members realized they had long overlooked the
potential of migrant workers in Hong Kong to be collaborators, both as artists
and partners in the fight against globalization. So when the APTFS prepared

its next project—a major new outdoor production with giant puppetry, "The Bursting of the Asian Economic Bubbles"—the participation of migrant groups was invited. The production was about globalization, the World Trade Organization, cultural imperialism, the information-technology revolution, poverty and migration. The migrant groups responded positively, in part because some of them had prior experience initiating cultural projects, including the organization of the First Migrant Cultural Festival in December 1999. The result was a first-ever cross-cultural collaboration where migrant workers and local artists performed together, expressing their common concerns. The play toured in Macao and Hong Kong to enthusiastic applause. After each performance, there was interaction with the mixed audience of migrants and locals, who were highly appreciative of the migrants' performances and receptive to the migrants who spoke, understanding their accounts of exploitation and discrimination.

Migration has always been a global phenomenon. But it has accelerated rapidly as a result of the globalization process, spurred by improvements in transport and information technology and increasing disparities between rich and poor on the national and international levels. Globalization of the international economy has limited the ability of the poor to earn decent livelihoods. As a result, the movement of people from the Third World to rich regions has grown continuously, as migrants move to find jobs as domestic helpers, construction workers, factory workers or in the entertainment industry—generally those that have been called "3-D jobs": dangerous, dirty and demeaning.

The number of migrant domestic workers in Hong Kong has increased exponentially, from just a few hundred in the 1970s to well over 100,000 in the early 1990s. Filipinas have been joined by Thais, Indonesians, Sri Lankans, Indians and Nepalis. By December 1995, the total of 150,000 included 130,000 workers from the Philippines. As of 1999, Asian migrant workers in Hong Kong totaled 218,100, mostly women: Filipinas numbered 147,400, followed by Indonesians at 46,000, Nepalese at 18,700 and Thais at 6,000. The rest—such as Sri Lankans, Indians, Pakistanis and the Bangladeshis— are estimated at not less than a thousand each.[1]

These thousands of migrant workers find themselves in harsh conditions, performing 3-D jobs and subject to many forms of exploitation. Indeed, they set off from their places of origin owing large sums to employment agencies in addition to other fees levied by their own government bureaucracies. While they are sometimes seen as taking jobs away from local workers, migrants and local workers have common interests in the universalization of workers' rights, one of the goals of the anti-globalization movement. Indeed, it is impossible to conceive of an effective anti-globalization movement that does not include migrant workers.

The collaboration between the APTFS and migrant workers in "The Bursting

[1] Statistics from Nicole Constable, *Maid to Order in Hong Kong* (Cornell University Press, 1997), xiii; and *Annual Report for Year 1999*, Asian Migrant Centre and Migrant Forum in Asia (Hong Kong); see www.migrantnet.pair.com /publications.html.

The author (left) and a Bangladeshi people's theater worker provide sound and musical accompaniment to the performance of "The Bursting of the Asian Economic Bubbles."
© Asian People's Theatre Festival Society, 2000.

of the Asian Economic Bubbles" led to a yearlong Theatre with Migrants Project that took us far beyond this first play. Working with local migrant organizations such as the Asian Migrant Centre, the Coalition of Migrants' Rights and other migrant workers' organizations involved in cultural activities, the APTFS offered workshops that led to staging a series of open-air perform-ance activities. In fact, the migrant workers' cultural movement had already begun on its own, so the collaboration with the APTFS and local supporters gave impetus to its further development.

The outdoor performances drew large audiences, ranging from several hundred to thousands. Performances usually lasted from midday to 6 or 7 p.m., featuring nonstop songs, music, theater, poetry and dances, ranging from the traditional to the modern and popular, and from individual ethnic groups (including the local Chinese) to cross-cultural efforts. They included the Workers' Bazaar on November 5, 2000; the campaign to Say No to Violence Against Women on November 26, 2000; the second Migrants Cultural Festival on December 17, 2000; an International Women's Day event on March 11, 2001; an International Labor Day performance on May 1, 2001; and Kartini Day on May 27, 2001. The grand finale for the 2000-01 program took place on July 29: the Filipino Migrants' Colors event was preceded by a cultural parade with slogans such as "Globalization Condemns Workers to Poverty."

In retrospect, this one-year collaboration with migrant workers achieved a great deal:

• An Asian Migrants' Theatre Company comprising domestic helpers from different countries has been formed and can be relied upon to devise showcases and performances for migrants' gatherings and campaigns.

- The migrant workers' movement in Hong Kong has become stronger and has significant cultural content. It is recognized that the empowerment of migrant workers is not just labor organizing, but also a cultural project with theater, songs, dances, poetry and so on. Groups are now eager to participate in cultural activities, with many specifically interested in theater. Given time and resources, other theater groups may be formed within different ethnic groups or organizations. In fact, the Asian Migrants' Theatre Company has since assisted the Mindanao Federation to form a theater group called Sining Mindanao Ensemble.

- Artistically, various ethnic groups have been contemporizing their traditional and folk performances to make them relevant to the issues of the day. For example, Indonesian migrants skillfully adapted a piece of traditional Indonesian monkey dance to tell their stories. In this allegorical play, the White Monkey was the oppressor and the brown monkeys stood for the people. The simple story of the brown monkeys organizing to end the White Monkey's years of exploitation was done with great artistry, with dance and movement extremely well executed and meticulous care given to costumes, makeup and props.

- With cultural diversity and cooperation being continuously promoted and affirmed, the project has helped strengthen migrant workers' cultural identity and pride without giving rise to narrow-minded nationalism. In fact, the partnership between migrant workers and local performers encouraged everyone to come up with their best in a spirit of solidarity. The project helped to strengthen the various ethnic workers' organizations: for example, the Indonesian Migrant Workers Union was able to stage a daylong event attracting 6,000 migrant workers, leading the Indonesian Consulate in Hong Kong to decide it is a force to be reckoned with. These experiences contributed greatly to growing solidarity among different ethnic migrant groups, and eventually to the creation of the Coalition of Migrant Rights.

- The project created such effective showcases for the rich cultural contributions of the migrant workers' movement in Hong Kong that it set a good example for Hong Kong's own workers' movement, which has never been very strong in the cultural dimension. It appears the project also paved way for the coming closer of the two movements.

- Similarly, in showcasing the diversity and excellence of migrant cultures in Hong Kong, the project enriched the local arts scene. The innovations of encouraging migrants' arts work and the full participation of the

Asian migrants' community in the development of Hong Kong's theater arts has been a breakthrough for both the locals and the migrants.

We hope that both the Asian Migrants' Theatre Company and the larger collaborative project with migrant workers can serve as models for other migrant communities around the world, helping to empower both migrants and local workers through the arts.

GLOBALIZATION: STAGE 3

Menan: Stop—it hurts!

Babul: We better get him to the hospital!

Ashesh: No—he's overstayed! If we go to the hospital, they'll catch him and deport him. Take him back to Chungking Mansions, ninth floor.

Migrant exits with Menan. Babul and Ashesh start back to work.
Two Hong Kong workers enter with signs: "Against wage cuts."

H. K. Worker 1: Get out, Ah-cha! You're cutting wages! You put us out of our jobs!

Babul: Look, brothers—we're just trying to get two good meals! You ever hear the saying, "Hand stops, mouth stops"?

Dance: They fight.

Factory Owner enters: Stop interfering with my workers! You don't work here anymore—get out or I'll call the police.

H. K. Worker 2: My whole family's waiting for their meals! You ever hear the saying, "Hand stops, mouth stops"?

Shouts of "Go home!" They shove them.

Factory Owner, going: OK, hurry up, get back to work. Oh, I almost forgot—from now on, 4 dollars an hour instead of 5.

He exits.

Babul & Ashesh (singing):
They love us here in Hong Kong.
They give us the easy jobs.
They house us like pashas,
And they welcome us like kings.
They wish we were invisible.
They call us "hairy monkeys."
They wish we'd go away, but
Their city would fall down.

Workers groan, follow him off.

Some of the 40 migrant workers performing in a production of "The Bursting of the Asian Economic Bubbles" in Macau.
© Asian People's Theatre Festival Society, 2000.

—FROM SCENE 4 OF "BIG WIND," A PLAY ABOUT MIGRANT
   WORKERS AND THE INTERNATIONAL MOVEMENT OF CAPITAL

Father: Friends, now my eldest son, Ah Keung, has two garment factories in California, America! And my second son has a handbag factory in Holland. And my daughter, the youngest, has just gone to New Zealand! Or wait… I think somebody's in Sri Lanka…is that Ah Wah?…Then Elizabeth must be in Australia…oh, no, where is Elizabeth?

Freeze.

Music. All sway as if in the wind.

Dance again, they are all blown offstage.

—FROM THE EPILOGUE OF "BIG WIND"

Workshops as Means of Empowerment

It should be stressed that the Theatre with Migrants Project included not only performances but also workshops that took place before most of the performances. While performances have positive and empowering effects, workshops are more effective means of bringing about empowerment, an educational process aimed at enhancing the individual's power, both in inter-personal relationships and politically. Empowerment enables the individual, family or social group to take action to change their own situation, building self-esteem through realization of one's abilities, learning and improvement of various skills such as communication, expanding political consciousness and social and political participation, imparting knowledge about rights and social responsibilities and so on.

Asian people's theater workers believe in theater by the people—that the people should be vested with the means to produce theater, speaking out for themselves. Through workshops, participants are helped to unleash their creative potential, mobilizing their artistic skills, sharing ideas, information and analysis of the conditions in which they find themselves, experiencing a process of artistic creation and becoming confident in using cultural means to articulate their demands and aspirations in a spirit of unity and solidarity. Our Migrants Project experience and its predecessors have demonstrated that workshops, properly facilitated, are very effective means of empowerment.

One of the chief organizer–coordinators of the Theatre with Migrants Project, Charito de la Cruz, herself a Filipina, described the workshops offered as part of the project:

> The workshops were carried out successfully as the training season ended in December 2000. In all the workshops (with different focus for each one), Nepalese, Indonesians, Filipinos, Thais and Indians and the locals shared their stories and explored artistic forms already known to them or learned new skills. The result was different highly impressive showcases. The pieces took the form of poems, short skits, allegorical plays, creative dance and creative movements. The performers had reviewed their own lives, and their performances gave an insider's view to the nonmigrants about migration. The showcases were performed during various migrants' campaign activities for the year and were also included in its performance season.

> The workshops organized have established a special kind of relationship between the migrants and the local workers. The migrants were led to appreciate their own individuality and their group capability, and they were encouraged to be creative and to become aware of the opportunity to be part of a cultural movement no matter how far they are from their homeland. As for the local Chinese people—artists and workers—the workshops allowed them to understand more deeply the situations of the migrants and the diversity of culture, and they were happily involved in the highly creative and artistic theater processes jointly with the migrants.

The Thai Women's Association chose creative dance and movement to focus its showcase, centering on the following story, which served as a guiding script:

> Thailand is one of only two Asian countries never colonized. The peace-loving Thai people worked in vast agricultural lands. Ironically, the process of modernization and industrialization which promised to provide employment and abundance left many in dire poverty, prompting them to leave their homes in search of greener pastures abroad.

> Migration became a lucrative business not only for the government but also for the scheming migrant employment and transport agencies. Migrants and their families faced all forms of exploitation, abuse, discrimination, including sexual trafficking in innocent young women. But this does not stop them from rising above the situation. Thai migrants organize themselves, providing

education on migrants rights, human rights and the struggle against oppression faced by many migrants. They work in solidarity with other Asian migrants and local workers in Hong Kong.

The Indonesian Migrant Women Workers' Union based its showcase on a semi-allegorical/realistic drama treating the following story in a fashion inspired by the common folkloric tale mentioned above, in which brown monkeys struggle against a powerful White Monkey oppressor:

> Indonesians back home faced various crises, from economic to political to social. The play presents the many difficult situations faced by Indonesian migrant workers the world over: highly repressive conditions in Saudi Arabia; undocumented workers in Singapore and Malaysia who are sent back in boats; and abuses in Hong Kong where many Indonesian domestic workers run away from the cruelties of their employers.

The Filipina group centered its showcase on poetry in motion, using this text:

> Migrant, woman sand worker,
> Are you really as lucky?
> You are intelligent and open-minded,
> But you toiled all day and night
> While you face a lot of difficulties
> And uncertainties in life.
> Migrant, wife, mother,
> You are a source of life
> To that fetus in your womb.
> You are the light at every home,
> Yet you need to leave your beloved family behind.
> To keep them together sand gives them a better future.
> Migrant, woman, heroine,
> Are you worth billions of dollars?
> Slapped with a thousand deaths,
> Chained for decades to poverty and exploitation?
> Because the rotten system of
> your society will forever chain you!
> Ha-ha–ha–ha–ha!
> Migrant, woman, dignified,
> Stand up and unite.
> Fight for your rights,
> For justice and equality.
> Migrant, woman, onwards!
> To international freedom and democracy!
> Long live the migrants!
> Long live the workers!
> Long live women!

These workshops were facilitated by Filipino and local artists who used the Basic Integrated Theatre Arts Workshop (BITAW) methodology developed by PETA, incorporating creative dance and movement, creative sound and music, visual art and creative writing. It is widely used by Filipino cultural workers and has been adopted by many people's theater workers throughout Asia. The BITAW process stresses orientation, artistry and organization through systematic use of various art forms and group dynamics so as to promote collective creative expression and group solidarity. Modules vary depending on the art form used, the type of participants and the focal issues. Integrated into the BITAW methodology are elements from the theory and practice of Viola Spolin, Augusto Boal, Rudolf Laban and others.

We have found BITAW a very effective methodology, but many others are useful in promoting empowerment, for example, Theater of the Oppressed as developed by Augusto Boal, playback theater as developed by Jonathan Fox, giant puppetry developed by Bread & Puppet Theater, playbuilding, process drama and other methods and techniques derived from drama-in-education, psychodrama and other therapies. We've found that the best approach is eclectic, depending on the circumstances, objectives, characteristics and needs of the participants. We ought constantly to update and improve our skills in facilitating workshops, clinging to one basic principle: if our workshops and activities are to empower and not to disempower, to educate and not to miseducate, they ought to provide a participatory and democratic mode of learning, neither authoritarian, one-way or top-down.

The aim of this type of training is to help participants develop, not do the work for them. The facilitator is to encourage a learning process neither rote nor spoon-fed but evocative. The process should be flexible. In participatory modes of learning, participants develop self-confidence, improve self-esteem and deepen their self-understanding. In this paradigm, everyone possesses knowledge, and the development of new knowledge is based on sharing existing knowledge and mutual learning. Inherent in this approach is a sense of shared responsibility to search together for new knowledge. The participatory mode of learning emphasizes collective creativity and sharing, acknowledging the value and contribution of each participant.

One essential way to wage continuous struggle against the negative effects of globalization is to work tirelessly to promote the empowerment of both migrant and local workers. This can be achieved through workshops conducted by effective facilitators, socially aware and responsive, comprehending how the world functions and in possession of a working knowledge of creating and staging theater. With these skills, they will be able to evolve a harmonious process of creation and implement participatory learning. But such skills require training. The need is urgent to train more effective artists–facilitators, calling for more systematic and frequent trainers' training, facilitated by international networking that can enable effective exchange of skills and ideas.

GLOBALIZING CULTURAL ACTIVISM

People's theater has been found effective in empowering migrant workers in Hong Kong. It provides powerful tools to expose and oppose the worldwide synchronization of human oppression and exploitation under the present process of globalization. Through participation in theater and other arts, migrant workers become aware of how they have internalized their oppressors. They begin to command the means of speaking out. By participating in arts among themselves and with the local people, migrant workers are no longer isolated, instead becoming active participants in the community life of their host countries. Through producing their own theater, they become part of the global movement to create a world that is truly ours.

Concerned theater workers in Hong Kong and elsewhere should be able to see that collaborating with migrant workers is as important and socially valuable as work with other sectors of the oppressed in society, whether persons with disabilities (who number half a million in Hong Kong) or marginal workers (who number more than half a million here). The commitment to theater and other arts as tools for societal transformation connects all artists, activists and the oppressed.

Our experience has shown that migrants, given the opportunity, can produce powerful art works that at the same time make strongly positive social statements. The continued blossoming of migrant theater and other art forms manifests a diversity that can be the antidote to the uniformity imposed by the present globalization process. This is diversity within the context of a cultural commonwealth in which real differences in culture are to be respected and appreciated. If migrant cultural projects are merely monocultural, they will only lead to narrow-minded nationalism. If cross-cultural exploration and inter-culturalism are enshrined and the process is carried out in the most participatory and democratic manner, I am confident it will produce exciting aesthetic outcomes.

I believe it is time to set up an international network of like-minded cultural activists to support and promote theater with migrant workers wherever they are found, and I hope readers will be inspired by these examples to join me in making this a reality.

Afterword

CREATIVITY UNDER PRESSURE

by Don Adams and Arlene Goldbard

Community cultural development is a global phenomenon, always manifest in highly specific, localized forms. Many, many more projects and organizations exist than could be mentioned in this volume, and many more will inevitably come into being.

The artists and activists included in this anthology typify the two principal paths into the community cultural development field, which in turn indicate the field's wide boundaries. Some of these practitioners have come to their cultural work through a commitment to social development. They have wanted to help communities articulate critiques and aspirations, thus raising their own voices and expanding social opportunities; they have focused on arts and media for their expressive and mobilizing power. Others always saw themselves as artists, but were disenchanted with the marginalization of conventional artistic expression and chose to use their gifts for community emancipation and development. Coming from remarkably different beginnings, the territory where they meet is the overarching subject of this volume— community cultural development.

In Africa, Asia and Latin America, support for community cultural development has always been scarce; elsewhere, even where support levels may have been significant in the past, public funding has shrunk in recent years as part of imposed austerity measures or in response to the global trend toward privatization. Yet around the world, community cultural development practitioners have demonstrated remarkable ingenuity under intense economic (and often political) pressure. An enormous amount of voluntary, small-scale work—including projects such as those described here by Maribel Legarda, Mok Chiu Yu and Nitin Paranjape—is sustained by little more than the passion and commitment of participants. Powerful arguments have been made for culture's essential role in development. Inventive community artists have taken advantage of the new attention to development issues galvanized by resistance to globalization's negative effects, successfully obtaining funding for, say, a participatory theater project that addresses a funding agency's interest in reproductive health or a participatory video project that serves another funder's HIV/AIDS education goals.

The upside of this new situation is that any funding is available at all, allowing some groups to continue their essential work. Working within limitations can be a spur to creativity, can even extend the work's impact. But the downside is that when the work is supported for some secondary purpose rather than its intrinsic value, funding entails distortion: the funder's priorities drive the work, leading to such dangers as David Kerr and Masitha Hoeane describe in their chapters.

It is now clear that one of the impacts of globalization will be ongoing (and perhaps expanded) attention to issues related to development—improving living conditions, strengthening social infrastructure, assisting violence-torn communities to rebuild, addressing both rural and urban needs in the face of accelerated migration and so on. There will be funding for nongovernmental organizations involved in such development work. The persistence and growth of both calls for democracy and critiques of conventional development approaches point to the need for a better way. Community cultural development practitioners pose a challenge and an opportunity for development funders: give culture its rightful place. Enter into a dialogue with the community cultural development field. Use the power of this practice to address questions of identity, autonomy and culture, ensuring that development efforts help rather than harm local capability and resilience.

We live in a new world. Everyone—everything, every place—is connected now. All our strategies and understandings must be guided by this knowledge. The either/or thinking of an earlier era must yield to a greater openness to experimentation, a greater willingness to enter into partnerships, if this useful work is to survive and flourish. Despite its persistence, community cultural development is in a precarious situation for reasons unsurprisingly linked to the phenomenon of globalization. Like other sectors of economic and social enterprise, this field must find balance in a period of restructuring.

In every region of the world, community cultural development's historic periods of growth and stability have come about mainly in response to the presence of public funding, but for reasons political, economic and social, we are still in a time of privatization. The more that governments are committed to enabling democracy, the more likely it is that their support of cultural programs will reach beyond sustaining prestige arts institutions to serve broader public objectives. Since World War II, public cultural policy in almost every nation has at least given lip service—and only occasionally much more—to the aims of broadening public participation and nurturing cultural diversity. But that is not to say there are many healthy public programs at this point to inspire and emulate.

The democratic embrace of community cultural development has been deepest—and its beneficial impact has been greatest—at times of widespread social breakdown, when culture's capacity to heal and unite has been seen as advancing broad social goals. In the 1960s, for instance, liberation movements of cultural minorities and youth throughout the world persuaded public officials to consider the question of social and cultural inclusion, re-examining public cultural institutions and programs with an eye to making them more responsive and effective in serving non-elite audience interests. It was this period of worldwide social ferment—anti-colonial struggles, movements for the civil rights of cultural minorities, of women, of gay and lesbian people and of local and regional cultures within nation-states—that brought the most focused attention to the emerging movement to promote community cultural development.

In response to the rising expectations and increasing population mobility that followed World War II, cultural ministers around the world had tried various means of democratizing existing cultural institutions. In the industrialized world, the aim was to lure more substantial cross sections of their populations into established museums and concert halls. But these efforts produced very little. As so many of the authors in this volume point out, cultural needs and aspirations of the disenfranchised are seldom satisfied by transporting the culture of the "center" to the "margins." In the post-colonial developing world, the aim was to shoehorn elements of heritage culture into colonial institutions such as the national theaters of Francophone Africa previously devoted to Molière and Racine. There, too, success has been limited unless policies have been deeply reconceived to reflect new realities. To paraphrase Paulo Freire, it became clear throughout the world that people were not content to listen to the words of the powerful, but wanted to "speak with their own voices and say their own words."

The hostility or boredom evoked by attempts to recruit wider participation for existing institutions led cultural policymakers to realize that larger forces were threatening the vitality of cultural life. Urbanization, the proliferation of commercial mass media and the other forces associated with Americanization or globalization of culture were discouraging active participation in community cultural life. Alarmed at the implications of these trends, beginning in the late '60s, policymakers articulated a new goal for public cultural policy: cultural democracy.

Cultural democracy envisaged a world where active cultural participation would become the overriding goal of policy. With such a policy, people are encouraged to engage in live, face-to-face cultural activities rather than entirely succumbing to passive consumption of cultural products. Instead of prescribing a presumably superior form of fine-arts culture, cultural democracy posits a goal of respect for cultural diversity—encouraging the preservation and development of diverse cultural traditions, as against the lionization of one culture (often a version of high-art Western tradition or top-dollar Western commercial culture). Cultural democracy also challenged policymakers to open up their own spheres of responsibility to democratic participation, enabling community members to exert a greater measure of control over conditions of cultural life, decentralizing decision making wherever possible and providing access to the means of cultural participation (such as facilities, artistic and organizational leadership and material support) rather than focusing solely on professionally produced end products. Key to the realization of these idealistic aims was the introduction of a new sphere of professional work: *animation socio-culturelle*, socio-cultural community development, what we call "community cultural development," the subject of the present volume.

These ideals were the centerpiece of a vigorous international cultural-policy discourse that lasted into the early '80s. But even during this time, once the cultural ministers returned home from their international meetings and stimulating collegial discussions, this dialogue seldom had much impact on domestic cultural budgets. The greatest share of public cultural subsidy continued to flow to mainstream, flagship institutions. Nevertheless, these new ideas inspired smaller-scale experimental initiatives in many countries to animate community cultural life. Even in the United States, where the public arts-support apparatus has been consistently unfriendly to the infusion of wider social goals in culture, public funding for nonarts purposes—for example, to redirect the energies of youth from rioting or gang violence, to stimulate new employment opportunities through public-service projects or to encourage community development—provided seed money to establish the kinds of projects described in this book and its companion volume, "Creative Community: The Art of Cultural Development."

Such publicly funded experimentation in cultural development is now largely a thing of the past. In the 1980s, the United States under Ronald Reagan led a backlash against such public funding. Reagan's Hollywood friends and other industry and ideological allies opposed UNESCO's role as a forum for criticism of the commercial cultural industries, its call for a "new world information order" to counter global centralization of news media and its moral support for liberationist movements of black South Africans, Palestinians and others. UNESCO's punishment for offending official U.S. interests was the withdrawal in the early '80s of several Western nations from the United Nations' cultural agency. Except for the United States, most have returned. But their actions forced a realignment in UNESCO that effectively quashed talk of cultural democracy in that primary international cultural policy forum.

Around the world, public cultural budgets declined through the 1990s. By the time UNESCO convened the world's cultural ministers for the first time since the U.S. withdrawal—for the World Conference on Cultural Policies for Development in Stockholm in 1998—the ministers' attention had been refocused on the privatization of former public institutions and support programs. The protection of cultural diversity against the homogenizing forces of globalization was put forward as a key theme of this meeting, but, in fact, more attention in the ministers' deliberations went to how countries where public funding had always been primary could refocus on stimulating private-sector support through earned income and private contributions.

The shift toward privatization does not bode well for community cultural development. When cultural subvention is an element of public policy, the questions that guide policy relate to public meaning: What aspects of our heritage should be preserved and extended? What cultural expressions exemplify our people? What makes up our nation's cultural commonwealth? How can artistic expression best represent our nation around the world? Although the answers will almost certainly be contested, the questions themselves are recognized as valid for the public sphere. But when privatization occurs, the guiding questions shrink: What artists are safe to support and likely to reflect well on the image of a corporation? What type of underwriting is likely to return the most value to the corporate or individual donor in the currency of public relations? Which projects advance the specific agenda of a philanthropic organization or individual, as opposed to the broad public agenda?

This has left the community cultural development field in a quandary. In one sense, community cultural work has always relied on nongovernmental initiative. Funding doesn't call culture into being; it merely supports what emerges organically from human creativity. Projects such as those described in this anthology have been created not by government fiat, but by public-spirited artists, by community leaders concerned about cultural issues and by issue-based organizations. But when it comes time to pay the bills, it has been hard to rely on private initiative, especially from marginalized and poor communities. Communities under stress are likely to lack surplus resources; while participants often contribute time and effort, they seldom provide much cash. Wealthier donors tend to prefer highly visible, concrete and noncontroversial

projects. Community cultural development work very often stimulates criticism of the status quo and, these days, few patrons—and this is true equally of governments and private individuals—are enlightened enough to see the long-term advantage in underwriting their own critics. The idea of a healthy opposition has clearly lost whatever cachet it might once have carried.

So while the community artists included in this anthology might dream of the kind of no-strings-attached public subsidy that would allow them to enter into open-ended collaborations with even the most impoverished communities, waking reality has forced most of them to improvise, and they have been remarkably resourceful. These essays describe market-based support systems (for instance, Gary Stewart's discussion of youth music workshops supported by a commercially successful music group and Trilby Multimedia's base of contracts from education and other agencies described in Tony Stanley's essay); work funded by international aid groups (such as the projects in Botswana and Malawi described by David Kerr); projects in social institutions (for example, the Brazilian prison work discussed separately by Paul Heritage and Bárbara Santos); commissions from arts presenters (such as the projects Liz Lerman recounts); community cultural development work supported by academic posts (like Mary Marshall Clark's); activities undertaken in partnership with activist organizations (for instance, Nitin Paranjape's account of his group's work in opposition to dam construction that destroyed villages); and even government subsidy (where, as Sarah Moynihan and Norm Horton recount, Australia currently leads the world). Approaches to finding support are almost as diverse as community cultural development groups, with just one common theme: the greatest contributions are always made by volunteers.

Taking a long view, it is quite certain that the spirit of community cultural development cannot be destroyed. Augustin Girard, the French cultural minister who wrote the leading primer on cultural policy back in 1972, put it thus:

> If cultural life is now to be dominated by cultural industries…will culture become merely another form of mass consumption, swallowed whole like the rest by a civilization unable to digest its leisure? This would be highly undesirable; but it is unlikely to happen.

> People have a profound need to communicate. …This can hardly be fulfilled by the mass media, which offer an abundance of material but no help in its choice or appreciation—nor any means of participation. …

> Man's higher purposes are creative: fulfillment with the means available to him, understanding and welcoming the creativity of his fellows which mirror and which mould him. Where this is lacking, the spirit dies. Art is not an optional extra, a frill, a luxury for the opulent. It is as basically human as morality and, like it, vital if man is to be at one with his environment. … Art is not life's final flowering and effulgence but that by which one becomes what one is.[1]

[1] Augustin Girard in collaboration with Geneviève Gentil, *Cultural Development: Experiences and Policies*, second edition, (Paris: UNESCO, 1983), pp. 62, 76.

Whether or not public programs can be sustained, the spirit that animates community cultural development will survive and find its expression even when repressive forces try to snuff it out, because apart from cultural development as a professional practice, the responsibility to preserve, cultivate and extend culture is universal. Good parents do this when they nurture their children's growth as autonomous beings and encourage the lifelong process of discovering and using their own unique voices. The dedicated teacher, the engaged librarian, the imaginative recreation leader and the democratic political leader will deploy community cultural development skills in their efforts to involve people in constructing lives of meaning and service. Wherever people struggle to shake off the forces of repression, community cultural development will be crucial to their success.

Writing from a dark time in the Marcos dictatorship, Filipino theater activist Karl Gaspar put it this way:

> It is a fact that no matter how remote a barrio is, there are local wise men who have kept the history, the richness and color of the local culture. There are men and women who have kept faith with the dreams of their people; have treasured these in their hearts. There are men and women who have kept the cultural ethos of their forefathers in terms of rich poetry, songs, dances and the like. It is there to be re-tapped, waiting to resurface and be appreciated as vital national treasures.[2]

[2] Karl Gaspar, "Creative Dramatics in Mindinao-Sulu (Philippines)," *Third World Popular Theatre Newsletter*, Dickson Mwansa, ed. (Kitwe, Zambia: *Third World Popular Theatre Network*, Jan. 1982), Vol. 1, No. 1, pp. 23–24.

Globalization's rapid progress thus far in the 21st century suggests that defenders of the human subject against the machinery of exploitation are in for rough times. This is the work of community cultural development.

Meeting in Bellagio in May 2001, community cultural development practitioners agreed that many elements of the field need support if the current storehouse of skills and knowledge is to be preserved and extended. One idea was to create an archive so that the teachings of seasoned practitioners don't dissipate as they age and become less active; this was described as "seed stock" for the future, to provide resources and ideas as circumstances change. Another was to underwrite peer-education, much more effective than top-down approaches to training; practitioners agreed support was needed to move to a larger scale, educating those who can train others to train still others, encouraging groups to multiply. Everyone stressed the value of new technology to aid networking among community cultural development workers from around the world. Translation capabilities are needed to forge truly international links. Exchange programs are essential. Above all, community artists—from those working under conditions of impoverishment in the developing world to those surviving in the industrialized world through a perpetual process of repackaging and reframing their work to attract short-term grants—ought to be richly supported—publicly, privately, imaginatively.

Toward the end of our meeting, Prosper Kompaore shared a proverb from his home country of Burkina Faso: "How is it that sky-high termite mounds can be made by such tiny insects?" he asked. The answer, counseling determination, endurance, commitment and plenty of sustenance: "It takes earth and earth and earth…"

About the Editors

This anthology comprises essays and interviews commissioned by the Rockefeller Foundation's Creativity & Culture Division from participants in the Foundation's Community, Culture and Globalization conference, held in May 2001 at the Bellagio Study and Conference Center on Lake Como in northern Italy.

The anthology's purpose and focus were shaped by an editorial advisory group comprising Dee Davis, Masitha Hoeane, Maribel Legarda, Nitin Paranjape and Martha Ramirez, each of whom has also contributed a chapter to this volume, and by the editors, Don Adams and Arlene Goldbard, who also wrote the opening essay and afterword. In addition, Brian Holmes took part in the initial editorial planning session.

Don Adams and Arlene Goldbard are founders of Adams & Goldbard, an organizational and cultural development consulting firm begun in January 1978. Over the ensuing 24 years, they have consulted with a wide variety of public and private agencies, most of them involved in cultural policy, artistic production and distribution, and cultural development planning and evaluation. Their work has integrated research, writing, planning, program and financial development, group dynamics, organizational restructuring and cooperative problem solving.

Their many clients in the community cultural development field have ranged from the American Festival Project to the Seattle Department of Parks and Recreation. In addition, they have done a great deal of work in the independent media field for dozens of clients such as the Independent Television Service, Web Lab, New Day Films and the Paul Robeson Fund for Film and Video. They have also spoken and published frequently on topics relating to cultural development and cultural policy. They may be reached via e-mail at icd@wwcd.org.

For additional resources on community cultural development, see contributing writers' suggestions at http//www.wwcd.org/action/resources.html.